SOCIALISM IN PROVENCE 1871-1914

Socialism in Provence
1871-1914

A STUDY IN THE ORIGINS OF THE
MODERN FRENCH LEFT

TONY JUDT
KING'S COLLEGE, CAMBRIDGE

CAMBRIDGE UNIVERSITY PRESS

CAMBRIDGE

LONDON · NEW YORK · MELBOURNE

Published by the Syndics of the Cambridge University Press
The Pitt Building, Trumpington Street, Cambridge CB2 1RP
Bentley House, 200 Euston Road, London NW1 2DB
32 East 57th Street, New York, NY 10022, USA
296 Beaconsfield Parade, Middle Park, Melbourne 3206, Australia

First published 1979

Printed in the United States of America
Typeset by the Alden Press
Oxford, London and Northampton
Printed and bound by Vail-Ballou Press, Inc
Binghamton, New York

Library of Congress Cataloguing in Publication Data

Judt, Tony.

Socialism in Provence, 1871–1914

Bibliography: p.

Includes index.

1. Socialism in Provence — History. I. Title.
HX270.P76J83   335'.00944'9   78-16419
ISBN 0 521 22172 2 hard covers
ISBN 0 521 29598 X paperback

FOR PAT HILDEN
IN RECOGNITION

Contents

Maps and tables

MAPS

TABLES

Preface

This book is an enquiry into the origins of a political tradition. It seeks to investigate why the peasantry of Provence turned increasingly to the socialist movement in the period from 1880 to the First World War. This question is of interest not merely for a clearer understanding of an important characteristic of modern France — the marked divergence in political traditions and affiliations between different regions, and the fidelity of French political allegiances — but also as the basis for a redefinition of the history of socialism. The latter is commonly treated as *either* a development inherent in the emergence of an industrial proletariat *or* as mere ideological camouflage for the continuation of older patterns of protest and conflict by other means. By setting out to establish who socialists were, and exactly when and why they became politically committed, this study aims to contribute to a clearer view of the modern French left, as neither a 'victime du marxisme' nor the latest in a succession of crypto-Jacobins.

Furthermore, by emphasising the extent to which socialist support came from the peasantry, I hope to rescue the latter from the twin identity usually ascribed to them: inherently conservative on the one hand, or ideologically nondescript on the other, following political movements with little concern for or interest in their content. Lastly, by limiting itself to a single period, and by stressing the importance of the events of that period, the book emphasises the centrality of a properly *historical* account of modern political divisions.

The book is arranged to respond to these concerns. Part One is a detailed study of one French department, the Var, in the first half of the Third Republic. As will become clear, I have chosen the Var both because it provides an excellent instance of the subject under investigation — an enduring political tradition — and because it has been the subject of much writing, especially for the eighteenth and early nineteenth centuries. As a result, there is a wealth of historical and social background which may serve as a context for the study of the years after 1870.

Whereas Part One is essentially descriptive, Part Two is conceived in terms of an argument. Having set out in the first part the political developments of the years 1870–1914 in the Var, emphasising the steady growth of socialist support in the region during this period, I have presented in Part Two various frameworks for an understanding of the strength of socialist affiliation in the rural Var during these years. Although Chapters 5 to 8 are separate in their theme and the evidence they deploy, cumulatively they result in a more general account of the growth of socialism in the Var, an account which is explicitly laid out in Chapter 9.

Thus Parts One and Two are devoted to a study of the Var, moving from a description of the region through an account of economic and political developments at a particular moment and ending in an explanation of these developments and their relation to the period, the place and the ideas in question. Part Three shifts the focus of the argument from Provence to France as a whole. Chapter 10 discusses the problems of relating regional to national history and considers the implications for the history of French society of some of the arguments presented in Part Two. Chapter 11 discusses the nature of the support which socialism found among the peasants and presents more fully some of the implications of the history of the Var for the study of rural communities in general, in France and further afield. Finally, in Chapter 12, I have pulled together the various threads which can be traced through earlier chapters in an attempt to offer some thoughts upon the history of socialism in France.

It will be seen that the book thus falls into two very distinct sections, that which deals with the Var and that which offers more tentative and personal reflections upon certain key areas of modern French history. The two are not unconnected, however. The book was always conceived in the form of a response to a particular question – why did the Marxist left in France implant itself so successfully and enduringly in the rural areas of the country? – and the order of the chapters is a reflection of my approach to answering this. Hence the choice of a limited region for close investigation, but hence too the decision to open the argument out, in Part Three, into its wider dimensions. It was never my intention merely to contribute a little more to the historiography of nineteenth-century Provence, but neither is it any longer possible to ask the kind of questions which interest the historian without recourse to this sort of detailed study. Thus Parts One and Two, taken together, form both a whole in themselves and, far more significantly, a justificatory underpinning for the otherwise rather adventurous reflections presented in Part Three.

Ideally, then, this book should be treated as a unity, in that it argues a thesis whose roots spread throughout the various chapters. The price paid for this approach is of course that any individual chapter, particularly the earlier ones, may seem occasionally opaque, depending as it does upon some later chapter for clarification of certain points. The alternative was to argue much of the thesis at each contentious juncture, which would have made for an even longer, as well as a very repetitive book. As it is, I have avoided the temptation to lead the reader by the hand through each stage in the argument, preferring to let my theme emerge as much through the arrangement of the material as from a reiteration of the case. Without in the least wishing to imply that I have dispensed with the apparatus of sociological or cliometric methodology only to lapse into literary structuralism, I would hope that by the time he or she reaches the conclusion, the reader will have been led by the form into an appreciation of the content. In the intellectual atmosphere of the late 1970s this would be the appropriate way in which to read the history of the French left.

Finally, to avoid or at least reduce confusion, I should add that I have referred to 'socialism' or 'socialists' when discussing either the idea, the complex of beliefs usually associated with the term, or those men and women who held them; where the reference is to 'Socialists', this denotes more specifically the political party which was formed in 1905, and its members and supporters. Because of the confusing multiplicity of parties and groups calling themselves 'socialist' in the previous generation, I have tried to avoid ambiguity by keeping references to these in the lower case.

Acknowledgements

In the preparation of this book I have incurred many debts, to institutions and persons, and it is a pleasure to have the opportunity to acknowledge these, however inadequately.

The nature of the present study has meant frequent and often lengthy visits to France. These have at various times been supported by grants from the Centre National de Recherche Scientifique, the Political Science Fund of Cambridge University, and the Electors to Fellowships of King's College, Cambridge.

In the various libraries and archives where I have worked I have always found generous advice and assistance. I am grateful in particular to the Librarian of the Ecole Normale Supérieure, and to the Archivist and his assistants in the Archives Départementales du Var in Draguignan. Here, surely, are the most congenial, as well as one of the best organised, departmental archives in France.

While in France I have benefited from the unstinting hospitality of a number of friends, and I am particularly grateful to Miriam and Jean Sarfati, and to Mimi Lloyd. As for Nicky and Clarisse Kaldor, were it not for them this book would have been much longer in the writing: my prolonged stay at their home in La Garde Freinet in 1977 enabled me to prepare the typescript and check local sources with a minimum of interruption.

Many of my ideas and approaches were developed while reflecting upon the work of Paul Bois and Alain Corbin, and I have also learnt much from reading the works of Daniel Chirot, Jacques Girault, Ted Margadant, Roy Sandstrom and Eugen Weber, as well as in discussion with a number of them. However, neither they nor Chris Andrew, Alan Baker and John Dunn, with all of whom I have discussed my work, need feel responsible for the book as it now emerges.

The same cannot in truth be said of the two historians to whom I owe the most enduring debts. It was Maurice Agulhon who, in person and 'par oeuvre interposée', first awoke my interest in the Var and its history, and the reader will have little difficulty in seeing just how much I have depended upon Professor Agulhon's own studies of the Var in an earlier period. Even in departing from his conclusions, I hope this book will render some small homage to the achievements of Maurice Agulhon. To Annie Kriegel, most prodigious and energetic of French historians, I owe a very special debt. It is Madame Kriegel's insistence upon the historian's duty to ask questions and to answer them with a proper consciousness of the historical moment which has inspired my own approach to the history of French socialism. I know of no other historian who has so consistently and courageously demanded a rigour and methodological awareness while remaining firmly and securely dismissive of the siren calls of quantitative or 'systematic' history. Many have written that history and sociology can have no separate existence, few have demonstrated how they might properly converge. Annie Kriegel is of that few. It is to her that I owe my belief in the historian's obligation to *explain*, and from her that I learnt how to do so.

Finally, I owe a multitude of thanks to the many people who have in various ways sustained and assisted me in the writing and preparation of this book. Frances Kelly and Patricia Williams have provided experienced and enthusiastic advice throughout the final stages, and been extraordinarily understanding in the face of what must often have seemed an annoyingly innocent and obtuse author; my parents have been unfailingly patient and supportive; as to other, close friends who must sometimes have wished for the Mediterranean to rise and swallow up the Var, peasants, socialists and all, I can only offer my gratitude for happy times and the thought that if it was not actually worth it, then at least it was for a purpose, which is more than was always clear at the time.

Cambridge   T.J.
February 1978

THE VAR

1 The regional setting

The environment

The department of the Var was created in 1790 from the eastern part of old Provence. Until the creation of the department of the Alpes-Maritimes around the newly acquired Comté de Nice in 1861 the Var included all of eastern Provence up to the Italian frontier, including the present arrondissement of Grasse. From 1861, however, its frontiers have remained unaltered, and it is with the area within the revised boundary that this book is concerned.

The Var, then, is framed by the Mediterranean Sea to the south and by the departments of the Alpes-Maritimes to the east, the Alpes de Haute Provence (formerly the Basses-Alpes) to the north, and the Bouches-du-Rhône to the west. The eastern and western frontiers of the department are for the most part arbitrarily drawn, but the northern edge of the department is formed by the gorges of the Verdon river as it runs down from Castellane to join the Durance below Manosque. The department was divided administratively into three arrondissements: that of Draguignan, the largest, covering the eastern half of the region and reaching from the Verdon to the coast; that of Brignoles, taking in the western part of the region but not descending to the sea; and that of Toulon, smaller in area, but administering the densely-populated coastal fringe and of course the city of Toulon itself. The departmental *chef-lieu* was Draguignan,[1] Toulon and Brignoles were administered by *sous-préfets*.

The outstanding characteristic of this region has always been its remarkably uneven topography, with hills, valleys and mountains following one another in rapid succession throughout the department.[2] Any description of the Var, then, must begin not by a division according to area but rather according to geological type; the essential variable is elevation: mountain—valley. The upland areas are of two kinds: the Alpine foothills to the north of the department, not yet themselves Alpine in character (the highest point in the Var

Map 1. France — departments

is only 1700 metres) but of the same family and sharing certain
features of the lower Alps to the north (not least their climate); and
the wooded hills which run, in three separate ranges, from west to
east in the southern half of the department. The first of these, the
Ste Baume massif, rises to a height of 1100 metres at one point and
is characterised by low but steep hillsides covered in thick forest. The
second 'coastal' range is that of the Maures, rising to the east of
Toulon and ending near Fréjus. The Maures are older hills, dark and
forbidding, with few peaks and a thick covering of cork-oaks which
for a long time provided the only source of employment in the

isolated hill villages. Finally, further to the east, the massif of the Estérel rises behind Fréjus and runs down to the valley behind Mandelieu. The Estérel, like the Maures, forms an older generation of hills, volcanic in origin, and of a porphyritic rock which is often reddish in hue and which gives the hills behind the coast from St Raphael to Cannes their distinctive character.

Between the Alpine plateaux to the north, and the Ste Baume, Maures and Estérel massifs to the south, the Var also boasts a variety of lesser hills which contribute their part to the region's topography. From behind Draguignan, and running east as far as Grasse, there is a ridge which forms the natural frontier between the southern Var, Mediterranean in aspect, and the northern, often bare, plateaux leading to the mountains. We shall meet this geological frontier post on more than one occasion when we come to consider the economic (and social) differences which characterise the region. Then there are the hills to the west of the department, lying to the north of the Ste Baume, and leading up into the most thickly wooded part of the Var to the north-west, where the forests occupy almost all of the available terrain.

Between these omnipresent hills and mountain plateaux there is a second Var, the Var of the valleys, struggling to survive in the midst of wooded hills and stony limestone mountains. The first and most important of these valleys is the depression which runs in a semi-circular groove from Toulon to Fréjus, separating the Maures and the coast below them from the rest of the department. This fortunate geological feature, never more than a few kilometres wide except where it meets the sea at either end, constitutes the central axis of communication and of settlement in the region, and is the source of most of the agricultural output of the department. A second valley, that of the Argens river, begins further to the north, near the village of Seillons, and runs in a south-easterly direction, entering the central valley near Vidauban, in the centre of the department. Together with the lesser valleys formed by the Gapeau and Issole rivers, both of which flow from west to east into the central depression, the Gapeau directly, the Issole via the Argens which it joins at Carcès, these form the main valleys which help give the Var its uneven topographical character. Numerous lesser streams flow through the hills to the north of the central depression, forming tiny dents in the folds of the Provençal hillsides.[3]

This chapter begins with a brief description of the physical geography of the Var department not merely in order to help 'orient' the reader, but because so much of the human geography of the region is conditioned by the environment. With so much of the region rendered uninhabitable, or at least uncultivable, by steep hillsides, thick forests and stony plateaux, the populations of the Var have perforce been led to make the most of the opportunities for habitation and agriculture offered by the many tiny valleys formed by streams or by geological chance. The reality of hill and valley, of mountain and plain, was ever present in the making of Provençal society, and is therefore worthy of emphasis from the outset.

Communications

The Var, until the very recent past, presented an interesting paradox to anyone passing through the area.[4] The geographical features described above militated against ease of communication within the department, and there is no doubt that inner Provence, bounded by Marseille to the west, Nice to the east and the sea on the southern side, was remote and highly inaccessible. The coast massifs

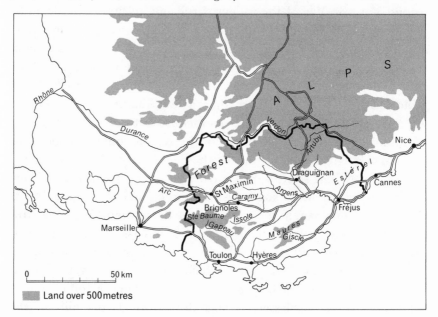

Map 2. Lower Provence – physical

to the south, the forests to the west and north-west, the inhospitable Alpine foothills (a bizarre misnomer — few would have assailed them on foot!) to the north, all seemed closed to the traveller; poor, isolated, with few roads, they neither invited nor received exploration from the outside. Yet the Var *was* surrounded by major centres of human activity in the form of the cities of the coast and indeed the coastal shipping, and as a result the area was from a very early date linked to the outer world in a number of ways.

From medieval times, the central valley of what would become the Var department was already a major trade route, as well as an important military link, between the Rhône valley and Nice (and thence Italy).[5] Indeed, earlier still, it had formed the Provençal section of the Via Aurelia. As a result, this east—west axis encouraged the growth of a string of tiny towns, bourgs with various functions, administrative or (more commonly) market, open to the wider world which regularly passed through them. Eighteenth-century maps show four major roads traversing the region which concerns us: the first of them runs eastwards from Aix, through St Maximin (to the north of the Ste Baume massif), Le Luc, Fréjus and Cannes to Antibes; that is, the route taken today by the National 7 which carries holidaymakers to the Côte d'Azur. A second road branches north from the first at Brignoles, thence to follow a parallel route, through Carcès, Lorgues, Draguignan and Grasse, meeting up again with the central route at Antibes. A third significant route runs from Marseille to Toulon via Cugès, and thence through Cuers and Pignans to meet the main axis at Le Luc. All three, then, run from west to east and along the valleys described earlier. Only one proper road is given as traversing the region from south to north, or more accurately from south-west to north-east: the royal road from St Maximin to Castellane, via Barjols, Aups and Comps.[6]

A century later, in 1837, the situation is unchanged in its essentials.[7] The main axes still run west to east, along the same routes, with the addition only of a further west—east route, from Toulon to St Tropez, cutting through the lower part of the Maures. By the mid-nineteenth century, then, eastern Provence continued to show the characteristics which had marked it for two millennia: in constant contact with the outer world which passed through its valleys on a horizontal path; but with virtually no internal links along a vertical axis, so that the communities only a few kilometres to the north or south of the valleys, and the rivers and roads which traversed them, might have lived in a different universe.

Habitat

Anyone who has had occasion to travel in Mediterranean regions will be aware of the special characteristic of communities in this region: their marked propensity to live in closely-agglomerated villages, 'urban villages', usually clustered together on some steep hillside. This special feature of human habitation in southern Europe was more than usually marked in the Var — even in the fifteenth century this part of Provence stood out from the rest of the region by virtue of the tightly-grouped dwellings of its population.[8]

The reasons behind this 'urban' propensity of the Varois, so different from the far-flung isolated farmhouses of northern and western France, are clear enough. With so very little cultivable land available, the peasants of inner Provence were little inclined to waste it by building their houses on what might otherwise serve as olive groves or vineyards. Villages would be squeezed up against the hillside, leaving for agriculture the valley and the few hectares of usable land on either side of it. There were other considerations as well: until quite recently, southern France lay exposed to raids from the sea, by Saracens and others, and the building of villages on hillsides and in a compact manner gave an extra margin of security. Then again, the narrow valleys and the proximity of the mountains exposed the Varois to a far from gentle climate (see below), and villages would often cling to south-facing hillsides for shelter from the violent winds from the north. Finally, the inhospitable hills and forests forced most people into the valleys, with the result that what relatively few valleys and plains existed were very early filled with communities, often separated by not more than a few kilometres from each other along the road which wound between the hills.

This urban context in which the peasantry of the Var passed their lives, in villages where the constant contact with others, the sense of being part of a community rather than an isolated *campagnard*, made them more like townsfolk than peasants, contributed to the development of what has been termed 'Provençal sociability', the inclination of the peasantry of the Var to live socially, in societies, in clubs, and in communal self-awareness. I shall have occasion to discuss the significance of this sociability later on. For the present, the reader's attention is merely drawn to the degree to which environment and habitat helped form a particular aspect of Provençal life.[9]

Not everyone lived in tightly-grouped villages, however. Just as the valleys and roads of the central and southern part of the Var helped condition a certain pattern of life, so the isolated communes of the uplands were also a product of their environment. The plains of the northern Var, and the lower but no less uninviting slopes of the rock-covered hills of the eastern Var, did not produce an agglomerated habitat. Quite the reverse. The tiny settlements of the mountains, many of which had only come into being with the population growth of the sixteenth century and the ensuing search for more land to bring under cultivation, these did not lack for land. Isolated, poor, and unable to support even the small population of the mountains, these villages saw their inhabitants spread out all over the hillsides. Since the colder regions in the north could not support the cultivation of vines, olives, fruit, the staples of the valley communities, they survived on the cultivating of poor-quality grain and the raising of sheep and cattle. In this respect resembling more the peasants of the rest of France than the villagers of lower Provence, they resembled the typical French peasant in their habitat as well. A majority of the inhabitants of a commune would live not in the commune itself, but in hamlets which might contain no more than a dozen houses, and which were often up to five kilometres from the village itself. The isolation resulting separated these populations very markedly from the inhabitants of the lower valleys, and helped produce differences in social and political attitudes which will be discussed at some length in Part Two.

It is perhaps worth observing, before leaving the description of Provençal habitat, that the manner in which the peasantry of Provence lived — itself a condition of where they lived — did not necessarily have any bearing upon the way in which they earned a living. This is not only true in the sense that many (perhaps most) Varois lived in a 'town' but worked in the countryside; it is also intended to indicate that, while men in Provence often *lived* collectively, they *worked* individually, often as independent small peasant proprietors. Out of this there resulted a certain tension, particularly

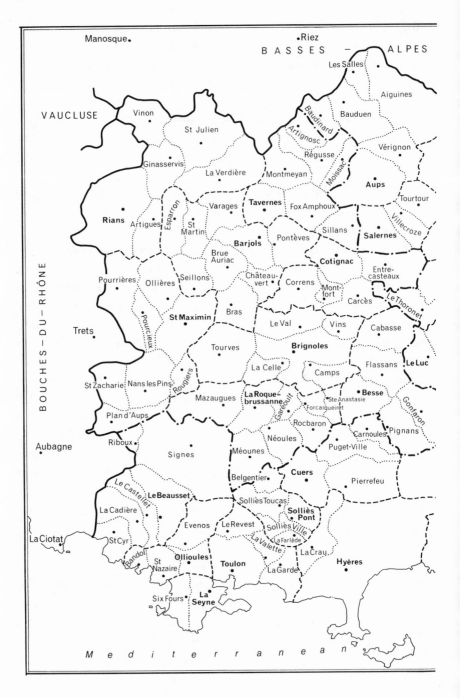

Map 3. The Var — communes

in the closely-grouped villages, between the collectivity and the individual, which manifested itself in the complex political affiliations of the late nineteenth century.

Agriculture

It is not intended here to give a full description of the agricultural structure of the Var, something which is discussed in the following chapter. However, in the context of an introduction to the region, it may be useful to present a very brief survey of the agricultural 'subregions' of the department, before going into greater detail at a later stage.

The same topographical features which conditioned the settlement of populations in the Var also dominated the way in which they earned a living. The steep hills and narrow valleys ensured that plough and fertiliser would never become central features of farming in eastern Provence; as for the higher areas, while they were often quite flat, the soil was so thin, so stony, that neither horse- nor mule-ploughing could really be used to turn over the thankless surfaces of shale and limestone. Consequently, Provençal farming was diversified from a very early date, the better to profit from any market for whatever could be grown, as well as to guard against the disaster which would result from over-reliance on a single crop in such undependable soil.

In the valleys, and on the lower slopes of the hills, where the soil was not so much better as more easily protected from erosion, terracing was employed and olives, nuts and vines were raised. The valleys of the Gapeau and the Argens were both particularly suited to such products, and it was in these two areas that the greatest concentration of peasant-villages came about, with the Argens valley concentrating on wine and olive production, and the Gapeau communes, further south, producing by the mid-nineteenth century an abundance of fruits — cherries, pears, peaches, apples — as well as flowers and of course wine.

In contrast, the peasants of the upper Var were constrained to rely on the raising of rather scrawny cattle and sheep (too high for coastal crops, the Haut Var was not sufficiently Alpine to boast rich grazing land), together with small quantities of wheat and potatoes. It is significant that the crops of the lower Var were ideally suited for market — wine, olive oil, fruit, flowers — both in their nature and because of the scale on which they were produced; the produce of the upper Var was sufficient neither in quality nor in quantity for marketing beyond the local region (unlike the semi-tropical produce further south, the agriculture of the northern Var merely duplicated that of French peasants everywhere, though in an impoverished manner). Thus the agriculture of the two Vars, the Var of the valleys and the Var of the hills, helped accentuate the division already marked in respect of communities, between the outward-looking populations of the valley and the isolated peasants of the hills. And far from being of recent date, this division goes back deep into the past — the old Provence of wines and olives was far more open a community than many of the more central regions of France.

The distinction between the two aspects of eastern Provence may be illustrated finally in two respects. In the first place, there was the vital contour beyond which the vine would not grow. Shifting slightly with the centuries, this line has always hovered along the curve bending from upper left to lower right, beginning around Artignosc, on the lower valley of the Verdon, and passing through Aups, Salernes, Draguignan and thence to Bagnols. To the north-east of this line, the vine could not be induced to grow regularly, in quantity, or with good results.

A second distinction, introduced here but discussed in the next section, concerns the size of property holdings. Small holdings, of 10 hectares or less, predominated in the Toulon region, notably in the areas of intense cultivation of the vine to the west of the city. Medium-sized individual holdings, ranging from 20 to 40 hectares, predominated in the central depression and the valleys which run into it. Large property, on the other hand, from 50 hectares upwards, was to be found mostly in the upper Var, in the Ste Baume massif, and in parts of the Maures. Moreover, whereas small- and medium-sized properties were often worked by the owner with little outside assistance, the large holdings of the north and the hills were commonly let, to tenant farmers or to sharecroppers. In this way, as the physical environment created economic differences, so these in turn produced social variations which we shall later find leading to important political distinctions. At this stage, however, it is sufficient

to observe that, like the frontier of the vine, the difference between
the Var of small and medium peasant property and the Var of large
holdings helps further distinguish the geographical divisions already
noted.

Climate

There is a common but mistaken belief, widespread among
northerners whose contact with Mediterranean France is normally
confined to the summer months, that Provence is blessed with a
balmy, near-perfect climate. This is far from being the case, and in
the time of the year which most concerned the peasant in this region,
that is to say the months of March to May, the unreliability of the
weather was a matter of common complaint. There were variations,
of course. The northern Var, higher than the rest of the department
and furthest from the coast, was consistently colder. It was not
unusual for the canton of Comps, the least favoured of all, to have
snowfalls in April and May, and this, together with its exposed
position, helped accentuate the impoverishment of the area, in
resources and people. The western half of the department, though
protected from erosion by a heavy growth of forest, was exposed to
the cold winds blowing down the Rhône and Durance valleys and
thus, despite its relatively low elevation, was an unsuitable environment for the fragile crops of the valleys, such as olives. The hills of
the Ste Baume, Maures and Estérel ranges do not rise very high, but
their northern slopes are regularly blasted by the mistral, and people
and crops thus tended to shun them. Only the protected valleys and
the coastal towns nestling into the southern fringes of the hills which
reach down to the sea could count on a normally gentle climate, and
even they were not immune from climatic disasters. In 1883 it
snowed in St Tropez (!) and in the previous year crops in the valley
around Cuers were severely damaged by frost.[10] What was worse, the
climate of lower Provence *could* be quite balmy in late winter,
encouraging into the open crops which would then be destroyed by a
stormy spring: all the more reason for the encouraging of the polyculture for which historic Provence had been famous. Climatic
disasters were recurring dangers, of course (although the later nineteenth century probably had more than its share of them); with the
coming of a specialised (wine-based) monoculture in this period,

extremes of temperature at inopportune moments were especially disastrous and had wide-ranging social consequences, as we shall see.

The physical environment of the Var, then, was harsh in many respects, lacking the navigable rivers and open meadows of the lands to the north, but compensating in part by the variety of its produce (along the coast, in the valleys and on the lower hillsides). The department was not, of course, a single unit; we have already considered the multiple differences between upper and lower Var. Moreover, it was not a 'natural' department (few of the administrative units created in 1790 were that) — some of the villages to the extreme west and north of the region looked to towns in the Bouches-du-Rhône, the Vaucluse or the Basses-Alpes for their contact with a wider world, attachments which reflected both physical proximity and economic logic. Nonetheless by the last third of the nineteenth century it is not altogether unreasonable to treat the Var as a unit distinct from the surrounding departments. But this identity which the Var and its inhabitants had acquired by 1870 was at least as much the achievement of history as of geography.

The historical context

The independence of Provence came to an end in 1480, when the region was formally incorporated into the French state. Despite its absorption into the national unit, however, Provence retained many characteristic features which distinguished it from other parts of France and which continued to mark it out well into the modern era. The Provençal language (a real language, not a mere patois) remained in use throughout the region, and with it a clear sense of difference between the Provençaux and the French to the north. Provence also retained its traditional contacts with the world beyond its frontiers. Throughout the sixteenth century Fréjus continued to play a significant part in coastal trade with the Ligurian ports, and Genoans and others were regular purchasers of the wines of the Provençal coast (around St Tropez), and of the Argens valley. Indeed, the local economy was sufficiently dependent upon trade with the rest of France and elsewhere that it was from a very early date sensitive to fluctuations in consumer demand, oscillating between frequent crises of overproduction (usually of wine) and acute shortages. Like other parts of the Mediterranean, it was a precocious commercial economy, in this as in other ways quite unlike the self-sufficient 'closed' economies to the north.[11]

This peculiar character of Provence (truer even of our region than of the Languedoc to the west)[12] was of course confined to 'lower' Provence; inner Provence, and the higher regions, shared in the commercial life of the rest of the area only to the extent that human and animal transhumance brought the people of the mountains down to the valleys and hillsides in search of work. Even here, the in-between character of the upper Var meant that it failed fully to share in the life of the Alpine communities, lacking on the one hand their homogeneity and on the other the scale of mobility which true Alpine conditions imposed. Lower Provence, then, went its own way.

The commercial, quasi-urban way of life of lower Provence had a number of by-products which came in time to influence the historical development of the region. With so many windows on the world — there were thirty-one full-scale annual fairs in the present Var department during the eighteenth century[13] — the populations of the region were naturally much exposed to new ideas and to any changes of which travellers and merchants brought word. Thus Protestantism acquired a certain following in the bourgs around the main lines of communication, bringing with it the ravages of the Wars of Religion, ravages which more isolated communities were generally spared. Later, the eighteenth century saw Provence exposed *both* to precocious 'dechristianisation' *and* to a not-ineffective attempt by the Church to re-impose religious practice upon the area. At first sight a paradox, this apparent openness to opposing tendencies was quite to be expected; an area open to secularising influences was no less accessible to missionaries. It was the isolated communities which clung, throughout, to a religious identity which has been termed 'crypto-pagan'.[14]

A further inheritance from the traditions of independent Provence was the considerable degree of municipal autonomy enjoyed by the communities of Provençal towns and villages. Whereas many rural bourgs in Europe had regular assemblies for the discussion of municipal affairs, these were in most cases 'open' forums, easily dominated and controlled by the local seigneur and by the representatives of the Church. Provence, and to a lesser extent Languedoc, had long since developed a tradition of independent municipal 'councils'. Often known as a 'syndicate', this urban self-government consisted of the whole community (sometimes but not always exclusively the *male* community) meeting together, often in the town square, to consider matters of communal interest.[15] This *laïc* local identity bequeathed to the communes of Provence a sense of municipal solidarity and independence of seigneurial authority which clearly distinguishes them from the rural and small-town communities in other parts of France. It also played an important part in the creation of that 'sociability' referred to earlier; the peasants and artisans of lower Provence did not merely live in closely-grouped communities, they lived *as* communities, accentuating thereby the habits of collective activity in administration and recreation which we shall later find influencing patterns of economic and political activity as well. Long after the old forms of Provençal sociability — *chambrées*,[16] town-square meetings, societies of penitents, religious brotherhoods — have passed, we find the style of social behaviour which they created and which created them still present, manifesting itself in modern ways.

Provence and the Revolution

Modern French history is most commonly taken as having 'begun' in 1789, and although, put thus, such a statement is clearly naïve, it bears a germ of truth. In Provence as elsewhere, the Revolution changed enough aspects of people's lives in enough ways for it to become a reference point for much of their future activities and choices. Nevertheless, just as the modern political history of the Var begins in 1790, with the creation of the department and the emerging evidence of political options, so it is worth reminding ourselves that the way in which the region reacted to the Revolution was in very large part conditioned by the kind of society already in existence when the events of the Revolutionary years came into contact with it.

Much of the response of the Var to the changes brought about by the French Revolution was conditioned by the characteristic features of *ancien-régime* Provence already described. Thus, as in some other parts of France, the Revolution often did not so much overthrow old structures as give proper recognition to changes which had already taken place. Communes such as Bagnols (one example — of many) had settled their scores with the local seigneur and established *de facto* independence of feudal authority long since — in this case in 1570, when the population of Bagnols bought back their powers of self-government from the local seigneur, a process completed in 1646 when the Bishop of Fréjus granted the bourg complete freedom from outside control.[17]

However, the comparatively 'un-feudal' nature of Provençal society did not prevent it from playing a full part in the events of the period. The Grande Peur and anti-noble revolts of the spring and early summer of 1789 had strong echoes in the region; significantly, the incidence of disturbance was greatest in those parts of the Var, chiefly in the west, where the concentration of small towns was greatest, and where the eighteenth-century *confréries*, manifestations of an active sociability, were most numerous. Similarly, the Federalist movement of 1793, very strong in the Var with its sense of a Provençal identity distinct from that of France (and Paris), acquired its greatest support from the same areas of southern and western Var, the Gapeau and Argens valleys and their tributary settlements.[18] Already by the 1790s, and accentuated by the heightened feelings brought about by the developments of the Jacobin Revolution, the geographical and social divisions within eastern Provence began to take on a more consciously political character. Nevertheless, in the simplest sense, Federalism was 'counter-revolutionary' (or seen to be such); *confréries* were manifestations of a certain religiosity; the Grande Peur and the attacks on châteaux were acts of a politically 'indeterminate' nature. The point, then, is not that the Var was in any clear sense dividing in the 1790s into left and right, 'red' and 'white'; more accurately, we are seeing the first signs of the split between a political and a non-political, or at least an inactive, Var.

This said, it remains true that by 1793 the populations of the Var had quite definitely identified themselves, taken as a whole, with certain sides rather than others. The sale of national lands in the region took on a form rather different from that obtaining elsewhere, by virtue of the associations of villagers which came into being expressly for the purpose of facilitating the collective purchase of the land which came onto the market.[19] This was very different from the situation in the west of France, for example, where these lands tended to be bought by the wealthier bourgeoisie of the towns, without any significant change taking place in the size of properties, or indeed in the social arrangements attaching to them. The small peasants were often the net beneficiaries of the land sales in Provence, both as communities and as individuals; elsewhere the reverse was not infrequently the case.

A further instance of revolutionary identification in the region emerged in the early stages of the Revolution with the promulgation of the Civil Constitution of the Clergy; the department of the Var could boast the lowest number of churchmen refusing the 'serment constitutionnel' in France. Since the refractory clergy were often encouraged in their stand by the support of their local parishioners, it is not unreasonable to suppose, given what we know of the region in later years, that the priests of lower Provence felt it prudent to accept the Civil Constitution, in view of the sentiments of the local population. Most significant of all, it was in the rural regions of Provence, that is the villages and small bourgs, rather than in the larger towns, that the percentage of churchmen taking the vow was at its highest.[20]

The Revolution, then, made its mark upon the Var. But the precise form in which the experience of the 1790s affected the social and political attitudes of the Provençal populations is not easy to distinguish. While it is clear, that is, that the Revolution helped bring about attitudes and affiliations which can properly be called political, the identity of these affiliations had not fully emerged by 1815 – or rather, a variety of identities had emerged, all of them congruent with the inheritances from pre-Revolutionary Provence. Thus the same department which welcomed so enthusiastically the Civil Constitution of the Clergy saw virtually every village turn out in the streets at the news of Waterloo, white cockades to the fore. What is more, fully 20% of those who voted in the elections of 1837 gave their support to the legitimist candidates.[21]

The Var in the nineteenth century

The history of the Var in the period from Waterloo to the fall of the Second Empire is dominated by the experience of the Second

Republic. A fairly quiescent, largely legitimist region from 1815 until the mid-1840s, the Var emerged during the brief life of the Second Republic as one of the most radical and 'advanced' departments of France. Maurice Agulhon has written a magnificent three-volume study of the process by which this department was politicised by the experience of the Republic, of how a rural society came to commit itself so fully to the Revolution, to the extent, finally, of rising up, in considerable number, against the *coup d'état* of Louis Napoleon in December 1851. It is not my intention here to recapitulate, however inadequately, Agulhon's argument, but merely to draw the reader's attention to the nineteenth-century developments which had created, by 1870, an image of a 'Var rouge', firmly attached to the political left, insurrectionist and extreme.[22]

The context of this development was the final blossoming of the old Provençal economy in these years. The region continued to produce a wide and profitable variety of fruits, flowers and wine, commodities for which the expanding and more articulated economy of nineteenth-century France generated a constant demand. The rural industry (of which more in the next chapter) also flourished in the early years of the last century, with the emphasis on those products which, though industrially produced, were closely inter-woven with the agricultural economy – distilled spirits, glass, cork and barrels, etc. The local population kept pace with the economic vitality of the area – a vitality assured by both the demand for local produce and the wide variety of the latter; the population of the Var rose rather faster than that of France as a whole, with the emphasis on the 'urban villages'; in 1851, over 50% of the inhabitants of the Var were employed in agriculture (the figure for France was 40%), but only 46% of them lived in 'rural' surroundings (that is, in towns or villages of less than 2000 souls), whereas three-quarters of all Frenchmen at the time were classed as *ruraux*.[23]

This flourishing and sophisticated (though not, of course, 'modern') society was all the harder hit by the crisis of the 1840s for being so dependent upon national developments, interwoven into the wider economy. A fall in national purchasing-power was as much of a crisis for the wine-growers of the Var as it was for the itinerant masons of the Limousin, perhaps more so.[24] Thus when the economic crisis developed into a political one, and the Orleanist monarchy was replaced by a Republic, we find the inhabitants of the Var largely in sympathy with these developments (the precise nature and meaning of this rural identification with an urban Republic is something to be considered later). In the elections of the spring of 1849, elections which historians have sometimes taken as a touchstone for modern political affiliations in France, the voters of the Var gave their backing very clearly to the radical list of Ledru-Rollin. Some communes (Flassans and Le Luc on the central highway, Cotignac to the north of the Argens valley, Bargemon to the east of Draguignan, La Garde Freinet in the Maures) offer evidence of over half of all registered voters putting their cross by the Démocrates—Socialistes list.[25] The Republic was firmly implanted in the villages. In 1851, with Louis Napoleon's *coup* of 2 December, we find many of the towns and villages of the department turning out to join the armed bands marching north to oppose the Prince—President in the name of the elections of 1852 and the defence of 'la République Sociale'. When the hopeless resistance had been crushed, the authorities condemned 2434 Varois in the repression that followed: 1152 from the Brignoles arrondissement, 931 from the Draguignan arrondissement, 335 from that of Toulon. While insurrection in a well-garrisoned region like that of Toulon was always difficult, it remains significant that the insurgents should have been most numerous in the western and central Var, those areas of small bourgs and clustered villages which we have already met in other contexts for an earlier period.[26]

The events of 1851 ensured that the imperial régime which ensued would keep a particular eye on regions such as the Var. Two and a half thousand insurgents had been condemned before tribunals, but many others had appeared before their judges only to be let off, a number had been killed during the clashes between the insurgents and the troops sent to quell the revolt, and there was little doubt that much of the rest of the population of the region sympathised with the victims of the repression. The result of the events of 1851 was that in the Var, as in the Nièvre and other areas which had risen up in defence of the Republic, the Second Empire saw very little evidence of opposition. There can be little doubt that the repression organised by the imperial authorities succeeded in its aim, so that those very regions which had been most determined in their identification with the short-lived Republic, or at least with their image of it, became the most docile thereafter.[27] It is important to stress this from the beginning, since there is an understandable inclination to see a continuity between the rural democrats of 1849 and 1851 and the socialist voters of the 1890s, just as it is tempting, though mistaken, to see a direct line running through the political history of the Var from the enthusiasm of 1790 to the republicanism of 1848. In the latter case, a period of legitimist affiliation intervenes and obliges us to see the developments of mid-century as, if not sui generis, at least dependent in part on their context. Similarly, the Var which emerges in 1870 and which is the subject of this study, is not simply the Var of 1851 awoken after a generation of silence. The structure of Provençal society will explain a lot; but we shall see that it will not, cannot, explain everything and that the events of the intervening years, the economic and political conjuncture, count for much.

Just what changes did take place in the region from the 1850s, and how they help us to understand later developments, will be discussed later. This chapter has been more concerned to provide a geographical and historical context, however brief, in order that the reader, like the inhabitants of the Var, may enter the last third of the nineteenth century with some sense of the identity and experience which the region gave to its population. Neither the environment of Provence, nor its history before and after the French Revolution, should be thought of as determining the pattern of events which this book describes. Nevertheless, without an awareness of them, it would be difficult accurately to distinguish between what was characteristic of the region and what was common to many departments of France in the later nineteenth century. And there are some senses in which the history of the region manifests its influence on later developments in the form of myth. Thus I shall argue that, whatever the significance of the history of this region from the earliest times to 1851, it must not be seen as in any sense 'explaining' the course of events after 1870 (nor indeed of explaining events, in itself, before 1851). Yet the myth of a 'red' Var, a belief at least as widespread among the Varois themselves as among the apprehensive administrators sent down to control them,[28] no doubt played some part in deciding the political choices of the 1890s. In so far as the region's 'self-image' became self-fulfilling, then, the shadow of history can be said to lie heavily across any account of local behaviour. But advancing from generalisations about the area as a whole to investigation of the affiliations of different villages, we shall find numerous instances of history failing satisfactorily to fulfil itself — sometimes to the startled surprise of its instruments!

A final point concerning the historical background. Ever since the later Middle Ages, the region of Provence which concerns us has been divided not just between the Provence of the hills and of the valleys, but also between the Provence of the hinterland and of the coastal settlement around Toulon. The city of Toulon, with its magnificent natural harbour protected to the landward by a providential outcrop of the Ste Baume massif, has long been a natural focus for the population and economy of the littoral. With the coming of the navy it acquired national prominence as one of France's two major naval bases (the other being Brest), and with the development of the arsenal it grew rapidly into a city of consequence, with a large working population and multiple outside contacts. The explosive demographic development of Toulon falsifies some general aspects of Var population data, just as its occupational structure, when not controlled for, distorts the otherwise agricultural orientation of the region. Perhaps most importantly, however, the presence of a garrison, a maritime *préfet*, a police force, indeed the whole infrastructure of a well-administered nineteenth-century city, produces a pattern of political behaviour in the city which, though not out of line with that of comparable communities of the period, diverges markedly from that of the small town and village populations in the rest of the department.

As a result of this consideration, and also because there exist already a number of studies of Toulon,[29] I have concentrated my attention on the Var as a whole, while not giving the coastal city the attention its size would seem to warrant. This seems justified not merely in that my concern here is essentially to explain the implantation of socialism among the *peasantry*, but also because most of the communes of the Var were little affected by the existence of Toulon, unless it were as a market for their produce or a magnet for their departing youth. Where Toulon does count is in the occasional problems its complex (and, in the context, atypical) intra-party disputes caused for the socialists and syndicalists of the rest of the department; here of course the city will receive our fullest attention.

But for the rest this book is concerned with the peasants and part-peasants of the bourgs in the valleys and the villages and hamlets in the hills. Having familiarised ourselves with the background to their world, it is to them that we must now turn.

2

Social and economic change 1871–1914

Between the collapse of the Second Empire and the outbreak of war in 1914 Provence saw immense changes in the way of life of its inhabitants. In that these changes were largely brought about by the economic depression of this period on the one hand, and by the social and political achievements of the Third Republic on the other, the region was of course sharing in a development common to all of France. But the way in which the region was affected by these events, and the manner in which the local population responded to them, were substantially conditioned by the social structure of the area, and to this extent the impact of these years in the Var was unique to the department. I have already made occasional references to the social and economic structure of Provence; since one of the chief concerns of this study is to establish the relationship between the economic changes of these years and the political affiliations which emerged, it is now necessary to look in greater detail at the scale and nature of the changes in agriculture, in rural industry, in communications and in population which took place.

Agriculture

The salient feature of Provençal agriculture as it entered the last third of the nineteenth century was the variety of produce grown in the region. Unlike the great wheat centres of the Paris basin, or the wine-growing regions of Burgundy and the Gironde, the Var was not yet committed to the growth and sale of a single crop, although this would soon become the case for some parts of the department. The major products of the region in 1870 were wine, olives (and thus oil), fruit, flowers, and, to a declining extent, silk. Cereals were grown, too, in the northern fringe of the department and the western area around St Maximin, but these were never very important, not least because such good land as there was had long since been given over to more profitable (and suitable) crops. Cattle, and more commonly sheep, were everywhere to be found, but only in the sub-Alpine regions to the north were they central to the local economy, and then largely because little else could be raised in their place.

Each of these products had advantages and drawbacks for the men and women who depended upon them, and in some cases these became sufficiently marked for certain crops to disappear, others to monopolise their environment. In order to understand what these factors were which militated against the survival of the complex polyculture of earlier years, it may be helpful to take each product in turn.

The olive, long a staple product and characteristic feature of Provençal agriculture, had entered an extended decline from the 1830s.[1] There were still 54 000 hectares of olive trees in the department in 1840[2] but within thirty years the olive and its by-products had ceased to be central to the rural economy. The chief reasons for this were firstly that the olive was peculiarly subject to blight; by the 1880s we find olive-growers complaining that the fruit seemed to be affected by one disease or another every two or three years. Since the cost of growing and harvesting the olives was substantially the same every year, growers were progressively discouraged from committing themselves to a future dependent upon them. This was all the more the case from the mid-1880s, at which time the market price for olives, as for much else, went into a lengthy and steep fall. Moreover, the olive was always a major victim of any freak frosts in the early spring – and poor spring weather, as we have seen, was an acute problem in Mediterranean France in this period. Finally, the olive was increasingly unable to compete as a profitable crop with the grape. From the 1850s olive-growers in the Var had begun to plant vines in among the olive groves, a form of Provençal economic diversification which could only work, in the long run, to the detriment of the weaker crop, thus leading to a loss of diversity. Thus by the 1880s the olive had lost its central place in Provençal polyculture.[3]

The growth and marketing of *primeurs* – fruit and flowers – present the obverse of the experience of the olive. Ever since the sixteenth century the Var region had been renowned for its fruit and flowers, which were sold far outside the region itself. With the coming of a modern urban market, and above all with the development of faster communications, this branch of local agriculture grew apace, favoured, in the coastal regions where it dominated, by climate (*primeurs* were not so vulnerable as the olive, coming to maturity at different periods of the year) and by demand.

The major centres for fruit production were the western part of the central depression — the cantons of Cuers, Solliès — the coastal cantons of Hyères to the east of Toulon and Ollioules to the west, and to a lesser extent the tributary valleys of the Argens. The specialities varied: from the middle of the century there were flowers in the eastern Var, near Grasse (for use in perfume and soap manufacture), oranges and other citrus fruits in Hyères, figs as far north as Salernes, plums in the valley behind Brignoles.[4] But the really substantial output of *primeurs* was the affair of the coastal area, and grew to a peak in the 1880s. By 1885, the department was exporting 4 100 000 kilos of *primeurs* (some vegetables — artichokes, haricots — but mostly fruit and flowers) in the months of April and May alone.[5]

Solliès and its canton specialised in the production and marketing of fruit, above all. Hyères was better known for its flowers. The labour force in the area was organised on an almost industrial level (the — predominantly female — agricultural labourers in Hyères were to the fore in strike activity in these years), and the scale of output was such that in 1901 the Var could boast 136 *jardiniers* (market-gardeners and their employees) for every 10 000 inhabitants; the figure for France was 42 per 10 000. An interesting confirmation of the national orientation of the product comes in the 1889 election campaign of Gustave Cluseret, who capitalised in Hyères on local feelings about Parisian price-fixing and conditions of purchase — 'On vous vole.'[6]

The boom in fruit, vegetable and flower production can in large part be explained by the expanding market and the improved communications in the years after 1860. But there is another factor. In the cantons of Solliès and Cuers, as in Ollioules, one man could live comfortably off the produce of a piece of land measuring no more than 3 to 7 hectares.[7] As a result, the small property of the Var, in those areas where climate and topography were suitable, was ideally adapted to this kind of agriculture. Furthermore, it was not normally necessary, except for the large flower-growers of Hyères, to employ hired labour for most of the year, a further advantage in a period of acute labour shortage and price uncertainty. This was in sharp contrast with the demands of the olive, which, like the vine, was a labour-intensive fruit, demanding much trouble and care, and a considerable hectarage to make it profitable.

Other *primeurs* shared in the reflected glory of the flowers and oranges and berries. Mushrooms were a popular crop, particularly in the upper Caramy and Gapeau valleys. In 1884 Mazaugues exported 70% of its mushroom crop, receiving for it a higher price in Marseille than could be obtained locally. The mushroom harvest in Pierrefeu in 1882 was just over four thousand kilos, and the bulk of it was sold in Toulon and Marseille, for around 35 centimes per kilo. Even Tanneron, up on its hill above Mandelieu, on the eastern border of the department, grew strawberries and mimosa to support its otherwise exclusively wine-based agriculture. Small-scale fruit and flower growing for far-flung markets, concerning whose fluctuations the Varois were thus very aware, was a developing and important feature of the agriculture of the region.[8]

In a quite contrasting way, an equally important feature of the agriculture of the Var was the paucity and poor quality of cereals grown there. This was not a new thing — the quantity of cereals grown in the department had been on the decline ever since the 1840s. In 1878 there were still 65 000 hectares of land under wheat. By 1915 this had shrunk to 19 700.[9]

The reasons for the virtual absence of cereals in the agriculture of the region are not far to seek. In the first place, the terrain was unsuitable. Where the land was good it was devoted to more profitable and marketable crops; in any case, it tended to be good in long, narrow strips, valleys and terraces, unsuited to cereal production and quite uneconomic for that purpose. Cereals were cultivated in the plains around Aiguines and Comps, to the north, where the soil was poor and the climate unsuitable, and where the means to import new techniques were quite absent — there were still not ten mechanical threshers in the department by 1871. As elsewhere in France, the poorest regions grew wheat and rye not because the land was suited to it, but because it was suited to nothing else. As a result, the yield was low — in 1885 the Var was the last department in France for both per capita and total production of cereals *and* industrial crops (e.g. beet). The 1881 wheat harvest in the department was 600 000 hectolitres — a mere 6000 hectolitres more than the mountainous department of the Basses-Alpes to the north. What kept the wheat production of the Var in existence at all was the need of the northern communes to grow their own wheat, being unable to grow any more marketable produce with which to enter the commercial economy, plus perhaps the traditional diversification of the local economy of some western areas, growing wheat as an insurance against the failure of other crops (the wheat crop expanded briefly, during the late 1870s and early 1880s, with the phylloxera crisis).[10]

The raising of livestock was another rural occupation uncommon in nineteenth-century Provence. All communes, villages and bourgs alike, had their share of pigs, goats, sheep, chickens, etc., of course, and the upper settlements in the Maures, the Ste Baume and the northern Var were well stocked with sheep in particular. But the numbers were on the decline; sheep were not profitable (see below) and, given the quality of their grazing, they could not be expected to provide much meat or wool, although they were kept with an eye to both. As with cereals, so with livestock; those who could live by some more profitable form of farming did so. The rest scratched a living from unsuitable crops and animals which could compete in neither quality nor quantity with those of their Alpine neighbours.[11]

Across the rise of a market-oriented agriculture on the one hand, and the decline of the olive and of cereals on the other, there falls the shadow of the vine. The Var had not always been a department dominated by the production of wine — the polyculture of the years before 1860 bears witness to this. But from the middle of the century until the 1870s the vine came progressively to dominate all other cultures in the area.[12]

The boom in wine from the mid-century onwards resulted indirectly from the falling grain prices (as a result of foreign competition) and the crises which affected the olive. More directly, the growing demand for mass-consumption wine, and the rise in wine prices which this helped induce, encouraged thousands of small peasants, here as elsewhere, to commit their land to the monoculture of the vine. It was a product which could be grown profitably on a very small piece of land, and it ensured a good livelihood for many until the 1870s. The threat of overproduction was averted for a long time by the residual polyculture of the region — even those who depended on the vine

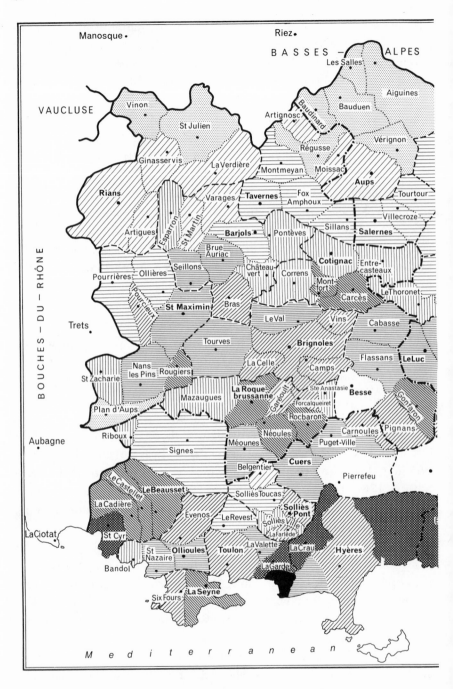

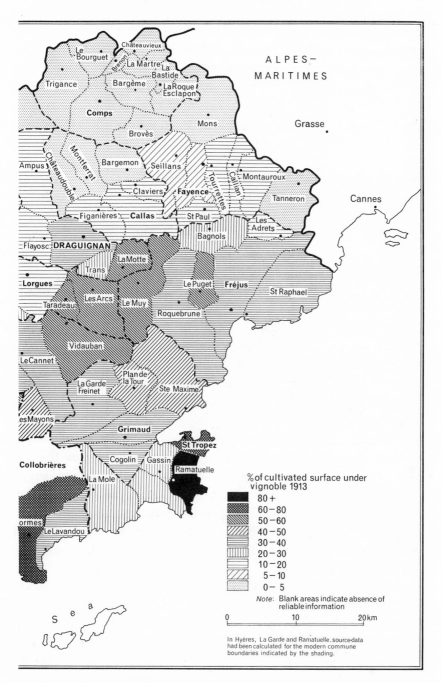

Map 4. Wine-growing in the Var — 1913

could not resist interspersing their vineyards with a few *oliviers,* some chestnut trees and perhaps an orchard. Like the *primeurs,* the wine was grown chiefly for a national market; as a result, the wine-growers of the department, like the fruit-producers of Ollioules and Solliés, became deeply involved with national price developments. Even had the phylloxera crisis not ravaged their crop, they would have suffered from the price fall of the late nineteenth century.

Phylloxera was a disease of the vine, caused by an insect which lived in and off the root of the vine, slowly killing the ceps. It first reached the Var in November 1871, at La Cadière, near the frontier with the Bouches-du-Rhône. Within fifteen years it had effectively destroyed the vineyards of the department, although it did not reach the central valleys until a little after it had ravaged the higher-quality wir es of the south-western Var.

Departmental wine output fell from 3 185 000 hectolitres in 1875 to 229 000 at the low point of 1885, to rise again to 1 753 903 hectolitres by 1907. But although the disease of the vine had a marked impact upon local communities, as will be seen, its quantifiable consequences were not enduring. The number of hectares under vine, 14 500 in 1873, had risen to 42 000 by 1890 and would reach 51 000 by 1914. In the meantime the new American ceps, imported for their immunity to the bug, pushed out all other growths (not least because uninformed peasants uprooted olives, fruit and the like, thought to harbour disease), and from the 1890s the vine, advancing steadily since the 1850s, began to take over the department and form those vine-filled valleys which greet the modern visitor. Even the 1907 crisis of overproduction, so traumatic in the Languedoc, did not impede the advance of the vine in eastern Provence; here the wine was usually a stronger one, $10°$ or more, and less susceptible to the kind of fraudulent mixing which had created the competition so damaging to the sales of weaker wines elsewhere.[13]

Thus between 1870 and 1910 the Var became a predominantly wine-producing department, though not on the scale of the Hérault, or even the Gironde, and different in a significant respect. In the Var, wine production remained for the most part the affair of the independent peasant producer — hence the non-industrial scale of the output. But with so many individuals separately involved in the monoculture of the vine, the market orientation which this implied and the cooperation which it demanded (individuals might grow their grapes separately, but after 1890 they found it advantageous to produce the wine in cooperatives) meant that this particular change in the orientation of Provençal agriculture would have very marked social consequences.

One other farming activity in the region is worthy of note. In 1883, the Var was the sixth department in France for the production of silkworms, raised for the most part on the mulberry trees of the hills behind Salernes.[14] In 1891 communes like Villecroze had 70% of their population directly employed in the raising of silkworms. This sizeable activity was nevertheless relatively insignificant for the economy of the region, since the major centres of silk manufacture were in the Rhône valley, and it was there that the silk was sent. Nevertheless, the department was still a significant producer in 1900 (with 518 000 kilos of silkworms it was fifth in France, after the Drôme, the Ardèche, the Gard and the Vaucluse), and the production of silkworms serves as a further reminder, were one needed, of the extent to which agricultural production in this region was directed to a wider market, with all that this implied.[15]

Property structure

The Var was substantially a department of small property. Of the four major categories of agricultural status in France (*propriétaire-exploitant* as distinct from absent landlord, tenant farmer (*fermier*), sharecropper (*métayer*) and agricultural labourer (*journalier*)), the first, farmers who owned and worked their land, predominated. During the early Third Republic, they constituted about 80% of those who worked the land. Sharecroppers accounted for most of the remaining 20%, tenant farmers being almost unknown in this department. Agricultural labourers — often small proprietors themselves, supplementing an insufficient income by hiring themselves out to larger farmers — were a declining force in most of the department, departing in large numbers during these years in search of work elsewhere.[16]

Despite the predominance of small peasants, however, a sizeable portion of the hectarage of the region was actually held in large properties of more than 100 hectares (about 45% in the 1880s), much of it in the forests and on the plateaux of the north. The small property was concentrated around the coast and the lower valleys, where a very small holding could still be a profitable undertaking. Medium-sized properties were on the decline in these years — outside the intense cultivation of the commercial crops only a large proprietor could survive the price falls of the depression, with the result that the Var came increasingly to be divided between a few large properties and a large number of very small ones. This ending of the process of *morcellement* also meant an end of the hopes of a *journalier* of acquiring a small plot of his own — a fact which helped accentuate the problem of labour shortage brought about by the departure of men who could no longer hope to establish themselves locally.[17]

A not inconsiderable quantity of the land surface of the region, particularly in the wooded areas, belonged still to the commune, an important factor both in helping to maintain the importance of the communal identity of many of the smaller towns and also in providing the occasional extra resource (rights of access to fuel, etc.) for the poorer peasantry during the perennial crisis which affected the crops of the Var in the later nineteenth century. The paradox of a region whose peasantry were both individual proprietors and members of strongly defined communities emerges once again.

Industry

To separate an account of the industrial activity of the Var from that of its agriculture is necessarily an artificial arrangement. Very few agricultural societies were ever completely without their industrial side, and the mixed and commercially-oriented agriculture of the Var would rightly suggest to the reader an active, if small, industrial sector. Nor did the two exist in the same place but independently of one another. Agricultural and industrial production were closely integrated, both in respect of the things produced and of the labour that produced them; many, perhaps most, Var peasants had a share in some partly-industrial activity such as distilling or cork manufacture, and most artisans and even industrial workers had some experience of agricultural work and often owned a small piece of land themselves. This was at least as true of Provence as it was for the rest of France, although in Provence as elsewhere rural industry was declining in this period and the industrial and peasant sectors were moving apart. As in other countries experiencing industrialisation on a major scale, the paradoxical consequence was a de-industrialisation of the countryside, with cottage industries and artisans failing through competition and local depopulation. Despite the continuing presence of many of the activities described below, the Var between 1870 and 1914 was becoming a more properly *peasant* society than it had been hitherto.[18]

The traditional industrial activities of the region fell into four general categories: mining and extractive industry, including quarrying; clothing industries; food production; finally, in so far as it was distinct from the last two categories, industry directly linked to agriculture.[19]

Mining had long since been pursued in the region, though never on a major scale. The Saracens had mined the lead and zinc of the Maures, and these same deposits, particularly around Bormes, continued to provide work right through our period. In 1894, 50 330 tons of zinc were extracted at the mines of Les Bormettes. Coal production was always on a small scale — 28 000 tons were produced in 1873 — and was exceeded both by anthracite and lignite (55 000 tons in 1873) and especially bauxite. The latter was a resource in a number of the communes in the centre of the Brignoles arrondissement. The east—west vein which ran through that part of the department produced 258 074 tons of bauxite in 1913. There were iron deposits, too, especially in the Maures, but they were far away from any communication by road or rail and thus were never fully exploited. The only other iron deposits, around Ampus and Châteaudouble near Draguignan, were linked for a time (until 1905) by cable to the Sud France railway line.

The making of bricks, tiles and pottery was a fairly active sector here as in many other parts of France. Eleven hundred people were regularly employed in this sphere, mostly in tile manufacture, in 1911, and many more worked in it part-time. The main centres for pottery and ceramics were St Zacharie and Varages in the western Var, but tile and brick manufacture were carried on over a much wider area; there were substantial establishments in Vidauban,

Flayosc, Aups, Salernes, Villecroze and Lorgues in the arrondissement of Draguignan, as well as in the canton of Solliès near Toulon.[20]

The clothing industries of the Var were, of course, closely integrated with the agricultural economy, and had been established in the villages and bourgs for many generations. In the 1880s they included a few surviving centres of cottage weaving, disappearing now in France as it had done two generations earlier in England, but above all the manufacture of shoes and hats, both closely linked to the tanneries which were still at work in the region. The census of 1911 records a total of 2148 people still occupied in the making of shoes, despite a generation of outside competition. Many of these people lived and worked in Bargemon and Flayosc, to the north-east of Draguignan, and we shall be hearing more of these two communes and their population of *cordonniers* later on. The manufacture of hats, an industry similar in structure and in its relationship to the countryside, dates back to the eighteenth century if not before, and ever since that time had been carried on principally in the communes of Camps, Carcès and Cotignac in the Brignoles region.

Even more directly linked to the rural economy of which they formed an integral part were the various manufactures such as those of paper, soap, spirits and, supremely, corks. Much more than the clothing industries, these products, often ancillary to the vine in some respect, were linked to the national market no less than oranges, flowers or the vine itself, and the steady decline which they underwent in these years was a reflection of this fact.

The manufacture of corks in the Var, generally in the cork-oak forests of the Maures and especially around the commune of La Garde Freinet, dates back a long way. The Maures region of the Var was the major source of cork-oak in France, and was equalled only by the resources of Sicily, Sardinia and Corsica in the Mediterranean. As the local output of wine increased, so the cork manufacturers and their employees grew in number. By their peak in the middle of the nineteenth century they numbered many thousands. Their decline began with the coming of the railway and of production on a modern, mechanical scale and it was hastened by the wine crisis of the 1880s. The rise and decline of the cork industry, with its effect on the population structure and political stance of the villages of the Maures, thus serves as an illustration in miniature of the sophisticated and thus vulnerable economy of the region and its collapse in the face of modern industry and economic depression at the end of the nineteenth century.[21]

The paper industry, essentially based in the wooded regions of the south-west and making packing materials for the produce of the valleys, survived on a small scale throughout our period. The production of soap, particularly luxury soaps, flourished in much the same way as the flowers whence came its perfume; in 1873 the annual value of the soap production of the Var was 2 700 000 francs, and this scale of activity remained undiminished throughout.

Two other industries linked to the vine, the making of barrels and the distilling of a kind of *marc*, both survived into this period, although the barrel manufacture of Bandol, where it was largely centred, was hard-hit by the phylloxera. More surprisingly, the milling of oil from olives remained a thriving activity, despite the decline of the olive itself (the drop in price may have helped, by making the raw material very cheap and enabling the millers to compensate for a low rate of return by an increased output). There were oil mills all over the Var, some of them (such as those at Barjols and Varages and in the Cotignac region) employing more than twenty men apiece. Many other communes clung on to their tiny local mill, producing an oil, which, in quantity and quality, could not hope to compete with the produce of the large mills, much less those outside the department. In some ways these mills atypically remained as truly rural industries, serving the local population alone, in a period and an area where such semi-autarky was always rare.

Aside from the activities of Toulon and La Seyne, where the naval arsenal and the shipyards respectively created an altogether different and quite un-rural industrial scene, there remained one 'industrial' activity conducted on a scale sufficient to be worthy of note. This was the bakery of the Var. Although most communes continued to bake their own bread locally, often privately, the department was equipped with a rather astonishing number of establishments of bakery and pastry-making. There were 77 people per 10 000 employed in the industry, making the Var in this field the third department in the nation. One consequence of this was that bakery workers became very prominent in the syndical movement of the Var from the 1880s onwards, and the wages in the bakeries often served as a touchstone for regional wages generally.[22]

The types of small-scale non-agricultural activity were thus rather heterogeneous; indeed they could be added to indefinitely, since quite apart from the sawmills at Le Muy and the railway workshops which came to Carnoules in the 1870s, every commune (barring only the truly isolated and tiny hamlets of the north-east) could boast its own carpenter, perhaps a locksmith, a blacksmith, maybe even a mason. Not perhaps industrial activity properly so-called, but these men were not precisely peasants either, though they may well have owned land and even worked on it, and their presence reminds us that if the leading characteristic of the Var was its agriculture, the industrial and artisanal side of the region was ever-present, albeit in declining numbers.

Most of this industrial activity was really more properly artisanal than industrial in the modern sense (that is, it was not concentrated under one roof nor even in one place). In the manufacture of shoes, for example, there were in 1911 three *patrons* for every two workers. In the same year the census tells us that the making of barrels was performed in the Var by 100 *patrons* and 82 *ouvriers* — as if, on that scale, the distinction can have meant very much. Only in the manufacture of corks (and, of course, the machine-tool and ship-building industries of Toulon) was there anything like an industrial concentration — 15 workers for every employer.

Thus the Var at the beginning of this century still managed to retain certain of the characteristic features of the old Provençal economy: a diversity of produce, much of it grown or made for sale outside the region; towns and large villages which retained an intermix of peasants, artisans, employees, workers and of course the bourgeoisie, with peasant — artisan — worker often describing the same man at different times of the year and in different stages of his life; above all production, in industry as in agriculture, which survived on a very small, individual scale, though increasingly at risk in the face of more efficient competition from France and abroad.

A changing population

The typical 'Mediterranean' community, urban in organisation and habitat, rural in occupation, was very well represented in the social structure of the population of the Var before 1870. The peculiarly

Provençal characteristic lay in the more than usually cosmopolitan mixture of occupations present in many of the bourgs of the Var. Not merely were there the 'urban peasants', the artisans, the café owners, the shopkeepers and tiny industries, there was also a considerable leavening of 'bourgeois'; *rentiers* for the most part, these men and women, whom censuses represent as 'living on their means', formed an educated urban nucleus around whom the social and political life of the community often turned. As late as 1891, when many of these people had departed the region, or died and not been replaced by a new generation, the Var still contained them in very considerable numbers. They constituted 8.3% of the resident population, whereas in France as a whole they were less than 5%. In earlier years their presence had been even more marked. Their disappearance is a factor to be taken into account when investigating the paths by which new ideas entered the villages once they had gone.[23]

The other Mediterranean feature well represented in most of the region was the agglomerated habitat. In 1891 fully 79% of the inhabitants of the Var lived in the urban commune itself, with only 21% dwelling in hamlets or isolated farms; this makes the Var substantially less 'rural' in this important respect than most other departments of France. It is all the more significant in that, still taking the 1891 census as our guide, we learn that 42% of the inhabitants lived in communities of less than 2000 persons. Some of these 'urban villages' were thus very small. Globally, the regions of tightly-grouped villages were the inland communes running east—west from Fréjus, through the central depression and up the Gapeau valley to Signes; the central part of the arrondissement of Brignoles from Pourcieux to Carcès; and the communes of the north-western Var from Barjols to Ginasservis. In all of these areas, the agglomerated population tended in the 1890s to number over 75% of the total.

The 'other' Var, the Var of more isolated, higher, spread-out habitation, was located chiefly in an arc running west—east from St Julien to Comps. There were smaller regions of sparse population — the coastal area around Bormes, and to the west, in the canton of Le Beausset, the individual communes like Le Cannet and Tanneron — where the general pattern of clustered villages was broken by a community of far-flung hamlets. In these areas the percentage of the

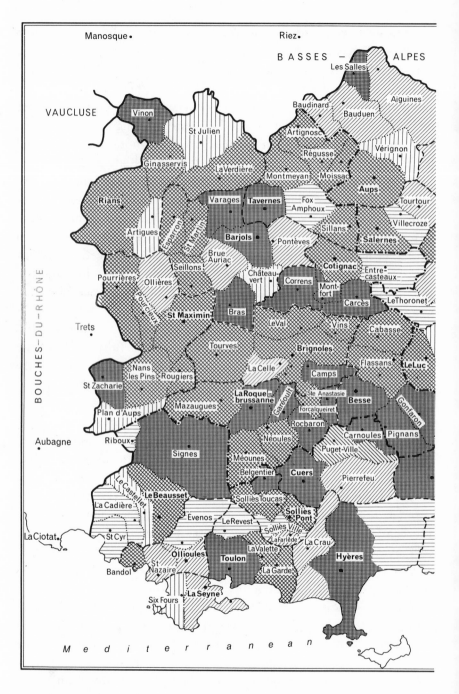

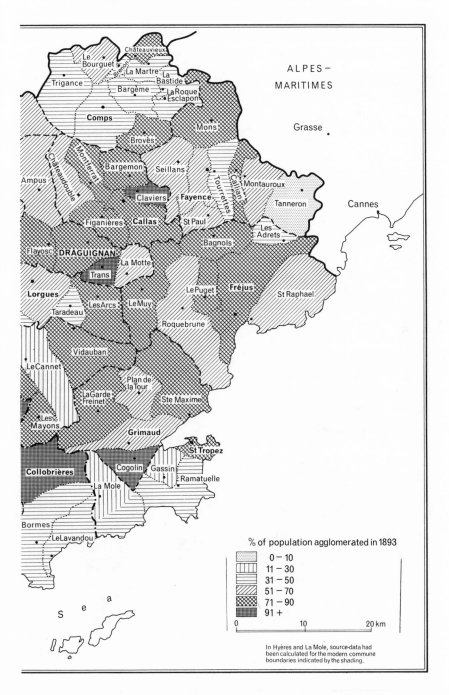

Map 5. Population by habitat — 1893

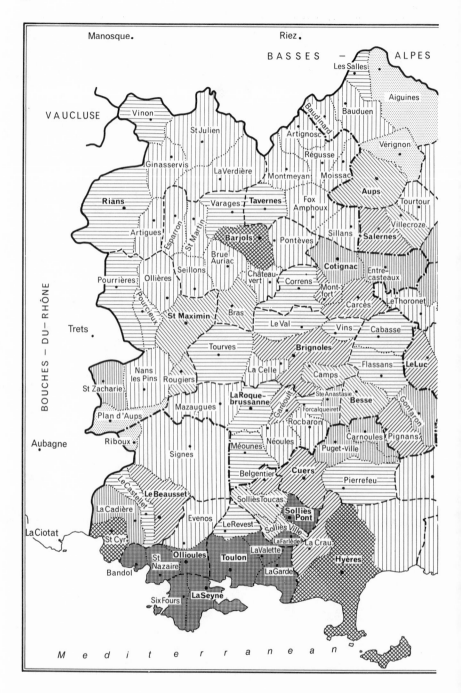

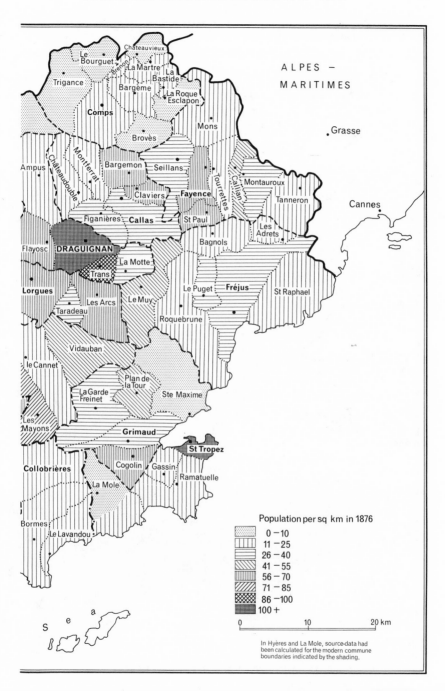

Map 6. Population per sq. km in the Var — 1876

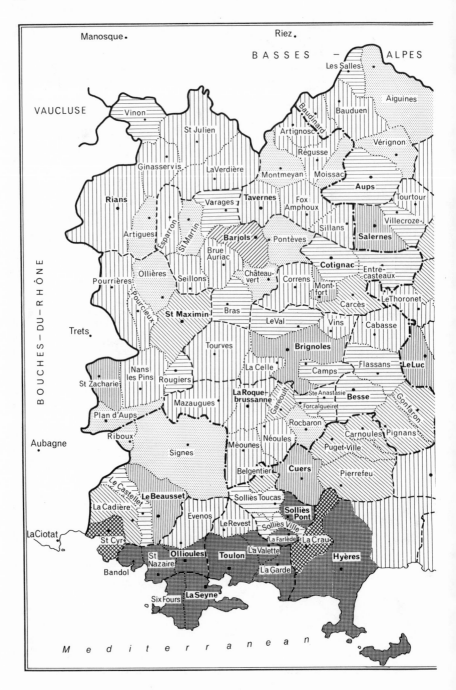

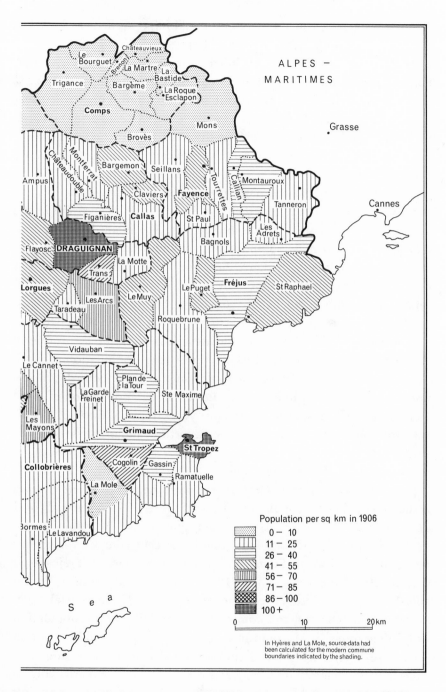

Map 7. Population per sq. km in the Var — 1906

population grouped in the *chef-lieu* could fall to as little as 10%, less even in Tanneron. The contrast between a commune such as St Julien, where 81% of the inhabitants lived in houses and tiny hamlets spread out all over the plateau, and Carcès, where all but 3% lived in the town itself, could not have been more marked. It was only in the bourgs like Carcès that the complicated social mixture, including that bourgeois wealth which made the Var the sixth department in France for the importance of rent in private fortunes, thrived.[24]

The great change in the pattern just described came about in the last twenty years of the nineteenth century, with a sharp fall in the population of the small towns of the Var. The main drop in population came between 1876 and 1886, coinciding as one might expect with the phylloxera pestilence and the more general agricultural depression. The chief victims, not surprisingly, were not the small, poor communities like Comps or Le Bourguet, though they too experienced a loss of population (Comps fell from 810 in 1876 to 622 inhabitants in 1906); the greatest loss came in the formerly thriving towns like Carcès, which declined from a population of 2667 in 1876 to 1775 in 1896, a population loss of one-third. An important market town like Aups could fall from a population of 2610 to one of 1892 persons in the twenty years from 1876 to 1896. This was not mere 'wastage' but positive departure, and on a considerable scale.[25]

Why was the fall so very steep? A clue lies in the fact that the department *as a whole* was out of step with the rest of France; it was actually growing in population from 1886 to 1911, at a rate (over 15% in that 25-year period) which put it in the same league as the Nord or the Rhône. This growth was centred upon the coastal region, from St Cyr to Fréjus, and was quite substantial; Fréjus itself grew by 20% in the period 1876–1906, and towns like Gassin, Hyères and St Raphael were developing even faster. These coastal communities, like the isolated communes of the hills whose population was falling more slowly than in communities in the middle, were in each case benefiting from circumstances absent in the bourgs and villages of the valleys. The coastal strip was actually experiencing an economic boom, while the mountain communes were being less drastically affected by the economic storms which were sweeping the richer communities lower down; that is to say, they were benefiting from the very economic and physical isolation which kept them small and poor in the first place.[26]

Those who departed were essentially of three kinds; the bourgeois rentier, the artisan and the young. A further category, the agricultural labourer, had already been a declining presence since before 1870. What was left, then, in so many of the small towns of Provence, was an older, more properly peasant population. Evidence of this may be seen in the composition of municipal councils. In Aups, for example, the municipal council of 1896 numbered 62% of peasant proprietors; in 1908 this category filled 72% of the seats. In Bormes, near the coast but economically linked to the Maures, the rise in the number of agricultural councillors was from 43% to 81% in the same period. In Le Luc, formerly one of the most complex and mixed populations of the central Var, peasants filled 67% of the municipal council places in 1908; in 1896 that figure had been 52%.[27]

The peasants who did remain (and they too of course were in decline) were for the most part victims of the agricultural crisis of these years; although the economy of these towns never remotely approached a return to autarky it did see the peasant cutting back his expenditure and turning to crops which might provide him with the means for survival rather than crops for cash marketing. Thus the local industrialists and the village artisans, already hard-pressed to compete with manufactured produce, found their *local* market rapidly contracting. It is not altogether surprising that it should have been they who first made the decision to leave. The significance of the growing presence of small farmers on municipal councils is precisely that it was the departing artisans who had formerly dominated in these assemblies. Furthermore, the fact that it was indeed the non-rural sections of the population which left helps explain the *relative* stability of the mountain communities – there had been few artisans and even less industrial activity in these parts to begin with.

Population movement had not of course been unknown in these parts. Regular temporary migration was part of the life of mountain communities, and even in the valleys it was not all that uncommon for young men to seek work in the town or city for a few years. What was new was both the scale of the out-migration and of course its permanence. The classic pattern of rural out-migration:

countryside—bourg, bourg—city, did not apply in the Var — the first stage was irrelevant. As a result it was precisely the bourgs, which had not been accustomed to population loss, which were the major victims.[28]

One major new feature of life in the small towns of the Var after 1890 was the steady increase in the number of people living there who had been born outside the department, and indeed outside France. The Var had of course always been a region of immigration, in the sense that, lying across a major network of communications from Paris to the coast and from France to Italy, it was a natural focus for population movement, the more so with the first intimations of its future career as a centre for tourism, a matter much discussed in coastal circles around 1900. Already in 1872, 21.8% of those living in the Var had not been born there, and this figure had grown to 25% by 1906. But what was new was the steady growth in immigrant labour, chiefly Piedmontese, which took place in these years. In 1884 there were 83 000 foreigners in the Var, 75% of them Italians. The problems posed were big enough for the Italian government to set up a special vice-consulate at Hyères in November 1882 to deal with the violent clashes between Piedmontese and local workers, provoked usually by the low wages which the Italians were forced to accept, and which kept down the wage rates of local workers. The influx of Italian labour altered substantially the balance of industrial to agricultural activity in the areas where they settled (chiefly along the coast and on the coastal fringes of the central depression), and also made an important contribution to the nascent socialist movement in the region, of which more later.[29]

This chapter has been concerned so far with describing in limited detail the main changes which took place in the economy of the Var in the last third of the century. Reference has been made on a number of occasions to the changes which account for these local developments, but it may be helpful to summarise these changes more precisely.

Promoters of change

Communications

The crisis of the Provençal economy really began with the growth of the railways. Although initially a boon to this market-oriented region, the railways helped produce the trap of monoculture — concentration on one profitable crop, with all that this meant in respect of lack of fall-back and dependency on weather, prices, the health of the crop, etc. For every market-gardener who made a living by sending his *primeurs* to Paris there were five peasant proprietors who had ill-advisedly put their land to nothing but the vine, and been rendered destitute by the coming of the phylloxera.

The railway grew most rapidly in this region in the period from 1878 to 1890, during which the existing 162 km of track was extended to 498 km. After that date, a mere 27 km was added, so that the essential change in the region's link to the rest of France was a feature of the 1890s, when it came in time simultaneously to complete the final changeover to the vine, hasten the ruin of the old polyculture, provide work (constructing the track) for those it had helped to make unemployed — and carry away the departing villagers to Toulon and Marseille.[30]

As the crisis deepened, many in the region came to see the new, rapid communications as in large part responsible for their woes. In some instances they were not without a case. Thus in 1888 the PLM railway company was charging 192 fr. 30 to transport from Fréjus to Paris a quantity of corks which a rival company would bring, weight for weight, from Madrid to Paris for 180 francs! Little wonder that the cork-makers, bosses and workers alike, demanded revised rail tariffs and an embargo on the export of raw cork (which would then be finished at low cost by cheap Spanish labour).[31] Similarly, the Chemin de Fer du Littoral, a project to build a railway line from Toulon to St Raphael, via St Tropez and Fréjus, was very unpopular everywhere except on the littoral itself. It would by-pass the villages of the Maures, would turn traffic away from the inland roads and towns, and would prejudice the chances of a railway link west—east across the upper Var, from St Paul to Draguignan, without which the inner Var was doomed, or so it was believed. The railway companies themselves were loath to construct inland — the terrain was thankless and the enterprise unprofitable. Even the railway link from Les Arcs to Draguignan (connecting the departmental capital to the Paris—Nice railway) was run at a loss; in 1880 it cost 114 000 francs in upkeep and redemption costs, but brought in only 67 000 francs. By 1890 the railway links through the Var and between the Var and the rest of France operated almost exclusively to the advantage of the coastal strip, particularly west of Hyères, which the littoral railway line had reached. This phenomenon, whereby modern communications can actually leave a backward region worse off than it was before, is not of course an unknown one. But for the Var, which had so long been anything but a backward region, the largely negative rôle played by the railways — bringing outside competition *in* rather than taking local produce *out* — was especially ironic.[32]

The economic conjuncture

Enough has already been said about the vulnerability of this region to outside competition for it to be unnecessary to repeat the point that the slump in prices and the collapse of the vine were major factors in promoting the demographic and economic changes so far described. However, it may be helpful to present a little more precisely the facts concerning these economic crises, since the exact rôle they played in promoting political change is something we shall want to look at closely in Part Two.

The fall in the price of wheat followed approximately the following pattern. Nationally, a quintal (100 kilos) of wheat fell from 30 francs in 1869 to 25 francs in 1882, reaching 18 francs in 1895. It stayed low, but steady, until 1907, rising thereafter to 1914. The significance of this lies in the fact that the experience of wheat runs quite counter to that of wine. In the Var, wheat prices began to fall sharply in the autumn of 1882 (between June and October of that year the price for a quintal in local markets fell from 26 to 22 fr. 80, a sharp drop even allowing for the usual autumn fluctuations). But the price of ordinary wine (most Var wine was of this class) actually *rose*, from 41 francs per 100 litres in 1882 to 47 francs in 1885 (March) and thence to 52 fr. 50 in March 1886. Since this rise was closely associated with the phylloxera-induced shortage, most local producers did not benefit; but when it was the turn of wine to experience a price fall, in 1907, the *vigneron* was to find that the price of bread was on a steep upward curve. The advantages of polyculture could hardly have been more clearly expressed — one generation late, however.

Other food prices also fell in the 1880s. Beef and mutton, which in the market at Les Arcs had reached a high of 1 fr. 80 and 1 fr. 90 per kilo respectively (on the hoof) in 1884, had fallen to 1 fr. 25 and

1 fr. 35 respectively by October 1887. But the worst fall was experienced by the olive. One kilogram of olive oil sold at 1 fr. 50 in 1871; it could still fetch 1 fr. 35 in 1886, although 1882 had been a bad year. But by 1899 the olive had slumped to 54 centimes per kilo. The olive-producers could not turn to the vine for help since, although phylloxera was past its worst by 1886, the new plants would not be profitable for a few more years. The late 1880s were the blackest period for the cultivators of the Var, with numerous bankruptcies and mass departures. They were also the formative years of modern political allegiance in the department.[33]

Not surprisingly, we find wages the major point of conflict in relationships between *patron* and worker in the industries of the Var at this time. The wage rates varied enormously in the region, between area and by occupation. Skilled hat-makers in Toulon could earn 4 fr. 50 per day in 1880; by 1912 they were commanding 7 francs per day in the city. At the other end of the spectrum, cork-workers (female) in Cuers in 1886 was striking for an increase on their 1 franc per day. The average wage in the Var outside Toulon was about 3 francs in 1910; in Toulon it was 40% higher. The significant point is that the rates in most jobs had hardly risen since the 1880s, when they had been kept low by competition from foreign labour, employers' falling rates of profit, and the falling price of staple commodities such as bread. But food and other prices were rising after 1900, and wages were lagging behind. Thus strikes of this period (and they were many in number) concentrated on raising wages, in almost every activity, rather than on improving conditions or gaining control of e.g. pension funds.[34]

A word concerning phylloxera.[35] Its direct effects were bad enough — it destroyed the livelihood of a large minority of the population of the department. But in certain respects its indirect effects were no less important. To begin with, it had a detrimental effect on the social life of the community. The *vendanges* had been the occasion for annual fairs, fêtes and festive events associated with wine and the well-being of the community. But the newspapers of the 1880s are full of reports of fairs and *vendanges* in the Var which had declined into hollow shams, with no one buying, no one singing or talking, eventually with no one coming. The mood of acute pessimism with which these reports are accompanied would eventually give way to doubtful optimism as the new vines took root. But the social effects of the decade of disaster were more durable, and the phylloxera must bear a major responsibility for bringing about a change in the way of life of the region — or perhaps, more precisely, for helping to channel Provençal sociability into angrier, more organised channels.

The indirect effects took other forms, too. Thus the produce of Hyères was affected for quite a while both by the stigma attached to fruit and flowers coming from a phylloxera-stricken region, but also by a government law forbidding the export of certain plants from an affected region to one which the disease had not reached. Or there were the barrel-makers of Bandol; their wine eventually recovered, but the skilled workers who had left when the industry collapsed did not return, and the unskilled Italians were no substitute; in any case, barrels were now being made elsewhere, more cheaply and in greater number. Finally, the phylloxera perpetrated a special injustice on the wine-growers, in that they continued to have to pay tax on their agricultural land even though they could grow nothing on it — excepting a few hectares of wheat and some unsaleable olives. The ravages of the phylloxera were many.

By 1870, the market for wine was showing signs of saturation, and had the phylloxera not come when it did, the disastrous overproduction of the years 1904—7 might have been anticipated by a generation. As it was, the blight set the wine-growers back, but only to advance the cause of monoculture still further by creating the need for American vines. These were distributed free by communes on the basis of communal decisions which often provoked cries of political favouritism in the early 1880s; by 1900 the American stocks had become the predominant and splendidly healthy strain. When the crisis did come, it was the small wine-grower, again more prominent in the Var than in, say, the Gironde, who suffered, because he did not produce enough to compensate for the slump in price per litre. The small wine-grower would learn, as his predecessor of the early nineteenth century could have warned him, that in growing as in drinking, an exclusive concentration upon the vine was not a healthy business.

The end of Provence?

Maurice Agulhon[36] argues that the decline of the small towns of Provence, and with it their specifically local character of 'sociability', meant the end of the region's separate existence: thenceforth it was 'normalised', integrated with the rest of France. Eugen Weber,[37] though he is not writing about Provence in particular, suggests a similar view for the generality of French rural communities as a result of the change they experienced in the years 1870–1914. The view is a seductive one. That the degree of change was startling is beyond doubt. The developments discussed in this chapter were also a matter for much sadness and anger in the Var at the time. The local newspapers were regularly carrying articles chronicling the sorry decline of the once thriving industry and agriculture of Brignoles and elsewhere. The municipal councils of the bourgs in the valleys sent regular pleas to the Minister of Agriculture for assistance; the coastal towns concentrated on finding new sources of revenue in tourism and intensive cultivation of selected cash-crops. The world was changing about them and they knew it.

Nevertheless, it is important not to exaggerate the perspective. On the one hand the northern Var underwent very little change — the *sous-préfet* of the Basses-Alpes who wrote of the remoteness of the Verdon region could as well have been writing in 1896 as in 1836,[38] and although the special characteristics of Provence were of course those of the valleys and not those of the *Alpes dégradées*,[39] the point is that the contrast which had been so important in 1840 had by no means disappeared by 1900 — in Chapter 6 we shall have occasion to see just how little it had disappeared. If the Provençal sociability of the small bourgs suffered a severe blow at the hands of the economy and the phylloxera bug, there are still some indications that it did not so much lie down and die as respond by new and different means. Thus it may be that Weber's contention that these peasants became 'Frenchmen' by 1914 takes insufficient account of the rôle their political choices played in their rejection of just such a development.

In some ways, then, the economic and social crisis transformed rather than destroyed the peculiar forms of Provençal social and economic life. There is, for instance, little in common between the reaction of the Var to the changes of this period, and the reactions of communities in southern Italy to not dissimilar pressures. Why the Var should have become a centre of political radicalism, rather than a deserted region of ghost-towns and impoverished peasants, is a question we can only answer by accepting, *ab initio,* that it has something to do with the social structure of the place; not just the structure that was, but the structure that must in certain respects have remained. To suggest otherwise is surely to imply that every significant characteristic of social life in peasant societies is a function of the presence of a non-agricultural sector. When it departs, nothing is left, or at least, nothing of what had been peculiar and important to the region. It is this dismissal of the specific identity of the peasantry which it is one of the aims of this book to argue against. We can begin by appreciating that the changes of the years 1870–1914 did not 'normalise' Provence by destroying its identity. They left it a more completely peasant, though in some ways no less urban, community. And it is in this context that we must now move on to an account of the growth of the Socialist movement in the region at this time.

3

Political developments 1871 – 1914

Most people are not particularly interested in politics most of the time. They are certainly not as concerned with political life as the preoccupations of historians might lead us to suppose. This truism has the force of paradox in France, where, despite the sharp and enduring political divisions, the concerns of the political parties arouse remarkably little interest except at moments of crisis. It is a commonplace that French men and women do not join political and social organisations to the degree that Germans or English do, and this has sometimes been held a contributory cause of the weakness of the left, given that left-wing politics depend in most instances upon a higher degree of popular participation.

At first glance, the Var appears a more than usually clear case of these characteristics of French political life. The rate of abstention at elections in the first half of the Third Republic was very high – one of the highest in France. Some 20 communes – and they are to be found throughout the region – consistently registered an abstention rate of more than 40% during the period. Many of the remaining communes registered such a voting rate, if not consistently, then quite often. Nor was there an increased interest as the Republic matured: in 1876 there were 49 communes where the turnout at the election of that year did not reach 60%; in 1898 the figure had leapt to 72 – nearly half the total number of communes in the department; it had reached 74 by the last election before the war. Of course, the reasons why people abstain may be just as political as the reasons they have for voting a particular way, although the former are harder to ascertain or indeed to formulate.[1]

We should not conclude from this that political life in the region was dormant, or that we are going to be dealing with the political activities of an élite. Although it was not unknown for a municipal election to be held and for no one to come – literally no one – this was rare; local elections, like national ones, were usually very active

occasions. And the reasons for both phenomena are hard to find: it
was in Salernes, where no one bothered to vote at the municipal elections of January 1883, that 686 people turned up at a meeting in
August of the same year to choose a Republican candidate for the
impending elections to the departmental council.[2]

There were, there is little doubt, too many elections for interest to
be sustained for long. As well as the general elections every four
years there were the municipal council elections, with the municipal
by-election every time a councillor died or resigned; the elections to
the arrondissemental council, and the elections to the departmental
council. The fact is that some of these bodies were virtually without
real function (the arrondissemental councils in particular tended to
meet, chaired by the *préfet* or *sous-préfet*, for a few minutes to discuss some anodyne technical matters, and then disperse again until
the following month).[3] Thus we should perhaps be surprised not by
the frequent apathy between elections, and the occasional apathy in
the face of yet another voting-booth, but by the generally high
level of enthusiasm for elections when they occurred – for the contemporary authorities assure us that interest in politics at election
time was 'avid',[4] and the pattern of local socialist meetings confirms
this opinion.

Abstentions or no, there were good reasons for taking an interest
in how a vote went. Until 1880, of course, elections had a real
bearing on the régime under which the French lived, so that the
higher turnout for the earlier period makes good sense. But throughout the period two points deserve stress. First, that it was actually
quite normal for peasants to express their thoughts and feelings
through elections – unlike industrial workers and of course the
middle classes, they lacked more regular and articulated channels for
making known their views. The high abstention rates we have noted
are in part explained by the active and urban political life of the
region, where organisation *was* possible, and where there were other
ways of expressing a grievance. There is some evidence, of a circumstantial kind of course, that abstention was especially high among the
artisans and the workers of the towns, rather than among the
peasantry of the bourgs.

Secondly, elections, especially local elections where the turnout
was usually (not always) higher than in national elections, were an

opportunity to continue the economic struggle by political means, just as the socialists would come to argue. The police in 1909 had little doubt about this, as witness this report from the town of La Seyne: 'Le parti révolutionnaire Seynois et la Direction des Forges et Chantiers se livrent une lutte sans merci, dont les phases principales sont marquées par la conquête des pouvoirs municipaux.' And it was in La Seyne in an earlier period (1880) that the Cercle des Travailleurs could bring together 400 people to draw up the extreme-left slate for the municipal elections at a meeting in December of that year.[5]

Political life flourished, then, in the Var – at least when immediate political choices were on the agenda. I shall have occasion later to consider just why so many Varois expressed their views by abstaining. For the moment it is merely necessary to remind the reader that the history of political events is just that, and that this chapter will therefore appear to place more emphasis on the purely political than would be justified in a more general history of the Var. At the same time, this book is not a political history of the Var, but an investigation of the strengths and weaknesses of one political movement within the region. The emphasis, then, is on the political history of the left, more precisely the history of the growth of the Socialist movement. It is necessary to begin, however, with a reasonably brief account of the general course of political events in the region after 1870.

Elections 1876–1914[6]

The first national elections under the constitution of the Third Republic took place in 1876. In the Var two Radicals were elected, Dreo in the arrondissement of Brignoles and Daumas in the city of Toulon. The other two arrondissements, Draguignan and Toulon 2ᵉ (for elections the city of Toulon was separated from its arrondissement), both returned moderate Republicans. In the elections of 1877, which followed upon the crisis of 16 May, the pattern was unchanged. In 1881 Radicals swept the board, winning in all four sections, although with consistently low percentages of the electorate in support of them (Maurel in Toulon 2ᵉ obtained only 28%, despite finishing first).

The 1885 elections were organised on the basis of *scrutin de liste*, rather than by single-member majority vote as was the case in all the preceding and ensuing elections. It is thus not possible to ascertain accurately the relative performances of each candidate in each region, but the Radical list, headed for the first time by Georges Clemenceau, came top with 41% of the total electorate. The next election for a national deputy took place in 1888, when Maurel, one of the 1885 Radical list, died, and had to be replaced by a department-wide election. At this election Gustave Cluseret stood as a socialist and won at the second round (for much more detail on Cluseret, see below, pp. 70–3). In the general election of the following year Cluseret stood for Toulon 2^e and was again victorious, obtaining 29% of the electorate and 56% of the vote, beating Radicals, conservatives and a Boulanger supporter. The other three seats were retained by the Radicals, with Clemenceau standing for the Draguignan arrondissement. This pattern was repeated in 1893, with Cluseret winning in rural Toulon and Radicals victorious elsewhere – although Clemenceau, tainted by the Panama scandal, was beaten into second place in Draguignan by Jourdan, a fellow Radical (the margin was 873 votes in 18 000).

The socialist breakthrough came in 1898. At the general election of that year, Cluseret (by now a fixture and no longer persona grata with the local socialists, though he continued to call himself one of them) again won Toulon 2^e, but was joined by Maurice Allard, a socialist who beat Jourdan by 776 votes in the Draguignan region, and by Prosper Ferrero, an independent socialist of left leanings who won in Toulon itself. Only Brignoles remained Radical, electing one Charles Rousse, but his success depended upon the socialist Vigne withdrawing in his favour between first and second rounds.

After the successes of 1898 socialism in the Var never looked back, although its internal balance underwent modifications. In the 1902 elections Allard and Ferrero again won Draguignan and Toulon (city) as they were to do in 1906. But Cluseret had died in 1900, and the Radicals recaptured Toulon 2e and held on to it in 1902 and 1906, in the person of Louis Martin, a popular local man. The significance of the socialists' persistent weakness in Toulon 2e, which takes in the prosperous coastal region and the towns of Hyères, La Seyne, St Nazaire, etc., as well as the suburbs of Toulon, is something to which I shall return. The socialists in 1902 finally won the Brignoles arrondissement, an area which they would retain control of, through Vigne, the local deputy, right up to the war.

In the elections of 1910 the Socialists, by now united in the local Federation of the SFIO, suffered a setback in Toulon occasioned by the internal divisions there among socialists. Allard had moved to Toulon for the 1910 elections (his place had been successfully taken in Draguignan by Gustave Fourment, the departmental Federal Secretary), but was beaten by a conservative Radical, Abel, by 132 votes. Pierre Renaudel, who would be a figure of national importance after the war, stood in Toulon 2^e for the first time but lost to a Radical Socialist.

In 1914, however, having dominated political life since 1898, the socialists finally succeeded in winning all four seats. Vigne and Fourment continued victorious in Brignoles and Draguignan (Vigne stood by now unopposed), while Renaudel won Toulon 2e for the SFIO for the first time since Cluseret. In the city of Toulon the victorious socialist was André Berthon, who was opposed by many of the local militants in true Toulon fashion, but who nevertheless won on a socialist ticket.

The general pattern, then, is clear. From 1876 until the late 1890s the Radicals dominated electoral politics in the Var, although it was rare for them actually to mobilise even a large minority of the electors behind them. From 1898 the socialists rapidly displaced the Radicals in rural regions, taking rather longer to defeat them in the city of Toulon and its coastal arrondissement. In describing a direct line of apparent inheritance from Radicals to Socialists, and in particular in being dominated by Radical politics in the first thirty years of the period, the experience of the Var does reflect some aspects of French history at a national level. But in excluding an active rôle for conservative, much less reactionary and monarchist politicians, the Var was of course behaving in a fashion which was very far from representative of the country as a whole. Having mapped out the political terrain, then, we must now move in a little closer and fill out the detail.

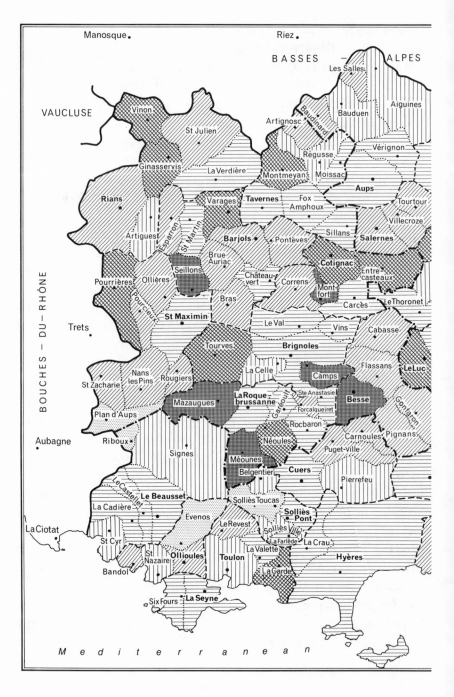

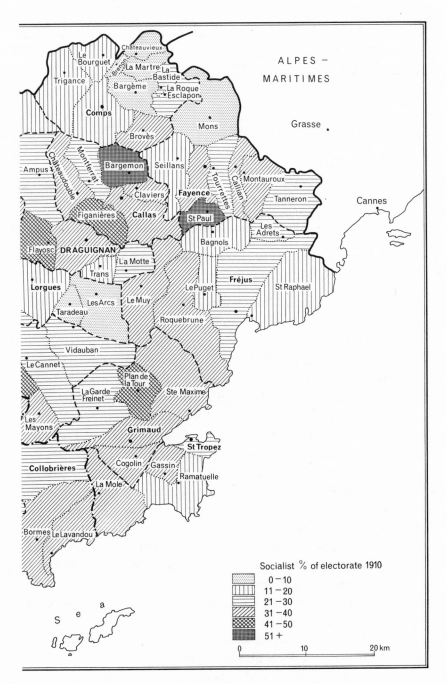

Map 8. Socialist vote – 1910

Table 1   *Socialist votes in the Var 1898–1914*

Year	Brignoles & Draguignan	Toulon 2^e	Toulon 1^e(city)	Total
1898	6584 (15.2%)	–	5600 (26.3%)	12 184 (19.0%)
1902	13 169 (31.1%)	–	7972 (33.7%)	21 141 (32.0%)
1910	12 396 (31.0%)	5141 (24.3%)	4200 (17.4%)	21 737 (25.5%)
1914	13 458 (36.0%)	6094 (29.6%)	–	57 971 (33.7%)

Notes
1. The total percentage in each year represents the Socialists' share of the electorate in those districts where there was a recognised Socialist candidate.
2. There was no Socialist candidate in the second Toulon arrondissement (which does not include Toulon proper) from 1898 until 1910.
3. For 1914 the Socialist votes in the city of Toulon have not been included. The reason is that the electoral district was sub-divided for that election, and a multiplicity of official and semi-official Socialists stood for election at the first round.

Republican politics 1871–1914

Despite the memories of the great rising and repression of December 1851, memories which kept the authorities more than usually alert to signs of discontent throughout the 1870s,[7] the Var experienced the coming of the Third Republic in a very low-key manner. The Commune found little echo in this region, despite the presence by 1869 of sections of the First International in five communes, Cogolin, Collobrières, Gonfaron, La Garde Freinet and St Tropez, all in the Maures region. Only one arrest was made in the spring of 1871 in connection with 'communard' activity: a man in Carcès, Ernest Roux, was arrested on 20 May for having distributed communard literature the previous week. He was sentenced to three months' imprisonment and a 25-franc fine. There was an outbreak of 'seditious writings' and 'encouragements to civil war' in Entrecasteaux, but even the nervous local police admitted that this meant little and led nowhere. Unlike the enthusiasms of the Second Republic, the support for the Communes of 1871 was confined to the people of the cities, and the difference is significant.[8]

The coming of the Republic, however, did evoke local enthusiasm. News of the events in Paris on 4 September 1870 reached the Var the following day, and on 5 and 6 September 1870 there were many spontaneous celebrations and much singing of the Marseillaise, in La Garde Freinet and elsewhere. The celebration of 4 September became something of a local 'cause'; during the early 1870s, when the government still banned republican activity, numerous local councils ignored prefectoral warnings not to commemorate the overthrow of the Empire. In September 1871 the mayor of Cuers, Pierre Andrieu, was suspended from his office because of this. September 1872 saw the 4th again fêted all over the departments, most notably in the communes along the central valley (Le Luc, Les Arcs, Le Muy). The *préfet* advised them to call off planned meetings, etc., 'because France is still in mourning', but only one, Lorgues, acceded to the request. There was little evidence that the Var was liable to rediscover its insurrectionist past, but much to suggest that republican sentiment ran deep.[9]

Further support for this view emerged during the crisis of 16 May 1877. During the period which followed, the Var was more touched than most by ministerial attempts to smother republican feeling. By July 1877 a total of 55 *cercles,* societies and *chambrées* had been closed by decree in the department, 41 municipal councils dissolved (out of 147), 44 mayors deprived of their posts. The Var did not 'become' Radical in the 1880s — in respect of national divisions at least, it was already on the far left by 1877, as the elections confirmed.[10]

The only obvious link to the divisions of the Second Republic came in the years 1880–2, when the question of pardons and compensation for the victims of 1851 was being considered. Around this time there were numerous local meetings of *proscrits* of 1851, and the deputies of the region, Radical or other, were very active in the parliamentary debates over the amounts to be paid in indemnity. Popular memory ran deep: the burial at Le Thoronet of Lambert Blanc, a militant of 1851, produced an attendance of 150 people from all around the region, while the unveiling in July 1881 at Aups of a monument to the dead of 1851 was the central republican event of that year. The memorials were somewhat marred, perhaps foreseeably, by bitter disputes between and within villages as to the amounts to be paid in compensation (the sharing out was often done on the basis of political or personal favour). Nevertheless, they bear witness to the local population's consciousness of its revolutionary identity of the 1840s, even if 1880 marked the end of an era rather than a point of continuity.[11]

In the Var, as in the rest of France, the Third Republic really came into being after 1880. The social and political freedoms which allowed the development of republican politics and divisions date from that year. It was in 1880 that the government amnestied the ex-communards, of course, but in most respects this was of less political importance than the releasing of certain constraints upon political life. In that year the government permitted the unrestricted opening of *débits de boisson,* requiring only that the owner register the fact with the town hall. The freedom of sale and circulation of political and other literature was also established.

Even more important, 1881 saw the law of 30 June which permitted the unauthorised holding of public meetings – previously forbidden; however, a prior declaration of the date and purpose of the meeting still had to be lodged with the police until 1907. It was only in that year, too, that *cercles* were permitted openly to declare themselves 'political' – a ruling consistently observed only in the breach. Finally came the law of 29 July 1881 (known to most Frenchmen through its regulations concerning the posting of bills, and advertised in that function on nearly every public wall in France) which gave much greater freedom to the press.

In the wake of these laws came the great period of proud republicanism. Everything was 'republican': Trees of Liberty were placed all over the Var, street names were altered (in Vidauban the Place de l'Eglise became the Place Nationale, Place de l'Eléphant became Place de la Montagne, etc.), the new pier at Le Lavandou was praised locally as 'the achievement of the republican ideal in this little bit of Provence', and so forth. The freedom to commemorate the great dates of the Republic produced a rash of celebrations: in 1881 24 February (birth-date of the Second Republic) was widely celebrated, and Bastille Day saw fairs and banquets everywhere. Only the minority of communes ruled by conservative or monarchist councils refused to join in these festivities – in St Nazaire the Ligue Ouvrière celebrated Bastille Day in isolation – but then St Nazaire, with its high quotient of foreign workers and low proportion of peasants, was and remained a reactionary outpost in a sea of republicans. And that sea had become quite a flood; by 1881, 88% of the municipalities of the Var were republican.[12]

Of course, 'republican' covered many shades of meaning. It is as well to remember that, until the 1890s, the *etiquette* included the sort of vague political neutrality which covered its programmatic nudity with lurid verbiage. Thus J. Gros, a candidate in the *conseil général* election of 1881 (I have retained the original French — the English language being badly adapted to the phraseology of Third Republican politics):

> Ce que je suis? Républicain de coeur, ennemi avoué de tout caractère pusillanime, de la monarchie comme de l'anarchie, n'ayant qu'un mobile, l'amour du bien public, l'amour de mes semblables. Mon programme est celui-ci: tout pour le peuple, tout pour le bonheur du peuple, dans le sens le plus large de la démocratie, m'inspirant toujours de la volonté de mes électeurs, ne perdant jamais de vue que je ne suis que leur mandataire.[13]

A 'programme' to be borne in mind when understanding the essential originality of what the socialists had to say a few years later.

It was not republicans like Gros, however, but Radicals such as Clemenceau who controlled the Var from the early 1880s. The Radicals had no party; even when the national Radical Party was formed in 1901 the Var Radicals remained unorganised, only forming a departmental Federation in 1909. Until then, they existed only at election time. Every major election was signalled by the calling of a congress at the town of Le Luc, meeting-point of roads and valleys and long-standing centre of regional Radicalism. The Congress of Le Luc, already a local 'tradition' by 1885, assembled delegates from every commune in the Var which could boast some republican group of Radical persuasion, even if it was only a few men meeting irregularly in a café. The delegates, one for every two thousand people in the commune they represented, would meet, discuss and nominate candidates for the four arrondissements (or, in 1885, put up a Radical list for the whole department). This list would then be presented as the official Radical slate, and would be, as we have seen, increasingly successful as the Republic matured. The names which came forward at Le Luc would be those which had been discussed in local groups and bars all over the region — with the natural result that names of prominent men, known to more than one village, tended to emerge successful. It was thus that Clemenceau, and others after him, were chosen.

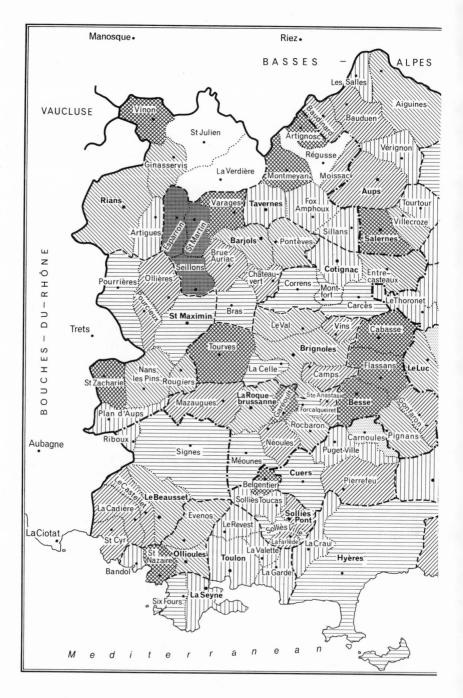

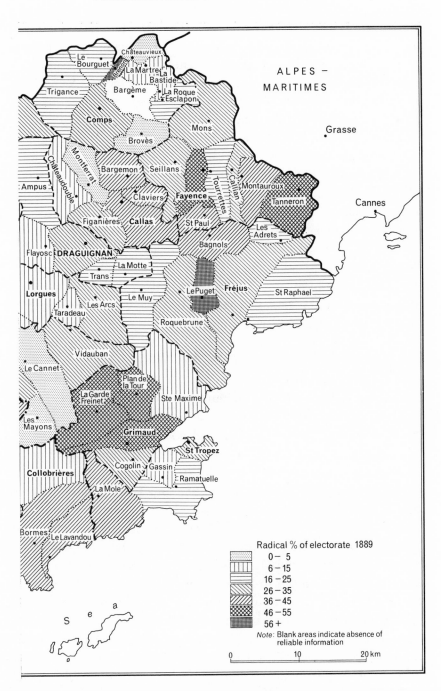

Radical % of electorate 1889

0 – 5
6 – 15
16 – 25
26 – 35
36 – 45
46 – 55
56 +

Note: Blank areas indicate absence of
reliable information

0   10   20 km

Map 9. Radical vote — 1889

Radicalism in the Var was thus genuinely popular and democratic — the same procedures, minus a full-scale congress, were used
to nominate candidates for local or cantonal elections. It was helped
by the same environmental factors which would later benefit the
socialists; but Radicalism had characteristics of its own, quite apart
from its programme, of which we shall be seeing more in Part Two.
The 1885 election with its system of list-voting favoured the growth
of a party-style presentation of candidates just as the foreign policy
of the Republic ('Ferry—Tonkin') gave the Radicals a political lever to
add to their social demands. Furthermore, there was the residual
local anti-clericalism (again, see Part Two) which benefited and
suited the Radicals much more than it would the socialists. Lastly,
there were the discussions of a possible revision of the Constitution.
These were widespread in the 1880s (the Third Republic had then, as
it would always have, the air of a compromise, unfinished), and the
Var was in fact the first department in France after Paris itself to
call, by means of a Radical committee formed for the purpose, for a
Revision of the Constitution in 1884.[14] As a result, perhaps, the
Boulanger crisis of the end of the decade had little impact in the
Var — the issues had lost their force. Boulangism collected some
support in a few coastal communes — notably St Tropez, which
began in this period its long career as a home for lost causes.[15] But
the strength of Radical implantation and, it should be added, the
fairly high degree of local corruption, meant that Boulangism passed
almost unnoticed — except in so far as the surprise victories of the
socialist Cluseret in Toulon 2e in 1888 and 1889, in just the place
and at just the time when one would have expected a Boulangist
upsurge, can be seen as having diverted it. Initially, as elsewhere,
local Radicals warmed to the general's cause; there were messages
and telegrams of support for him throughout 1887. But by 1888 the
threat had passed, and in his new incarnation (no longer the martyred
minister, more the aspiring Bonaparte) Boulanger was quite
unacceptable to majority sentiment in the Var. However, the ease
with which some Radicals had swung from side to side on the matter
certainly earned them little local credit. Reports from many villages
in these years carry word of a developing local cynicism with respect
to Radical pronouncements. The growing abstention rate dates from
this time, too.[16]

From the early 1890s Radicalism stagnated in the Var, thereby experiencing a pattern of events which Radicals elsewhere would undergo a full half-generation later. The Le Luc Congress continued to function, Radicals continued to win elections (until 1898, when their support dropped very sharply), and local conservatives dwelt on in a political wilderness. But the problem for the Radicals was that on the one hand they were identified since the early 1880s with the Republic under which the Var was experiencing a major economic crisis; on the other their criticisms of government and their proposed reforms seemed increasingly irrelevant to the concerns of the local peasantry. Social, not political, issues, moved people after the first heroic years of the Republic. The Dreyfus affair and even the anti-clerical legislation that followed had remarkably little impact in Provence; the papers and public meetings were full of sad tales of dead vines and unsaleable olives, or outside competition and population decline. Not surprisingly, Radicals maintained themselves rather better in the towns and in Toulon, where the old political debates and squabbles over municipal control still ensured a certain pattern of allegiances. But in the inland areas, particularly in the formerly thriving bourgs in the middle Var, genuine political interest was now overlain with more urgent social issues. By the early twentieth century, the Radicals were as politically ineffective in these areas as the monarchists had been two decades earlier. It was not that the socialists were not concerned with the old political debates — their stand over Dreyfus and their consistent acknowledgement of better-placed Radicals in election run-offs put them unambiguously on the republican side of the divide. Nor were the socialists above municipal squabbles — we shall see that it was precisely internecine disputes which weakened them in Toulon. But in the emphases they placed on certain kinds of solutions to the problems of the region they emerged not just as an updated Radicalism but as something rather more precise and quite different — and they were elected in those terms. From the late 1890s, then, the Var was becoming a socialist department.

Socialism in the Var 1870–1904

The Var had been visited by socialism before the coming of the
Third Republic. Utopian socialists had been active in Toulon in the
1840s and emissaries of the First International had succeeded, as we
have seen, in setting up a few sections in the area. Indeed, they had
been surprised at their own success, remarking on the fact that in
this region above all they had been able to attract some peasant
support. But the repression of the Second Empire had caused a
definite break with the past in most respects, and the socialist
movement which emerged at the end of the 1870s was for all
practical purposes breaking fresh ground.[17]

The first sign of activity came in Cuers, which in October 1879
received a visit from Auguste Blanqui. As a result of this visit, a
Cercle Socialiste was formed in the town, and thirty-three citizens
signed their names to Jules Guesde's newly published programme, as
printed in L'Egalité. In general, it was in conformity with the national
experience that the first full statement of 'scientific' socialism in
France should have been supported by a group of Provençal townsmen – two-thirds of the signatories to Guesde's programme at this
time came from south-eastern France. But it is interesting that the
first backing for socialism in the Var should have come from Cuers.
Situated in the central depression, a little to the north-east of Toulon
and easy of access (it was just off the main road from Toulon to
Nice), Cuers was something of a natural focus for speakers from the
extreme left in these early years. It was slightly larger than the average
Provençal bourg (just over 4000 people in 1876), but its population
lived largely by agriculture, notably, at this time, the growth of olives;
the only 'industrial' occupations were the manufacture of corks,
which employed 25 people in 1884, and the olive-processing industry;
60 men and women worked in a number of oil mills. For whatever
reason, the town had acquired a precocious reputation for left-wing
political leanings, doubtless a factor in bringing first Blanqui, then
Guesde, to visit it. In August 1877 the local authorities reported that
the town of Cuers 'continued . . . to remain the setting for riots and
demonstrations of an essentially revolutionary nature; every meeting
is an excuse for politics – and such politics!'. The official presidential-
election notices in 1877 had to be guarded night and day to prevent
them being destroyed, the local population being 'devoted to the

republican ideal'. This is all the more interesting in that in later years Cuers never became a socialist stronghold, but remained one of the few communes in the area which supported Radicals consistently up to the war.[18]

Nevertheless, the extreme republicanism of Cuers was a suitable terrain for the birth of socialism in this region, and it was a delegate from Cuers, Louis Dol, a member of the newly established Cercle des Travailleurs Socialistes (the revised version of the 1879 Cercle), who travelled to Marseille to attend the Socialist Congress there in 1880. In the following year the Cuers Cercle broke from the Radical alliance which predominated elsewhere in the region and put up its own candidates both in the national elections and the municipal ones. The man whose candidature was presented on a 'collectivist' ticket for the national election in Toulon 2e, Casimir Bouis, actually received a majority of the popular vote in some communes of the cantons of Collobrières, Ollioules and Cuers itself, although his total support only reached the figure of 1590 votes. In the municipal elections, by standing separately from the Radicals, the Cuers socialists helped permit a victory for the reactionary list, a development not calculated to smooth relations with the defeated Radicals. There is certainly no doubt that the socialists of Cuers were perfectly frank about their political identity – even the *Petit Var*, the Radical– Socialist daily usually sympathetic to local left-wingers, described them as 'ceux qui se vantent de professer les doctrines de la Commune et revendiquent la révolution sociale'.[19]

The socialist plant did not at first take root elsewhere as it had in Cuers, although the Cuers group acted as an organisational nucleus for the isolated socialists of Toulon and the rest of the southern Var. In 1885 it was again Cuers and its Cercle des Travailleurs which organised the socialist presence in the elections of that year. The Cercle chose as its slate for the list which the new electoral laws required two local men and two national figures. The local men were Frédéric Gambon, a retired ex-communard, and a certain Joffrin, a local mechanic. The national figures were Edouard Vaillant, communard and national leader of the Blanquist tendency in French socialism, and Henri Rochefort, journalist and also associated with the Commune. The list was presented everywhere in the Var, of course, but very little propaganda was undertaken on its behalf. As a result it did very badly in the department generally, but in Cuers itself, and in a few local villages, it did sufficiently well to force the Radicals into second place, and to contribute to their defeat at the hands of the conservatives.

After these elections, socialist activity in the area picked up quite noticeably. Toulon was already becoming a centre of socialist activity, with local and national speakers addressing crowded meetings in the popular quarters of the city, and then making forays into the Cuers valley and beyond. There was still very little sign of any formal or regular socialist organisation, although this was in keeping with events elsewhere; between 1884 and 1890, for example, the Parti Ouvrier Français (POF, the Guesdists) made no attempt to organise any congresses or national meetings. It is thus extremely difficult to measure the degree to which the presence of a socialist list in 1885 had helped stimulate the growth of socialist groups in this region – there is little enough evidence for such a development in either official or newspaper sources, although part of the difficulty was that with political discussion still heavily circumscribed it was not easy to tell just what *did* go on at meetings of a Cercle des Travailleurs in Bargemon, or a Cercle Social in Aups. However, socialism was most assuredly gaining some kind of support in the period 1885–8, and not just in the immediate region of Toulon, and as evidence of this we have the electoral success of Gustave Cluseret in the by-election of 1888.

Cluseret, who was 55 years old when he stood as a candidate in this election, was not attached to any particular 'school' of socialism. He was associated with the Commune, of course, he called himself a socialist, and it was at a private meeting of socialists in Toulon in October 1888 that 'General' Cluseret's name was put forward. The idea was picked up by Vincent, the mayor of Flayosc, who had headed a victorious socialist list in the municipal elections in that commune, and Cluseret was promoted as a candidate for the seat left vacant by the death of the Radical Maurel – Vincent and other Var socialists also thought that Cluseret might have a good chance of defeating the rising Boulangist challenge too.[20]

The Radicals, significantly, were furious. Maurel had been elected on the Clemenceau-led Radical list of 1885 and they had hoped to replace him with Clemenceau's 'man', Fouroux. As a consequence, there began a stream of Radical attacks and calumnies on Cluseret which helped bring about both a clear separation of identity between Radicals and socialists, and also a bitterness in local relations which helps account for the premature split in the republican front in this region. The *Petit Var* began by referring to Cluseret as a 'condottiere', but as his campaign gathered strength they spoke of him as 'the man who made the Commune disreputable', and finally as having been paid by Bismarck to blow up the Vendôme Column![21] A few socialists also had qualms about Cluseret, and in the arrondissement of Brignoles a rival socialist, a local tanner by the name of Ventre, was put up instead.[22] But the 1885 election laws required that the candidate stand in all four arrondissements, so local candidates stood virtually no chance of success. Conversely the Radical congress at Le Luc, in early November, gave a reluctant and partial endorsement to Cluseret – thereby assisting his candidature and consecrating a division between Radicals and those who would come to be known as Radical Socialists.

In the election of November 1888 (under the newly-reintroduced *scrutin d'arrondissement*), Cluseret came top in the first ballot, with 12 744 votes out of 31 138 votes cast. This beat Fouroux into second place by just 700 votes, a small but very significant change in the balance of forces in the Var. Cluseret did best in the arrondissements of Draguignan and Toulon 2[e] – the latter causing some surprise, being such a traditionally conservative area. In the second round, backed by many (but by no means all) Radicals as well as his own supporters, Cluseret won easily and entered the Chambre as the first socialist deputy from the Var.[23]

Cluseret's personality and his apparent lack of clear doctrinal stance worried many local socialists – the Cuers Cercle, for example, gave him their backing with great reluctance. But there is no doubt that his victory in 1888 served as the springboard for future electoral success. Full-scale legislative elections were held in the following year, with the return of *scrutin d'arrondissement* – dual-ballot single-member elections, preferred to the experimental list system of 1885 which had produced a certain conservative revival in 1885 in many parts of France. In Draguignan the various little socialist groups could not yet put together an organised campaign, while in Brignoles the local socialists did manage to find a candidate, Isnard, who obtained less than 1000 votes (of which 276 were in Cotignac, centre of what would later be the most determinedly socialist canton in the Var). But in Toulon the impetus provided by Cluseret had some immediate effects. In the city of Toulon, at the municipal elections held earlier in 1889, the various socialist groups met and agreed to present, for the first time, a list of their own, distinct from that of the Radicals. There was some discussion of the wisdom of such a move (reference was made to the experience of Cuers), but the Guesdist views of Josué Milhaud, an emerging local figure, prevailed. The Radicals were furious, the left-wing vote was divided and a reactionary candidate headed the victorious slate. But the socialists were unrepentant — proud, said one of them, Vauthier, to have presented the full socialist programme in uncompromised fashion.[24]

Adopting the same line in the general elections later in that year, the Toulon city groups put forward the name of one Lullier as a socialist candidate, while Cluseret was officially re-adopted as the socialist candidate for Toulon 2[e] (which covered both the conservative coastal towns to the east and west of Toulon and the radical rural bourgs and towns immediately behind — including Cuers). Lullier was defeated in Toulon by Camille Raspail, the Radical, by a quite small margin (less than 1000 votes out of 9255 cast). Cluseret, aided by campaigns on his behalf by a number of prominent figures, including Jules Guesde and Paul Lafargue, carried Toulon 2[e] at the second round.[25]

Cluseret, once elected, began soon to move away from the Guesdists and Vaillantists who had helped him. In the Chambre he voted with the Boulangists, to the disgust of the socialists and many of the Radicals, and when interviewed in November and asked what his programme was, replied

Cluseret, Candidat Républicain, Révision, Constituante.[26]

His standing in the second Toulon arrondissement was nevertheless assured and he would continue to be re-elected there until his death in 1900, but the local socialists rapidly came to see him as an opponent. By 1895 Jules Guesde, at a speech in Hyères (in Cluseret's constituency), was speaking of him as 'that false socialist'.[27] But false or no, Cluseret had played an important rôle in getting the local socialist movement off the ground, and in 1889 at least he was still a popular local figure — the artisan boot-makers of Bargemon gave him a rousing welcome when he visited the town in that year, and the experience was repeated everywhere he went. The corollary of his achievement of course was that during his lifetime and after his death the organised socialist movement always found it difficult to gain a foothold in the arrondissement he dominated. But this probably owes at least as much to the nature of the coastal region as it does to his own behaviour; in a strange way, Cluseret was really more of a substitute Radical than a socialist: when he died it was the Radicals who inherited Toulon 2^e — long after they had been pushed into second place elsewhere.

In the aftermath of the elections of 1889 it is possible to see a little more clearly the state of the socialist movement in the Var. That there were socialists, if not exactly a socialist movement, is quite clear. Both the authorities and the local press were quite careful to distinguish between socialists (sometimes called *collectivistes*) and Radicals or other republicans by the early 1890s.[28] It is very difficult still at this stage to know precisely how many socialist groups there were — and totally impossible to make the remotest guess at how many people actually belonged to properly socialist organisations. Such data come only with the birth of the national party organisations, and at this stage even the Parti Ouvrier Français, by far the best-organised of the national movements, still allowed its local groups considerable autonomy of organisation and activity, and had no idea how many members they comprised.[29]

To judge from the membership of the committee which was set up in 1893, under the chairmanship of Vincent, the shoemaker mayor of Flayosc, to organise a socialist candidature in the elections of that year, there were ten socialist groups in the arrondissement of Draguignan. These were located in Draguignan itself, in Lorgues, Le Luc, Taradeau and Vidauban along the central axis of the department, in Salernes, Flayosc, Figanières and Callas in a semicircle to the north of Draguignan, and in Ste Maxime on the coast of the Maures.[30] Most of these communes also figure on any list of socialist electoral strongholds in these years (see the next chapter), so these groups were probably quite well established. In the arrondissement of Brignoles things were still unclear — there were probably the same

number of socialist groups, chiefly in the canton of Cotignac, but
their existence seems to have been ephemeral — Brignoles itself does
not figure on a map of socialism in this region until rather later. In
Toulon, on the other hand, the initial successes of socialism in Cuers
and the electoral victories of Cluseret, together with the natural
impulsion given to left-wing activity by a large and militant urban
work-force, meant that the city had more than a dozen flourishing
socialist sections by the 1890s, and there were also sections in other
parts of the arrondissement — Cuers of course, but also Hyères,
Bormes, Ollioules.[31]

The Guesdists were best established in the Toulon region, where
even the *sous-préfet* acknowledged the presence of the 'marxistes' by
1893.[32] Guesde himself made frequent visits, helping on one of them
to found the socialist section in the town of La Seyne. The Blanquist
groups, nationally organised into the Central Revolutionary Committee and led by Edouard Vaillant, were also strong in Toulon, but
their real base lay in the rural areas of the Draguignan arrondissement,
where Maurice Allard was their local leader and where by the end of
the 1890s they had set up organisations in Bargemon, Le Luc and
Roquebrune. The independents, that is to say those socialists
professing no particular doctrinal stance and loosely identified with
the ideas of Alexandre Millerand and Jean Jaurès, were nowhere near
as well rooted in the region as might be supposed; it was quite clear
from an early date that the socialist movement in the Var was not to
be a warmed-over Radicalism. Most of those who did profess
'moderate' socialism in these years were to be found in the region of
Hyères, where they were well established, and Draguignan itself. It is
not without significance that Draguignan, a Radical (later Clemencist)
stronghold from the 1870s, never became an important centre of
socialism, while Hyères, at the heart of the conservative coastal belt,
consistently gave socialists some of their lowest support in the whole
department. When Jean Jaurès came down to the Var, it was not to
the moderates of Hyères, but to an audience of would-be Guesdists,
1200 of them, in Toulon that he spoke. The Radicals, and the police
informers, were not far wrong in their characterisation of local
socialism as 'collectivist' and extremist.[33]

The growth-rate of the local socialists, although at this stage not
particularly handicapped by doctrinal divisions, remained slow. The

successes of Cluseret in 1888 and 1889 helped bring about the foundation of many socialist groups, particularly in the Toulon region, and once in existence these groups remained in being, if not always flourishing, throughout the next decade. But the absence of any major election in the next three years, and the continuing strength of the Radicals, expressed in victories at local elections, inhibited any further development. Thus the elections of 1893 were little more than a reflection of those of four years previously. Cluseret again won in Toulon 2ᵉ, although he was run rather close by a Radical, Vivien. The local socialists conspicuously failed to endorse Cluseret, all of them, but could not for all that put up a candidate of their own.

In the city of Toulon Milhaud stood on a full-blooded Guesdist ticket, but received a mere 683 votes, a figure which cannot have much exceeded the total membership of socialist groups in the town. This is an interesting confirmation of the point that in large cities the extreme left was often well organised but disproportionately weak at elections, where the traditional (Radical) allegiances endured. In the countryside, the left was precociously successful at elections on the base of very little actual membership. Thus in Draguignan Vincent, who had been nominated by the committee referred to above, did not do particularly well, but he certainly outstripped Milhaud. In his own village of Flayosc he swept the board, with over 60% of the votes. Elsewhere he did well in bourgs with socialist groups (such as Lorgues, Le Luc, Bargemon and Figanières) but also in unlikely communes such as Mons. All told he improved the standing of the socialists in the Draguignan arrondissement, paving the way for the success of 1898. He was aided, it must be said, by the Panama shadow hanging over his opponent Clemenceau, who was finally beaten by another radical, Louis Jourdan.[34]

The elections of 1898 represent a breakthrough for the socialists which cannot easily be explained. The Radicals were still a strong force in the department — no socialist could yet be assured of victory at the second round without at least some switching of Radical votes — and they continued to hold the majority in the region of Brignoles. But between 1893 and 1898 the continuing growth of the local socialist organisations in Toulon (much aided by visits from prominent national figures) and the steady worsening of the situation of the peasantry in the Draguignan arrondissement contributed to a clear break with the pattern of the past. The election of 1898 did not benefit from any marked change in the pattern of socialist organisation; the Socialist federations only came into being in the enthusiastic aftermath of the victories. What happened was that a strikingly large number of voters chose to support the socialist candidates, who, it is true, worked rather harder at acquiring their support than had formerly been the case. Whether these electors had formerly voted Radical, or whether they were new young voters, or whether they were men who had previously abstained, is something we shall later have to assess.

At all events, the socialists won three out of the four local seats at the 1898 elections. In Draguignan Maurice Allard (a supporter of Vaillant) and in Toulon 1^e Prosper Ferrero (an 'independent' of Guesdist leanings) both defeated Radicals at the second round. In Toulon 2^e Cluseret was again victorious, but this time a socialist, Stroobant, had been put up to oppose him and had obtained 3483 votes in the first round, nearly one-third of the total vote.[35] It was this 'great leap forward' in electoral terms which helped hasten the coming together of the socialists in the Var under the umbrella of a departmental Federation.

It was on the initiative of the POF militants of Toulon, led by Milhaud, that a Congress was held there on 25 November 1900 to form the Socialist Federation of the Var. Delegates were invited to attend from every socialist group in the department (all known groups were contacted directly; advertisements were also placed in local Radical newspapers as well as the national press of the Parisian socialist groups); most prominent, however, were the half-dozen Guesdist cells in Toulon itself, all of whom had been represented at the Japy National Congress of 1899, where the first steps had been taken, under the impulsion of the Dreyfus campaign, to form a national organisation. The organisation of the Toulon Congress doubtless benefited from this national move to unification, the more so in that Jules Guesde toured the whole department early in 1900, urging the case for unity.

It was the following year, at the second Congress in April 1901, that the Var Federation, now a loosely-grouped organisational umbrella covering every socialist group in the department but with little impact upon their local activity, voted to adhere to the Parti

Socialiste Français (PSF), the new national body which had emerged from the Parisian meetings of the previous year. The PSF was essentially Jaurèsist in outlook, and it is doubtful whether the Var Federation, with the Toulon Guesdists at its heart, would have adhered had it not been for the death of Milhaud in 1901, leaving the Federation in the hands of Ferrero and other less committed Guesdists. At any rate, the link to the PSF was soon severed. Jaurès' policies, in particular his support for the Waldeck-Rousseau and Combes governments, and the undisciplined structure of the PSF with no clear doctrinal line and a strong penchant for parliamentary action, were uncongenial to most of the socialist militants in the Var. At a further Congress, held on 23 February 1902 in Draguignan, the Var Federation left the PSF and declared itself an autonomous socialist federation, a position it maintained until 1905.

Meanwhile, the national disputes between Guesde and Jaurès had resulted in the creation of a second national organisation, the Parti Socialiste de France (PSdeF), whose members were the former Guesdists and Blanquists of the POF and the Comité Révolutionnaire Central. This organisation reflected Guesdist doctrinal and organisational positions, and it attracted a number of Var socialists, discontented with the initial support of their Federation for the reformist PSF. Early in 1902 they broke their links with the Var Federation (at that time still a member of the PSF) and formed a Revolutionary Socialist Federation of the Var, affiliated to the PSdeF. They were led by Maurice Allard, the Draguignan deputy, and it is important to note that, although they represented the 'extreme' fringe of local socialist politics, they came mostly not from Toulon but from the smaller towns. Apart from La Seyne, with its strong Guesdist links, the Revolutionary Federation was based on support in Draguignan, Les Arcs, Vidauban, Le Muy, Puget-Ville and Flayosc — the central depression and the Draguignan region, the areas of original socialist implantation a decade earlier.

From 1902 until 1905 the two Federations, the Autonomous and the Revolutionary, existed side by side in the region. Once the former had left the PSF there was relatively little difference of opinion between the two, and they collaborated on election lists and public activities. In so far as their annual congresses, held separately in 1903 and 1904, are any indication of what it was that distinguished them from one another, there seems to have been some sense that the Revolutionaries were based on the bourgs (all their congresses were held in the communes of the inner Var), while the Autonomous Federation was stronger in the city — Claude, the secretary, was a Toulon municipal councillor, and a leading light in the Autonomous Federation was Ferrero, the Toulon deputy. Otherwise, the subject matter of their congresses converged — what sort of control to exercise over parliamentary socialists, how to further the cause of socialism in the region, etc. The Revolutionary Federation perhaps devoted a little more time to considerations of a doctrinal nature, as befitted its Guesdist origins. In these respects their respective careers parallel quite closely the differences and similarities between Guesdists and Jaurèsists at the national level. And, like them, they found themselves, by the end of 1904, drawn together by a popular desire for the final unification of the multiple streams of socialism in France.[36]

From unification to the war

Just as the SFIO was created out of decisions at an international level, so the Var socialists were drawn together by events in Paris. Left to themselves, they might have taken a little longer to achieve their unity. As late as September 1904 Maurice Allard, in a speech at Draguignan, was still critical of the way in which the PSF had 'slavishly' followed Combes, and he implied that he believed that some of the local 'autonomists' had supported this view. Nevertheless, even he conceded that the Guesdists could live with Jaurès and his followers, as long as there was agreement on the fundamentals: no compromise with existing governments and commitment to the class struggle.[37]

The Revolutionary Federation held its last Congress in August of 1904 at La Seyne, and the Autonomous Federation was invited to send representatives to be present (which it did). Both sides would henceforth benefit from the support of a new local weekly paper, the *Cri du Var,* founded on 10 July, and committed to socialist unity on the principles of Jules Guesde, but with 'room for all'. The paper was organised on a cooperative basis, and sold at 10c. a copy (later 5c.) in order to attract the maximum readership. The process of unification was now firmly under way; according to the *Cri,* there was a strong undercurrent of support for unification among the socialists of the region, so long as Autonomists and the local individual members of the PSF remembered the need for doctrinal solidarity and a stress on militant, not parliamentary, socialism.

Both Var federations sent delegates to the founding Congress of the SFIO, held in Paris in April 1905. They returned together, and met immediately afterwards in an impromptu local Congress in Toulon, on 14 May. Here the organisers of the two federations voted unanimously to recommend adherence to the new national party (this was not by any means a foregone conclusion – the Jura Federation, for example, chose to remain autonomous). At this Toulon meeting (held, significantly, at the headquarters of the Parti Ouvrier Français, the Guesdists), a temporary joint committee of both federations was established in order to liaise with the Commission Administrative Permanente (CAP) of the national party. This committee also undertook the planning of a definite unification of the two federations at a later date. This event finally came about at a formal Congress, held in Toulon on 3 September 1905. Here, where seventeen socialist groups from the region were represented, the two federations merged into one, Gustave Fourment was made Federal Secretary (a post he retained until 1920), and the united Socialist Federation of the Var, bound by the statutes of the SFIO, came into being.[38]

The new Federation was already a force in local politics. Its membership varied somewhat from month to month, but in September 1905 it stood at 405 paid-up members, a figure which would increase rapidly in the coming years. It was the sixth federation in the country, expressed in terms of socialist militants per head of the departmental population (only the Nord, the Seine, the Gard, the Loire and the Gironde did better); it had a weekly newspaper of its own, as well as an (initially) sympathetic ear from the daily *Petit Var*, and three of the four electoral districts in the Var were in its control (for fuller details of the socialists' electoral implantation, see the next chapter). The *préfet* of the Var was sufficiently conscious of the importance of the local socialist movement, and the rôle of the Guesdists within it, to spend some of his time cutting out from *L'Aurore* reports of speeches made by Jules Guesde from all over the country![39]

Between 1905 and 1914 the Socialist Federation of the Var grew
in size and influence. We have already discussed briefly the electoral
successes and setbacks it experienced between 1906 and 1914.
In organisational terms the pattern was broadly similar. Membership
rose from the original 400 to 755 by 1908, whereupon there was
a stagnant period caused largely by the intra-party crisis in Toulon
(see below); but by 1911 the movement had picked up again, achieving a membership of 1535 in that year. By 1913 the membership
stood at 1403, one member for every 154 inhabitants of the region.
Members appear to have been fairly diligent in their obligations;
SFIO regulations required that every member buy a monthly stamp
to place on his or her annual card, but few cards were ever completely filled. An average of 8 stamps per card was taken by the
party treasurers to be an acceptable minimum. In the Var the number
of stamps per card varied from 9.8 to 10.6, consistently above the
national average.[40]

The local party experienced two important crises during this
period, one over the disputes in Toulon, the other over its attitude
to Georges Clemenceau, although in reality the two issues were
closely interwoven. It is worth devoting a little space to them, as
they are interesting sources for an insight into local political life.

Socialist leaders throughout France faced a dual problem when
establishing their movement. Disciplined parties were unknown in
France, and keeping members in line was a delicate matter: too much
insistence on adherence to party ordinances and there might be
provincial splits; too little, and the SFIO would degenerate into a
coterie of parliamentarians loosely attached to a sympathetic but dis-
organised base. The second problem was that of the Radicals. From
1848 until the 1880s, perhaps later still, socialists and Radicals had
acted together — and had often been quite indistinguishable. Now
the SFIO, like the various socialist movements before it, was asking
members to treat the Radicals, if not quite as enemies, then at least as
no more than occasional allies, separated from true socialists by an
ocean of doctrine and discipline. This was a difficult matter, and
many of the extreme left of the party felt that it was never quite
successfully achieved — hence one of the reasons for the post-war
schisms.[41] But socialist—Radical relations were especially bedevilled

Table 2   *Socialist membership 1896–1914*

Year	Var Federation	SFIO total
1896	475 (est.)	–
1905	425	35 000
1906	1410	40 000
1907	700 (est.)	53 000
1908	755	57 000
1909	1550	58 000
1910	1501	69 000
1911	1535	70 000
1912	1515	73 000
1913	1403	75 000
1914	1478	93 000

in the Var by the presence of the personality and influence of Georges Clemenceau.

Clemenceau was a wildly popular figure in the Var, where he had been a Radical deputy since 1885, and the Panama scandals and his stand on Dreyfus did not diminish that popularity. Everywhere he went he was cheered and welcomed; even his opponents conceded his widespread popular support. Until he came to power in 1906 the Socialists remained broadly sympathetic to him, declaring themselves optimistic that he would bring about real reforms at last. He was a popular guest at socialist meetings — Vincent in Flayosc gave a banquet for him in September 1904, Collomp in Le Luc followed suit the next day.[42] Opposed politically as a Radical, he was welcomed by Socialists in personal terms — not least, perhaps, through their legitimate desire to be seen to be, in the broadest sense, *with* him rather than against him in local politics.

Things changed with the formation of the first Clemenceau ministry. The SFIO, not constrained of course by local consider-ations, insisted that, while he be given every opportunity to imple-ment his promised reforms, Clemenceau should still be regarded as a class enemy, no less than any other bourgeois minister. At its Federal Congress in September 1907 the Var Federation disagreed, and gave members permission to attend Clemencist banquets in the region. This was a breach of national discipline, however minor, and local leaders were at pains to explain their position. Earlier in the year Gustave Fourment, the Federal Secretary, had written that

Clemenceau's support for nationalisations showed that he was in advance of his Radical colleagues and should receive Socialist support. Fourment stuck by this line in July; Clemenceau was on the wrong side, yes, but he was still a true republican underneath. He was the ᵢₒₛt hero, wrote Fourment, for whom many Varois still had almost a cult.[43]

The decisive turning points were Clemenceau's use of troops against miners' strikes in Calais in 1906 and again in Draveil 18 months later. The Var Socialists were forced to declare their opposition to the man and his government. The Federal Congress of July 1907 attacked him bitterly for his anti-worker policies, and also — for the wine crisis had begun — for his indifference to the sufferings of the small peasants of the Midi. 'Where', lamented Fourment in August 1907, was 'the Clemenceau of our youth, the man who had incarnated the republican faith of a generation?'[44] There was a tone in Fourment's articles, and in others of their ilk, which went beyond mere embarrassment at having to oppose the local hero, with all that this might cost the Socialists in support. The real bitterness arose from the fact that some of the local Socialist leaders had never quite been able to adjust their doctrinal sights in order to focus on individuals. They firmly believed that Jules Guesde was correct and that the real divisions were ones of class, and that the Radicals were on the other side of the barricade, their rhetoric just that. But that this should also apply to Georges Clemenceau? No one denied that it did, and the Socialists in the Var achieved the really rather remarkable feat of cutting themselves free of the Clemenceau link fairly cleanly. But it was a painful business.

By 1908, the *Cri* was able to refer to Georges Clemenceau as that 'senile despot', and in February of that year the local Federation organised a major demonstration in protest at Clemenceau's policies. In Toulon, in August 1908, a socialist section unanimously voted a motion to work 'to send Clemenceau back to the Vendéen *bocage* whence he came'.[45] These were brave words, because the man still had widespread popular backing in the region. In 1909 he was re-elected to his seat in the Senate, in an election in which the Socialists had supported anti-Clemencist Radicals in the hope of unseating him. Soon afterwards, however, he fell from power, and the vexed question of Socialist relations with a Clemenceau government disappeared.

There were still occasional signs of nostalgia for the Clemenceau of better days, but by 1909 the question had been resolved. As an editorial put it in the *Cri*: 'Ceux qui, au milieu de la tourmente Clemenciste, sont restés du bon côté de la barricade sont maintenant des militants sur qui l'on peut compter.'[46]

This was said with all the more feeling in that the Clemenceau issue had helped stoke the fires of a major row in Toulon in these years. The issue itself was almost wholly personal at first, but it had widespread effects. In 1905, when the two separate federations first met in the spring and agreed to form a temporary liaison with a view to unity, the man appointed secretary was Claude, a Toulon councillor. But a group of Toulon Socialists, led by Marius Escartefigue, intrigued against Claude, had him replaced by Fourment (a Draguignan man) and got Escartefigue appointed as a delegate to the National Council of the SFIO.[47]

Claude wrote an article about this minor matter in the *Petit Var*, and was censured by the Federal Committee, at a meeting in March 1906, for washing the Federation's dirty linen in front of a non-Socialist public. The whole affair appeared to be over. However, Claude and his supporters continued to rail against Escartefigue, both within the Toulon sections and on the municipal council, where Escartefigue was mayor. The 'Claude case' was brought to the attention of the rest of the Federation, causing as it was such disruption within the socialist movement in Toulon, and at the Federal Congress held in Brignoles on 7 July 1907, Claude and his supporters were formally expelled from the party. They refused to leave the meeting, and the Congress degenerated into a rowdy squabble, with Claude calling Escartefigue a 'fraud' and a 'liar'.

However, 1907 was the time when the local Federation was beginning to take a strong line against Clemenceau and his ministry, and the same Federal Congress which expelled Claude also required of all members that they commit themselves to opposing Clemenceau, take no part in meetings organised on his behalf, and themselves arrange anti-Clemenceau demonstrations. Despite this ruling, Escartefigue in Toulon continued to support Clemenceau, and the divisions re-emerged in August 1908 when he and his supporters on the Toulon municipal council opposed an anti-Clemenceau motion raised by the Claudistes, now operating independently of the main party. The rest of the Federation, by now thoroughly bored with the behaviour of the Toulonnais, cried scandal at such indiscipline, and a special Federal Congress was called for September 1908 to discuss the matter. At this meeting on 6 September, from which Escartefigue absented himself, the Var Federation voted by 39 to 3 to require every member to sign within fifteen days a motion condemning Clemenceau and all his works. Meanwhile, the Federal Committee officially 'chided' Escartefigue for his attitude and his absence.

Fifteen days went by, Escartefigue did not sign, and he was formally expelled from the party, at a meeting of the Federal Committee on 12 October. With him went 21 of the 25 Socialist municipal councillors in Toulon, and an unknown number of Toulon sympathisers. As if to emphasise the split, Escartefigue appeared with Georges Clemenceau himself on the platform at an anti-SFIO meeting in Bandol that same month.

Although the Toulon socialist movement was soon put back together, much was affected by this episode. Toulon lost its importance in the local movement – Fourment discovered that its membership had in any case been overestimated deliberately in order to boost its representation at Congresses – and all Toulon socialists were thereupon required to leave the party and have their applications for re-entry thoroughly vetted. Claude was welcomed back into the party in March 1909, after providing evidence of good faith by supporting Renaudel in a local election, but the urban section remained weak and was defeated in the 1910 general elections. The *Cri* lost many subscribers – it had acquired a wide readership in Toulon – and even the newly-cleansed local groups remained susceptible to quarrels and divisions. Most important of all, Marius Escartefigue remained mayor of Toulon, carrying with him through the power of his office much local support, just as Cluseret had done in Toulon 2^e. The departmental Federation was not fundamentally damaged by all this, despite the fall in membership. What happened, though, was that the centre of gravity of socialism in the Var shifted even further away from the coast and into the villages, as the election results of 1910 confirm. As for Toulon, it remained until very recently a city whose left-wing majority was crucially divided by past and present conflicts. I was able to raise a heated discussion at a gathering of elderly militants in Toulon merely by mentioning the name of Escartefigue – and this was in 1971![48]

With the passing of the Clemenceau and Escartefigue episodes, the last few years before the war were fairly quiet ones in the region, dominated by national political issues, notably the threat of war. Anti-militarist sentiment was widespread in the Var; not the anti-militarism of the anarchists (see below), but rather a residual dislike of conscription and the economic and social costs of war, a dislike common to all rural communities, and compounded in the Var by the fact that small peasants could ill afford the loss of the labour-power of their sons; they could not afford to hire agricultural labourers, and in any case few were available.

It is not surprising, then, that the Keir Hardie–Edouard Vaillant motion, committing socialists to opposing war by a general strike, should have been so widely supported in the Var from 1910 onwards, nor that the *Cri du Var* should have come more and more to emphasise the threat of war and to give space to articles condemning the militarist foreign policy of the government. But what catalysed local feeling was the proposed increase in the period of compulsory military service to three years. In March 1913 Socialist groups all over the Var passed motions attacking the proposal, and the Federal Congress of that year spent much time discussing the issue; it was not of fundamental doctrinal importance, but the party would have to devote a lot of attention to it – the issue provoked deep feelings in the region. There were clashes with the authorities throughout the Var during the summer of 1913; when the Brignoles *sous-préfet* ordered the removal of a Socialist poster in Tavernes attacking the three-year law, the local Socialist group received fourteen new members who joined in sympathy at its stand.[49]

The agitation of 1913 undoubtedly prepared the way for the electoral success of 1914. In that year Draguignan and Brignoles were retained yet again by Fourment and Vigne, while Ferrero won back the old district of Toulon. The old arrondissement of Toulon 2[e] was now divided into two parts, Renaudel standing in the coastal region and the hinterland, Claude in the newly-created district encompassing the communes of La Valette, Le Pradet, La Garde and Le Reveste. Only Claude was unsuccessful, and he was beaten by Berthon, a renegade socialist of Escartefiguian persuasion. In 1914, the SFIO in the Var was the dominant local political force. It had numerous groups, covering 31 communes and comprising a total of nearly 1500 members. But its real force was on the one hand its electoral strength and on the other the influence that its organised groups exercised over political life even among the unorganised sympathisers in the region. The degree to which the Federation of the Var dominated all aspects of political life cannot easily be measured in numbers. Oblivious to the coming catastrophe (the *Cri* welcomed Sarajevo — 'another despot falls'), the Socialists in Provence in 1914 were celebrating their political success in the region. Before we move on to try and measure that success in more detail, we must first step back to consider briefly the mechanics of Socialist organisation in this period.

The organisation of the party

From the date of its adherence to the SFIO in 1905, and its adoption of the statutes of the party, the Var Federation was constrained to follow the organisational and doctrinal lines laid down from Paris, even though in principle it, like all the other departmental federations, had the final power of deciding, at the National Congresses, what its organisation should be. The party machinery operated in much the same way as that of the old POF; instructions or advice on a given topic would come down from the Commission Administrative Permanente (CAP) in Paris, would be transmitted to the sections, and after being voted on at section meetings would then return to Paris in the form of motions or proposals for the next National Congress. The whole system was closely articulated, emphasising discipline and uniformity of action. The modern French Communist Party does not operate very differently.

Party life at the organisational level was the affair of section and federal meetings. Sections met infrequently; ideally they gathered once a week, more commonly once a month. Unless there was an election pending, the turnout was not usually very high, and discussion desultory. The meeting of the Collobrières Section of the SFIO on 20 June is a good case in point. The year was 1908 and there was no burning issue to discuss. Twenty-four of the thirty-six members came (a good number — most sections could not do as well); the remaining twelve were absent in the cork woods or in the fields.

There was a short discussion of the Draveil strikes, and 5 francs was voted towards the strike fund being collected by the party. A further brief discussion concerning impending local elections in Draguignan then ensued, a further 5 francs was voted to assist in propaganda in the election, and then, after a break, the date for the next meeting was arranged, for 30 July. The subject for discussion would be national politics. The meeting broke up after just over an hour. It ought to be said though that this was high summer and to hold a meeting at all was an achievement.[50]

The Draveil episode is significant – Socialist sections in isolated communes like Collobrières often discussed major national issues and were active in their support of outside causes. In February 1906 there were subscriptions from all over the Var in aid of exiles from the 1905 Revolution in Russia, and the execution of Ferrer in Spain in 1909 provoked angry and genuinely spontaneous motions from all over the region. But though the meetings were thus concerned with major events, they were infrequent. Often a section would be brought into existence by an electoral success (Allard's victory in 1906 helped create a group in St Tropez), or by a visiting speaker (Cabannes came down from Paris in May 1907 and left new groups in his wake in Pignans and Fayence), and would then lie dormant until the next election. This was the fault of the local secretary, often a man with a full-time job and in any case ill equipped to organise the content of a political meeting. Instead the members would meet in their chosen café, so that the absence of formal meetings does not betoken an absence of political life in the village.[51]

Above the sections came the Federal Congress. This met one or more times per year, in a central town or large bourg, and comprised the standing Federal Committee (elected at each congress), and delegates from every group in the region who cared to send a representative. The Federal Congress fixed the price of membership stamps (that is, it could fix the price of *its* stamps above the national price – it could not charge less than the nationally-fixed figure); it approved motions to be sent forward to Paris for the next National Congress; and it decided Federal policy on organisational business, on local elections, propaganda activities, etc. These were implemented until the next Federal Congress by the Federal Committee. But the chief concern of Congress and Committee alike was party discipline.

We are sometimes told that the Socialists of the Midi lacked 'discipline'; that they ignored party rulings in all kinds of things and were merely 'Radicals in Socialist clothing'. This is to take, in this as in other matters, the verbal style of the Midi for its substantive content. In fact, as we have already seen, the local Federation kept a strict control on its followers, cautioning and even expelling them when they transgressed fixed positions. In many respects the Federation of the Var was more disciplined, more rigid, than a lot of other Socialist areas.

Discipline was exercised in a number of ways. The Federal Congress and the Federal Committee kept a firm control over membership of the party. Any group or member who was more than six months behind with subscriptions was excluded from the Federation, following a decision to that effect in May 1906. Candidates for local or national office had to be fully paid up and to have been in the party for at least one year; they must also undertake to accept without fail any decisions taken by National or International Socialist Congresses. All candidates for office from within the party had first to be approved by the Federal Committee, be they standing in a municipal by-election or for the Senate.

The Federation was also very firm about participation in non-Socialist activities. In keeping with the national rules of the SFIO, rules drawn up to avoid the confusion of identities which had existed before 1905, no member of the Var Federation was permitted to attend meetings of other political parties, *or* of non-political groups such as the Ligue des Droits de l'Homme, without permission from the Federal Committee; this permission was rarely given. In October 1905, only a month after unification, the Federal Committee chided the Collobrières group for making local electoral alliances without the prior approval of the Federation. And when a local Socialist, one Dr Varenne, protested at Fourment's arbitration in the matter, he was expelled from the party. Whatever the subject of a meeting or society, no Socialist could attend without permission. The declared aim was to keep the identity of the party quite distinct from that of all other groups – especially other left-wing groups.[52]

Two exceptions were made to this ruling. In 1912 a Federal Congress at Carnoules agreed, after much debate, to allow Socialists to belong to the freemasons; this decision was in keeping with national policy, but all the same it encountered strong opposition from the rural groups — only Toulon was firmly in favour. The other exception was the acknowledgement that, where there existed no organised local group, a Socialist might attend meetings of the local Radical *cercles* — but only then. From 1911, meanwhile, all local Socialists were required to belong to their syndicate or cooperative — an important requirement, which was not easy to oversee, and it is thus all the more significant that it should have been insisted upon. Nothing could look less like the casual, quite informal, occasional gatherings of the Radicals of the Var who did not even have a federal structure, much less a federal discipline.[53]

The Federation might affirm its authority, but it was in other respects quite weak. Financially, it never succeeded in achieving a secure position. Like all Socialist federations, it depended upon subscriptions and the occasional sale of a pamphlet or booklet. But just as the sections were subordinated to the authority of the Federation, so the latter was in thrall to the national organisation. In 1906 every militant paid 1 fr. 15 per year (25 c. for his card, $7\frac{1}{2}$ c. per stamp). Of this meagre sum, the Federation received 30 c. the remaining 85 c. going to the coffers of the SFIO in Paris (where admittedly there were a lot of expenses to meet). As a result the Federation barely covered its costs — in June 1907 it had fully 197 francs in its account. Even when this sum had risen to 1005 francs by August 1908, the Federation was still constrained to cancel the Congress planned for March 1910 in order to meet the electoral costs of that year. The resources of the Federation were no help — the newspaper *Le Cri* was persistently in debt and sold an average of 600 copies per week throughout the period, but needed to sell at least 1000 to show a profit.[54] The Federation, then, was a shell, so to speak, whose authority was effective because militants chose to accept the Federation's rules. It had no coercive force to hand other than expulsion, and this was hardly a punishment it would care to use too often.

As the party grew, so did the problem of relations between elected representatives and militants. As elsewhere, the militants resented the fact that deputies were elected through local effort, but then spent their time in Paris with (so it was claimed) little thought for their fellow members in the provinces. There was a certain degree of criticism of this kind levelled at Fourment and Vigne in 1910, and

again at Renaudel in 1913. In each instance the charge was that the
deputy was not seen often enough in the region – a real problem in
areas so far from Paris. However, although this division between the
party élite and the rest would become a vexed question after the
war – Renaudel in particular falling victim to it – the Federation of
the Var survived without too much disruption until 1914 – no doubt
on account of the large degree of *local* electoral success. It was an
obvious demagogic ploy to stir up militant feeling against the parliamentarians, especially in areas of economic decline; in Aups the local
Socialists resented Fourment's enthusiastic support for reaffores-
tation; 'theoretically competent people know nothing in practice',
and the local Radicals tried, without success, to make electoral capital
from the dispute. But the Var does seem to have been a rather united
Federation, the Toulon business once completed, and the elected
Socialists continued to meet with warm receptions all over the
department right up to July 1914.[55]

The character of the party

Certain characteristics of the socialist movement in the Var help
make it unique in the region, and need to be emphasised in order to
avoid giving the impression that on the one hand the Var was much
like any other local socialist movement, or on the other that socialist
movements elsewhere in France may have been much like the Var.

To begin with, there was the undoubted tendency of the Var to
lean to the left within the party after 1905. Because of the large
number of independent socialists there before 1905, because this was
an old Radical region, and because the predominant local activity
was agriculture, there is an understandable inclination to view the
'extremism' which emerges in so many of the pronouncements of
Var socialists as merely surface-deep. It was not. The Var regularly
supported far-left motions at National Congresses and, perhaps more
important, local socialist propaganda was hardly ever 'watered down'
for popular consumption (for a reasoned case for this view, see Part
Two, Chapter 9). Why was this so?

Apart from the arguments from context, which I shall be investigating in Part Two, there were two political reasons for the nature of
socialism in this area. The first is the deep division between

Draguignan and Toulon, or more generally between the rural and semi-rural Var and the urban area around Toulon. The Toulonnais disliked the rest of the population – a local prejudice little diminished today – and the feeling was reciprocated. Had the socialist movement in Toulon come to dominate the region, as it easily might, then the character of the Federation would have been very different. The weakness of the socialists in Toulon, despite the presence of a large proletarian sector, meant that they were inclined to play second fiddle to the Radicals and modulate their doctrinal tone considerably. Actually, the working population was not particularly socialist in inclination; anti-political syndicalism established itself in the town from an early date. But Toulon's Socialist groups were torn apart and much reduced by the squabbles of the years 1905–9, with the result that the organisational and ideological initiative passed to the rural areas. And these, at first sight paradoxically, proved more doctrinally firm than their urban counterparts.[56]

The second factor was the presence of an important leavening of Italian socialists in the department.[57] From the 1880s these had been active in the area; in 1885 Matteucci, an Italian socialist and printing worker in Draguignan, was expelled from France for spreading 'revolutionary' propaganda. By 1888 there were regular meetings like the one at Les Arcs in July, addressed by the Italian Cannioni on the subject of socialist theory and the need for international socialist cooperation. The Italian activity continued right through into the twentieth century. There were Italian socialist sections all along the central valley, and in May 1907 the *Cri* carried an announcement of the coming Fifth Congress of the *PSI in Francia*. Clemenceau expelled the organiser, Ugo Nanni, on 13 May, but the Congress went ahead and there were meetings all over the Var that year and in 1908, including an address given in Italian at Bargemon by De Giovanni of the Turin labour movement.

These Franco-Italian exchanges were important, because they brought to the French a taste of the PSI's interest in doctrinal matters, and also its experience of organisation and labour activity. The widespread presence of Italian workers, industrial and agricultural, in the Var brought economic conflict of course, but also ideological exchange, yet another dimension in which the Provençal peasantry gained access to new ideas and movements. And it is interesting to note that the Italians concentrated much of their activity in the small towns; the socialist movement in Toulon, in La Seyne and in Hyères was much less influenced by Italian propaganda and organisation, even though there was no shortage of Italians in these towns.[58]

Another aspect of socialism in the Var was the tension between electoral success and party membership. The socialists had little choice but to fight the unending elections which faced all French political parties, but they never became in that sense an electoral party. The costs of fighting elections were prohibitive, and even after 1905 the Federation often did not bother to present candidates at elections for the *conseil général* or the *conseil d'arrondissement*. Throughout the period, Socialist local electoral activity was concentrated at the municipal level, where the Federation encouraged the sections to try and take part whenever possible. But cantonal election lists of a socialist leaning seem to have been regular features *only* in those cantons where the party could be sure of a good showing: Barjols, Cotignac, La Roquebrussanne in the Brignoles arrondissement; Aups, Callas, Draguignan, Fayence, Le Luc and Salernes in the Draguignan region, and La Seyne and Toulon itself in that region. Elsewhere they left such contests to the Radicals. Now this reflects in part the absence in many regions of a strong local group; similarly local successes were usually evidence of the presence of a thriving socialist *cercle*; but there is no doubt that the Federation tried conscientiously to diminish the importance of some local elections. The *Cri* was at pains to stress that elections were largely a nuisance, deflecting the party from its real tasks of organisation and education, while sections like the one in Draguignan bitterly criticised those who only attended when an election was in the offing – 'we are not an election committee'.[59]

However, while politics may have been a peripheral concern for many Varois most of the time, elections did matter, and so we must take note of them. It was at elections, especially national elections, that the health and standing of a party were measured, just as it was municipal elections which decided the daily matters of real importance. Thus the Var Federation was not without wisdom in concentrating its effort in these areas, and its performance in them is some kind of a gauge of its local standing. It may only have had a membership of around 1500, but by 1914 it controlled fourteen municipal councils and had the largest minority in many more. In fact it had one mayor for every 108 members. And 1500 was not a small figure measured by French standards — the Var was always near the top of the SFIO's list of federations measured by per capita membership.

The party, then, was not an 'electoral' party, like the Radicals, who only 'existed' in the weeks before an election, but nor was it a membership party like the German Sozialdemokratische Partei Deutschlands (SPD). Its strength has to be measured in terms of its vote, because politics in rural areas are that much more electoral than elsewhere. Section attendance could lapse to nothing in the harvest time, and then bloom again in the winter.[60] And in any case, much local political discourse, in these 'urban villages', took place in the street and in the café. Formal meetings are the affairs of the city. Thus the next chapter, and much of Part Two, will be concerned with asking questions of the electoral data available to us, and only secondarily investigating the social geography of party membership. Socialist voters were not, of course, 'socialists', though they might easily call themselves such. But the same is true of Communist voters today. Why people vote for a movement they do not choose actually to join may indeed be the most interesting question of all.[61]

Syndicalism and Socialism

The detailed history of the syndical movement in the Var is not my immediate concern in this book. But certain features of the growth of syndical activity in this region helped fashion the Socialist movement which was developing alongside, and these must now be considered.

There is little about the history of the syndical movement in this region to distinguish it from the growth of labour organisation elsewhere in France, and in this respect it differs of course from the local history of socialism. From the 1870s the major concerns of workers in the Var were first that they should have control of their own mutual-aid funds, and secondly that their wages and conditions should be improved. The first led to a rash of *sociétés de secours mutuels* in the early years. These were often the only form in which workers' organisations could receive official consent — thus the Bandol

Syndicate of barrel-makers began in a mutual assistance society formed, after much official misgiving, in 1872. There were 55 members, most of them in their early thirties and 19 of them unable to sign their name. They remained unique for a while, though — police and prefectoral authorities were loath to allow any forms of worker organisation until 1880.[62]

Thereafter, the main emphasis was upon the organising of syndicates, which were given legal rights in 1884. By 1889, Toulon had its own Bourse de Travail, with 9497 members organised in 23 syndicates, from port-workers to teachers. Other towns followed suit in the next few years, so that by 1910 the Var had 86 workers' unions comprising 10 352 members. Agricultural syndicates took rather longer to organise — the first to emerge, in 1881, the Fédération Rurale of Carqueiranne, remaining unique for some years. But the speed with which syndicates of farm-workers, small wine-growers, employees in the market gardens, etc., came into existence thereafter was quite remarkable. In 1910 there were 9410 peasants and *journaliers* organised in syndicates, almost as many as in the industrial sector.[63]

Just as elections determined the rate of progress of the Socialist movement, so the growth of organised labour movements in this region was largely a function of strikes in certain key sectors. Two such sectors might be taken as examples. The first is the cork industry, centred in the Maures, and suffering by the early 1880s from outside competition and price falls. On 9 August 1881, the cork-workers of La Garde Freinet struck, demanding an increase of 25 centimes per 1000 corks. The *patronat* refused, and as other cork-workers in the region joined the strike there was talk of lockouts and expulsions. Meanwhile those still working paid money into a strike fund to support the strikers. By 17 August the strike had affected every establishment in the commune. Three days later, some of the small employers began to concede increases and their workers returned. The rest stuck it out.

By January 1882, the leaders of the strike were working to set up a union of cork-workers. They organised a meeting at Cogolin at the end of the month and a syndicate was formed. The declared aim was to enable the cork-workers to organise themselves, so as to avert future strikes by bringing pressure to bear on the owners. The subscription would be 12 francs per annum, and membership would be extended to all cork-workers in the Var. The initial membership of this Syndicat des Ouvriers Bouchonniers was 400 men and women. The syndicate came too late to save the strikers in La Garde Freinet, who finally returned to work, defeated, in April 1882, at the old piece rates. Many had meanwhile left the region and gone in search of work elsewhere, never to return (the population of the commune fell from 2651 to 1872 between 1876 and 1896). But the syndicate survived, and helped mobilise the remaining cork-workers in their own defence until the virtual disappearance of the industry after the war.[64]

The other case was that of the agricultural workers. There had been strikes by agricultural labourers in the market gardens of the coastal towns on a number of occasions before 1907. What was significant about the short but violent strike of December that year in Hyères was that it involved female farm labourers – an important group in the region – and carried political overtones. The women, most of them working in the flower fields around Hyères, struck on 19 December for a wage increase to 1 fr. 50 per day, and a reduction of the hours of work (twelve per day). Two hundred of them came out, and on 20 December they marched through the streets of Hyères, waving flags and singing the Marseillaise. By 24 December the Toulon arsenal workers were taking up collections for the strikers of Hyères, and on the same day there was a skirmish between strikers and police, after the arrest of one of the leaders. A general strike began in the town that same evening. This brought the *sous-préfet* hurrying in (on Christmas Day), and the employers were persuaded to grant an immediate rise and an eight-hour day. Within three weeks the former strikers, now back at work, had formed a syndicate and affiliated themselves to the Bourse at Toulon.[65]

Strikes, then, helped determine the expansion of the syndicalist movement. But there was little contact with the Socialists. Where a strike took place in a municipality controlled by the Socialists, the mayor would intervene and work for a favourable settlement, but it was rare for Socialists actually to be involved in the *organisation* of strikes. This does not mean that there were not Socialists among the strikers – some of the *cordonniers* in Bargemon were members of the socialist groups there, so that economic conflicts inevitably involved the local party.[66] But it did not play a leading rôle. The Socialist

Federation in the Var remained apart from syndical organisation in the region, just as the SFIO and the Confédération Générale de Travail (CGT) operated independently of one another in the nation as a whole.

Apart from the apolitical, indeed anti-socialist views of the syndical leaders in Toulon, for example, where anti-socialist views were circulating as early as 1884,[67] other factors helped keep the two movements apart. The electoral successes of the local Socialist movement placed it in an ambivalent position in the eyes of the syndicalists — indeed control of a municipality could not but damage relations between Socialists and syndical militants. But there was another factor. Socialism in the Var, as we shall shortly see, was firmly rooted in areas of rural small peasant property — indeed its success among smallholding peasants was one of its special characteristics. But this tended to preclude it from taking very much interest in the centres of syndical activity — among which Toulon was prominent, and there, as has been shown, the Socialists were weak for other reasons. Of course, implantation in areas of small property did not preclude support from day-labourers and rural workers. But it was just these groups which were declining most rapidly at the time, and while this led naturally to a greater militancy and political radicalisation, it also meant that their effective presence in the Socialist movement was much diminished. When agricultural syndicalism developed in the Var, it took the form, increasingly, of cooperation. Here the Socialists played a very much more important rôle; the concept of cooperation, because it did not preclude political activity and because of its collectivist implications, was welcomed by Socialists in a way that full-blooded syndicalism was not. Furthermore, it was small, vulnerable peasant property, rather than landless labourers, that stood to gain most from cooperatives for the sale of wine or the purchase of fertiliser,[68] and thus cooperatives tended to flourish precisely in those areas which were also proving most fertile soil for the Socialist movement. The map of cooperation and the map of Socialist electoral strength overlap considerably, whereas syndical activity followed a route of its own, much more closely linked to centres of large-scale employment, or else to regions where traditionally militant occupations still flourished. These, on the other hand, were only centres of Socialist support under certain conditions – the shoemakers of Flayosc and Bargemon were active on both the economic and the political front, but the bakery workers of Le Muy were politically moderate, for all their syndical militancy. And, like all bakers, they were unpopular with the same peasantry which bought their bread and voted for the Socialists. The degree to which Socialist areas and syndicalist areas differed is suggestive, one might argue, of the very politicisation of the Socialist movement and its support. Unlike the movements to the north of the Loire, Socialism in the Var was not a reflex action of organised workers. It was the political representation of men whose economic circumstances and social position alone might well lead us to expect them to have behaved differently.

Anarchism

The character of the anarchist movement in the Var may serve as an extra element in an understanding of the nature of the socialist movement with which it competed. If the standard *canard* about meridional socialism were to be taken at face value, we would have to suppose that the penchant of the populations of this area for movements of the extreme left, whatever their nature, would have produced widespread success for the anarchists in the Var. But this did not happen. The Var did not slide from republicanism to Radicalism, from Radicalism to Socialism and thence, logically, on to anarchism. It stopped, quite unambiguously, with the Socialists, which is why the rest of this book is concerned with discovering why this was the case.

That the anarchists failed to establish themselves in the Var is something for which we have their own word. At a meeting in Toulon in October 1886, anarchists from Cogolin, Aups and Cuers reported that they had found it impossible to organise anarchist groups in their localities, although socialist groups flourished there. When a Toulon anarchist militant, Fougue, went to speak at Lorgues the following year, he was laughed and jeered at by what a police reporter called a 'diminishing' audience.[69]

In Toulon, on the other hand, anarchism flourished. The typical Toulon anarchist was a manual worker or else a small shopkeeper, usually on the verge of bankruptcy. Initially the foreign element was quite large, but after 1904 local manual workers replaced foreign artisans. Anarchists tended to be mature men, in their early forties during the 1890s, and they were nearly all inhabitants of Toulon. All of these are characteristics which distinguished them from Socialists (who were younger, often peasants, and rarely Toulonnais, especially after 1908).[70] Why was there this marked difference – and why did the anarchists not succeed in spreading their influence to the countryside?

In the first place, the anarchists in southern France were peculiarly counter-suggestible to any form of organisation, even within their stronghold of Toulon. This is why they never succeeded in converting their support among the workers of Toulon into a political force. And their distaste for organisation, their emphasis on the individual and the individual act, far from appealing to the southern temperament, was quite out of keeping with the communal life-style and shared interest of the peasants outside of Toulon.

Secondly, anarchism in this region was deliberately and consistently anti-political. In the 1890s anarchist speakers scorned the 'inanity of universal suffrage', spoke of the perfidy of all governments, the need to dismantle all national frontiers. These were positions which had little appeal to the peasantry or even the small-town artisans, for both of whom politics represented the only means by which they could protest their situation. Abstention at elections was something that many Varois practised, but hardly as a point of principle.

Finally, the anarchists deliberately eschewed programmatic statements, whereas the Socialists, much more than the Radicals, went in for detailed promises of the reforms they hoped to bring about. This often caught them in conflict with some of their own doctrinal positions, of course, but in general both their doctrinal stance and their detailed electoral platforms were precisely in tune with the views and interests of the small towns which dominated the political life of the region. Anarchists had nothing to offer (anti-militarism apart, and this was a theme that Socialists were quick to adopt after 1911) except their position on the extreme end of the political spectrum; and it is precisely my point that this alone did not qualify them for political success in Provence any more than elsewhere. The traditional loci of anarchist success in the countryside, in Spain or in Italy for instance, were regions of large landholding, latifundia worked by landless rural labour. There was some landless rural labour in the Var – in Hyères, for example, as we have seen – but there were no latifundia (except on the high plateaux to the north, where there would have been other factors working against anarchist success, even had they attempted to achieve it) and much of the truly landless agricultural proletariat was female (not that this made it any the less militant – arguably the reverse – but it reduced its political impact).

Thus it was socialism, political socialism, which took root in the Var in these years. Not a new kind of Radicalism, not the latest incarnation of an amorphous tradition of extremism, but also not an outgrowth of the urban or rural labour movements. By political I mean not merely electorally oriented, but identified with a particular political doctrine and organised quite clearly in a distinctive political movement. We are now in a better position to investigate precisely what the nature of its success consisted of, and in what social and economic sectors its support rested.

4

The social geography of the left

The aim of this chapter is to discover the areas where support for Socialism was strong, and then to identify as closely as possible the characteristic features of such areas, and what distinguished them from regions of conservative support, or regions where Radicalism did well but never gave way to socialism. In order to do this, it is clearly necessary to decide what constitutes a region of 'strong' support for socialism, and this is not an altogether easy matter.

The first point to make clear is that the criteria must of necessity be electoral. It would be very pleasing to be able to discuss the nature of socialist support in the Var in terms of the membership of the socialist movement. Such a procedure would enjoy a precision that electoral geography inevitably lacks. Unfortunately, this is not possible. Information concerning socialist membership is scanty. Ascertaining both where the socialist movement's members lived, and what they did for a living, is difficult; we do have occasional information but it is almost certainly not complete, and it is not possible to use it for comparisons over time. Electoral data – which communes voted for a socialist candidate – are fully available for the whole of the period under investigation. We must at the least begin by assessing what they can tell us.

If we are to rely on election results, it is imperative that these be as detailed as possible. Election results analysed by department are hopelessly uninformative (although, sadly, they are the usual basis on which students are taught of the political affiliations of the French);[1] but even cantonal divisions are often seriously misleading. There are between three and seven communes to a canton in most parts of France: as a result the political predilections of a majority of them may camouflage the ways in which the communes differ very sharply from one another in their voting patterns. Thus in the canton of Aups the majority in our period leaned away from the Socialists. Yet within this canton lay the commune of Les Salles, resolutely

Socialist from an early date, though surrounded by communes of the right. It is by comparing Les Salles with its neighbours (and by repeating this process in other cantons) that we have some possibility of discovering what might explain the differences in political behaviour.[2] It would be absurd to write the history of France in terms of its 13 000 communes, of course, but to answer some of the questions posed in this study the commune is without doubt the correct starting point.

It remains to establish *what* level of support constitutes a 'Socialist' commune. There can be no fixed criteria for this: in some areas a consistently low turnout meant that socialism could be regularly victorious at elections with the support of only a small minority of the electorate. Elsewhere a large number of committed socialists in a commune might be unable to ensure their side's success against an even larger minority of people of a different persuasion. In what follows I have compromised to the following effect: 'strong' socialist communes are defined as those districts where the Socialist candidate consistently received the support of a percentage of the electorate above the departmental average for his party over the period 1902–14 (i.e. covering the first four legislative elections of this century).[3] I have tested this concept on a variety of communes for each of the four elections in question, and have found that it provides a fair account of the areas in which socialism was actually successful at elections. Furthermore, few communes where a Socialist was ever successful (i.e. received a local majority) in more than one election are absent from this list. It is thus a nearly comprehensive account of the communities of the Var which preferred Socialist candidates to all others in this period.

In order to confirm or refute patterns which emerge from a study of those communes which were Socialist-inclined, I have asked the same questions of two other categories: communes which were strongly pro-Radical in the earlier years but which never became Socialist, and communes which, throughout the years 1871–1914, failed to support either the Radicals or the Socialists. For the former I have chosen communes which gave the Radicals 40% or more of their votes in 1876 (expressed, as always, as a percentage of the electorate), but which failed thereafter to provide either the same

Table 3   *Socio-economic and political characteristics of Var communes*

CODE

A. Population loss of 25% or more in the period 1876–1906.
B. Population loss of less than 15% in the period 1876–1906.
C. 70% or more of the population lived in the central commune in 1893.
D. 50% or more of the population lived outside the central commune in 1893.
E. Central commune situated at a height of over 300 metres above sea level.
F. Estimated 80% or more of the agricultural population were property-owning farmers in 1891.
G. 40% or more of the cultivable land under vine in 1913.
H. 40% or more of the electorate voted Radical in 1876.

I. 40% or more of the electorate voted Radical in 1889.
J. 10% or more of the electorate voted socialist in 1893.
K. 40% or more of the electorate voted socialist in 1902.
L. 40% or more of the electorate voted Socialist in 1914.
M. Less than 25% of the electorate voted Socialist in 1914.
N. Socialist vote consistently above departmental average 1902–14.
O. Socialist vote consistently below departmental average 1902–14.
P. 40% or more of the electorate voted Dém.-Soc. in 1849.
Q. 40% or more of the electorate abstained from voting in 1876.
R. 40% or more of the electorate abstained from voting in 1898.
S. 40% or more of the electorate abstained from voting in 1914.

	A	B	C	D	E	F	G	H	I	J	K	L	M	N	O	P	Q	R	S
Barjols																			
Bras	*		*			*		*				*			*	*			*
Brue Auriac		*	*			*	*	*				*					*	*	*
Esparron			*		*	*						*							
St Martin	*		*					*	*			*							
Pontevès						*		*	*		*	*		*					
Varages	*		*					*	*			*		*					*
Seillons	*		*					*	*		*	*		*					*
Châteauvert	*			*				*	*		*						*	*	
Besse																			
Cabasse	*		*			*		*	*			*		*		*	*		*
Flassans	*		*					*	*						*	*	*	*	*
Gonfaron		*	*				*	*	*				*		*		*	*	*
Pignans	*		*			*	*	*	*										*
Brignoles																			
Camps	*		*				*	*	*		*	*		*			*		*
La Celle							*							*		*			
Tourves	*		*					*			*	*				*		*	
Le Val			*			*	*		*			*	*				*	*	*
Vins		*	*			*	*	*										*	*

Commune	1	2	3	4	5	6	7	8	9	10	11	12	13	14	15	16	17	18
Carcès	*												*		*		*	*
Correns	*												*		*		*	*
Cotignac	*												*		*		*	
Entrecasteaux	*											*		*		*		*
Montfort		*										*		*	*		*	
St Maximin	*												*		*		*	*
Nans	*												*				*	*
Ollières			*												*			
Plan d'Aups										*				*		*		
Pourcieux	*											*			*		*	
Pourrières	*											*					*	
Rougiers	*											*		*			*	
St Zacharie			*									*		*		*		*
Artigues		*											*		*		*	
Ginasservis		*										*		*		*		*
St Julien														*		*		*
Rians												*		*	*		*	
La Verdière												*		*	*		*	
Vinon												*		*	*		*	*
Ste Anastasie												*		*	*		*	
Forcalqueiret		*												*		*		*
Garéoult														*		*		*
Mazaugues														*		*		*
Méounes														*		*		*
Néoules														*		*		*
Rocbaron														*		*		*
La Roquebrussanne														*		*		*
Artignosc														*		*		*
Fox Amphoux													*		*	*		*
Moissac														*		*		*
Montmeyan														*		*		*
Régusse														*		*		*
Sillans														*		*		*
Tavernes														*		*		*

Table 3 *Socio-economic and political characteristics of Var communes (cont.)*

CODE

A. Population loss of 25% or more in the period 1876–1906.
B. Population loss of less than 15% in the period 1876–1906.
C. 70% or more of the population lived in the central commune in 1893.
D. 50% or more of the population lived outside the central commune in 1893.
E. Central commune situated at a height of over 300 metres above sea level.
F. Estimated 80% or more of the agricultural population were property-owning farmers in 1891.
G. 40% or more of the cultivable land under vine in 1913.
H. 40% or more of the electorate voted Radical in 1876.

I. 40% or more of the electorate voted Radical in 1889.
J. 10% or more of the electorate voted socialist in 1893.
K. 40% or more of the electorate voted socialist in 1902.
L. 40% or more of the electorate voted Socialist in 1914.
M. Less than 25% of the electorate voted Socialist in 1914.
N. Socialist vote consistently above departmental average 1902–14.
O. Socialist vote consistently below departmental average 1902–14.
P. 40% or more of the electorate voted Dém.-Soc. in 1849.
Q. 40% or more of the electorate abstained from voting in 1876.
R. 40% or more of the electorate abstained from voting in 1898.
S. 40% or more of the electorate abstained from voting in 1914.

Commune	A	B	C	D	E	F	G	H	I	J	K	L	M	N	O	P	Q	R	S
Aiguines	*				*	*		*							*		*	*	*
Aups	*		*		*	*					*	*			*		*	*	
Baudinard	*				*	*	*							*	*	*			
Bauduen	*					*	*	*			*	*		*					
Les Salles		*	*	*									*						
Vérignon	*		*			*	*	*				*	*		*	*	*		*
Bargemon			*							*		*		*		*			
Callas	*		*		*			*	*	*	*	*				*			
Châteaudouble	*			*						*	*	*		*			*	*	*
Claviers	*		*					*		*	*	*		*					*
Figanières			*			*					*	*	*	*					
Montferrat	*		*					*											
Bargème	*				*			*							*	*	*	*	*
La Bastide	*			*	*	*		*					*		*		*	*	*
Le Bourguet					*	*					*				*	*	*	*	*
Brenon	*		*	*	*				*			*	*				*		
Brovès	*		*		*	*		*			*							*	*
Châteauvieux	*		*		*	*		*									*	*	*

	1	2	3	4	5	6	7	8	9	10	11	12	13	14	15
Comps	*														
La Martre						*			*						
La Rq. Esclapon								*	*	*		*			
Trigance	*								*	*	*	*			
Ampus									*		*	*	*		*
Draguignan	*	*							*			*	*	*	*
Flayosc															
La Motte	*	*							*						
Trans										*					*
Callian	*								*	*		*	*	*	*
Fayence	*	*	*								*				
Mons	*	*	*							*				*	
Montauroux									*	*			*	*	*
St Paul									*	*	*				
Seillans									*	*	*				
Tanneron	*			*	*				*	*	*				
Tourrettes															
Bagnols					*	*	*								
Fréjus					*	*	*								
Le Muy					*	*	*								
Le Puget					*	*	*								
St Raphael						*									
Roquebrune						*									
Les Adrets						*	*								
Cogolin	*				*		*								
La Garde Freinet	*				*	*									
Grimaud	*	*													
Ste Maxime	*	*			*										
Plan de la Tour	*														
Les Arcs	*				*										
Lorgues	*														
Taradeau	*						*	*							
Le Thoronet	*						*	*							

Table 3   *Socio-economic and political characteristics of Var communes (cont.)*

CODE
A. Population loss of 25% or more in the period 1876–1906.
B. Population loss of less than 15% in the period 1876–1906.
C. 70% or more of the population lived in the central commune in 1893.
D. 50% or more of the population lived outside the central commune in 1893.
E. Central commune situated at a height of over 300 metres above sea level.
F. Estimated 80% or more of the agricultural population were property-owning farmers in 1891.
G. 40% or more of the cultivable land under vine in 1913.
H. 40% or more of the electorate voted Radical in 1876.
I. 40% or more of the electorate voted Radical in 1889.
J. 10% or more of the electorate voted socialist in 1893.
K. 40% or more of the electorate voted socialist in 1902.
L. 40% or more of the electorate voted Socialist in 1914.
M. Less than 25% of the electorate voted Socialist in 1914.
N. Socialist vote consistently above departmental average 1902–14.
O. Socialist vote consistently below departmental average 1902–14.
P. 40% or more of the electorate voted Dém.-Soc. in 1849.
Q. 40% or more of the electorate abstained from voting in 1876.
R. 40% or more of the electorate abstained from voting in 1898.
S. 40% or more of the electorate abstained from voting in 1914.

	A	B	C	D	E	F	G	H	I	J	K	L	M	N	O	P	Q	R	S
Le Cannet								*		*	*	*		*	*	*	*	*	*
Le Luc		*	*					*			*	*		*		*		*	*
Les Mayons			*				*	*			*					*			
Vidauban	*	*	*			*	*	*	*						*	*		*	*
Salernes	*	*	*		*			*	*		*			*		*			*
Tourtour					*	*								*	*	*	*	*	*
Villecroze				*		*	*	*					*					*	
Gassin		*		*							*								*
La Môle		*		*		*	*		*				*				*		*
Ramatuelle		*		*		*	*	*					*		*	*		*	*
St Tropez		*	*				*	*							*	*		*	*
Le Beausset			*	*			*			*				*	*			*	*
La Cadière		*		*		*	*	*	*				*	*				*	
Le Castellet	*			*			*	*	*				*		*			*	
St Cyr				*	*								*	*	*				
Riboux	*	*		*	*										*				
Signes	*		*			*		*		*					*			*	*

	1	2	3	4	5	6	7	8	9	10	11	12	13
Le Lavandou				*					*			*	
Bormes		*		*		*	*	*		*		*	*
Collobrières		*	*		*			*		*		*	
Carnoules	*		*		*	*		*				*	
Cuers	*		*		*		*			*		*	
Pierrefeu		*				*				*		*	*
Puget-Ville	*		*		*			*				*	
Hyères		*	*			*			*		*		*
La Crau		*				*		*			*		*
Bandol		*	*		*						*		
Evenos				*	*	*				*		*	
St Nazaire		*			*		*			*		*	*
Ollioules		*			*			*	*		*		*
La Seyne		*				*		*				*	*
Six Fours		*		*		*		*				*	*
Belgentier	*		*			*		*				*	*
La Farlede		*			*	*		*			*	*	*
Solliès Pont		*	*		*	*			*		*		*
Solliès Toucas	*		*			*			*		*		*
Solliès Ville	*			*			*			*		*	
La Garde		*	*			*						*	*
Le Revest				*								*	*
La Valette		*	*								*		
Toulon (1e and 2e)		*	*			*					*		*

level of support for the Socialists, or even to raise their support for the Socialists above the departmental average for the years 1902—14.

The second category comprises communes which at no time gave to Radicals or Socialists 40% of their votes; furthermore, in all of these, the Socialists were supported by less than 25% of the electorate in 1914 — a good test, since that election saw the Socialists sweep the board in the department. Less than 25% of the electorate meant in each case that the Socialist candidate was defeated by a conservative no matter how low the turnout.

The final section of this chapter moves on from electoral data to a consideration of Socialist membership and an assessment of the occupational background of Socialist militants.

The geography of Socialist support

Although the Socialists lost some support in the elections of 1910, in the aftermath of the Toulon schisms and the Clemenceau ministry, the pattern of Socialist support at general elections varied little. Forty of the one hundred and forty-seven communes in the Var gave the Socialists a higher than average percentage of their votes at every election from 1902 to the war. These communes are shown on Map 10, and it is with these that I am now concerned.

Of these forty, sixteen were in the arrondissement of Brignoles, eighteen in the arrondissement of Draguignan, six in the arrondissement of Toulon. More usefully, perhaps, they fall in five distinct regions: seven of them lay in the wooded area of the north-west, near the lower reaches of the Verdon; ten were tucked in the valleys which run from north-west to south-east in the region north of Brignoles; a further eight were ranged in an arc around Draguignan, to the north; nine more lay on the fringes of the Maures or in the hills themselves; four communes were in the Toulon region and there were two further communes unattached to a particular region.[4]

What, topographically speaking, is distinctive about these particular communes? A number of things. In the first place, they represent a disproportionate number of low-lying communes (a random sample of forty communes in the Var ought to provide many more villages from hills and mountain plateaux). Next, they are remarkable, as a bunch, for their closely-grouped habitat.[5] A comparison with Maps 6 and 7 in Chapter 2 shows how few of the communes whose population was loosely grouped in isolated hamlets figure on this list. Compared, then, to their share of the department as a whole, communes situated on high ground and with far-flung populations are under-represented in the list of Socialist strongholds.

As well as being predominantly 'urban villages', then, and mostly situated in valleys or in forest clearings, these Socialist communes were remarkable for their size. They include none of the towns of over 4000 inhabitants (taking the 1896 census as our base); instead they are grouped predominantly in communes whose populations varied between 500 and 3500.[6] These forty communes were large villages, or small towns for the most part, rather than hamlets on the one hand or sizeable urban concentrations on the other.

They were also, as one might by now expect, communes whose population was on the decline. While there does not appear to be a close link between a falling electorate and a growing Socialist vote, it is the case that Socialists did disproportionately *badly* in the towns and villages where the population was steady or rising (for all of these points, see Table 3). This confirms some suggestions made earlier, both because it was primarily the coastal strip, from Fréjus to St Cyr, where the population was growing (and where Socialists complained of the innate conservatism of the local communities), but also because it was areas of acute population fall which were experiencing the worst crises and thus most likely to respond to a movement of social protest.

The structural and demographic characteristics of these forty communes are easier to ascertain than are reliable data concerning the occupations of their inhabitants. Nevertheless, it is clear that most of them were communities which had been very mixed in character, with complex occupational patterns − typically 'Provençal', in the sense described in Chapter 2. Taking the Statistical Enquiry in 1885 as a base, only ten of the forty villages and bourgs reported a complete absence of industrial activity. And even in these cases it is likely that there was still some manufacture, but on a very small scale, and employing men and women whose primary occupations were agricultural.[7] Apart from these ten communes, and a further four where industry survived at the minimal level,[8] the other twenty-six com-

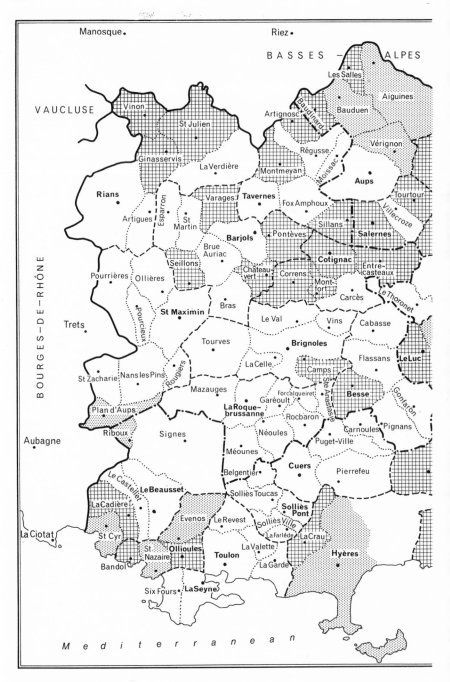

Manosque.

Riez.

BASSES — ALPES

Les Salles

Aiguines

VAUCLUSE   Vinon

Artignosc   Bauduen

St Julien

Vérignon

Ginasservis   Régusse

Moissac

LaVerdière   Montmeyan   Aups

Rians   Tourtour

Varages   Tavernes   Fox Amphoux   Villecroze

Artigues   St   Sillans   Salernes
Esparron   Martin

Barjols   Pontèves

Brue   Cotignac
Auriac   Entre-
Seillons   Château-   Correns   casteaux
vert   Mont-   Le Thoronet
Pourrières   Ollières   fort

Carcès

Bras

St Maximin   Le Val   Vins   Cabasse

Trets   Tourves   LeLuc

Brignoles

LaCelle   Flassans

St Zacharie Nans les Pins   Camps
Rougiers   Besse

Mazauges   Forcalqueiret
Garéoult

LaRoque-
Plan d'Aups   brussanne   Rocbaron   Carnoules Pignans

Riboux   Signes   Néoules   Puget-Ville

Aubagne
Méounes

Belgentier   Cuers   Pierrefeu

Le Castelle   LeBeausset   Solliès Toucas

LaCadière   Solliès
Pont
Evenos   LeRevest   Solliès Ville
La Ciotat   LaFarlède LaCrau
St Cyr   LaValette
St   Ollioules   Hyères
Nazaire   Toulon   La Garde
Bandol

Six Fours LaSeyne

Mediterranean

BOURGES—DE—RHÔNE

Baudinard

Pourcieux

Ste Anastasie

Gonfaron

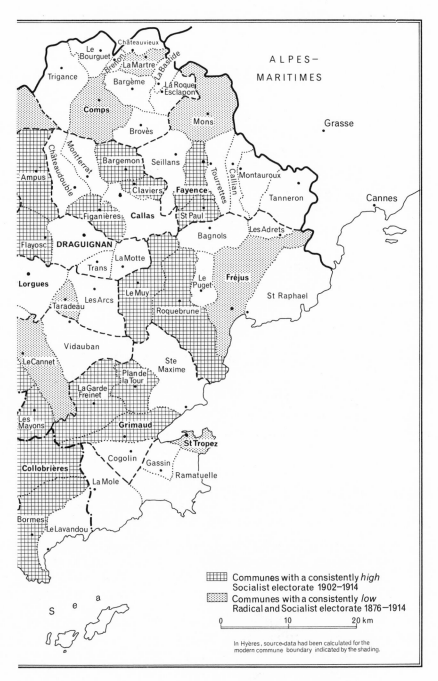

Map 10. Left and right in elections — socialists and conservatives

munes seem all to have employed a part, at least, of their adult population in some artisanal or manufacturing rôle.

Three industries dominate the list. The first is cork manufacture. This is no surprise, since cork production was the main nineteenth-century activity in and around the Maures, and it was in the Maures that much of the Socialist support was to be found. In the communes lower down, on the edge of the hills, there were 53 people employed in cork production in Plan de la Tour, 57 in Roquebrune. Higher up, there were 177 men working in eight different establishments in Collobrières, while at the top, in La Garde Freinet, 404 cork-workers were counted in 1885.

The second major industry in these communes was shoemaking. Still pursued on a predominantly artisanal scale, the manufacture of shoes and boots employed 5 or 6 men in Fayence and Ampus, but was based primarily in Flayosc, with 246 masters and workers, and in Bargemon, with 270. Like cork manufacture, this was a well-established local industry, deeply rooted in the wider rural economy. The third predominant activity was the manufacture of bricks and tiles. This was pursued on a smaller scale than the first two but in more places. A half-dozen men worked in tilemaking in Pontèves, another dozen or so in Figanières. But there were 90 men employed in brickmaking in Flayosc, which with its shoe manufacture and still quite sizeable olive crop was a mixed and still fairly large community.[9]

The only other occupation which employed a large number of people was the manufacture of (felt) hats, but this was almost exclusively the affair of the inhabitants of Camps, where in 1885 there were 195 men and women (out of a population of 1120 altogether) employed by ten different establishments of hat-makers. But even Camps, like Bargemon, Flayosc, Pontèves and the rest, was never an 'industrial' town — very far from it. The vast majority of the adult population worked in the fields — indeed the industrial workers often did likewise from June until August. The industrial production described above contributed an important social variable, of course, and its decline, already begun and quite marked by 1885 in the cork industry for example, would play an important rôle in preparing the ground for socialism. But these were primarily peasant communities all the same — though by habitat and through the presence of these industries predominantly urban in tone. What is more, the cork and shoe industries were confined almost without exception to communes which appear in the list we are currently discussing. It can thus be stated with confidence that a further characteristic of Socialist strongholds was the fact that they had until very recently been active centres of small-scale industry as well.

Only four of the communes in my list could be described as having complex as distinct from mixed economies. In Cotignac in 1885 there was a variety of small industries: brickworks employed 10 men, the manufacture of oil a further 65 men and women, there were two tanneries which employed 30 people altogether; there was also a branch of the hat manufacture, employing some 22 people, and 19 women were engaged in the spinning of silk. Le Luc and Le Muy, both in the central depression and on the main through road, were also small but complex towns. They both had a number of cork-workers (12 in Le Luc, 74 in Le Muy); in Le Luc there were also some hat manufacturers (15), a few shoemakers, a small cannery (employing 14 people) and some oil mills. Le Muy was dominated by a large, mechanised sawmill, which employed 48 men.[10]

None of these three compares however with Salernes, the only town on the list which might remotely be called industrial. Although there was the usual range of semi-artisanal occupations (oil-milling, potteries, flour-milling, etc.), what made Salernes unique were its factories and workshops devoted to the production of bricks and, especially, domestic tiles. In 1885, just under 1100 men were employed in this industry. In a town with a total population of 2800, this probably represented not merely the vast majority of the adult male population of the town itself, but also many workers who travelled in to live, temporarily, in Salernes, but who were registered in their communes of permanent dwelling. Only in Salernes does it seem likely that the Socialists were gathering their support from men who were not particularly peasants — a point which thus confirms the earlier assessment of the fundamentally rural basis of socialism in this area.

If peasants, then what kind of peasants? Here there are real difficulties of evidence. In principle it ought to be easy to determine the property structure of a given commune, to discover how many peasants were owner—farmers, how many sharecroppers, etc. But the data on this which were collected by enquiries and statistical surveys were normally provided by local elected officials, and they do not appear to have been overly conscientious in their task. There are discrepancies in the figures available which suggest either that some men have been recorded under more than one category, or that they have been left out altogether — or, most commonly, that the categories changed in certain respects between enquiries. In order to obtain some idea of the property structure of this area which might be reliable enough to use, I have compared data from two sources, an enquiry of 1872–6, and a statistical survey of 1891.[11] Only where they confirm one another have I used the resultant data (see Table 3). Nevertheless, what emerges seems quite clear; the presence of a predominant number of small peasant proprietors appears to favour the Socialists, though not to a very marked degree. Similarly, areas where Socialists received *below* the average for the department were less likely to be areas of small peasant property than was the case for the department as a whole. Except in special cases like Ollioules, with its numerous and mostly female farm labourers, the areas of Socialist success were areas of the Var where small peasants, rather than large holdings with sharecropping or day-labourers, were predominant.

What these peasants produced is easier to ascertain, but not particularly informative. One assumption, readily made by many, including myself, needs modifying. This is that areas of intensive cultivation of the vine were *ipso facto* areas of strong leftward inclination. In taking the *vignoble* of 1912 and setting it against our grid of forty communes, we find that the latter were actually disproportionately non-wine-growing areas. Bearing in mind that over half of them lay in a belt across the central Var on the very outer fringe of the vine, this should not come as a surprise. There are also particular reasons for limiting the significance of the comparison, however.

In the first place, wine-growing in the Var, once the vines had recovered from the phylloxera (or been replanted with American ceps), became heavily concentrated in the Toulon region, as well as in the Argens valley and the central depression. The relationship between wine and socialism, so to speak, is thus distorted in this department by the conservative politics of the Toulon coastal region, conservative politics whose origin must be sought elsewhere. If we control for the arrondissement of Toulon, areas of *vignoble* then appear slightly over-represented among the Socialist communes. There is a further point to be taken into account; the relationship between wine-growers and the extreme left in these years was, I would argue, one of anger and protest. The *vignerons* who were protesting loudest were those most affected by the crises of this period. And these, in almost every case, were not the largest growers, but those who grew small quantities and found their vines first destroyed, then under-priced. Measuring the vine in terms of hectares or of hectolitres produced (as we must) tends to bury such small peasants in the great and flourishing *vignobles* of the coast.[12]

On the other hand, *none* of the forty communes in question were centres of grain production. Even the flour mills of the north were in every case fed by grain from elsewhere. Vinon may have employed men in flour mills, but in 1885 it boasted only 320 hectares given to grain (out of a total land surface in the commune of 3500 hectares). Elsewhere the figure was lower still.[13]

So what was the basis of the agricultural economy of these places? More than elsewhere in the department, it seems, they lagged behind in the switch to monoculture (except in respect of the vine, but the phylloxera had probably produced a temporary and unsuccessful reversion to polycultural habits). To take the example of Grimaud: as well as its cork-workers, Grimaud had a few flour-millers, twenty men working in the making of olive oil, eight workers in an artisan shoe manufacture, and five brick-workers. The rest of its population of 1100, saving only the *curé*, the teacher, a blacksmith, a postman, an innkeeper, two café-owners, the *garde-champêtre* and occasional *fonctionnaires*, lived directly off the land. In the 1890s the commune's arable land was put to the following uses: 400 hectares of wheat, 5 of rye, 315 of barley and oats. There were 20 hectares of potatoes, 10 of lucerne and 3 of beetroot (that it should be three is not surprising — both the soil and the climate were quite unsuited to beet-growing: someone was clearly desperate). There were also 200 hectares of natural grazing land. Then came the orange groves, the chestnut plantations, the mulberry trees (for silkworms) and above all the olives, by now a hopelessly unprofitable crop, though Grimaud still produced 20 000 quintals per year, in the late 1880s. And of course there were the vines of which in 1885 all but 200 hectares had been destroyed, but which would one day return to replace everything else and dominate the commune (as they still do). The animal population of the commune provided further diversification. As well as 88 horses and 36 donkeys, the population of Grimaud kept 136 head of cattle, 632 sheep and 200 pigs in 1886. Nor did this catholic outlook disappear overnight. In 1913 Grimaud still boasted almost as many horses and donkeys, a few fewer cows, but over double the number of sheep (1500); and 100 goats had been acquired meanwhile.[14]

Grimaud was not particularly remarkable for its variety of produce and resources, though few could match Grimaud's olive production, a consequence of its favoured south-facing situation near the coast. But all of these forty communes, with the exception of industrial Salernes and perhaps tiny Les Salles, shared this anachronistic economic structure, and in this respect they most certainly stand out from the department taken as a whole. The arrondissement of Toulon to the south, or the canton of Comps to the north, had either passed on from this old rural economy, or never attained its complexity.[15]

To turn, briefly, back to certain political characteristics of these forty communes we have been considering. Although a high abstention rate (especially at the first round of elections) was a strong characteristic of local political behaviour, it does not seem particularly to have contributed in any way to the success or otherwise of Socialist candidates. The twenty communes of the department where the abstention rate was 40% or more in the elections of 1876, 1898 and 1914, the rate remaining consistently high throughout, show no marked relationship either to communes of the left or to more conservative ones. Since they are scattered all over the Var, from Méounes in the south-west to Le Bourguet near Castellane, it seems reasonable to infer that electoral abstentionism, if not an entirely random matter, had little to do with geographical or political factors of a general kind. It is certainly true that the turnout was higher in coastal areas, but it is not easy to establish an explanation for this. Communes of agglomerated population did vote a little more conscientiously than those whose populations were widespread, and this makes obvious sense, given difficulties of transportation. But the link is not so very strong as to make it a likely explanation in itself — if it were, and given the relationship established above between agglomerated habitat and

Socialist voting, we should probably have found high rates of abstention linked to conservatism. But this is not the case. At any rate, Socialists seem neither to have benefited nor to have suffered from low turnouts at the polls.

Finally, how far were Socialist candidates the beneficiaries of established political traditions? It may be possible to answer this question in part by seeking a parallel with the elections of 1849 and the Démocrates–Socialistes vote of that year, and perhaps also with Radical successes in later elections. In the first case (see Table 3 again) the left vote of 1849[16] (where it can be determined – some communes voted by canton in that year), is a good but far from perfect guide to later behaviour. More precisely, it is a good guide to the pro-Socialist leanings of communes in the eastern and southern parts of the Var. But the Socialist communes of the Brignoles arrondissement did *not* have their roots in the leftism of the 1840s: of the twenty-one communes in this arrondissement which figure on the list of forty, only two voted strongly (over 40% of the electorate) for the Démocrates–Socialistes in 1849. This evidence of a late flourishing of socialism and its lack of historical links to the 'seminal' elections of 1849 ought at least to give pause to those who might too readily see the latter as a reliable indicator of later political allegiance in France.[17]

So much for a very brief account of the social and economic features of the forty communes of the Var in which the Socialists scored consistent electoral successes in the years before the First World War. The purpose of this chapter being to sketch out a profile of the Socialist-inclined communes of the Var, it is necessary now to raise a rather different question: what link was there between the early successes of the Radicals and the later rise of electoral socialism? How far, that is, can a profile of Radical-inclined electorates help explain the particular circumstances which favoured a vote for the Socialists?

From Radicalism to Socialism?

Seventy-three communes in 1876 gave the Radical candidate at the elections of that year votes representing more than 40% of the local electorate. All seventy-three were in the arrondissements of

Manosque.   .Riez

BASSES — ALPES

Les Salles

Aiguines

VAUCLUSE   Vinon   Bauduen

St Julien   Baudinard

Artignosc   Vérignon

Ginasservis   La Verdière   Montmeyan   Régusse

Aups   Tourtour

Rians   Artigues   St   Varages   Tavernes   Fox Amphoux   Villecroze

Martin   Sillans   Salernes

Pourrières   Ollières   Seillons   Brue   Barjols   Pontèves

Auriac   Cotignac   Entre-

Château-   Correns   casteaux

vert   Montfort   Carcès

St Maximin   Bras   Le Val   Vins   Cabasse

Trets   Le Thoronet

Tourves   Brignoles

St Zacharie Nans les Pins   La Celle   Camps   Flassans   Le Luc

Mazaugues   La Roque-   Besse

Plan d'Aups   brussanne   Ste Anastasie

Forcalqueiret

Riboux   Roquebron   Carnoules   Pignans

Aubagne   Signes   Néoules   Puget-Ville

Méounes

Belgentier   Cuers

Le Castellet Le Beausset   Pierrefeu

La Cadière   Solliès Toucas   Solliès

Pont

Evenos   Le Revest   Solliès Ville

La Valette   La Farlède

La Ciotat   St Cyr   La Crau

St   Ollioules   Hyères

Bandol   Nazaire   Toulon   La Garde

Six Fours   La

Seyne

M e d i t e r r a n e a n

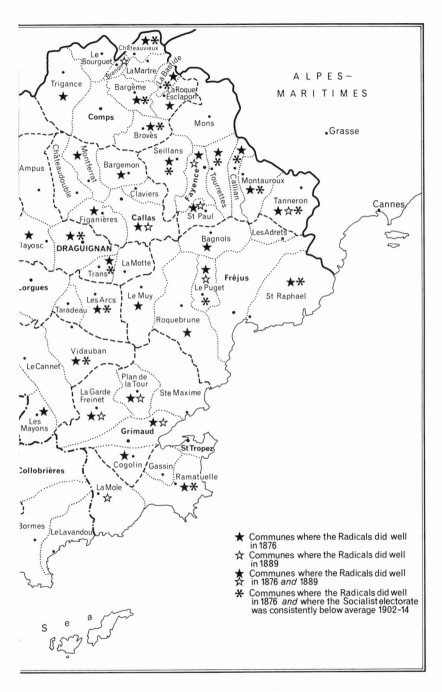

Map 11. Radicals in elections — 1876/1889

Brignoles and Draguignan (in 1876 as in some later elections the
voting pattern in Toulon is blurred by a proliferation of candidates
and labels; this section is thus confined to the two rural arrondissements). In 1889, 25 out of the 30 communes which gave the Radicals
over 40% were among the original 73 (see Map 11). There was thus a
certain continuity within Radical support throughout the 1870s
and 1880s.

Yet of the original 73 Radical-leaning communes, fully 36 never
gave a socialist candidate 40% of their electorate's support, nor did
the socialist vote in these 36 communes ever rise above the average
socialist vote for the department as a whole. Furthermore, 7 of the
strong socialist communes in the two arrondissements in question
had never been Radical strongholds, as defined above.[18] Thus in the
two rural arrondissements of the Var, there were only 27 communes
among those which we have defined as socialist which had once been
Radical. This is not incompatible with the view that Radicalism led
to socialism in many areas, but it certainly suggests at least the possibility that the two had different roots — a possibility heightened by
the high levels of abstention; even communes which had once been
Radical and became socialist later need not have been switching
allegiances — we may be seeing former abstainers coming in to vote,
or even a new generation behaving differently from their elders.

There is no easy way of testing these possibilities — ecological
correlations merely confirm that there *is* a relationship between
Radicalism and socialism in respect of their electoral geography. But
a slightly closer look at one election may be more revealing. In 1898
the socialists for the first time broke through into a leading position
in local electoral politics, winning two seats and improving their
standing in the other two. Conversely, this was the year in which the
Radical hold in the Var was decisively weakened. The figures from
this particular election may help to indicate how the process worked.

In 1898 in the arrondissement of Draguignan, at the first round of
voting, the turnout was 60%; very close to the turnout in a year of
Radical success (1889) when 59.3% of the electorate had voted. In
the first round of the voting, the Radical candidate (Clemenceau)
obtained 28.7% of the electorate in 1889. In 1898 the Radical
(Jourdan) received 23.1%. But this 5% drop in Radical support does
not account for the success of the socialist candidate (Allard) who in

1898 received 17.2% at the first round of voting. In the second round, Jourdan increased his share of the electorate to 32.7%, Allard improved his to 35.7%. The turnout as a whole had risen from 60 to 69.7%.

Those figures alone suggest not so much that Radicalism was declining as that socialism was advancing. However, by referring to matters at the commune level we can see the process more clearly still. Table 4 shows the results and developments between rounds in each election for five of the communes which figure on our list of Socialist strongholds. The pattern they reveal seems too regular to be pure chance. In 1889 the total vote fell between rounds, but the Radical share of it grew, usually by a small amount. In 1898 the total vote rose between rounds (except in Figanières), and in every instance the Radical share grew, again by a small amount. The number of socialist voters also rose, by a slightly larger amount. Now it is possible that the increase in the socialist vote, taking Allard ahead of Jourdan in each case, was a result of conservatives playing the *politique du pire*. But this cannot hide the really significant fact: in every example except that of Figanières, where there is a discrepancy of 30 votes, the combined total of Radical and socialist votes at the first round in 1898 exceeds the number of Radical votes in 1889. The Radicals were *not*, therefore, losing voters to the socialists – or if they were, they compensated among other voters; the Radicals were not in decline, they were being overtaken, and this suggests that within those communes we have been considering there was a different group (or groups) of people who were now voting socialist having never voted Radical. When we further consider that the period 1889 to 1898 saw the final years of the rural economic crises and the end of the old Provençal economy, it becomes at least very plausible to suggest that the socialists were receiving the support of the peasantry, in ways which the Radicals never had been able to do.

This may be confirmed by the geographical distribution of the Radical communes of 1876. There are far too many of them (73) to analyse them separately, and it is in any case clear, from a glance at the map, that they are much more widely distributed than are the socialists. But this is of course precisely the point: the Radicals' support was far more socially and geographically heterogeneous than that of the socialists. We find over 40% of the electors turning out for the

THE VAR

Table 4   *From Radicalism to socialism 1889—1898*

| Commune | | 1889 | | 1898 | | |
		Votes	Radicals	Votes	Radicals	socialists
Bargemon	1st rd	312	218	399	71	185
	2nd rd	261	253	438	95	329
Figanières	1st rd	222	107	222	54	23
	2nd rd	134	129	218	70	149
Le Luc	1st rd	617	255	616	134	449
	2nd rd	414	372	680	181	494
Ampus	1st rd	158	79	188	72	46
	2nd rd	86	84	254	115	139
Roquebrune	1st rd	328	158	241	60	159
	2nd rd	191	175	363	150	210

Note

Note that in four out of five cases the Radical and socialist votes together at the first round in 1898 exceed the 1889 Radical vote. This is representative of the rural Var generally and suggests that although Radicals *were* losing votes to the socialists, the latter were also gaining votes from elsewhere; this was not from conservatives, who in the first round voted for their own candidates.

Radicals in 1876 in all kinds of places: the communes of the central Brignoles region, in valleys and hills alike; in many more of the far north-western communes, rather than in a select few like the Socialists in the next generation; even in six of the ten communes of the canton of Comps, the wildest, most remote and poorest region of the Var, where the Socialists never established themselves even as late as 1914. And this geographical heterogeneity applies no less to the social and economic distinctions. Radicals culled votes in areas of intense viticulture, of substantial industry and of none at all, and so forth.

Nevertheless, some things stand out. Radicals were not as unsuccessful as socialists in areas of loosely-grouped habitat, nor did they seem to be as much put off by high places. They benefited from the traditions of 1849 to about the same degree as did the socialists, although here too 1849 was another world and the political behaviour of the 1870s and 1880s is best explained in its own terms. But in general the Radicals' success appears to be less easily related to social and economic contexts than does that of the Socialists two decades later, and this no doubt reflects both the intervening economic crisis and the greater emphasis in the Socialists' propaganda on social and economic change of a decidedly radical kind. To that extent at least, the continuity on the French left looks a lot less predetermined than a first glance at the departmental map might suggest.

A conservative Var

Radicals nevertheless shared much more with the Socialists in respect of their social and geographical implantation than either had in common with those parts of the Var which remained firmly conservative in their politics throughout this period. Map 10 shows 16 communes which at no time gave the Socialists a percentage of their electorate above the departmental average for the Socialist candidate, and which moreover never gave the Radicals more than 40% of their electorate's backing. These criteria in fact coincide with those communes where neither Radical nor Socialist candidates *ever* emerged victorious throughout this period. What distinguishes these 16 communes from the rest?

To begin with, nearly half of them are located in the northernmost part of the region: Bauduen, Vérignon and Aiguines in the canton of Aups, La Martre and Comps in the canton of Comps, Mons on the northern edge of the neighbouring canton of Fayence. A slight lowering of our criterion would bring in all but two of the remaining eight communes of the Comps region, so this area was clearly the preferred soil for conservativism. Four more communes in this group lie in the Toulon region – St Nazaire (Sanary on modern maps), St Cyr and Evenos to the west, Hyères to the east. A little to the north come the isolated communes of Riboux and Plan d'Aups on the border with the Bouches-du-Rhône. Finally there come two coastal towns, St Tropez and Fréjus, and two small towns on the northern fringe of the Maures, Le Cannet and Taradeau.

Asking of these communes the same questions we asked of the earlier, Socialist ones, we find the following points emerging: these sixteen communes are decidedly over-represented in two kinds of sub-region – the coast and the hills. A glance at Map 5 will show just how strongly these non-left communes are represented among areas of sparsely grouped population. On that map, Plan d'Aups and Riboux in the west, Comps and its hinterland in the north-east,

St Cyr, Le Castellet and Evenos in the south-west, all stand out for their loosely-grouped populations in areas where the dominant habitat is clustered agglomerated villages and bourgs. And in the centre Le Cannet in particular emerges as remarkably spread out across its valley, surrounded by some of the most tightly-knit communes in the region.

The next point to emerge is that, in contrast to the areas discussed earlier, these communes are predominantly high up. Riboux and Plan d'Aups are the highest communes in the western Var, just as the canton of Comps, rising up towards the Alps, is the highest in the department. And in the canton of Aups, only Les Salles is closely grouped and situated on low ground — and it stands out as a centre of leftism in a sea of reaction. The conservative regions of the coast, from Fréjus to St Tropez and on to St Cyr, form an exception in this instance, of course.

In certain other respects, though, they form a contrast to the Socialist communes discussed earlier. Whereas the latter were small in size, reflecting the Provençal norm of between 500 and 3000 persons, the sixteen conservative communes were either particularly tiny or much larger than the average.[19] Furthermore, they were notably communes whose population was on the *increase* — again in contrast to the tendency evinced by the left-leaning bourgs.[20]

Furthermore, just as the Socialist communes had inherited very mixed economies, even if the mixture was much thinned by the 1890s, so of the sixteen right-leaning communes, nine reported a total absence of industrial activity of any kind in 1885. These nine include the communes of the north, together with Taradeau just off the central valley and Riboux and St Cyr in the south-west. Two more, Plan d'Aups and Evenos, reported a single 'industrial activity'; in the former there were seven men working a zinc-mine, while in Evenos the production of olive oil employed eight full-time workers. At the other extreme Hyères and St Tropez both boasted a wide range of activities, much greater than that of any of the Socialist communes except Salernes, while in conservative Fréjus the dominant occupation (after fishing) was the mines — 110 men worked in the mines situated behind the town. There was also the special case of Aiguines, deep in the rural Var but with one specialist activity — small-scale metallurgy – in this case the regional centre for the manufacture of *boules* for *pétanque*.

In general, then, the economy of the 'conservative Var' was less varied than that of the leftist villages. On the one hand it included communes which had not known any industry for years, on the other the large coastal towns of an economic character altogether distinct from that of the inner valleys. This does tend to confirm the view that the erstwhile presence of many small crafts and industries was a significant factor in forming a Socialist electorate in the closely-grouped villages of these valleys.

The contrast emerges again with respect to the peasantry. Whereas smallholding property predominated in the areas of socialist support, the otherwise small number of sharecroppers and tenant farmers were over-represented among the sixteen communes on the conservative list, in eleven of which more than 20% of the landholders were either *métayers* or tenant farmers. These too were regions of wheat-growing and cattle-raising – again, activities generally under-represented in the Socialist villages and bourgs. The tiny conservative commune of Riboux (35 people in 1886) lived entirely from the proceeds of 40 hectares of wheat, 5 hectares of oats, 4 hectares of sainfoin and a flock of 615 sheep. There was nothing mixed or poly-cultural about economic resources here, any more than in Plan d'Aups, and the same applies to the impoverished (and conservative-voting) regions on the plateaux overlooking the Verdon.

In political matters, conservatism seems to have been a more deeply implanted and enduring tradition than was Radicalism of any hue. Of the sixteen conservative communes, only one, Le Cannet, had given its votes to the Démocrates–Socialistes in 1849. The rest were as staunchly non-Radical then as they would remain for the next seventy years. Nor was this the conservatism of indifference. It is true that Mons and Aiguines were areas of high abstention throughout this period, but all the other conservative areas showed no particular inclination to avoid voting. Indeed, some of them show remarkably high voting figures: in 1898 Plan d'Aups turned out to vote in a proportion of 72:28, the highest percentage in its canton and one of the highest in the arrondissement. Taradeau and Le Cannet steadily presented over half their electorate to the polls at legislative elections throughout this period, and coastal towns like St Cyr,

Evenos or St Nazaire did better still. The last named, one of the most staunchly conservative towns in the region, provides voting figures which show a turnout of 60–70% every time. Just as the socialist peasants were positive in their commitment, so were the conservative townsmen and the passively obedient sharecroppers. This last point is confirmed by a further piece of evidence: there existed a very high negative relationship between communes which were consistently conservative and communes where socialist groups thrived. The two hardly ever overlap. To put it differently, there is good reason to suppose that the presence of a socialist group or groups was closely related to socialist success at the polls. This is not of course to posit a causal relationship – more likely they were both consequences of other factors. But it is clearly time to take a look at what we know of Socialist *membership* in the Var, in order to establish what link it bears to the electoral divisions I have been describing.

The pattern of Socialist membership

I have already referred to the problem of sources in assessing the social structure of this region. The problem is compounded when attempting a survey of Socialist membership. In the first place, of course, the data is serial in form only from 1905, the date of the founding of the SFIO and its local Federation. From that year until 1914, annual congresses published details of membership, giving the numbers of militants and groups in each commune. Even this evidence has to be treated with care – often it did not include communes where a group existed but had for some reason failed to send a representative to the congress. It is thus necessary to use other sources – newspapers, police archives, etc. – to confirm and fill out the party documents. But for the years 1876 to 1904 the historian of French socialism is completely dependent upon such random sources – the records of the various parties existing before unification are incomplete and very unreliable; with no central and permanent secretariat, their knowledge of provincial membership was based on optimism more than on solid information. It is thus not possible to draw up a complete list of socialist groups for this period; the best that can be hoped for is a list which is accurate as far as it goes, rather than exhaustive.[21]

Furthermore such a list will tell us little of the *occupations* of socialists at this time; or more precisely, we learn of their occupations in a manner which is little better than random; occasional police records of the occupations of a given socialist *cercle* or society, a newspaper report providing similar information. But for most of the time we must rely on detective work — thus for example the membership of a municipal council whose majority is socialist may be compared to the list of names (where known) of the members of the local socialist group. Since it is usually possible to ascertain how municipal councillors earned their living, some insight can be gained concerning the structure of socialist membership — but only, of course, in communes where socialists did well.

Finally, as with other such source material, there are difficulties in distinguishing one occupation from another. The end of the nineteenth century was a period of considerable terminological flux, and it is by no means clear in 1890, as it would have been two generations earlier, what precisely distinguished a *propriétaire—cultivateur* from a *cultivateur,* a *ménager,* or even a *propriétaire.* The latter was not necessarily an absentee landlord, nor does the term *ménager* imply in every case that the man in question did not own some property. And to complicate matters further, many men, as I have pointed out already, could be and sometimes were entered under a number of categories: a *cultivateur* might also be a part-time *bouchonnier,* the local butcher almost certainly raised a few cattle or sheep, olive-growers were sometimes down in census records as being employees in a *moulin à huile.* All of this makes it unwise to be too definite in statements of a sociological nature regarding the occupational grid of socialist militants; and it most certainly makes any kind of attempt at a sophisticated statistical analysis quite foolish — it is important to emphasise the complexity and interdependence of economic life in these years, not to camouflage it.

With these caveats borne firmly in mind, what do we know of the membership of the SFIO in the Var? In 1895 the total number of socialists belonging to one organisation or another was probably between 375 and 400. By the time of the birth of the united Federation, in the autumn of 1905, the figure had hardly risen — there were 425 members represented at the founding Congress. But unification proved a spur to propaganda and organisation, and by the following year the membership had blossomed to a figure of 1410. This seems to have been about par for the period; although some 730 members were lost through the divisions and expulsions in Toulon in the next two years, reducing membership to 755 at the 1908 Congress, things had reverted to normal by 1910, when membership reached 1500, making the Var Federation the sixth in the party in terms of per capita membership in its department. There was little change in the next four years; at the beginning of 1914, membership had slipped a little to just over 1400, but the department had retained its place in the national rankings.

Membership of the local party, then, was stable but far from widespread. From 1906 to the war, the relationship between membership and electorate remained steady — expressed as a percentage of the Socialists' electorate the membership figures ranged from 6.2% in 1906 to 6.9% in 1910, slipping back to 6.0% in 1914. Fifteen hundred men and women were far too small a number to be in any sense representative of their social or geographical background, but it is therefore perhaps all the more interesting to discover, so far as it is possible to do so, where they came from and what they did.

Map 12 shows those communes where a Socialist group, however small, flourished consistently in our period. The year marked represents the year from which the existence of such a group can be dated beyond doubt. It is quite possible that some of these communes had socialists living in them before the date given, but we have no firm evidence for this.[22]

From this map a number of interesting points emerge. The sixty-four communes where a socialist group is certain to have existed evince certain of the characteristics of the forty areas of Socialist electoral success, but in a much more marked fashion. Thus the socialist groups were located in almost every commune in the central depression, running in an arc from Toulon to St Raphael; then there was a string of communes running down the lower Argens valley, and to their east a network of socialist groups in a semicircle to the north of Draguignan, from Moissac to St Paul. Moreover, socialists were well implanted in the villages of the Maures — La Garde Freinet, Cogolin, Bormes, Collobrières. Only in one respect does this map differ from our map of Socialist electoral support — the socialist groups are also to be found in a cluster along the coast on both sides of Toulon.

This suggests a further and important distinction between voters and membership. It is quite clear, from the briefest glance at this map, that socialist groups flourished in the larger towns. Whereas the forty electoral areas were predominantly small, typically Provençal bourgs, with a population in 1896 varying from 500 to 3500, socialist *groups* flourished in the larger communes.[23]

This is the only sharp contrast between the geography of electoral Socialism and that of Socialist membership, and it should not come as a surprise. Membership was very much a function of organisation — and of convenience; large communities had the advantage here, particularly communities with substantial artisanal or industrial activities, where, as in the case of the shoemakers or cork-workers, an activist in the workshop or factory could organise a socialist group composed in large measure of work-mates. What is more, larger communities quite simply offered a wider scope for attracting members — smaller towns and villages might *vote* Socialist, but there was less likelihood of finding enough people willing to overcome the traditional antipathy to *organised* politics in order to form a stable group. And lastly, of course, towns where there was a permanently employed urban population did not face the problem of village socialists during the summer, when peasants lacked the time to attend political meetings on a regular basis.

This importance of a large community for the formation of Socialist groups is confirmed in a very different way by the 17 communes of our original 40 which show no evidence of an organised Socialist group before 1914. Of these 17, 10 are in the arrondissement of Brignoles, where Socialist groups appeared much later than in the other two arrondissements. And it was the communes of Brignoles which were among the smallest in the department. Not one of the ten communes in this arrondissement which voted Socialist but failed to join the Federation could boast a population of more than 1100 people in 1896.[24]

Another way of seeing this pattern is to compare the 64 communes with a Socialist group with my earlier list of 16 communes which regularly voted conservative. Of these 16 communes (see Map 10), 11 had no Socialist group in these years. What is more, the remaining 5, where the Socialists had an organised group but where the electorate voted right, were *all* sizeable coastal

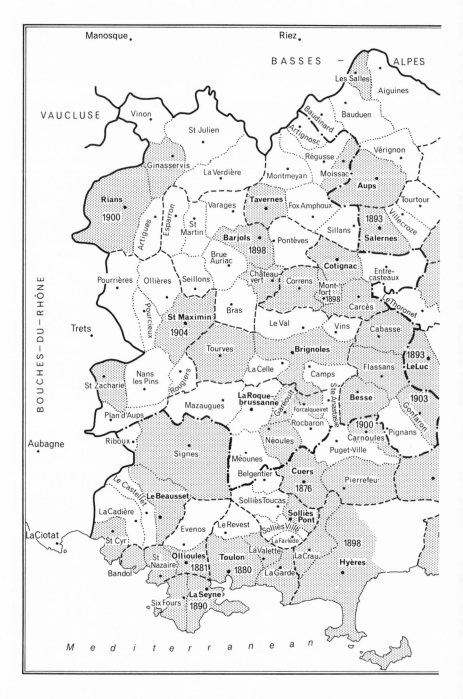

Manosque.   Riez.

BASSES —   ALPES
                              Les Salles
                                        Aiguines

VAUCLUSE   Vinon   Baudinard   Bauduen
                      St Julien   Artignosc
                                        Régusse   Vérignon
              Ginasservis   Moissac
                      La Verdière   Montmeyan   Aups
Rians   Varages   Tavernes Fox Amphoux   Tourtour
1900   Artigues Esparron   1893   Villecroze
                      St   Barjols   Pontèves   Sillans   Salernes
                      Martin   1898
                      Brue   Cotignac
                      Auriac   Entre-
Pourrières Ollières Seillons   Château- Correns Mont-   casteaux
                      Pourcieux   vert   fort
                              Bras   1898   Carcès   LeThoronet
Trets   St Maximin   Le Val   Vins   Cabasse
                      1904
                              Tourves   Brignoles   1893
                                  La Celle   Camps   Flassans   LeLuc
          Nans   Besse   1903
St Zacharie les Pins Rougiers   La Roque-   Forcalqueiret
                      Mazaugues   brussanne   1900   Pignans
Plan d'Aups   Rocbaron   Carnoules
Aubagne   Riboux   Néoules   Puget-Ville
                      Signes   Méounes
                              Belgentier Cuers   Pierrefeu
                      Le Castellet   1876
                      LeBeausset   SollièsToucas
          LaCadière   Solliès
LaCiotat   St Cyr   LeRevest Ville Pont   1898
                      Evenos   SollièsVille
                                  LaFarlède
              St   Ollioules Toulon   LaValette LaCrau   Hyères
              Nazaire 1881   1880   LaGarde
Bandol
                      La Seyne
              Six Fours 1890

M e d i t e r r a n e a n

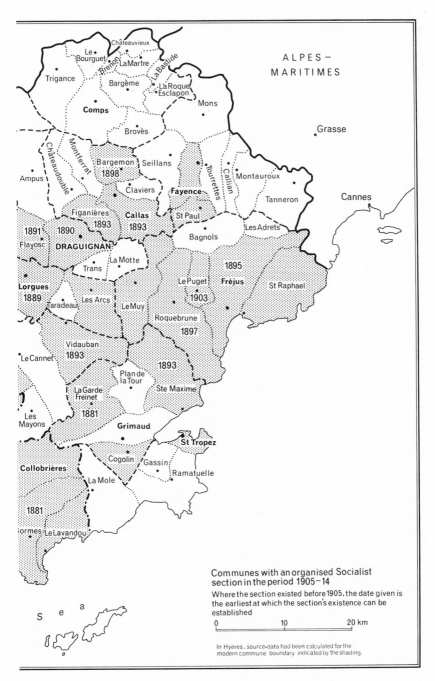

Map 12. Socialist membership 1905–1914

towns (Fréjus, St Tropez, Hyères, St Nazaire and St Cyr). The other 11 were all small villages, with no industry and scattered dwellings. Furthermore, with the exception of Le Cannet, Taradeau and Evenos, they were high up on the Ste Baume massif or the sub-Alpine plateau.

It is thus plausible to suggest that the geography of the Socialist electorate and that of Socialist membership were broadly similar. Even where Socialist groups existed in the coastal towns, they were very small: in 1913 in Fréjus there were just 28 paid-up members of the SFIO in a population of 4200. In Hyères, with a population of over 17 000 in 1913, the Socialist Section stood at 81 members. There is a marked contrast between these figures (respectively 0.7% and 0.9% of the populations of Fréjus and Hyères) and those of Socialist villages such as Montfort, where there were 34 members in 1909 (4.2% of the population) or Cotignac, whose 101 members represented 5.2% of the 1906 population of 1940. The influence of the Socialist groups in the coastal towns, compared with that of the inland bourgs, was negligible.

The difficulties of discovering the occupations of the members of the socialist movement in the Var have already been discussed. They are further compounded by the strong likelihood that such information as we *do* possess is very misleading. Socialist candidates at legislative elections, men like Claude or Allard, Renaudel or Fourment, were professional men of one kind or another, teachers, doctors, engineers. Renaudel was not even a local man (he was born in Normandy). But the further down the party hierarchy we go, the nearer to the basic membership, the fewer data there are. We must thus take our information as we find it, with the result that the next few paragraphs cannot hope to do much more than add occasional details to the pattern we have been inferring from the electoral geography of the movement.[25]

The first point to make is that, where a local industry dominated a commune, the Socialist group in that town or village was very likely to have an over-representation of workers from that industry among its members, for reasons already suggested. The Bargemon Cercle Socialiste of 1901 had 41 members, of whom 36 were workers in the shoemaking industry which was centred in the town. In fact there were many more *cordonniers* than this (the local branch of the

International Shoe-workers Union had 150 members in 1912), and local militants complained at the large number of men who were *syndiqués* but not party members; it was admitted, however, that most of the shoe-workers voted Socialist, but that only a minority actually agreed to join the movement.[26]

Similarly, in nearby Flayosc we find that in the Cercle du Progrès Social (a socialist group) of 1891, 18 of the 26 members were shoe-workers, and indeed the chairman of the Cercle was a 27-year-old worker in a shoe factory, Allarty. The socialist vote in Flayosc – 415 ballots cast for Vincent against Clemenceau in 1893 – partly reflects the fact that Vincent was the local mayor as well as the socialist candidate for the arrondissement of Draguignan. But Flayosc gave Allard 348 votes in 1898, so the socialist electorate was fairly constant. This suggests two things. Firstly that personality was relatively unimportant in these elections – Allard had never even been to Flayosc before 1898. Secondly that, as in Bargemon, the solid majority of the *cordonniers* must have been voting for the socialist candidates, but were not joining the party in anything like the same number, though nevertheless they were the dominant group in the local section. According to a report in *Le Cri*, this pattern of the 1890s still obtained in 1906.

Another rural industry which dominated local politics was that of cork extraction and manufacture in and around the Maures. Seventeen of the thirty-four members of the Garde Freinet Cercle de la Fraternité (later Cercle des Travailleurs) in 1881 were represented as cork-workers, and this is probably an underestimate. At least seven of the others appear in the census of the period as cork-workers (the Cercle records list them as *cultivateurs*). And the predominance of cork-workers among socialists in this part of the Var reflects the information we have for the local implantation of the First International: of the twenty local men known to have been active in the workers' movement of 1869, ten were cork-workers, seven of them living in Gonfaron; a further two were shoe-workers.

Cork manufacture and shoemaking, however intensively pursued in the Maures and the Draguignan hinterland respectively, were not typical of the pattern of regional activity. Most communes of the inner Var were predominantly peasant in orientation, and this characteristic grew more marked with the decline of all the artisanal trades and industries after 1880. Many of the areas where the socialist vote grew most rapidly were regions where the local bourgeoisie and the artisanat that depended upon them had all but disappeared. This much is clear. But did the peasants actually *join* the socialist movement, as distinct from voting for a socialist candidate at local and legislative elections?

It is extremely difficult to tell. There was only one peasant among the 1869 list of First International activists, yet Bastelica in 1869 spoke of his astonishment at the local support for socialism among the Var populations, 'mi-paysannes, mi-ouvrières'. But what little evidence we may cull from surviving membership lists suggests that peasants in the Var *did* join the socialist movement, if not out of proportion to their share of the local population, then certainly to a degree out of keeping with socialist support among the peasantry elsewhere in France. As early as 1884 the Cercle des Travailleurs in Cuers, one of the first in the region, had at least 29 *cultivateurs* among its 40 members; four more men were not described as having any occupation, and one or more of them may well have been a peasant as well. Similarly with the Bargemon Cercle of 1901 described above: all but two of the remaining members, once we subtract the shoe-workers, were described in the membership list as *propriétaires* or *cultivateurs*.

The same pattern obtains elsewhere. Seventeen of the twenty-three members of the Cercle de l'Union des Travailleurs in Roquebrune in 1897 were *propriétaires* or *cultivateurs* as were 14 of the 30 members of the Cercle des Travailleurs in Lorgues in 1890. More significantly, the Cercle de l'Union Ouvrière in Lorgues in 1896, successor to the Cercle des Travailleurs, had 13 peasants out of 39 members; but of the six men whose membership spans the whole period 1890–6, four were *cultivateurs*. These examples are by no means statistically significant; but they do suggest that, excepting special cases such as towns where a single rural industry predominated, it was often the peasantry, more exactly the property-owning peasantry, who formed the nucleus of socialist groups in the commune. Nor was this a tendency confined to the bourgs of the central valleys. The newly-formed Socialist Section in Aups in June 1910 was composed almost entirely of peasant proprietors; its first act was to set up an agricultural cooperative for the mutual benefit of its members, 'because this is the first step on the road to socialism'.[27]

Two final points. The average age of these socialist groups, where it can be ascertained, appears to have been younger than that of, for example, the anarchist groups in Toulon, and it appears also to have fallen over time. Thus the average age of a 'revolutionary' Bargemon Cercle closed down in 1877 was 44 years, whereas the 1901 group averaged 37 years. The Cercle de la Fraternité in La Garde Freinet in 1881 had an average age of 52, whereas the Roquebrune Cercle of 1897 had an average age of 38. This may tend to confirm the hypothesis suggested earlier that socialist supporters by 1900 were not necessarily the same people as their Radical predecessors of the 1880s – politics appears to have become the preserve of a slightly younger generation by the time the Socialists came on the scene. But there is hardly enough evidence to make this more than a suggestion.

What is rather more certain is that the professional classes were *not* very well represented in the socialist movement in the Var. The *Cri* in 1907 was inviting primary-school teachers to think of joining – after two decades of support for the Radicals it was time they had the courage of their convictions and transferred their allegiance to the Socialists – the more so in that, as the editorialist observed, schoolteachers had been unionised since 1884, and must now be more 'logical' in their politics.[28]

Nor was it just schoolteachers who avoided the socialist movement. Successful socialist candidates at local elections were always less likely to be doctors, notaries, merchants, than were their Radical or conservative opponents.[29] The more isolated the commune the more likely it appears to have been to be dominated in local matters by one of the few bourgeois families that lived there. In the small, mixed communes of the valleys where the left was dominant, the decline of the Radicals saw the departure from local politics of that stratum of businessmen, artisans and professional people who had dominated local life since the 1840s. In their place, on socialist committees, standing at local (but not legislative) elections, we find the urban peasant, able through his presence in the bourg to take part in political life, and compelled by his economic situation to protest against the way things were going. Unlike his forebears, the peasant in the Var appears not to have required a filter of literate townsmen in order to be made receptive to new political ideas.

Thus the Socialist election committee in St Paul, in 1910, meeting
to decide which name it wished to see go forward to the departmental
congress, was composed entirely of peasants, all nine of them
propriétaires. In Aiguines, despite the presence in the town of eighty
metalworkers, full- and part-time, the 1910 election committee of the
Socialist group was composed of one carpenter, one *débitant de
tabacs*, one turner, and the rest were peasants.[30] The municipal
election lists of the Radicals and Socialists in the town of Draguignan
in 1908 cast a further light on both the social basis of the Socialists
and the ways in which this distinguished them from the Radicals.
The Radical list included five businessmen, two *lycée* teachers, a retired
officer, but only two peasants, one of whom was specifically described
as not working his own fields. The Socialist list included just one
businessman and one schoolteacher; the rest were either local artisans,
railway workers or *cultivateurs*, of whom there were seven, that is
just over 30% of the list. This is not conclusive evidence, of course,
but it tends further to confirm the view of socialism in the Var as
both distinct from local Radicalism and more securely based among
the peasantry – even in a town the size of Draguignan.[31]

In this chapter I have tried to bring out the main and characteristic
features of those communities which consistently voted Socialist in
the years before the First World War. I have done this both by
enumerating the chief features of those communes which *were*
Socialist, and, in contrast, by considering what distinguished them
from other communes, communes which voted Radical and communes which supported conservative candidates. I have also discussed
the geographical and occupational basis of Socialist membership in
the Var, and contrasted this with the evidence already discussed
regarding Socialist electors.

What I have *not* attempted so far is any proper explanation of the
things described. As with Chapters 1–3, this chapter has been
concerned with laying out the evidence for an argument which will
be pursued in Part Two. Thus all that has so far been attempted is a
detailed account of the social and economic changes which affected
Provence at the end of the nineteenth century, an account of the
political history of the region in this period – with the emphasis
upon the growth of the local socialist movement, and an initial
summary of the social and geographical location of that movement.

What has emerged, I hope, is some sense of the *sort* of relationship which has been identified between economic change, peasant protest, Provençal social patterns and the nascent socialist movement. It is now time to undertake an investigation into the various possible historical *causes* of this relationship.

5 The economic crisis

The socialist movement in the Var, while generally following the same pattern of development as elsewhere in France, was by the early twentieth century much more successful than in other regions, measured by its support at elections. I have shown that this support was forthcoming most notably in the small towns and villages of the lowland areas of Provence, the coast excepted, and that within these communities it is plausible to suppose that the bulk of Socialist support came from those who worked on the land. Indeed, given the departure of artisans and *rentiers* in this period, the 'peasant' hypothesis is more than merely plausible. Finally, the property structure of these areas, and the shortage of agricultural labourers, suggests that the peasantry who voted Socialist were substantially property-owning farmers, though of small- or medium-size holdings.

In view of this, it is tempting to ascribe this pattern to the geographical, historical and economic context of Provençal society as described in Chapters 1 and 2. The temptation lies not merely in the residual assumption that it is factors such as these (production relations, local political traditions, environmental considerations) which are in fact the determining characteristics of political choices, but also in that the relationship between the conditions of Provençal life and the political attitudes of the local population seems so obvious.

This approach has formed the basis of recent studies of French rural political behaviour in this period. E. Le Roy Ladurie and his collaborators have observed the coincidence ('peut-être fortuite, peut-être révélatrice') between, for example, regions with a large population of stonemasons, and areas of dechristianisation.[1] Alain Corbin,[2] dealing in immense detail with similar questions in nineteenth-century Limousin, has noted the relationship which apparently connects a high degree of literacy with areas whose habitat is closely grouped, where small private property predominates, where birth and death rates are lowest and health relatively good. But Corbin is also careful to observe that the relationship observed by Le Roy Ladurie is just that — a relationship — and that causal accounts of the link between 'involuntary' social characteristics (health, literacy, property structure) and political options will require an awareness of the historical and political events of the day. Nevertheless, Philippe Gratton, observing, with Corbin, the radical proclivities of the mountain populations of the Corrèze, lays the stress firmly on the fact that the mountains (unlike the valleys) are regions of monoculture (cattle, in this instance), and goes on to conclude 'D'une façon générale, en effet, une monoculture rend la région qui la pratique plus perméable à la pénétration des idées révolutionnaires, ou du moins extrémistes.'[3]

This tendency to a kind of ecological determinism is taken much further in a recent study of left-wing politics in the Midi by Léo Loubère. Laying aside Corbin's strictures, and ignoring even Gratton's cautious phrasing, Loubère makes his position clear from the outset. 'Most of the important variables we can investigate (in the Midi) in order to understand political evolution are dependent upon wine, or its opposite, nonwine [sic]'.[4] This crude position forces Loubère into such arguments as that which explains the radicalism of the inner Hérault compared to the conservatism of coastal districts in terms of the fishing industry ('a non-progressive factor'), and in general into a refusal to do more than pay lip service to considerations of tradition, habit or ideological choice in the region he is studying. Moreover, his association of wine-growing with political leftism leaves him no space for an understanding of what might distinguish one form of 'leftism' from another. In short, his model is mechanistic in the extreme, and fundamentally unhistorical.

These points are made here to serve as a reminder that any attempt to account for political choice which seems to isolate one factor, in this case the nature of rural production, and ascribe ideological options to it, does violence both to the complexity of a historical explanation, and also of course to the voluntaristic element in political choices. The peasantry of the Midi did not respond to left-wing politics in such a Pavlovian fashion, and the diversity of any explanation of their behaviour must be even more marked in Provence, where the monoculture of the vine was much less developed than to the west of the Rhône. Limited correlations between geographical factors, occupation, production, even local tradition, taken as a static 'variable', lead almost inevitably to fallacious and oversimplified accounts of the reasons why people make the political choices they do. What is more, the relationships described in Chapter 4 are far from self-evident — nothing about the history of the Var would suggest that there was one, or even a few, dominating variables which conditioned people's responses to change and crisis. Even some of the more obvious characteristics can be misleading; thus Juan J. Linz has argued that the leftist tendency in Mediterranean France arises from the disproportionate number of very large holdings (fifty hectares and more), which creates rural class cleavages, pushing the resentful small proprietors to the left. This of course carries the implicit assumption that, other things being equal, the small proprietors would not be so politically radical — a view I dispute. But more immediately, Linz's otherwise attractive theory breaks down simply because, in the Var at least, small and large properties were hardly ever located in the same region, very rarely produced similar crops, and were thus not conscious of one another in the way he suggests. What he says may be true of parts of the western Languedoc — but that still leaves us in need of some more subtle account of the phenomenon for Provence and elsewhere.[5]

I shall begin, then, with a discussion of how far, and in what respects, economic considerations helped condition ideological responses in the Var after 1870. Chapters 6–8 will then look at the influence of other characteristics of Provençal life and how far they may be adduced as explanations of the pattern already noted. Finally Chapter 9 will return to the question of the ideological 'colour' of socialism in this region, and will attempt to construct an historical account of the relationship between Provençal society and this particular variant of radical politics.

Politics and the Provençal economy

The market orientation of much of the produce of the Var was clearly of some importance in bringing the small producers of the region into contact with the wider political and economic community. There were still upwards of two hundred fairs in the department by 1884, all of them primarily occasions for the sale of rural produce and the concurrent purchase of food and other necessities not produced domestically or in the region. The major fairs in the 1880s were at Aups (eleven annual fairs in this period), Barjols (seven annual fairs), Draguignan, Lorgues, Rians, Salernes and St Maximin. These were important occasions — the September fair in Aups was devoted exclusively to the sale and negotiation of future prices of wool; the early spring fair in Bargemon was the natural point of sale for the produce of all of the tiny rural communes in the mountains to the north, while the fairs at Vidauban, almost all of them centred around wine, were the focal point for all the wine-growers of the valley, and the prices obtained there determined the condition of local *vignerons* for the remainder of the year. These fairs exhibit two characteristic features, one perhaps obvious, the other less so. All the major fairs took place in small towns situated at important road or river junctions — Aups, Barjols, Le Luc, Salernes, St Maximin; but they were also predominantly located in the middle Var, the central regions of the arrondissements of Brignoles and Draguignan. Of the seventeen towns which held three or more annual fairs in 1884, only one, Cuers, was situated in the Toulon arrondissement.[6]

Of these seventeen major market centres of the rural Var, only nine — Salernes, Bargemon, Le Luc, Camps, Entrecasteaux, Flayosc, Seillans, St Julien and Vinon — were also communes which figure in our list of Socialist strongholds; significantly, these are the smallest of the market towns, with the exception of Salernes. If a complex and outward-looking economic structure helped bring about the acceptance of new and radical ideas, this was a development which affected the peasants who visited the market, rather than those who lived in the economic centre itself. This is confirmed if we observe the political developments in those smaller communities which lived in the orbit of the market towns. Barjols itself was a busy market and commercial town, albeit small. But the villages and bourgs which most depended upon it for their link to the wider market, Varages, Pontèves, Châteauvert, Correns, all within a few kilometres of the bourg itself, were overwhelmingly socialist by 1900. Similarly, Aups and Vidauban were the two major marketing centres for the northern and central Var respectively. Yet their large and mixed communities appear not to have moved to the left nearly as much as communes such as Baudinard, Tourtour, Le Muy or Les Mayons which depended upon them.

All this would tend to suggest that the rôle of a commercialised economy in bringing modern political issues into the villages was important but in a special sense. Such town as Aups or St Maximin, Vidauban or Lorgues, all in the central valley, with regular markets and much passing traffic, were consistently more moderate politically than the relatively isolated communities, in touch with a wider world but socially more homogeneous and self-contained. The men and women who visited (regularly but infrequently) the market towns might hear news and rumour from abroad, and would almost certainly take part in animated discussions during their visit. But what mattered was the rôle they played upon their return in propagating new ideas in the village, where in many cases, to judge from the election results at least, such ideas would become the common property of the vast majority of the enfranchised adult population of the commune.[7]

It is very plausibly the case that the radicalisation of the villages reflects the predominance of small peasant proprietors in the communities of the valleys of the central Var. A theoretical account of this pattern was offered by Wolf in his conception of the revolutionary 'middle peasant'.[8] Unlike the sharecropper, who is constrained both by his poverty and his fear of eviction, and the landless labourer who lacks both economic independence and the opportunity for political expression, the small peasant proprietor is free of domination by landlord or employer, aware of political and economic developments through his links to the market, but radicalised by his vulnerability in the face of competition. Consequently it is he who is most 'available' to revolutionary ideologies of change.

This is an attractive thesis, the more so in that it does seem to reflect both what is known of the geographical divisions of support for left and right in the Var, and because it is internally plausible. But it, too, can easily be made to answer for everything, when in fact its application needs to be considerably limited. Above all, the relationship between small peasant property and left-wing politics needs to be controlled for product. The dairy-farming small peasantry of Normandy have voted a conservative ticket consistently since the 1870s, and the small proprietors of Old Castile, growers of wheat in the main, have been traditionally so well served by protectionism and import quotas that they have remained economically viable — and politically conservative.[9]

What may have helped produce the radical colouring in the political life of the Var in our period was not so much the independence of the small peasant *per se*, but the way in which the nature of his produce forced him into a collective pattern of existence which actually reinforced that independence of local notables and authority, while blocking any tendency to individualism and isolation of the Breton or Norman kind. Vines, olives, fruit trees, the maintenance of earth walls and terracing, all created in Provence a constant need for agricultural interdependence, in an area where the property structure and static population produced a shortage of landless labourers. Provençal farmers had to work steadily for 8–9 months of every year, and in lieu of employed labour they often worked for one another. Fertiliser, always in short supply and desperately needed in the thin soil and unreliable climate of much of the region, was purchased communally from an early date, and in the 1890s there were still very rigid local regulations governing the gathering of animal manure. The coming of a local monocultural economy, mostly *vinicole,* strengthened this tendency towards cooperation, without in any way lessening the individualist structure of property. The result was a community of small peasant proprietors, producing crops whose survival depended upon a communal collectivism, initially in informal ways, later through organised cooperative groups. In *this* way, the property structure of Provence, with its traditionally collective organisation, and reinforced by the close grouping of peasant dwellings, certainly provided a potentially favourable basis for political movements which appealed to collective interests.

There is a further point, of perhaps greater importance, concerning the particular nature of small property in the Var. Until the 1870s many of these small peasants were simultaneously themselves artisans or even industrial workers of one kind or another. I have already noted the difficulty this poses for the student of the demographic structure of the region, but this very confusion of occupational identity may well have been a vital feature in the creation of a later propensity to radical politics. Broadly speaking, there were three kinds of community in pre-twentieth-century Provence: the isolated rural village, normally sparsely inhabited, usually found in the poorest regions of the mountains and coastal hills; the large towns (upwards of 3500 inhabitants) of the valleys and coastal regions, with industrial, commercial, non-productive populations, as well as a leavening of peasants on the outskirts; finally the large village— small bourg, situated in the inner valleys and on the lower slopes of the hills, with small trades, rural industries, a scattering of bourgeois *rentiers* and many urban-dwelling peasants. It was this last category which most typified the region and lent it its enduring characteristics; it was also this last category which stands out for the complex intermixture of rural and urban occupations. The socialists of the 1890s were very conscious of their support among the part-peasant, part-worker populations of these bourgs, though they do not appear always to have grasped the precise basis of the enthusiasm they evoked in such communes.[10]

It was in these mixed communities that we find an important organisational rôle being played by social groups defined by occupation. Just as in Lyon the *canuts* (silk-weavers) achieved political awareness through their work-based organisations,[11] so the workshop-based organisation of the shoemakers of Bargemon, or the hat-makers of Camps and Carcès, was clearly vital in forming the political awareness of the local population. Generally speaking, it seems to have been the activities pursued in small workshops, rather than the larger industrial centres, which first generated political consciousness. Thus the master shoemakers employed an average of less than two men per shop; the hat manufacturers of the Cotignac region and in Camps averaged eight employees per establishment. In these places, the local peasantry were often employed on a seasonal basis and were introduced to political discussion within the shop. Conversely the cork-workers of La Garde Freinet, organised into large establishments averaging 15 per unit by 1911 and often in fact employing more than 50 men and women in a full-time factory, increasingly lost contact with the local peasantry, as did the railwaymen who were employed in the repair shops at Carnoules. In each case this clearer division between industrial and rural work appears to have produced a lower degree of left-wing politicisation among the peasantry in later years.[12]

However, one must be wary of reading this pattern as an indication of the importance of socialism. What emerges clearly in the Var at least is the extent to which, although it was in *formerly* mixed communities that the socialists achieved most success, by the time they came to political prominence, the artisan element in the community had all but disappeared. Thus the relationship between the small peasant and the artisanal activity of the bourg was, by 1890, a historical one, but no less important for that. The contact with urban life and with workshop organisation reinforced in certain areas of the Var the habits of political independence and social collectivism which the market-oriented polyculture and small property had in any case encouraged here as in other such communities.

In so far as political 'extremism' flourished in specifically rural areas, then, it was in communes such as Cotignac, Claviers, etc., which, while predominantly rural and small-peasant-based by 1900, had once possessed a sizeable artisanal community (engaged in clothes or shoe manufacture, milling, pottery, barrel-making, etc.), closely integrated into the rural economy and often employing small-property-owning peasants and their families. Varages, by 1900 a socialist stronghold whose population was almost completely dependent on the marketing of wine and olives, had once been a thriving centre of earthenware and pottery manufacture, with a market all over France. This was fast disappearing by the mid-1880s, undermined by competition from northern France and abroad. But although socialism flourished in areas which were *by 1900* overwhelmingly rural and peasant, it did very badly in communities which had *always* been so — that is, in the first of our three classes of Provençal settlement. Where there had never been anything other than a single class of peasants, left-wing political allegiance was consistently low. It is also the case that areas such as these (in the Comps regions, to the west of St Maximin, in parts of the lower Maures) saw a predominance of large holdings and sharecropping, and this doubtless played an important rôle in blocking the development of local political life. This confirms the theme first raised at the beginning of this chapter — that economic structures cannot serve as much more than indications of a pattern of political behaviour — they are neither determinants of political choice nor sufficient conditions for an explanation of political change. Taken in purely static terms, the evidence discussed would indicate that some purely agricultural communities are conservative, others radical; understandably, the

historian feels obliged in such a case to look to questions of production or land tenure for the distinguishing variables. But I would
argue that the conservative rural regions were consistently areas
where agriculture had *always* been the dominant local activity,
whereas socialist communes of a predominantly peasant nature usually
turn out to have been, *at one time,* areas of complex mixed
economies. The distinguishing difference, then, is the experience of
change undergone in the years 1870–90, that is during the economic
crisis of these years, and it is there that we must look for a fuller
account of the developments described.

Economic crisis and political change

Whereas the economic structure of Provence, its diversity and
sophistication, may serve as the primary explanation for the radicalism
of the Second Republic, a radicalism which was itself a reaction to
economic crises which affected most acutely the more advanced and
thus exposed sectors of the economy, such a structural account is
not sufficient to account for the much more fundamental re-
alignment which took place after 1880. To understand the later
development, which was much less atavistic, more ideologically
'positive' in nature, we have to consider not so much the basic
elements of Provençal society themselves as what happened when
they were threatened and disappeared. For just as it was the most
advanced and 'cosmopolitan' bourgs which responded to the appeal
of the Démocrates–Socialistes in 1848–51, so it was the areas which
were most affected by the economic changes of the last third of the
century which responded to the arguments of the socialists.

The economic crisis of the years 1870–90 took three inter-related
forms in lower Provence. In the first place, there was the impact of
industrialisation and modern communications upon the tiny rural
industries. This was not a development confined to the Var, of
course. Rural industries and urban artisanal production everywhere
were falling a victim at this time to the industrialisation of the
continent. But the artisans of the Var were particularly sensitive to
the economic conjuncture partly through the nature of their produce,
partly through their presence throughout the region. Hat-makers,
shoemakers, barrel-makers, potters, cork manufacturers, leather-

workers, all had markets which reached well beyond the limits of the department, and they were to be found in the majority of the small towns of the region. The crisis affected them in two ways. Their sales declined as outside competition and falling prices forced them out of wider markets; but the local village economies were also contracting as a result of the falling purchasing power of the non-artisan population. The peasantry were facing a crisis of their own, and the traditional class of bourgeois *rentiers* and retired professionals which gave Provençal villages their peculiarly complex social character, and much of their purchasing power, was dying and not being replaced. Artisanal and even industrial activity disappeared altogether in some villages, declined significantly in others.

A telling witness to this is the loss of combativity of the tradition-ally militant organisations of *ouvriers cordonniers* and *ouvriers bouchonniers*. Men who had been at the forefront of syndical activity in the early 1880s were soon to be found in alliance with their employers, jointly demanding solutions to their shared plight. The shoemakers of Bargemon abandoned a strike in April 1886 after the *patrons* pleaded their inability to pay higher piece rates 'in the present situation'. By 1891 the Garde Freinet cork-workers, who a decade previously had been at the forefront of a major strike and had founded the regional cork-workers' syndicate, were petitioning jointly with their employers for a lowering of transport costs and the imposition of a duty on raw cork exported for manufacture.[13] Just as the peasants were becoming politically militant, so the local rural industries were exhibiting all the signs of massive decline. And this decline was of course most marked in precisely those villages and towns where artisanal life and its organisational and political conse-quences had been most prominent. In consequence, the relationship between economic crisis and political response was at its closest in these communes — just as it was often these communes which had been at the forefront of the radicalism of the previous generation. But the reasons were different, and the militancy had shifted from artisans to peasants.

The effect of these years on agriculture was considerably more complex. The tendency to monoculture from the 1860s, consequent upon the decline of the olive and the attractions of a growing market for cheap wine, left the Provençal peasant much more exposed to

climatic and economic fluctuations. The same development of communications and international markets which did so much to undermine rural industry was initially a boon to the peasants, able to sell
as much of their market-linked crops as they could grow. But the
price fall, beginning in the early 1880s and lasting for most products
until the end of the century, sharply reduced the rate of profit on
everything from olives to flowers, so that only the most diversified
holding, or the very large producers of the coast, could survive
without difficulty.

Worst hit, clearly, were the wine-growers. They would in any case
have suffered like the others from price falls, and overproduction
after 1885, but the phylloxera gave a special character to their crisis.
Whereas wine-growers everywhere suffered from the difficulties of
these years, the small-scale producers of the Var, like those of the
Beaujolais, experienced the crisis in an especially acute form.[14] The
phylloxera hit the vines of Provence at the end of the 1870s and
in the early 1880s, although there had been signs of it from as early
as 1871. The small producers borrowed wildly in order to save their
vines, employing all manner of patent cures and expensive insecti-
cides. As a result, they were the very last to replant, hanging on to
their old vines until the last possible moment, before taking the difficult decision to uproot the whole plantation. Replanting cost more
money (communal distribution of American ceps was usually insufficient to replace existing hectarage), which meant more borrowing. In
the Var, this meant that most small *vignerons* were not back in full
production until the late 1890s; as a result they had missed the
profitable years of 1891–7, when the large growers had been able to
benefit from the huge demand and high prices caused by the shortages
of the previous decade. The small *vigneron* tried to compete by over-
planting, all the while increasing his debts thereby; and found that
his expanded production coincided tragically with the overproduction
and price falls of the years 1904–7. Crippled with debts, unable to
sell his huge crop, the small-property-owning peasant, exclusively
dependent upon his vines, was both the major rural victim of these
years and a natural candidate for revolutionary politics.

That it should have been revolutionary politics, rather than a
Poujadist reaction, is explained by the emphasis placed by the
socialists (and by them alone) on a collective or state solution to the

rural crisis. This appealed to the small *vigneron* not merely because of the residual Provençal tradition of collective economic interests, but because by 1906 the only option left to many small peasants was cooperative agriculture aided by state subsidy, regulation of production and prices, and control of overseas competition. Thus for many of the local peasants, the specific nature of the economic crisis of these years produced a sympathy not merely for anti-governmental politics in general, but for a programme of state intervention in particular.[15]

Harvey Smith has described a similar process of radicalisation as a result of economic crisis in the Hérault.[16] But there he regards the *vignerons'* demands (for customary wage rates, the removal of 'middle men') as initially atavistic, but giving way by 1911 to attitudes essentially identical to those of the working class. The crisis had converted the wine-growers into an agricultural proletariat; whereas mid-century 'leftism' was a passing reaction to crisis, the developments of the 1890s and 1900s were the consequences of a secular decline in occupational status and social mobility. The difference between his *vignerons* of the Hérault and those of the Var is thus a significant one: the wine-growing peasants of the Languedoc became socialist because their conditions rendered them effectively indistinguishable from the urban proletariat. But in the Var, the *vignerons*, like many other economically depressed peasants, came to share the attitudes and ideals of the working-class movement without abandoning their identity as property-owning peasants or their economic independence, however fragile.

This identity with the interests of the urban worker was further encouraged by the purchasing pattern of the peasantry of Provence. As in other regions of monoculture, the peasant in the Var was often constrained to purchase many of his basic requirements, saving only that which he produced himself. This had led to a precocious development of a money economy in the region even in the time of polyculture, since at no stage did the Provençal peasantry grow sufficient wheat or raise sufficient cattle for their own requirements, and the market price of meat, and especially of bread, was always a highly sensitive affair. With the collapse of the market in olive oil after 1886, and the crisis in the vineyards, many of the peasantry of this region were often without the means to purchase their basic needs, the more so in that the decline of local industry meant that alternative non-agricultural employment was harder to find. Hence, the local villages were much moved in opposition to the tariff laws promulgated in 1891. Protection on cereals meant higher bread prices — hence the many meetings and petitions against protection from the villages of the central Var in these years.[17] Here too the socialists' stand against protection, based on the urban population's interest in cheap food, was very favourably received in the countryside of Provence. The Radicals took a more ambivalent stance — much of *their* rural support in France came from wheat-producing regions.

The local industrial crisis, and the peasants' own difficulties, combined to produce a third significant feature of the economic conjuncture, the decline in population. I have already noted the difficulty of seeing a clear link between demographic decline and political choice — except in so far as the already depopulated mountain regions and the flourishing littoral were both areas of conservative politics. But the drop in the population of the inner valleys, where the sharpest falls were experienced, produced important changes in the character of these communities. In this respect, as in others, what matters is not so much that Provençal economic structure in itself as that structure in a period of rapid change.

One feature of the changing demographic balance in the villages was the democratisation of authority. The departure of the bourgeoisie and the artisans, the decline in the number of shops, inns, professional people, meant that political power and political influence in the community devolved upon the remaining population, predominantly peasant. Thus Le Luc saw between 1896 and 1908 a 15% increase in the number of *propriétaires—cultivateurs* on the municipal council. Whereas in 1896 there had been on the council doctors, small shopkeepers, a miller, some artisans, two wine merchants, a businessman and others, by 1908 there were no artisans, no professional people and fewer commercial entrepreneurs.

In Lorgues, by contrast, the non-agricultural representation on the council remained strong. Along with the peasants who formed just over half of the council in 1908 (they represented just under half eight years earlier) there were still some doctors, *négociants*, carpenters, potters and also some retired men from outside the region. Unlike Le Luc, Lorgues was no centre of socialist activity, and its relatively complex social mix as late as 1908 both reflects this and helps to account for it.

Socialist councils tended in any case to be more homogeneous in composition, reflecting the dominant occupational pattern of any given community; nevertheless, conservative communes showed a persistent tendency to favour traditional local élites. Communes such as Le Val and Comps were themselves socially homogeneous, lacking any industrial or artisanal admix, but authority remained firmly in the hands of the local bourgeoisie, small as it was. But then these were not communes which had lost their social complexity through crisis and depopulation – they had always been largely peasant and rural in character, and the pattern of peasant subordination to a tiny urban ruling class remained fixed. In *newly* homogeneous communities it was the peasants who themselves controlled the life of the bourg and represented its interests.[18]

The age of the socialist members in Provençal *cercles* at this time tended to average just under 40 years. This was considerably younger than the average age of active members in many urban groups on the left, but it was quite significantly older than the average age of those who were brought before the tribunal for their part in the uprising of 1851. The average age of those condemned for their share in the uprising in Bargemon was 31; in La Garde Freinet 32; in Flayosc 31.[19] By the 1890s political radicalism was much more the province of mature men, and this too reflects the departure of the young, the disappearance of a whole class of artisan apprentices and journeymen, and the emergence on the political scene of the peasantry. Peasant proprietors did not usually become such until the death or retirement of their father or father-in-law, and it is clear that they did not play an active part in local political life until they had come into their inheritance. This may reflect again the extent to which the turn to the left in these years was a consequence of the practical experience of peasants struggling to survive in an economic whirlwind. The younger men departed for the towns or for other regions; the older men stayed put and became politically militant. Similar patterns would emerge in later years in parts of southern Italy.

The demographic pattern of these years affected inner Provence the more in that it had never been a region of marked geographical mobility. Whereas the populations of the mountains were accustomed to seasonal and temporary migrations, and the coastal communities had been regions of regular immigration since the mid-century, the population of most of the inland towns and villages had been rather stable. The local economy could and did support a static or slightly increasing population, and there had been little of that movement away to the towns or cities which had characterised less favoured parts of rural France. The sudden changes of the two decades after 1876 — and they were sudden, taken in comparison to what had been before — had all the more traumatic an effect. If anything, local commentators tended to exaggerate the losses — in La Garde Freinet there was much talk of disastrous population losses a good few years before the major decline actually came about.[20] A *sense* of decline and decay prevailed, which helped underpin the socialists' reiterated propaganda concerning the need for collective action to ensure the survival of the community. It is certainly not the case, in the Var at least, that population decline, by ensuring greater resources and security to the remaining inhabitants, helped promote an insular conservatism.[21] The local response, conditioned by the extent to which a shortage of people was seen to be as much a cause as an effect of the economic crisis, was to turn to the government and demand measures to halt the slide. Failing this, the peasantry of Provence reacted by a reaffirmation of their traditional communal identity and solidarity. In both instances the socialist movement was a logical and popular vehicle for the expression of such sentiments.

Taken in these terms, we can see how the same economic crisis, acting upon different communities, would produce quite distinct reactions. The subsistence and wholly rural economy of a town like Comps, or villages such as Plan d'Aups, Bauduen or La Martre, made it easier, paradoxically, for the local population to withstand the difficulties which were destroying the basis of social and economic life lower down. It was not because they were sharecroppers, or because they did not grow wine, or because there were no left-wing artisans among them, that these peasants did not turn to the socialists. It was because these structural elements in the world of the mountains produced a very different *conjunctural* reaction to the crisis. The populations retrenched — the per capita consumption of meat in Comps falling sharply in these years; as elsewhere, subsistence-level economies were less exposed to economic downswings. This is far from being any kind of a sufficient account of the conservatism of these areas of course – there was also the socialists' own self-fulfilling belief in the reactionary character and geographical inaccessibility of the northern Var, for example. But there is little doubt that the stability of poverty, like the buoyancy of wealth and resources on the coast, provided unfavourable conditions for radical politicisation, in the countryside as in the towns.

The crisis of the French economy at the end of the nineteenth century, a crisis whose major symptom was a secular fall in agricultural prices (and a growth of foreign competition), was thus central to the creation of the conditions for a flourishing socialist movement in the Var. But just as the economic conjuncture helps explain the chronology of political developments, so we must allow for the importance of the existing economic structure of Provence in order to grasp why those political developments took the form they did. The same conjuncture, after all, produced a given result in the Var and quite different effects in other regions.

In this respect, my argument differs from that of Maurice Agulhon, who writes convincingly of the complex relationship between the Provençal economy of the mid-nineteenth century and the political divisions in the region during the Second Republic. It is clear that the political divisions of 1849 are only a rough guide to later ideological cleavages. This suggests that there were changes within the social basis of Provençal life which must be accounted for, and these changes seem to be most closely linked to the departure of the village artisanat and bourgeoisie, the crisis of the rural economy and the turning to a more modern form of protest by the peasantry who were left behind. On the other hand, to understand the differing responses of varying regions means referring back to earlier social and economic patterns, and this I have tried to do. However, 'Provençal society' was more than just the means by which the men and women of the region kept themselves alive – cultural 'structures' also helped influence people's reactions to crisis, and it is now time to look at what these structures were.

6

Provençal sociability

Between the economic organisation of people's lives – the way they earn their living, the rôle they play in the chain of production relations – and the political choices they make there lies the important element of social and occupational organisation, the way in which they arrange their daily relationships with one another, both at work and during their leisure time. The importance of this as a determinant of ideological choice is easily understood with reference to the industrial working class, whose hierarchies within the factory, trade-union activities in the factory and outside, and meeting places in the evening (pub, café, club) all played central rôles in bringing working people to a consciousness of their economic situation and helped mobilise collective protest, of both an economic and political kind. The very nature of rural life makes the identification of equivalent social forms rather harder, but they are present nonetheless, and played a no less central rôle in guiding the political choices of peasants.

The ways in which social life served to bridge the gap between individual experience and collective political identities are all the more important in the case of the peasantry of southern France, where a sociability based around the community was traditionally of greater importance than in more dispersed and anomic parts of the countryside. That the life of the collectivity in many parts of Provence was peculiarly diverse and vital is not in doubt; as a historical characteristic of the region it is extremely well documented, and no one who has spent evenings in the town squares of villages in various parts of France could fail to be impressed, even today, by the marked difference between the silent, empty villages of Picardy or Anjou and the noisy, crowded street life of the typical southern bourg. What is harder to determine is the precise way in which this penchant for a public rather than a private society affected men's political options; we may agree that an active social life, allied to other factors to be discussed, tends to the creation of a greater political awareness, or at least a wider interest in political matters. How far such sociability determines the precise *direction* of political opinion, and why this is so, is a quite different and altogether more complicated matter. Not all complex and lively communities are politically radical, for example – there are good grounds for supposing that, above a certain size, towns develop political patterns owing little or nothing to the presence or absence of active political debate among the populace. Other factors intervene, notably the predominant local occupations and the way in which *they* are organised, and the ideas and identity they help impose upon those who work in them. Sociability, the tendency to active public life rather than an isolated private existence, appears to have been most significant in small communities where the population was, if not economically homogeneous, then at least closely economically interdependent.

In this chapter, then, I am interested less in discovering some explanation for a given political choice than in describing the changing preconditions of the very possibility of choice itself; to the degree to which we can establish the importance and the particular forms which sociability had in Provence, we shall be better placed to identify what was determinant, what merely contingent, in the social structure of a region whose political options were so strongly marked.

Historical sociability

A commonplace among students of Mediterranean societies in general is the very active level of social life which characterises the villages and small towns around the western fringe of the sea.[1] However rural the occupational pattern, the context of life is remarkably urban. Communities live in closely-grouped habitats, existing and acting very much as communities, traditionally meeting in public to discuss problems of common interest, sometimes retaining large areas of 'communal' land, and frequenting societies and cafés where all manner of concerns are discussed in lively and open fashion. This interesting aspect of small-town life in Mediterranean Europe has been studied in great detail and with immense sophistication with reference to southern France in particular. As a result, the historian of modern Provence is especially privileged in having an unusually clear understanding of the historical background to the region and to its social relations.[2]

This privilege is not without its drawbacks. It is tempting to see the social structure of old Provence, as described by Vovelle and Agulhon in particular, as so deeply a part of local life as to be almost as immutable as the topography of which it is largely the result; as a consequence one may overlook the subtle ways in which social life in Provence altered both in form and content in the years 1850–80, producing new forms of sociability. These in turn played a central rôle in determining the politicisation of the region, but in ways which were rather different from the political influence exerted within the old forms.

The older, classic, specifically Provençal sociability, may best be defined as a decidedly un-French tendency to join others in various societies. The most common of these societies in the eighteenth century were the brotherhoods of penitents and, to a lesser degree, freemasons. These substantially masculine communities, normally confined to a single commune and limited for the most part to the small bourgs of the central Var, were originally religious in function, but there are good indications that by the later eighteenth century their religiosity was much reduced. Clerical observers found their piety 'more ostentatious than real', and the 53 communes in the Var region with penitent brotherhoods (23 of them in the future arrondissement of Brignoles) were already becoming, before the Revolution, social rather than religious centres, their initial function much overlain with the more secular rôle they had acquired within the towns where they were to be found.[3]

Less formally, the social peculiarity (in France) of the south lay in something I have already mentioned, namely the importance of the community in people's lives. With so many Provençal communes free of seigneurial constraint, either through communal repurchase of rights or as a result of the timeless absence of any dominant local notable, the self-governing municipality of Provence was already a regional commonplace well before the 'municipal revolution' of early 1789 gave the matter political significance. The populations of many Provençal communities were thus accustomed both to discussing matters of common concern – common land, the regulation of prices, the traffic of goods, the distribution of fertiliser – and to seeing the interest of the individual in terms of the notional interest of the collectivity. This combination of freedom from seigneurial constraint and an unusually developed sense of community may help explain the later paradox which concerns this book: the otherwise mysterious juncture of individualist small peasant proprietors and the collectivist doctrine of a modern socialist movement.

In the early nineteenth century new forms of social life emerged. These, the *chambrées* and *cercles*, were in part the inheritors of the *confréries* and the societies of freemasons, in part the more direct result of the politicisation of village life during the radical years of the Revolution. Broadly speaking the village and small-town bourgeoisie met in private *cercles*, societies which tended increasingly to an interest in radical politics during the 1840s. The artisans and peasants, the *petit peuple*, gathered in *chambrées*; these were of a more public nature, less restricted in membership and often meeting in a café or *cabaret,* with premises and newspapers provided by the proprietor, himself often a political radical, as well as the beneficiary of the societies' custom. Both *chambrées* and *cercles* were to be found predominantly in the larger villages and small bourgs of the western and central Var, above all in the valleys and around the main axes of communication. Their membership was reflective of the social structure of such communities: *rentiers*, bourgeois, many varieties of artisans, and a multitude of peasants, 'vivant socialement bourgeois', or at least urban. Strangers were not often welcome in these very exclusive sub-societies, so that despite the significance of their close contact with outside news and opinions, via the important human and commercial traffic of the nearby roads and cities, these socialised villages confined the stranger, however politically sympathetic, to the café or inn, keeping their rich communal life essentially closed, and somewhat rigidly structured by social class.[4]

Just as the Great Revolution found a fertile breeding-ground in the dechristianised societies of the communes of Provence, so the Revolution of 1848 drew powerful and enduring support from the *chambrées* and *cercles* of the region – often in the self-same communes. Agulhon argues that the sociability of the 1840s took the form of the drift of radical ideas from bourgeois *cercles* to popular *chambrées*, via the politicised and organised artisanal cadres of the latter. There is little doubt that it was from within the *chambrées* that the last great burst of pre-modern radicalism in southern France emerged — the widespread and desperate insurrection of December 1851 in protest at the *coup* of Louis Napoleon. That the form and content of social intercourse had undergone important changes in the years between the popular Jansenism of the early eighteenth century and the political radicalism of the Second Republic is beyond doubt; how else account for the mysterious 'gap' from 1815 to the 1840s during which time southern France became a refuge of popular royalism and conservative reaction? Clearly the repression of the late 1790s played some part here, but the fact remains that the changing forms of sociability were accompanied by changing political attitudes as well, and not always in a consistent direction.[5]

A new sociability?

The important shifts in the economic base of Provençal life which occurred in the years 1850–80 also took their toll on the social organisations just described. Although old forms of sociability and old attitudes did not completely disappear, they were largely replaced by new contexts for a continuing sociability. Thus the resentment expressed in La Seyne in 1887 at the action of the mayor, M. Fabre, in paying women to collect for him from the forest straw which had once been, by tacit consent, the common property of the commune, was largely formal — the protest was registered but the communal right had been lost. Similarly, the Société des Pénitents Blancs in Le Beausset, although still in existence in 1881, and maintaining its old traditions, was attended exclusively by old men in their seventies, and was in effect controlled by a few local bigwigs.[6]

Maurice Agulhon ascribes the shift in patterns of social and community life in this period to a demographic development.[7] During the second half of the nineteenth century, he argues, the villages of Provence lost *both* their 'micro-aristocracy' of bourgeois *rentiers and* the very poorest workers and farm labourers, who departed in search of urban employment. Meantime the mass of small peasant proprietors and rural artisans saw their own conditions of life undergo improvement, with the result that village life, while remaining no less socially active, became democratised, with the artisans introducing the peasantry to modern forms of political affiliation within the societies and clubs to which artisans and peasants jointly belonged.

While this theory lays a proper emphasis on the democratisation of social life in the last third of the nineteenth century, it appears to underestimate a development noted in Chapter 4; namely, the close relationship between communes of declining artisanal population and areas of socialist electoral advance. What is more, it is difficult to see how such a view can be squared with what we know of the crises which afflicted most categories of small peasant at just this time. In other words, the structure of social life may serve as an important and necessary condition for the flourishing of political activity generally: but as a means of accounting for more specific developments within the political life of a region, it has a limited scope. There is a suggestion of social determinism in the idea that regional sociability was in some sense a fixed variable, only the social mix of the population varying over time. In fact, as we shall see, the very ways in which people organised their lives were altering considerably in the period we are considering.

The contexts in which men (and increasingly women too)[8] met and exchanged opinions in the communities of Provence were becoming more varied during the early years of the Third Republic. Although there was much overlap of membership and function, we may separate the organisation of social experience in this region into five categories: fêtes and their attendant communal celebrations and traditional holidays; musical societies; social and political *cercles*, incorporating aspects of early-nineteenth-century bourgeois and popular societies; the life of the village café; and, increasingly important, syndicates and especially cooperative societies.

The communal festival

The dominant festivals were those celebrating the local patron saint. In itself this serves as an index of the degree to which traditional religiosity and communal identity had been merging since the eighteenth century. Most communes had their own saint — Ste Cécile in La Valette, St Maur in Cogolin, St Quénis in Besse and so forth. The whole commune would set aside one or often two days every year for the celebration of the local patron saint; there would be races and games, for children and adults, banqueting, singing and dancing. By the 1880s such public holidays had become well-organised, semi-official events. To take one example, that of Gonfaron, which fêted its local saint in the first week in June: there were marches through the streets, public orchestral performances, competitions in such diverse skills as shouting, story-telling and the like; horse races and children's games were also popular and organised by the municipality. Such was the fame of the Gonfaron fête that, helped by the town's position on the main road from Toulon to Draguignan, people travelled in from many neighbouring villages to take part. In 1881 the railway company serving the area even arranged for reduced tickets to Gonfaron for all communes on the line linking Toulon to Brignoles and Draguignan.[9]

Many local patron saints were celebrated at this time of year; *fêtes-champêtres*, doubling as local holidays, were a common feature of May and June throughout the department during the 1870s and 1880s. Most of these holidays were simultaneously 'religious' celebrations, although the properly sacerdotal element in them was much diminished by this time; in Tourves, the holiday in honour of St Probace, traditionally held under the auspices of the local clergy, had become thoroughly 'laicised' by the early 1880s, and even in the relatively clerical commune of Le Beausset, the *fête-Dieu* had lost much of its properly religious overtones — the procession still took place, and observers of a certain age claimed that it was still much as in 'les vieux temps de la Restauration', but the *curé* was no longer at the head and the penitents who dominated the procession were mostly men not noted for their assiduous attention in church. The enduring character of such festivals was their seasonally determined nature; planting the 'May' was still a popular activity among the youth of many of the communes, and the celebration of mid-Lent was marked in Fayence by an annual *farandole*, with much sporting of historical masks, Henri IV to the fore.[10]

Overlapping with these seasonal and local festivals were the celebrations organised by particular trades and guilds. Two instances from 1882 will serve to illustrate this aspect. On 25 August, in Vidauban, the local corporation of hairdressers and barbers, *patrons*, *ouvriers* and apprentices, marched around the town, singing and dancing, before sitting down to an 'intimate dinner' which lasted all night. In December of the same year the miners of Châteaudouble celebrated the festival of Ste Barbe by attending mass, then marching through the village with drums and flags, on their way to a banquet paid for by the Marseille mining company which employed them. What is interesting here is the degree to which this particular form of sociability crossed social and class barriers for the occasion; indeed it is an instance where the ancient traditions of social life, crossed with the specific traditions of the occupations in question, militated *against* radical politicisation, by drawing workers and apprentices into a vertical community which contrasts sharply with the more horizontal relationships normally associated with popular celebration.[11]

Despite this evidence of a considerable element of traditional activity still informing local pastimes and leisure, the old festivals were in decline at this time. Compared with the high peak of rural and village activity of the early nineteenth century, in the Var as elsewhere, the patronal, religious and corporate holidays of the last decades of the century were fewer in number, poorly attended and lacking in spirit. The municipal festivals in particular had become movable feasts; the original inspiration and date had been forgotten, and often we find the holiday in fact falling on a date which marked a more recent political event, or simply on a date of local economic convenience (the appropriate market day for a given crop, for example). By the end of the 1880s there were many complaints at the quiet and somewhat perfunctory character of many local festivals — 'où sont les masques d'antan?'. The reasons for this change are not far to seek. Political divisions in the bourgs, together with the departure of the youth and the tighter financial situation of municipality and populace alike, all worked against the survival of lengthy, costly, and public celebrations of an identity which the commune was fast losing. Where the holiday was not actually falling into disuse (as in La Motte, where in 1891 St Quinis' Day was not celebrated for the first time in generations), it was developing quite new implications. As early as 1872, the communes of Roquebrune and Le Muy, forbidden to celebrate 4 September for political reasons, instead held huge public demonstrations on St Aigulphe's Day. Since this was a traditional local feast which fell on the first Sunday in September, the *préfet* could not very well ban the planned celebrations, even though it was manifestly the case that the old forms were being used to commemorate a quite new (and political) cause. Significantly, of the organising committee for St Aigulphe's Day in Le Muy in 1872, all but one of the thirteen men were artisans (7) or peasants (5). The continuity of popular sociability in this form depended upon its transfiguration into something politically and socially very different from what had gone before.[12]

Musical societies

The frequency of public festivals in the villages of Provence resulted in one rather specialised form of social activity – the communal orchestra or band. In the mid-nineteenth century such an orchestra, however small, was to be found in the vast majority of the small towns of the Var, and membership of the local musical society was often synonymous with a particular stance in village or even national politics. In Brignoles there were two 'Musiques' – the republican and the reactionary; during the early 1880s they often gave competing performances, and would be called upon by local political factions to provide musical accompaniment to the appropriate political or historical occasion – the reactionary society taking part in religious and monarchist activities, the republican one playing the Marseillaise on 14 July.[13]

The musical societies were important not just because they were yet another context for public meetings and collective identification with a particular party, but because they offered a means of displaying the growing tensions within village life in the early years of the Third Republic without resort to physical violence. Not that such violence was ever very far away: when the Correns 'orphéon réactionnaire' came to perform in Montfort on 9 April 1882, local republicans were scathing – showering it with rotten vegetables and abuse. The attacks on the musical skills of the performers were quite inseparable from the local rejection of the political views which the band represented. Similarly, when the commune of Auriol, in the Bouches-du-Rhône, celebrated in 1880 the installation of its first republican municipal administration, the local orchestra and choir were passed over in favour of the *corps de musique* from St Zacharie, seven kilometres distant, whose sympathies (and melodies) were deemed more appropriate to the occasion. The local musicians responded with a noisy boycott of the proceedings. In Brignoles, in

1886, there were disturbances and arrests at a festival on 20 August, when the visiting orchestra from Pignans, invited by the priest, refused to play the Marseillaise. According to the *sous-préfet*, similar instances of cause and effect had happened before, on more than one occasion.[14]

Although membership of musical societies remained high throughout the last third of the century, the political associations which had, for example, caused the *corps de musique* of Gonfaron to be closed down on 16 May 1877, were of declining prominence. By the 1890s, with the Republic securely established and the clerical issue apparently resolved, membership of musical groups, like participation in village festivals, lost the political bite of earlier years. Nevertheless, the overlap of membership between, say, the Société Philharmonique of Cogolin and the left-wing circles within the town, remained considerable. But during the 1880s the region saw, for the first time, the development of forms of sociability whose function was *primarily* political, where the old forms had been political only by implication or as a result of the discussions which they generated.

The cercles

Whereas all village life contained an element of the political, what distinguished the Mediterranean community from, say, the Castilian *pueblo* was the presence of associations, societies within the society, which helped focus political and social divisions which were otherwise diffuse and ineffectual.

Provençal communities were especially precocious in this respect, with *cercles* and *chambrées* forming the nuclei of political and social divisions and serving as informal schools for the political education of their members. With the coming of the Third Republic, political choices could increasingly be made in the open, at the same time as the economic divisions within many of the villages were often much diminished. As a result the old pattern of bourgeois and popular clubs changed in favour of more formal and overtly political clubs, dividing men not by status but by opinion.[15]

The great period for such clubs was the decade from 1881 to 1890, when many of the Cercles des Travailleurs, Sociétés Républicaines and so forth came into being, often born out of a society which had survived, in muted form, from the repressive years of the Empire. The more politically divided the commune, the greater the number of such societies, and the more active their membership. In communes such as La Crau, where the republicans exercised an absolute hegemony over local politics, the distinction between republican societies and the commune as a whole was often blurred. Thus in June 1882, candidates for the forthcoming municipal by-elections were chosen at an open meeting held in the Café de France. A committee was formed, composed exclusively of the members of the Cercle Sociale, but the hundred or so persons present at the meeting were all invited to express their views as to a favoured candidate.[16]

More commonly, however, it was within the local political clubs that such choices were made. Membership was formal, with dues and regular attendance required of all, although in the summer many of these *cercles* fell into tacit abeyance while their members were at work in the fields. But in the winter, and during the periods of critical elections, much of the social life of the village took place within the walls of the club. In this way, some form of political commitment was often an essential precondition for a share of the social activity of the village; this is the obverse of the situation two generations earlier, where active sociability via membership of the appropriate sub-community was the only means of partaking in political debate.

Membership of the multifarious *cercles* of Provence does not appear to have been in any way socially exclusive by the mid-1880s. These societies were often the basis of what would later become Socialist sections, affiliated to a wider socialist movement, and their members were usually a representative cross-section of the village itself; thus their heterogeneity declined in the last fifteen years of the century as the artisans and bourgeoisie disappeared from the small towns. There were conservative *cercles*, of course, not easily identified on account of their careful adoption of republican labels, but usually biased in their membership in favour of the wealthier members of the community — and thereby small and few in number. As for the villages of the forests and Alpine plateaux, they showed a much lower proclivity to form groups from amongst themselves, a reflection both of the absence of a tradition of sociability, and the enhanced difficulties of communication and transport in these dispersed habitats. Finally, it is perhaps not without some significance that so many of these *cercles* would later become formalised into socialist groups: the informal and irregular basis of Radical politics, for example, was much less in keeping with the regional tradition than was the Socialists' insistence, with Jules Guesde, on highly structured, formalised and doctrinally homogeneous local cells. In this way the traditional sociability of Provence, by 1890, was converging with the occupationally-based socialist groups of the Nord and the Pas-de-Calais, both of them particularly appropriate and fertile soil for a highly articulated political movement.

Cafés

If the *cercle* was the form which public life was coming increasingly to take in this period, then the evening meeting in the local café was the preferred context, and this fact is not without its special significance. We are naturally less informed about the content of discussions and gatherings in a local café than we are about the membership and aims of the *cercles*, which were legally obliged to declare membership and activities to the authorities. But it is beyond doubt that by 1880 the café in Provence had ceased to play a merely residual rôle in a society whose social life was conducted in formalised clubs and discussion groups, but had become the very epicentre of the community.

Why was this the case? In the first place, the increased consumption of alcohol in France during the course of the later nineteenth century resulted in an expansion of the number of cafés, bars and *débits de boisson*, in the south as elsewhere.[17] Then there was the economic crisis of the last years of the century; in many rural areas peasants found themselves increasingly obliged to borrow money against optimistic expectations of future improvements, and the café often served as something of an informal bank. Although money had long circulated within the market-oriented economy of the south, the shortage of specie and the hardships of the peasantry gave a special importance to the café-owner, with his ready cash and access to the sums which his clientèle wished to borrow.[18]

Furthermore, the café-owner, like the *cabaretier* before him, would often subscribe to one or more newspapers (a habit still frequently found in French café-owners today) as a means of attracting custom. More commonly still, particular cafés would take newspapers of a given political bent, thereby both reflecting the views of their clients and encouraging the spread of certain political ideas among them. As a consequence, cafés in Provence were very often at the centre of political life, and would become strongly identified with the political colour of their regular customers. When a collection was taken in Nans les Pins towards the establishment of a school for the poor in June 1883, the Café National and the Café Tartan (?) both gave generously. But the *habitués* of the Café Apollon gave not a sou — the conservative and clerical clientèle who frequented it disapproving of the aims of the appeal and in any case reacting against the fact that the notices had originally been posted in the other, 'republican' cafés. Similarly, bonapartists, republicans and monarchists in Salernes in 1873 all had their 'own' cafés, taking the appropriate journals and excluding all but fellow sympathisers. However, Salernes was a local commercial centre of some importance, and, as the *préfet* observed, there was also a 'neutral' café for strangers and visitors to the market.[19]

The cafés were thus the focus of the political divisions of the commune. An official Enquête of 1873 observed that the population of Draguignan spent much of their spare time in cafés, either alone, *en famille* or, more commonly, in societies and clubs, musical, political or whatever, which regularly met at a given bar. The authorities were already worried at the political implications of such social activity; the 'Café Concert' of Varages (where there were regular performances of popular music and occasional bursts of political singing) was held to be a 'bad influence' and it is certainly the case that this same café, by the 1890s, would be serving as the locus of socialist organisation and propaganda in the village.[20] The café was becoming a 'contre-église', with public readings of left-wing papers in place of the Sunday sermon, and visiting speakers from Marseille and Paris in place of the regular episcopal visitations. To the extent that *cercles* and cafés had come to overlap — the Cercle des Travailleurs in La Garde Freinet in the 1880s was in effect a semi-private café frequented exclusively by the local population and is still so today — political and social life in Provence had lost its rigid and stratified nature and, becoming democratised in form, was tending to reflect this change in its content as well.

Cooperation

The relationship between economic solidarity and social cohesiveness might too readily be supposed to work in terms of the priority, historically and causally, of the former. In fact, the pattern of events in Provence suggests the reverse — that the traditions of sociability, particularly once they had acquired a more open and democratic nature, losing the exclusivity of brotherhoods and private *cercles*, favoured the development of economic cooperation. This was all the more the case in that the broadening of the forms of social intercourse was accompanied in this period by an economic crisis which forced collective defence upon the peasantry.

The propensity to join clearly worked in favour of a rapid growth of syndicalisation in this region; union membership here easily outstripped the organisations of the under-unionised east and northeast of France.[21] That this was the case for bakery workers, corkworkers, shoemakers, leather-workers and the like is perhaps not so very surprising. The drive to syndicalisation in these rural industries reflected both the *compagnonnage* traditions of the occupations in question and the crisis of competition which was afflicting them all after 1880. Of much greater significance, precisely because it is so out of keeping with patterns elsewhere, was the highly-developed mutual cooperation among the *peasantry* of this area. The explanation appears to be threefold. In the first place, there were the ancient traditions of collective interest — the sort of mutualism which made men purchase with their limited means various parts of an injured or diseased animal belonging to another — a form of unwritten rural insurance common among those who raised cattle in southern France. Taken with the widespread survival of common lands and the collective association which accompanied them, this historical identification with the interests of others, of the community, had long marked out the peasantry of Provence and the Languedoc as unusually given to a consciousness of their mutual interest — irrespective of the individual property structure of the region.[22]

The second element encouraging cooperation in the area was the very extent of artisanal mutualism just described. The importance of the close intermix of peasant and townsman in the crowded villages of Provence is most clearly seen in this context; through informal (and formal — viz the early-nineteenth-century *chambrées*) links with the artisanat, the Provençal peasant was introduced to the forms of mutual aid and organisation long before the peasant of, say, Brittany, so enduringly suspicious of joint activity.[23]

Thirdly, there was the crisis of the phylloxera and the price collapse of the ensuing decades. In these circumstances a natural sympathy for collective solutions became an economic necessity for many of the smallholders of Provence — hence the rapid growth and efflorescence of agricultural and above all vinicole cooperatives, whose imposing structures still dominate many villages of the region today. Most of these cooperatives, formed with the advice or assistance of local syndicalists but comprising exclusively peasant membership, were founded during the years 1890—1909; the few agricultural syndicates which antedate this period, founded in the 1880s, were almost all located in communes which would show an early and enduring sympathy for the socialists — Ollioules, Flayosc, Montmeyan, Le Luc. There is little doubt that the link between economic cooperation and support for political collectivism was a close one. It is also reasonable to suppose that, given the respective chronologies of cooperation and socialist movements, the former was often the means by which the peasantry were introduced to the latter. The emphasis on cooperatives and rural syndicates, usually organised for the processing of crops and their sale, and to a lesser degree for the purchase of material, helps explain the marked antipathy shown by the peasantry of Provence towards the efforts of the Toulon anarchists to propagate their ideas beyond the city. The whole history and structure of social life in the villages ran counter to the emphasis on individual acts and the rejection of authority and organisation which informed the anarchist ideal.[24]

The geographical conditions of sociability

Whatever the form of sociability, its presence was consistently conditioned, in earlier times as in the 1880s and 1890s, by certain considerations of location and habitat. The fairs around which so much of early modern Provençal society revolved were to be found clustered in those same small bourgs of the valleys where, a century later, cafés and cercles would be at their most dominant. As in other respects that I have considered, it was not so much the major markets themselves as the constellation of villages dependent upon them which were most representative of these characteristics. The main roads, such as the communications networks from Aix to Fréjus and Toulon to Le Luc, were probably important for the communication of news; but the towns lying directly on these roads — St Maximin, Tourves, Brignoles, Vidauban on the west—east axis, Solliès, Carnoules, Les Arcs and Trans on the south—north route — were too open, perhaps also too well policed, for the development of that special combination of accessibility and separation which nurtured the local societies out of which sedition would grow. Thus in 1851, of the thirteen communes in the Var with the highest percentage of their population arrested for their part in the insurrection of December, nine lay in the wooded valleys around Barjols — within easy reach of the main routes but sufficiently apart to initiate and nourish a local political radicalism.[25]

By the 1870s radicalised *cercles* and *chambrées* were to be found in two types of environment, to judge by the list of societies banned during the repression of July 1877:[26] in the large towns themselves — Toulon, Hyères, Draguignan — and in the selfsame bourgs which had sheltered penitents in the eighteenth century and Démocrates—Socialistes in the 1840s: Besse, Carcès, Correns, Ginasservis, Bargemon, Claviers, etc. Of small to medium size, with a smattering of artisans but a predominance of peasants, and in easy reach of important centres and roads, though not themselves significant markets or junctions, these communes continued to fertilise a sociability whose geography, at least, was remarkably stable. We find them a generation later at the forefront of the Socialist electorate.

Negative considerations, working against the growth of an active social life and an awareness of wider issues, were also fairly constant. Those mountain villages which had been so inaccessible in the eighteenth century remained as untouched by the changes taking place lower down a hundred years later. Most of them were at least twenty kilometres from an urban centre, and their badly maintained roads and paths served as a further discouragement to travel.[27] Even so relatively accessible a commune as Callian, forty kilometres north-east of Draguignan, was complaining in 1880 that its elected representatives scarcely ever deigned to make the journey to the town;[28] how much more so was this the case for the upland villages of the

Alpine foothills. In any case, a consistently conservative electorate in these regions served as a further disincentive for Radical (and later Socialist) deputies to make the long and tiring journey. It is noteworthy that much of the northern Var was quite without public transportation throughout the early Third Republic; the two main bus lines ran from Sisteron to Marseille and from Gap to Nice, thereby completely by-passing the upper regions of the arrondissements of Brignoles and Draguignan. Even the local departmental buses only covered three basic routes: east—west from Draguignan to Brignoles; north—south from Aups to Toulon via Brignoles and from Draguignan to Toulon via Le Luc. Only with the coming of the Popular Front did matters improve in this respect. Formal communications thus reinforced the distinction already created by natural topography between those areas of easy accessibility and those locked in a remote fastness no less complete than that of the genuine mountain villages of the high Alps.[29]

If geographical location helped determine the degree of access to modern ideas — an access which was not in itself a determinant of politicisation, since only two of the seven towns *on* the Route Nationale 7 appear on our original list of Socialist electoral strongholds — the extent of the impact of ideas encountered in the market and from newspapers and at meetings was largely a reflection of a rather different geographical factor, that of habitat. The point has already been made in an earlier chapter that there was a very close relationship between communes of closely-grouped population and left-wing voting: it remains to account for this link.

The obvious starting point is the simple matter of the difficulty experienced by peasants in areas of dispersed dwellings in meeting one another. No one in Les Salles, up near the Verdon, had more than a few hundred metres to cover between his home and the centre of the commune. But in the surrounding communes of Aiguines, Bauduen, Vérignon, many people lived at quite a distance from the communal *chef-lieu*. In Vérignon, 72 of the 1893 population of 94 people lived outside the commune itself (which with 22 people could hardly have been a lively centre of social or political life). In these circumstances we should not be surprised to find Les Salles alone from this area appearing not merely on our map of socialist strongholds, but also on a list of communes with 'suspect' *cercles* in 1877.[30]

This distinction between *habitat aggloméré* and *habitat épars* in Provence dates back to the sixteenth century. Until then the dominant, close-grouped form had been the norm; but with the population growth of that period and the search for new and marginal land for cultivation, people moved into the plains and hills to the north, where it took a far larger hectarage to support a given population. As a result, families scattered all across the upper Var, forming a pattern of settlement quite distinct from the crowded and wealthier regions to the south.[31] The distinctions in patterns of sociability between the two kinds of habitat date from this period. Access to one another's company and opinions was so very much easier in the tightly-grouped villages of the valleys that with the greater ease of social intercourse came a smoother path for the introduction of new political conceptions. Thus the public readings of the *Démocrate du Var,* the organ of the left in the Second Republic, depended upon the ready audience which only a peasantry living in the style and conditions of townsmen could provide. Similarly, the insurrection of 1851 was limited in its scope in the Limousin by the dispersion of the population into numerous tiny hamlets, delaying the spread of news and retarding the emergence of local political leadership.[32] Of course, a population which was technically dispersed might in fact be grouped into numerous tiny communities, hamlets of a few dozen souls, rather than being isolated in individual farms. But such dispersal, with the communal church in one hamlet, the school or the *mairie* in another, was just as effective a barrier to sociability — tending if anything to the formation of tiny conservative communities much more easily dominated by local notables, conservative or radical.

Within the grouped habitat of the valleys, the size of the population also mattered. There were the occasional exceptions, such as Les Salles, where a tiny village would nevertheless generate an active social life around the sole café, but as a rule the enduring centres of Provençal sociability were bourgs whose population lay between 500 and 2500. This order of population provided for politicians an audience worth the effort of a special visit, as well as helping ensure the survival of well-attended and competitive *cercles* and cafés. The attendance at political meetings was often extremely high. When Gustave Fourment (Secretary of the Var Socialist Federation) visited

Barjols in May 1909, over 500 people turned out to hear what he had
to say. There were only 688 electors in the commune (in a population
of 2300) and, in the 1910 elections, 541 of them voted – 231 of
them for the Socialist candidate. Presumably some people came in
from the surrounding villages for Fourment's speech (further evidence
of the importance of proximity – all the neighbouring villages were
staunchly Socialist), but it is nevertheless clear that a remarkably
high proportion of the enfranchised population attended such
meetings. Furthermore, 1909 was *not* an election year, nor Fourment
a candidate. Nor was this an isolated instance – in the following year
over 400 people gathered to hear Fourment speak at Cogolin (population 2200) and there were many more such instances.[33]

Ease of access, both within one's own commune and between
communes, was quite clearly an essential precondition for political
participation. There is no record of Fourment, for example, having
ever visited La Martre, or Châteauvieux in the remote north-east of
the department; with two Socialist voters between them in 1910
they were hardly propitious environments for Socialist propaganda.
But even had he done so, it is hard to imagine the impoverished
sharecroppers of the Comps canton trudging across the plateau to
hear him.

It is thus difficult to accept Paul Bois' view that *no* peasant was
completely remote from politics, whatever his physical isolation.
Bois argues that voting, for the remote *campagnard,* was often an
excuse for a visit to the communal *chef-lieu,* a distraction from his
lonely existence.[34] In the Var, the consistently high rates of abstention in these remote parts suggests otherwise. Ten of the twenty
communes with above-average rates of abstention in the elections of
1876, 1898 *and* 1914 lay north of a line running from Barjols to
Draguignan. It is certainly true that the church continued to provide
a focus for companionship and encounter in these parts – but the
influence of the priest worked against the development of the newer
forms of social intercourse, including politics.[35]

If geographical isolation played an obvious rôle not merely in
retarding the growth of modern social and political intercourse, but
in orienting political affiliation in a particular (conservative) direction,
aided by the survival of a dominant local bourgeoisie and an impoverished class of propertyless peasants, the relationship between

geographical proximity and radicalisation is perhaps not quite so obvious. We have already seen that as a causal relationship it is not valid for larger towns; but is it not the case that the economic crisis, allied to traditional forms of sociability of a politically neutral nature, was much more important in laying the path for socialism than the mere fact of closely-grouped habitat? Perhaps — although habitat and sociability were so closely intertwined in Provençal life that distinguishing them for explanatory purposes may be a pointless task. It is more likely that, just as isolation and economic retardation seem to lead to a certain continuity of political tradition — whatever that tradition may be — so 'urban peasants' were much more likely to be fickle in their choices, influenced by new ideas and changing circumstances. Thus we should understand the largely conjunctural turn to the left at the end of the century as a result of the wider options available to the populations of the bourgs at a time when their local experience was making them sympathetic to collectivist ideas. That socialism then becomes an *enduring* political characteristic of the area — as enduring in the valleys as conservatism was in the hills — may be explained by the stagnation of the old Provençal bourgs during the twentieth century. Radicalised during the last years of urban sociability, they stagnated in their (Socialist) affiliation in later years, when so many of these villages retained their urban form but had lost much of their urban function and character.

Such a perspective enables us to understand the enduring importance of the traditions of sociability in this region as a determinant of political life, while also making due allowance for the properly historical and circumstantial importance of the developments of a particular period. The specially Provençal character of local life as described earlier in this chapter was definitely much diminished by the 1890s; but transformed into the various kinds of sub-society I have described, it could still play an important part in accounting for the map of local political divisions. Organised left-wing activity (syndicates, cooperatives, socialist groups); left-wing political leanings as a communal identity — replacing the religiosity of earlier times and often coming close to absorbing the whole of the communal electorate; specifically peasant gatherings of a democratic nature in open forums; all of these were in some degree the descendants of the brotherhoods, the *chambrées* and the freemasons, and were conditioned by the ways in which their forebears had organised *their* public life. This was probably true even to the extent to which sociability in this region led in practice to a greater degree of social conformity, whatever the ideological form of the activity; as the social mix was reduced, so the pressure to conform to the dominant local tendency was probably increased.

But that all of these developments should have led in the direction of modern socialism is at least as much a reflection of the circumstances, economic above all, in which the changes were taking place — just as Provençal sociability in the years 1815—40 showed a fundamentally conservative face. And then, despite the traditional distinctions (underlined here) between social bourg and isolated hamlet, the two drew closer together after 1900, as the former lost, through that same economic stagnation and crisis which had brought it to socialism, the very social variety which had helped determine that political choice. By 1914 both parts of the Var were firmly rooted in traditional political stances — the only difference being that the crisis of the village economy, and the historical collectivism of the region, had created in one part of the area a tradition which had grafted itself on to the ideology of the extreme left.

7

Education and an absent Church

A casual glance at the geography of religious practice in France cannot fail to reveal the frequent overlap between areas of apparent dechristianisation and departments with large Radical and Socialist electorates. Most of the classic interpretations of post-Revolutionary French history accordingly lay emphasis upon this evident relationship between religion and politics, and not a few of them have ascribed the one phenomenon to the existence of the other.

While such a link appears likely not merely through the confluence of shaded areas on a map but also in logic (religious practice tending to political conservatism or moderation), the easy ascription of cause and effect which this sort of electoral and religious geography encourages is not without its problems. In the first place, such maps tend to describe the phenomenon at the departmental level. In this way, variations of religious practice and political affiliation between different sub-regions, between and even within villages, become blurred. By any global standards the Var was, as we shall see, a very non-practising department, and appears as such on all maps of religious observance in France. But there were quite a number of villages and towns within the department which did not conform to type in this way. As a result, any account of French society which was tempted into describing Provence, or the Limousin, or any other *generally* dechristianised area, as characteristically hostile to the Church would be seriously underestimating the complexities of the matter.

Secondly, such geographical studies of religious practice depend of necessity upon the sort of data which document not religion but attendance at religious ceremonies — mass, baptism, the annual festivals, etc. There exists a body of more impressionistic data culled from the observations of local clerics, but even if separately reliable these reports are rarely comparable for the historian's purposes. Thus we are ill-informed as to the degree of religiosity in France. We might even posit three 'levels' of religion: overt Catholicism, judged by attendance in church; passive Christian observance — difficult to measure but quite distinct from a third level, that of an almost pagan faith in patron saints, local shrines and the like. The latter often flourished in those areas which appear most 'dechristianised' on maps; the Var might be such a case. In this instance, then, failure to attend the local Catholic church becomes important evidence about the decline of the Church's social rôle (or perhaps, in some areas, it never really achieved one?); but it is far from being prima facie proof of the secularised character of a region.

Even if we accept such limitations upon the heuristic value of religious sociology, however sophisticated,[1] there remains a further nagging difficulty. Both the religious 'traditions' — in respect of geographical variations — and modern political divisions in France date for the most part from the Revolution. For politics the dating is self-explanatory; but for the Church it is less a matter of the chronological onset of dechristianisation, more a question of the fact that the Revolution first raised the sorts of issue — separation, lay education — which enable us to see religion emerging as a socially divisive factor. But this very overlap between the historical origins of modern political debate and those of the nineteenth-century clerical issue surely makes it very unwise to suggest that the one in some sense helped determine the other. They might rather more plausibly be seen as twin symptoms of other and deeper social divisions which the Revolution helped create — or to which it gave a newer, secular form. To say that Frenchmen in some regions voted for the candidate of the right because of the influence of the Church, itself allied socially and ideologically to political conservatism and the local notables, is not on the face of it implausible. But one could reasonably argue, *mutatis mutandis*, that a sympathy for the right helped prolong a practising faith which conservative ideology so fervently espoused.

One might resolve the issue by claiming that, in the years when such traditions were forming, religion was the more important social issue, and that ideological choices were fashioned by the influence of the priest — or by his unpopularity. But it is not in fact clear that, even in the 1790s, religion *was* more important for many Frenchmen than politics (in so far as they cared much about either in an abstract sense). And even if it were so, we should still wish to know why some parts of France took more notice of their priest than did others. The answer to this question would then surely have to be couched in terms of social, perhaps territorial or even economic considerations. And if this is the case, why should it not be the case for the post-Revolutionary years? That is, may not religious practice *and* political choice be affected by other factors even after the divisive years of the Revolution? There is certainly no doubt that there were places and times where religious practice increased in the last century, so that we are not necessarily dealing with patterns set once and for all.

These points are made here by way of introduction to a brief discussion of the conflicts surrounding the Church in the Var after 1870. In the Var as elsewhere the Church, and with it the question of the control of education, was a lively issue at the end of the nineteenth century. But lower Provence was also, in the usual sense, a very dechristianised or non-practising region, so that it is an interesting locus for the discussion of the relationship between a weak Church and a penchant for left-wing politics.

There is much evidence that the Church was a topic of absorbing local interest in these years, more particularly from the end of the 1870s, when opinion could begin to be expressed freely, until the late 1880s, by which time the education issue at least had been for the moment resolved. There would be a revival of interest and feeling on the subject in the early twentieth century, with the Combes ministry and the separation of Church and state. Feeling was high on both sides, not merely among the anti-clerical left whom I shall be considering. In 1882 the Bishop of Fréjus refused to unlock and illuminate his palace on 14 July — and when he visited rural villages, certain citizens would be conspicuous for their expenditure on lights and flowers, in contrast with the darkness which shrouded their homes on republican anniversaries.[2]

This perennially lively character of the clerical issue, such as it was, is all the more surprising in Provence because of the traditionally non-practising nature of the area. It was a matter of common accord that very few men in the region attended church. The police in Cuers and Pierrefeu reported as early as October 1877 that the local churches were attended exclusively by old women and girls from 'well-heeled familes'. When the cholera epidemic raged in Toulon in

the summer of 1884 and a procession of some 400 people from
La Garde Freinet climbed the hill to pray at the shrine of Notre
Dame de Miramar, the correspondent of the *Petit Var*, admittedly
not an unbiased source, estimated the attendance as exclusively
female but for three men and a number of children. The parties of
the left certainly had no illusions as to the specific character of the
Church's audience: at a meeting of the POF in Toulon on 25 February
1901, Mlle Marie Henry, a socialist and feminist speaker, urged on
her listeners the 'vital' task of ending their wives' attendance at con-
fession.[3]

Anti-clericalism, then, represented in the Var not so much a
struggle for men's hearts and minds, that battle being long since won;
the issue was much more substantively political, and perceived in this
way. Even the opposition to female churchgoing was couched in
political terms, notwithstanding an exclusively male suffrage: as
Mlle Henry explained, it was the mother who formed the child's view
and thus helped condition his future choices.

This local dislike of the Church and all its works ran deep. It has
been calculated for 1877 that, expressed in terms of diocesan
'vitality' – attendance at church, in effect – the diocese of Fréjus
(which covered the Var) came at the very bottom of the list of
dioceses in France. The contrast with such areas as those covered by
the dioceses of Luçon (Vendée), Vannes, Laval, Arras or Cambrai
was more marked in Provence than in any other part of the country.
A small, 'folklorique' example will illustrate this. On the local road
between Tourves and La Roquebrussanne, just south of the Aix–Fréjus
highway, there is an unusual formation of three rocks, resembling a
trio of hooded monks. Local tradition has it that there was once a
convent in the area, where were committed all manner of suitably
salacious indiscretions and impieties. On one All Saints' Day God, to
show his wrath, cast a thunderbolt at three of the sinning monks and
caused them to be for ever petrified where they stood.

This tale is interesting for its combination of pagan and Christian
conceptions – as well as for the significant fact that it implies a very
religious form of anti-clericalism. But my point is that such a rock-
formation in Brittany, for example, would almost certainly have
acquired a rather different origin and might well have become a place
of pilgrimage. Certainly the part-religious part-pagan use to which the
menhirs were put in Brittany suggests such a likelihood.[4]

All manner of sources testify to this local isolation of the official Church. In February 1873 a young *voiturier*, Louis Long, drove through a funeral procession in Salernes to the cheers of onlookers, and then poured scorn and invective on the priest, Bouchard. He was arrested and sentenced to 14 days' imprisonment under a law of 1822; but the police commented that this was hardly a unique instance. In Barjols, stones and animal dung were regularly flung at the door of the school run by the Frères des Ecoles Chrétiennes, and at the brothers themselves. At 9 a.m. on 4 September 1876 two windows of the classroom were smashed by a bullet, during class. Despite an attempt at an enquiry, the police despaired of finding the culprit — the whole population was in sympathy with the anonymous gunman and no one would say a word. Little wonder that the *curé* of Rebouillon, near Draguignan, had taken to carrying a revolver![5]

If religious influence was low even in the period of Moral Order (*c.* 1873—8), it would be even less with the coming of the secular Republic. In the last year of the Empire the Brignoles arrondissement was reported as quite beyond the influence of a clergy who took care to avoid prominence; an official enquiry of 1874 found the *patronat* of Belgentier advocating Sunday work — the local workers did not attend church, but spent their leisure in idle and dangerous pursuits. There was 'no religion' in the commune, or so it was believed. By the 1890s, the strength of feeling had diminished — but so had the influence of the Church. The Bishop of Fréjus might easily have endorsed the impressions of Mgr de Cabrières, the Bishop of Montpellier, whose diocese covered the neighbouring area of western Provence and the Languedoc, when in 1892 he reflected on twenty years' service in the region: 'Je suis frappé des progrès que l'indifférence — une indifférence absolue et presque dédaigneuse — fait dans notre pays. On se retire de nos églises même dans les campagnes; ou si l'on y vient . . . c'est le lointain souvenir d'anciennes habitudes, c'est un sentiment vague et indéfini.'[6]

A special and rather interesting instance of the further decline of the Church's influence is the increase in the number of civil burials, particularly during the 1880s. This is the more significant in that religious burials were often as important to those whose religiosity was of the non-practising, informal kind, as they were to the official Church. From 1883 onwards, announcements of the 'first civil burial' in a given commune or canton became a regular feature of the radical press, material evidence of the growing secularisation of the peasantry. The geography of this particular development is a fairly faithful reflection of certain other characteristics of Provençal sub-regions already described.

Once the Republic had established a firm control over both primary education and the polling-booths, a control whose achievement came early in Provence, other issues arose – notably the economic crisis, the question of protectionism and, by 1900, increasingly acerbic conflicts *within* the once-united republican front. But the Combes ministry and its legislation reawoke the dormant debate over the Church – or more precisely, the momentarily hushed attack on what remained of the organised Church in lower Provence. The real issue now was the control of Church property after separation. This was a particularly significant issue in the Var because of the traditional claims of the communality upon public land. Beginning in Le Luc, and then spreading to many other places (Lorgues, Le Muy, Collobrières, Barjols, Vidauban, etc.) there were petitions in 1904 requesting amendments to the separation law. These municipalities disliked the obligation imposed upon them to rent property to the Church for a period of ten years. They also opposed the granting of special police privileges to the Church for processions and the like, and demanded more thoroughgoing reduction of the Church's residual claim to special status of any kind. By 1906 this overt antagonism had again muted, but not without reawakening many village hatreds and accusations. Weak or no, the Church remained a favoured target, particularly of Radical politicians, in the first half of the Third Republic. In this the Radicals of the Var differed little from their *confrères* elsewhere. But it is noteworthy that the political use of the clerical issue did not depend very much on the actual degree of conflict which it generated. In many parts of the Var, the reactionary and powerful *curé* was a straw man by 1890 – which did not prevent him being burned, as such, in effigy.[7]

Even within such a secularised region, however, there were considerable if subtle variations. The geography of anti-clericalism, or of religious affirmation, was as complex at this level as on the national scale. The degree of attendance at church, and the influence of the priest in local affairs, was far stronger in the northern fringe of the department than it was further south. The incidence of civil burials there was far lower, and aroused a considerable opposition. Whereas there had been 96 civil burials in Cuers by mid-1882, Montmeyan (near the border with the Basses-Alpes) experienced its first such occasion in December of that year – indeed it was the first civil burial in the whole of the surrounding canton of Tavernes. Significantly, the deceased person who had broken with tradition in his request for a non-religious ceremony was a former insurrectionist and *proscrit* of 1851.[8]

Whereas the northern Var represented a region where religious practice and secular conservatism went hand in hand, such was not always the case. The hills and forests of the southern Var, while distinguished from the radical Provence of the valleys in many other ways, shared the latter's anti-clericalism. Neither the incidence of civil burials, nor the impressionistic reports of local officials and journalists, suggests that there was much clerical influence in the Estérel, the Maures or even the Ste Baume. Outside of the Verdon region, only the coastal towns west of Toulon showed an enduring religiosity, and in their case this was not infrequently the traditional semi-pagan religiosity of processions, penitents and saints' days, rather than a deep respect for the authority of the established Church. Only the communes of the northern plateaux were truly under the influence of the organised clergy, and this confirms both the religious geography established for the eighteenth century by Vovelle, and the map of religious practice in 1877, which shows the departments bordering on the northern and north-eastern fringes of the Var (the Basses-Alpes and the Alpes-Maritimes) as considerably less dechristianised than the Var itself.[9]

The distribution of feeling on the subject of the Church may be further illustrated by reference to the impact of the law expelling the congregations, which came into effect in late 1880. Whereas Marseille, Avignon and Aix all experienced considerable disturbances over the summary ejection of the congregations, the expulsion of monks and nuns in Toulon, begun on 30 October 1880, provoked no opposition at all. And the same was true all across the department. The major centres of the local congregations were Lorgues, with a community of Capucins, and St Maximin and Fréjus where the Dominicans were based. The Capucins were removed without difficulty. In St Maximin a crowd of women, children and some priests attempted to block the way to the cells, whose inmates had barricaded themselves in, but nowhere else did the issue create the slightest stir, although it is interesting to note that both St Maximin and Fréjus stood out in the 1880s and in later years for their conservatism in political affairs – in Fréjus the Church's control over education was relatively well established, and the commune is one of the few in its area which figures on my list of consistently conservative communes. Clearly the presence of the Bishop, like that of the Dominicans in St Maximin, had played its part in controlling local politics and influencing local opinion, especially through the schools. But since both Fréjus and St Maximin (like Lorgues) were largish towns in the regional context, and all three of them on major axes of communication, they were distinguished from their radical neighbours by more than the mere presence of a religious community or diocesan headquarters.[10]

One dimension of the religious conflict in France seems largely to have been absent from the Var. Protestantism is sometimes seen as a factor in determining the leftist leanings of a region, if only in that it encourages the sort of anti-Catholicism which characterised a certain left in nineteenth-century France. Even this relationship may be questioned – Protestantism in Alsace or the Gard was often strongest in business *milieux*, where moderate republicanism from the 1860s onwards was the political expression of a liberal bourgeoisie, whose Protestantism was as much consequence as cause of their traditional antipathy to governments and nobility. Such was not the case in the Var. It is true that Le Luc, with Manosque in the Basses-Alpes, had been a privileged area for local Protestants, who had been granted freedom of worship there from the 1590s. But the strongholds of seventeenth-century Protestantism in lower Provence, chiefly Le Luc itself and the canton of Solliès Pont, never spread their influence very wide in the region, and, by the mid-nineteenth century, formal communities of Protestants survived only in Draguignan, Fréjus (hence the strength of local religious feeling there?) and Toulon. Even Le Luc could no longer boast a reformed church. Indeed, by 1900, the government's own publications record the presence of only two Protestant pastors in the whole of the department.[11]

Thus formal religion of any kind was at a very low ebb in the Var at the end of the nineteenth century, and the attacks on Church and clergy, by Radicals especially, represented above all an adherence to the traditional forms of political discourse in French public life. Attacking organised religion was a sure and simple means of establishing one's identity in local political conflicts. Some socialists even levelled accusations at 'international Jewry' — a depressingly common target of a certain tendency on the European left in this period — though they were not slow to remind their audiences that *all* religions served essentially the same opiate function. It was on this account that the formal organs of the socialist movement were occasionally apologetic about following the Radicals' lead to anti-clerical agitation; as *Le Cri* put it in 1913, there are more important things to do than 'bouffer le prêtre'.[12]

Thus religion, despite the prominence on occasion of the clerical question, was not really a central issue in local political life. The reason for this seems perhaps to have been that very religiosity which kept the local population so actively traditional in their social life. In a region where the rest of the community formed an ever-present basis for the exchange of opinions and for ideological reassurance, the Church was sharply reduced in its potential rôle and influence. And with so much popular religiosity of an informal kind, the Church was far from being that guardian of traditions and practices which it so often became in other parts of France. If anything, the very obsession with local celebrations and anniversaries *both* conserved an ostensibly religious but non-clerical sensibility *and* favoured the transplantation into these celebrations and public activities of a more secular, ultimately political identity.

What is more, it is worth considering the possibility that, in rural areas at least, religion in whatever form was ultimately a rather super-ficial thing. Peasants' concerns were in every sense more earthly. Religion took the form of a structured account and explanation of those seasonal and climatic matters which dominated the conscious-ness and working-life of rural society. This is not to deny the consid-erable importance of this interplay between religion, myth, popular belief and practical daily cares. Quite the contrary. But it helps us appreciate that the Church and debates concerning it were much less important than the faith they represented. How far the two were separated in the minds of the peasantry was largely a function of the local economy and topography. Where the church was the natural (and perhaps the sole) focus of *social* activity — with the weekly market held, for instance, in the shadow of the church and in the presence of the priest — then its influence was great and the distinction between faith and practice unclear. Where, as in the Var, there were alternative meeting places, other forums for discussion, no shortage of occasions for social intercourse, there faith and clergy were far from synonymous. Thus the clergy were without much influence in Provence, except in the somewhat 'un-Provençal' hills to the north. But we must not deduce from this any very ambitious conclusions about the relationship between religion and politics at the level of local perceptions. The peasantry of Provence were not of necessity Voltairian in their view of the compatibility or otherwise of being both religious and socialist. But they did take a very clear view of the distinction between two kinds of local authorities, and that choice is really the one I have been describing.

This can be more clearly seen in the importance attached to the question of primary education, particularly in the 1880s. It is here that we may see just how functional and immediate, rather than profound or ideological, was the clerical issue for most Frenchmen. At its simplest, it was a matter of establishing the maximum of control over the education of the next generation. Hence the extent to which this issue mobilised Radicals rather than socialists, since it was the former who were most committed to the image of the crusading Republic, a state with a duty to orient its citizens in a given direction, not least in order to ensure its own survival. The secular education of the Third Republic was fundamentally concerned with establishing in people's minds a proper understanding of the relationship between state and society, between government and citizen, freed of intermediary authorities such as the Church (but also, it would later emerge, such intermediaries as trade unions). In this respect, the Republicans of the 1880s were the direct descendants of the legislators of the 1790s, concerned to clear away everything that lay between the free citizen and the secular state — and determined to use compulsory education as a form of conscious social engineering to that end. It was because the Church owned and controlled so much of French education, and was both able and more than willing to exercise this advantage to counter the 'civic' education of the Republican ideal, that anti-clericalism became so substantially a matter of securing hegemony over primary education. And in *this* respect, at least, the conflict in the Var as elsewhere was by no means one-sided.

Although lay control of education within the Var was rather greater than in many other departments, it was far from being complete, and this was particularly so in the case of the education of girls. In 1873, only 22% of schoolboys were being educated in religious schools, whereas in the same year 41% of girls attending school were taught by nuns or attended Church-controlled schools. These figures had not diminished by so very much a decade later: in 1882 the Church still taught 17% of those local boys receiving a primary education, and 34% of the girls. The big break came in the next two decades. By 1908 the figures would be 11% and 18% respectively — figures which remained little changed until 1914.[13]

The Church's control over the education of the female population of the Var was thus considerable, even after the steep decline following the developments of the 1880s. In 1898 there were 130 primary schools in the arrondissement of Brignoles, of which 23 were private congregational establishments. Of these 23, no fewer than 17 were for girls. Not surprisingly, it was over the education of girls, especially in the wake of the introduction of compulsory primary education, that the major battle was waged. In a conservative community like Fréjus, there was fierce opposition in the early 1880s to the introduction of laïc education for girls — an opposition which was by no means ineffective. One resource in the conflict was municipal expenditure on education. The (Radical, then Socialist) municipality of Le Muy spent more on public education than did Fréjus, despite having a revenue only two-fifths that of the diocesan capital. The conservatives' control of the local authority kept public (and even private lay) education very backward in Fréjus, as in a number of the larger communes to the north, thereby ensuring the prolonged survival of the Church schools.[14]

Hence the importance of electoral struggles for control of the municipality — and with it the education budget. The government might oblige a commune to educate all its citizens, but it was limited in its ability to force the council to spend its money in such a way as to implement the law. Hence the significance of the electoral programme of the Carnoules Radicals in 1882, which consisted of a single proposal: if elected they would construct a municipal primary school (lay of course).[15]

Whether or not control of education *actually* mattered is of course a different question. I would certainly take the view that local political choices were not very much determined by the influence of the school; the village context, occupation, the economic conjuncture, dominant local opinion, were probably all more important, and conditioned political choice just as they helped fashion religious practice. But Radical politicians in particular chose to see control of the school as a vital political and ideological struggle. Was this in part because it was the only remaining issue on which the old republicanism could still present a united front? Without the Church question, there is little doubt but that the Radicals and socialists, to take just the leftward end of mid-century republicanism, would have moved apart even earlier than they did. For both sides in French public life, control of education provided a useful, perhaps vital, focus for divisions which were increasingly unreal — the real conflicts now appearing between the various classes which had once shared a common opposition to clerical reaction.

This is not to deny the reality and acuity of these matters in the eyes of participants. How else account for the anger and resentment incurred by the *curé* of Ste Anne d'Evenos when, in May 1882, he railed against the local *laïc* girls' school from his pulpit. It was not as if his view were unknown, nor was his audience likely to be swayed away from an anti-clericalism which they clearly did not espouse — their very presence in church bears witness, in the Var, that the priest was preaching to the converted. The extraordinary height of feeling on this issue also explains the sort of humourless pedantry which characterised a letter from a correspondent in St Julien in the *Petit Var* in 1889. Little girls in the village, he wrote, spend their leisure time in games which included a variant of hopscotch played to the accompaniment of the chant 'Un, deux, trois, Vive les Rois'. This he found disgusting. These children should be taught of the sacrifices which the Republic was making in order that they might be educated, and not kept enslaved in the ignorance which had surrounded their ancestors! This incident testifies to the character of the informant, perhaps, but it is not untypical of much correspondence in the local press at this period. It illustrates therefore an important point: the extent to which political and doctrinal issues of national importance — or taken to be such — were of real impact in the smallest and most remote communes. The interaction between national and local politics, which has been so much a theme of my account of Provençal life, is again manifested, overlain here with the bitterness which surrounded the Church and its works.[16]

The impact of the schools

No discussion of the coming of compulsory education in France would be complete without an initial consideration of the accompanying religious issue, but for the student of political change both imply the eventual question, how important *was* education in determining political choice? This question is all the more worth asking in that it was, as I have suggested, the consideration which lay behind the obsession of nineteenth-century radicals and their opponents with controlling the organisation and content of the school system.

Considerable attention has been paid in recent years to this question, and more specifically to the rôle played by a growing literacy in populations formerly unable to read and write. The apparently obvious assumption, that economic backwardness and illiteracy go hand in glove, and that together they provide an unfavourable context for radical politics, turns out to be false, on at least two counts. In the first place, areas of economic and social backwardness or isolation were often, as we have seen, regions where the influence of the Church was strong. But before the last third of the nineteenth century, the Church was the major source of whatever education was available to the poor. As a result, remote rural areas of strong religious practice were not necessarily regions of highest illiteracy.

Secondly, literacy and radicalisation or even politicisation seem not to have had a very marked historical relationship. This is partly for the reason just suggested — that literacy could often be a function of an active local Church; partly too, through the means by which politics and new ideas came to rural areas, means which did not necessarily exclude the illiterate.

The data in support of such arguments are extensive. Michel Vovelle, discussing the spread of *sociétés populaires* in Provence in the Year II, observes the 'paradoxale divergence du pourcentage des sociétés et du taux d'alphabétisation'. Paul Bois, in his study of the Sarthe, takes care to emphasise the high degree of *scolarisation* in the western fringe of the department — that area where religious practice and conservative politics were most pronounced. In modern Spain, Edward Malefakis has observed that illiteracy was at its highest in those areas where the Church's influence was least pronounced — and where a weak and unconcerned state did not provide compensating facilities. He also points out that these areas are the very ones where revolutionary sentiment would have been at its most strong in the Spanish Second Republic of the 1930s. In the Mâconnais, a high level of dechristianisation (by the standard measure of church attendance) was accompanied by a high incidence of illiteracy among nineteenth-century conscripts. Finally, there is the well-documented case of mountain communities; isolated, poor, usually firmly religious and politically conservative or uninterested, they demonstrate a remarkably consistent and high level of literacy, ever since records have been kept. There are special reasons for this, of course — the very isolation tends to an emphasis on education during the winter months, the children not being required for any more productive employment. But as in other instances cited above, we are seeing an example of the impossibility of establishing any sort of simple correlation between religious practice, educational standards and political options.[17]

Bearing this caveat in mind, what was the impact of education on the populations of the Var at this period? Taken on a departmental scale, it appears to have been rather successful. Whereas 6% of the conscript class of 1901 in France were *illettrés*, I calculate that only 3.6% of the 1899 conscripts from the Var (1901 figures not available) were unable to sign their name, although some of these could read, or so it was claimed. Of course the intra-departmental variations were considerable. Table 5 shows the official survey of the 1899 conscripts, arranged by canton. From this list it emerges that, by the end of the nineteenth century, most young men in the region could read and write, though few had achieved the distinction of passing the certificate of primary education. It is also clear that, although some isolated and poor regions such as Comps had a high degree of illiteracy, and some Radical or socialist areas such as Barjols had a higher than average percentage of literate conscripts, there is absolutely no correlation between literacy and political behaviour. The canton of Grimaud had a particularly high number of

Table 5 *Literacy of Var conscripts in 1899*

Canton	Totally illiterate	Able to read but not write
Draguignan	3.1%	0
Aups	0	0
Callas	3.4%	3.4%
Comps	7.1%	7.0%
Fayence	0	1.9%
Fréjus	2.8%	0
Grimaud	9.3%	0
Lorgues	7.7%	0
Le Luc	3.8%	1.9%
St Tropez	0	2.8%
Salernes	2.9%	0
Brignolès	4.9%	0
Barjols	2.0%	0
Besse	0	0
Cotignac	4.8%	0
Rians	6.7%	0
La Roquebrussanne	3.7%	0
St Maximin	1.7%	0
Tavernes	0	0
Toulon (1e)	3.6%	0.7%
Toulon (2e)	0.8%	0
Le Beausset	4.4%	0
Collobrières	0	0
Cuers	7.8%	0
Hyères	2.5%	2.5%
Ollioules	1.6%	0
La Seyne	3.1%	0
Solliès Pont	5.7%	0

Average percentage of children completing primary education in the Var

Arrondissement	1889	1899
Draguignan	61.0%	81.9%
Brignoles	72.5%	78.2%
Toulon (rural)	63.0%	68.5%
Toulon (city)	73.5%	82.2%

SOURCES: AN F^{17} 14270; *Le Petit Var* 30 December 1889.

illiterate conscripts — yet three of the five communes in the canton
(La Garde Freinet, Plan de la Tour and Grimaud itself) appear on my
list of Socialist strongholds. The canton of Cuers, first bastion of
Provençal socialism, had a degree of illiteracy well above both the
local and national average — but so did Lorgues, a traditionally
conservative canton and with a well-established religious community.[18]

Conscript data, while reliable, tell us only about the male youth
of a community, the beneficiaries of the Ferry legislation. What of
the older generation? We do have some evidence regarding the degree
of literacy of the adult population, but it is based on returns
completed by local officials, often mayors, and is thus of questionable
value. But for what it is worth, we learn that, for example, 54% of
the men and 38% of the women in Comps (the commune, not the
canton) could read and write in 1872. In Le Luc the figures were
37% and 31% respectively. In Les Salles they were lower still — in
1872 only 21% of the men and 10% of the women were deemed to
be literate. Comps of course was a very conservative area, Les Salles
and Le Luc bastions of socialism in later years. But in case we were
tempted to posit a link between literacy and conservatism, we are
reminded that in Tanneron, high on its hill in the east and never
noted for its left-wing sympathies, only 26% of the men could read
and write in 1872. As for the women, a mere 2.9% (12/404) were
classed as literate. We thus learn that the agglomerated communes of
the valley such as Le Luc show a much lower differential between
male and female literacy than do the villages of the hills (the figures
quoted are representative of many other examples), but that otherwise literacy is a poor guide to anything, certainly a hopeless guide to
political leanings, likely or actual.[19]

We can be fairly certain, however, that certain kinds of habitat and
certain sorts of economy were more or less favourable to educational
progress. Dispersed habitats posed a difficulty of transport. Of the 24
schools whose construction was deemed a matter of urgency in 1900,
nearly all were in regions of dispersed habitat. Thus there was no
school in the hamlet of Les Anges in the commune of Aiguines, a
region of very scattered population. Yet 217 of the 549 inhabitants
of Aiguines lived in or around Les Anges, and their school-age
children had to travel 14 kilometres each way to attend the nearest

primary school — which few of them did, understandably enough. Other areas affected in this way were La Martre in the north, the interior hamlets of the Maures, and many of the villages in the Seillans–Callian district in the east-central region of the department.

Economic considerations also counted. Unlike the Alpine villages with their winter period of inactivity, the communes of the lower Var especially had need of labour for much of the year. In Cuers it was rare for the children of the peasantry to attend school in late February on account of the exigencies of the olive harvest. The semi-skilled labour of a young adolescent in the *vinicole* areas was much too precious to waste on an education which in any case bore little relation either to his environment or his future concerns. Thus observers in Le Cannet, for example, a region which combined dispersed habitat with intense cultivation of the vine, affected to be quite astonished at the success of compulsory school attendance in their commune. Notwithstanding the distances involved and the interests of the domestic economy, children were attending school with 'remarkable' regularity.[20]

A further local barrier to the effective implementation of a modern system of education was that of language. As in many parts of France, a national system of *French* education was being imposed on a population whose natural form of communication was a local dialect or language. Thus Provençal came to be the language of the uneducated, French that of the young. This has a distorting effect on statistics of literacy, of course — many older men and women especially could read Provençal but not French; indeed not a few of them must have experienced great difficulty in simply handling questionnaires and official enquiries phrased in bureaucratic French. It is tempting to suppose that, after the initial difficulties experienced by the first generation of children who passed through the primary schools, a distinction developed between the young who spoke French and had access to new ideas, and the old, held back by their inability to communicate in the national language. In fact this appears not to have been the case: partly no doubt because some impact had been made by the primary schools which dated from the Guizot legislation of the 1830s, but more because, in the Var at least, the long-standing links to the outside world, through trade and communications, had reduced the importance of Provençal relative to

that of French, at least in the urban villages of the lower Var. The
language question was clearly much more important in every way in
the Languedoc or the Pyrenees, not to mention Alsace or Brittany.
In Provence the conflict over language was linked with an atavistic
and in any case largely literary movement associated with the poet
Mistral, and it is significant that as an issue it never surfaced in the
propaganda of the socialists – though there is some evidence that a
number of local socialist groups conversed in Provençal at their
meetings. This confirms my sense that socialists' supporters were
often older men, and casts further doubt on the hypothesis of a
division between Provençal traditionalists and politically advanced
francophones.[21]

Despite the dust which it aroused, then, the conflict over the
control of education, once reduced to a question of measuring the
results of the chief benefit of education at this level – literacy – seems
not to have been in the least bit crucial. The Var, like the Limousin,
offers no evidence of a relationship between literacy and political
tendencies, nor does the degree of education available appear to have
varied in any way as a function of political considerations. Just as the
clerically-dominated, *notable*-run communes of Comps in the north
or Fréjus on the coast varied sharply in the degree of literacy of the
youth emerging from their schools, so the politically-advanced town
of Le Luc boasted a Cercle founded in 1887 which would be active
in socialist politics, and half of whose 26 members signed their
adhesion with a mark. I cannot, then, accept Roger Price's conclusion
(admittedly in reference to an earlier period) that commerce, Protestantism, good communications and a relatively high degree of literacy
tend 'to a high level of political awareness'. Or, more accurately, I
can only find evidence of the first and third elements in such
tendencies in Provence at least. The fact that the Var was traditionally
an area of relatively high illiteracy seems in no way to have reduced
its various forms of political awareness; the northern Var certainly
conforms to a limited type – neither Provençal nor genuinely Alpine,
but a 'société Alpine dégradée', lacking the communal solidarity and
the traditions of education of the true Alpine community, but also
bereft of the compensating sociability of the bourgs down
below. But we have seen that there are exceptions even here –
and in any case a linear relationship (isolation – clerical

hegemony — low literacy — conservative politics) has little heuristic value without evidence of its inverse in the valleys. And such evidence is not forthcoming.[22]

Of course, there is more to education than mere literacy. Also at issue was the content of what was being offered to children by way of instruction, irrespective of whether or not they could read it for themselves. Hence such incidents as the outburst by the *curé* of Vins in 1880 against the textbook in use at the local primary school, the *Eléments d'éducation civique et morale*, and his warning to parents to burn it and withdraw their children from any school where it was in use. The debate over the content of the educational syllabus raged throughout this period, and it was a real conflict, concerning as it did the means by which competing ruling élites strove to impose their ideological domination upon a newly-educated and socialised mass electorate.[23]

But such issues are not strictly my concern. They are, after all, perennial sources of conflict, and in a rather changed guise they informed much of the educational dispute in France during the 1960s. I am more concerned with a narrower question, concerning the ways by which a political doctrine takes root in the consciousness and political habits of a given region and social class. Since, clearly, there was no question of socialism being presented as a dominant ideology, in the schools or from the pulpit, what mattered were less formal, more voluntaristic forms of 'indoctrination'. Thus my interest in the growth of compulsory primary education in France lies in the extent to which it gave to peasants the tools required for access to modern political communications. But the attainment of literacy appears in itself not to have been a significant prerequisite for radical politicisation. How, then, did the rural populations of the Var gain access to modern ideas? By what means did they absorb the doctrines which would move them in a particular political direction?

Artisans, peasants and politics

For most of human history, myths, popular tales and the like have been transmitted orally. The advent of the printing press changed little, since access to the printed word, both in terms of availability and comprehension, remained the privilege of a tiny minority of even the most advanced societies. It was through the long fireside sessions of the winter, therefore, that peasant women passed on old stories and popular wisdom to their children and grandchildren, and by means of informal social intercourse in fields and village squares that men acquainted themselves and one another with occupational skills and such news as filtered through to their remote communities.

The coming of a modern system of education did not bring about any substantial or immediate changes. Literacy, measured by the minimum standards which were applied in the early years of the primary school, did little to ensure a person's ability to read a newspaper, much less a book. By the middle of the nineteenth century, it is true, the availability of popular literature was much expanded, and in France especially there was quite an active trade in popular almanacs, simple novels and (where permitted) political pamphlets. Nevertheless, these, particularly the last, were never read or even seen by the vast majority of the population. Their sales were understandably greater in artisanal towns and (to a lesser degree) industrial cities; not so much because of any higher level of literacy, particularly in the cities, but rather through a greater degree of opportunity. Modern forms of lighting took a long time to reach the private dwellings of the remote countryside — gas lighting was comparatively unknown in many mountain areas of France even at the very end of the nineteenth century, and as for electricity, it would not reach even some quite accessible parts of the country until the last years of the Third Republic.[24]

And yet, there is little doubt but that much modern thinking, suitably popularised, was entering the consciousness of the peasantry in some parts of France; Provence is a notable example. The first explanation for this relates to earlier observations concerning sociability. It was the very proximity to one another and to the outside world which established for the populations of the Var, from quite an early date, their links with political propaganda and the like.

The link between a peasantry 'vivant urbain' and modern ideas and movements of protest was the café, or in earlier years the *chambrée*, where many, often a majority, of the local working population would meet, sometimes in lunch-breaks, usually in the evenings and on Sundays, to drink and talk. But not just to drink and talk. A centrepiece of many such gatherings was the reading aloud by one of their number of the newspaper to which the *patron*, or perhaps a prominent (and slightly wealthier) member of the society subscribed. Such readings were often lengthy affairs, whole articles being read out with care, often accompanied by a commentary from the reader, his audience or both. Few of the assembled number could have afforded to subscribe to the journal in question, nor would they have thought of so doing. The chances were high that they would have had difficulty in making sense of much of the French (the commentary not infrequently took the form of a translation), but in any case such things were traditionally and best done in a group. Private reading was (and of course remains) an essentially unsocial activity and thus ran counter to the dominant habits of the Provençal community.

The newspaper, and the arguments which accompanied and followed its public perusal, was thus in some sense the 'collective organiser' of populations which it helped to politicise. The rôle is well documented for such periods of rapid and acute political development in the provinces — such as the Second Republic. But the increased prominence of the café, and the liberty of expression and of the press enjoyed after 1880, meant that the rôle of public readings, far from diminishing, probably increased, at least until the early twentieth century.[25]

At this point we encounter a fascinating and tricky problem. *Who* were these readers? *Their* literacy and knowledge, the respect which their opinions earned for them, surely made them vital intermediaries between national politics, strange and new doctrines and theories, and the community of which they were a part but which they also stood just a little outside. One theory is that this vital rôle in the politicisation of the peasantry was performed by rural artisans. In much of France the period 1840—80 had seen the decline in status and means of the traditional artisan. In many trades and skills, the artisan had retained the form of his work — cottage or workshop rather than modern factory — but had seen it deprived of much of its content. He was now not very different from the cottage worker, taking on out-work from merchants or manufacturers, specialising in part of a given product rather than in the manufacture of the whole item, paid by the piece and often short of work for periods of the year. Alternatively his skills might have been preserved, but his income diminished by direct competition from large-scale urban manufacture, in France or abroad. In either case, his reaction might plausibly have been to turn to various forms of social protest — of which cooperation was a favourite — and, in rural areas, to try and carry with him the surrounding peasantry.

Thus Maurice Agulhon suggests that whereas in the early nineteenth century artisan leadership of radical movements was confined to the small communes of hills and forests, while the liberal bourgeoisie dominated political protest in lower Provence, by the later years the village bourgeoisie having disappeared, the artisanat played the central rôle in the political conflicts of the early Third Republic. But this view of the matter has its own problems. We know that in many of the most radicalised villages the artisanat itself was a disappearing class; what is more, many rural artisans (shoemakers, carpenters, cork-workers, even tanners and millers) might equally be described as part-time peasants. Their leadership, if such it was, thus came in some sense as much from within the peasant community as from an educated and distinct class of skilled craftsmen. In rural areas, particularly in Provence where rural occupation and urban habitat overlap so much, the occupational distinctions are often without much meaning.[26]

Agulhon would seem to be inferring for the later period a pattern of social relations which really only fits a slightly earlier era. In 1851 there is absolutely no doubt but that artisans both took the lead and formed a substantial part of the following in the Montagnard movement of that year. In the arrests which followed the insurrection in the Var, artisans (52.6%) were disproportionately over-represented, just as the local bourgeoisie were notable for their absence (4.9%). Even allowing for selective arresting by the authorities, these are relevant data. Similarly, Bezucha's observation of a high level of literacy among the *canuts* of Lyon in the 1830s is obviously important — in artisanal circles within cities such as Lyon there was a high degree of participation and educated political awareness, for example among the protesting silk-workers, and in these early modern revolts the skilled artisanat played a central rôle.[27]

But in later years the pattern is rather different. It was only the most economically backward or isolated communities which appear to have been dependent upon leadership coming 'down' to them from above – either in the form of advice and direction from the local wise-men in Andalusia, or from the distinctly better educated and more socially independent blacksmiths or masons of the Alps and the Limousin. By the 1880s the artisan was the vital political link only in the most archaic and closed economies, where the peasantry by themselves lacked means and will to mobilise collectively. In the open communities of lower Provence, the peasantry seem not to have needed such leadership by the end of the nineteenth century – doubtless in part because it was no longer readily available. Thus the complex artisanal base of the population of Lorgues seems to have had no discernible radicalising effect on the surrounding peasantry, while the Cercle des Travailleurs in Cuers in 1876 was already 83% (33/40) peasant.[28]

This is not to deny that the man reading the newspaper in a village café may very well have been at one time a skilled artisan of some kind – perhaps still was. In the same way, the peasantry of the Beaujolais often met and held their discussions in the local forge – with the surprising result that blacksmiths emerged frequently at the head of political movements in the region, bonapartist and republican alike. But herein lies the crucial point. Because of their natural advantages and status, artisans not infrequently served as the focus for political life in many rural communities – but the precise direction in which they led their peasant following was not thereby determined. The political prominence of the artisan, that is to say, was not a function of what he had to say, but of who he was and what he did. It was circumstances and political developments in a wider sphere which brought the peasantry to protest movements, to radical clubs and socialist groups. That we often then find prominent within these organisations the informal dominance of one or more local tradesmen or master craftsmen is a result of the advantage they enjoyed in being able to convey news to the illiterate and spread ideas rapidly among their colleagues in the shop. But the presence of a peasant audience for what they had to say was only very indirectly a result of their own achievements. In the Limousin, rural artisans played an important politicising rôle – but they were also the major source of recruits into the Church.[29]

Thus, in sum, the informal leaders of village discussions and political meetings were frequently men whose primary occupation set them apart from their audience in respect of their work and their education. But what they actually said and advocated in these meetings was almost always a reflection of the interests and concerns of their (peasant) audience. I shall consider this point in more detail in Chapter 9. But it is worth noting here that in Flayosc, for example, where there was a heavy concentration of *cordonniers*, masters and employees, the socialist Cercle in 1891 was understandably dominated by their presence (the president was a young man — aged 26 — and skilled: a cutter). But the peasant members of the society seem not to have been at any kind of a disadvantage thereby, and the emphasis on cooperation, attacks on high food prices, and sympathy for collective solutions to problems were areas of wide mutual agreement. In so far as artisans led and peasants followed, this must only be construed in the purely formal and organisational sense — and even there it was of limited applicability. So far as the content of such gatherings was concerned, the socialism of the Var was no less a reflection of the peasantry's interests and preoccupations for being occasionally refracted through an artisanal prism.[30]

In this way, then, education and its by-products were important sources of friction within the village community during these years. But the direct link between peasant interest and political literature and ideas was very little affected by the fact that educational reforms were slow to have much impact upon the rural community. To suggest otherwise is to diminish the independence and autonomy of rural society. Just as in the early nineteenth century the peasantry had reacted in atavistic ways for reasons and from fears of their own, acknowledging and needing the leadership of artisans and bourgeois to strengthen the cohesion of inherently disparate rural protests, so in the economic crisis of the last years of the century the Provençal farmers developed their own awareness of a necessity for radical change, their own resentment at their reduced income and prospects. They, too, required an artisanat which could serve as a source of information and education and sometimes of organisation. But they imposed their own needs upon the shoemakers, masons, carpenters and blacksmiths in their villages, making demands upon them, insisting that they subscribe to a particular journal or explain a particular issue, rather than responding passively to the views of the artisans. Nor is this very surprising — by the 1880s many rural artisans had departed, and those who remained were much impoverished, reduced in professional status and totally dependent upon the local community, whose problems they thus shared to the full. They spoke much of the Church, of education, of cooperation and of the need for legislation in various fields. But their audience filtered out the traditional, Radical dogma, taking heed instead of the increasing social element which was entering such political debate. In this way one might almost suggest that, the traditional leadership and access to ideas of the small-town artisan notwithstanding, it was the peasantry which brought the latter to socialism, and not the other way round.

8

Feuds and personalities

All studies of political behaviour are bedevilled by a psephological variant of the Uncertainty Principle. Even where the investigator is in a position to ask of the voter the reasons for his or her choice, the response can at best only approximate to an accurate account of what motivated a particular choice in a given situation. The supposition that people make political choices on the basis of rational (and conscious) criteria remains far from proven. Nor should the investigator assume that the voter shares the specialist's interest in politics and political behaviour. Few questionnaires have been devised which are capable of taking account of political allegiance based on tradition, ignorance, passing sentiments, sudden impulses, etc. And there remains always the uneasy sense that the voter who bases his choice on irrational, self-serving or thoroughly empirical considerations may actually have a more accurate perception of the nature of politics than has the historian or political scientist, with his concern to identify doctrines, programmes, ideological distinctions.

These matters are sufficiently complicated for the political behaviour of the modern urban electorate in countries such as England where ideological factors in politics are fewer in number, or at least where they are much blurred. The problem of accounting for political choice in regions of acute doctrinal conflict, such as Latin Europe, is somewhat more complex. Even harder to assess, of course, is the political behaviour of men in pre-industrial or largely agricultural societies, where the chasm between local interest and national politics may be assumed to be all the greater.

One view of the matter is that in practice political ideas, divisions which seem so distinct and significant in the city, are of little real consequence in the life of the peasant. The latter has his own concerns, his own local squabbles, his own interests, which rarely if ever meet those of the politicians who are appealing for his vote. Where, for reasons of their own, urban politicians introduce the countryman or villager into the *polis* through the granting of universal manhood suffrage, they are in effect superimposing their own concerns on those of the rural community, which remain unchanged thereby for many years to come. Thus, it follows, we can only truly grasp the bases of rural political life by ignoring the formal ideological divisions which emerge in village voting and by seeking behind them the true, apolitical issues which move the village voter; issues of a traditional nature (local feuds, family conflicts), of an economic nature (common lands, disputes between competing artisans, etc.), or of a personal nature (support for a prominent local personality, whatever his political colour). It is the argument of this book that, while these matters were clearly of real importance to the peasantry of Provence, they did not prevent a large number of men from making political choices which appear substantially to have been responses to contemporary stimuli, among which political propaganda and ideology were a far from negligible element. In practice, it seems, local and national politics were not separate and distinct areas but had become, in the first generation of the Third Republic, almost indistinguishable. To see how this was the case, it is necessary to devote some space to a consideration of the nature of local issues and conflicts.

Feuds and conflicts

All communities form 'clans', divisions, both within themselves and between one small community and another. To say this is by no means to deny the importance of politics in the affairs of the inhabitants of such villages or towns. Quite the reverse — political divisions serve as an important means of identifying one group from another; what is of particular interest in France after 1870 is the extent to which overtly political differences came to be accepted as a faithful representation of divided interests which had, in more repressive times, expressed themselves in less obviously ideological or political terms.

The most obvious form of local conflict in Provence was that between communes — usually between communes within easy reach of one another. A famous example is that of the rivalry between Le Luc and Le Cannet. The former was already a town of particular prominence through its precocious association with religious non-conformity. It had been sacked by the Catholics during the Wars of Religion, and the Edict of Nantes gave its Protestant community special privileges (unique in the Var) in the seventeenth century. Already thereby distinguished from the surrounding communes, it seems first to have come into open conflict with its nearest neighbour, the smaller community of Le Cannet, during the Revolutionary Terror, when the Cannetois took in and sheltered the *curé* of Le Luc who had been chased from his parish by the local *sans-culottes*.

This incident was, of course, less a cause for conflict than clear evidence of existing antagonisms, but it is from the Revolution that one can most easily date the close relationship between village feud and political divergence. Le Luc, despite its location on a main thoroughfare, became a prominent, later a dominant centre of regional Radicalism (the traditional meeting to choose Radical election candidates was always held there); it also emerged as a stronghold of the local socialist movement from the 1890s. Le Cannet, on the other hand, was consistently conservative, a characteristic doubtless aided by its very dispersed character – the commune was spread out all across the stony plain which runs down from the Maures to the central valley. It even appears on my list of consistently conservative communes (those which *never* gave Radicals or Socialists even a large minority of their votes), unique in the central area. Moreover, the conflict between the two communities was little abated even by the later 1880s. In 1886 there was much bitter resentment in Le Cannet at the refusal of the municipality of Le Luc to contribute part of the cost of constructing a railway station at Le Cannet (from which both communes must benefit). It is significant that, by this time, the Cannetois found it politic to express their anger in modern terms: they accused the 'démocrates' of Le Luc of having been 'misled' by the monarchist element in their commune![1]

Such inter-village rivalry abounded in the Var. Another example was the old dislike between Cuers and Pierrefeu, some 6 kilometres apart on either side of the valley leading north from Toulon (Le Luc and Le Cannet were separated by no more than 3 kilometres of main highway). The Cuersois were reported to have 'molested and condemned' the men of Pierrefeu from time out of mind, and here too the origin is likely to have been religion (or rather, the original symptom of the rivalry was religious conflict; the cause is a different question – rival producers of wine for the medieval coastal market?). The population of Pierrefeu was certainly far more *pratiquante* than that of radical and secular Cuers; Pierrefeu was also just a little more remote from communications and trade than was Cuers, a cause for resentment even today. In any event, the Third Republic saw a feud which was commonly expressed in terms of the character defects associated with the other community translated into marked political divergences: Pierrefeu did show a propensity for mild Radicalism, but never more, while Cuers was the initial centre of regional socialism.[2]

This form of very ancient dislike between neighbouring communities often took the form of a heightened rivalry over more immediate issues in the last years of the nineteenth century. The construction of a railway station refuelled the Le Luc–Le Cannet dislike. Similar issues provoked similar clashes elsewhere. St Raphael, a town which had overtaken Fréjus in size and importance by the end of the century (in 1846 the population of Fréjus was three times that of St Raphael; by 1906 it was only 85% of that of the coastal resort) resented the fact that the old Roman town still conserved the status of *chef-lieu* of the canton, and with it certain privileges. One of these was the provision of gas to the rest of the canton, and in 1881 a storm blew up over the refusal of the municipality of Fréjus to provide gas to the casino at St Raphael – the centrepiece of its profitable tourist trade.

Similarly, the cantonal elections of 1883 in Rians were dominated by the demand of Ginasservis that it be considered as a future cantonal capital, in replacement of Rians. In terms of size this was ridiculous (in 1886 the population of Rians was 2391, that of Ginasservis 791), but Ginasservis was better placed to serve the other four communes of the canton, and thus received their backing. Nothing came of the conflict, in that Rians remained the cantonal *chef-lieu*, but by the early twentieth century Ginasservis and three of the other four communes were firmly established as Socialist electoral strongholds, while Rians oscillated between Radicalism and moderate Republicanism.[3]

Issues such as these, of real economic consequence in the locality (the cantonal capital could be assured not only of better trade for its shops, inns and cafés, but also of more sympathetic consideration

for its special needs and interests), probably superseded older disputes — unless they came to reinforce them, as with the station at
Le Cannet. Typical was the case of the millers and bakers of Salernes,
who were being squeezed out of the market at Aups where they had
long been accustomed to purchase their stocks of wheat. From 1891
they resolved to 'look elsewhere'; in practice, what was happening
was that Salernes, a large and thriving town, was progressively
replacing Aups, a shrinking community, as the market centre for
north-central Var, and that the economy of Aups could no longer
support its traditional rôle as provider for the whole region. But the
symptoms of this development were economic conflicts which, again,
emerged eventually as political divisions — Salernes becoming a
stronghold of the socialists, Aups losing its old standing as a centre of
political radicalism, a rôle which it had performed most notably
during the 1851 insurrection.[4]

Thus both ancient rivalries and more modern conflicts of interest
came to be expressed in terms of political divisions between communities. To this extent, it is true, traditional local issues remained
dominant in men's thinking — or, more precisely, remained dominant
to the degree to which they coincided with changing needs and
interests. Where no new bone of contention was available, the old
issues not infrequently subsided. Conversely, new issues could easily
replace old allegiances where the two conflicted. Thus when Pierrefeu
and Brignoles were in contention for the (highly profitable) construction of a new asylum in the region, in 1881, the traditionally conservative and clerical municipality of Pierrefeu was not above attacking
Brignoles as 'reactionary and monarchist' — and hence unsuited to a
republican institution like a lunatic asylum.[5]

Rivalries between adjacent villages were common, but even more
rooted in the rural community were rivalries and feuds within the
village itself. The origins of this sort of intra-communal feuding are
extremely difficult to locate. On the one hand it may be a conflict
between two dominant local families which has its roots in ancient
disputes over property or local pre-eminence; on the other hand rival
factions may date back only a few years, to some quite recent dispute
over grazing rights, or even to commercial rivalry between competing
cafetiers or bakers. On the whole it was rare for Provence to offer
examples of the sort of clan feud which so characterises certain Italian

(or Corsican) regions. Most of the local feeling of this kind in Provence can usually be traced, if not to some first cause, then at least to a fairly recent focus of conflict.

Moreover, conflicts *within* the village nearly always took on some political colour, in a way that was less immediately true of disputes *between* villages. They can almost be reduced, in many cases, to battles between 'ins' and 'outs', as determined by control of the local municipal council. Accusations of 'clerical' or 'reactionary' were usually voiced by those in the political wilderness against those who had gained a position of power, however temporary. It was much rarer, incidentally, for the accusation of 'collectivist' or 'revolutionary' to be levelled against those in office, however unpopular their actions. This reflects, of course, after 1877, the dominant ethos of the Republic — the right being a more acceptable and easily-labelled threat — and also the extent to which, in much of this area, only accusations of acute conservatism carried the appropriate opprobrium. The fact that the mayor or council in question was (usually) as republican as its accusers does not lessen the political significance of the labels; through consistent use of such ticketing, men came to identify unpopular local actions with a particular position in national affairs. Within a very brief span of time they would come to reverse the process, and give local power to men of the appropriate national political identification.

Such developments took a variety of forms. During the boom years of the mid-nineteenth century, but also continuing into the later period, a number of the villages of the Var, perched high on their hillsides, came to be duplicated by a 'replacement' community, built on a lower, more accessible site, sometimes a few hundred metres from the original settlement. When this happened the *mairie*, and with it the focus of the commune, usually shifted as well. Simultaneously with the local consequences — resentment on the part of the upper villagers at the loss of their central place and importance to the new commune below — came certain national overtones: on more than one occasion the mayor of the old commune (associated, say, with the Moral Order of the 1870s) would be opposed by a new municipality representing the 'republican' interest, which came to be linked to the new settlement, the beneficiary of a new road, perhaps a railway station, almost certainly a primary school, all achievements

of the Republic. This national political colouring would again be
related back to local issues because of the profits accruing from the
development of the new site — to builders in particular, often friends
of the new council, if not members of it themselves.

Local power meant local prerogatives, such as the appointment of
local officials. When the municipality of Puget-Ville in 1891 appointed
a new *garde-champêtre*, friends of the unsuccessful candidate for the
post accused the council of favouring a known reactionary over a
true republican. By 1891 this sort of thing was no longer the burning
issue it had been a decade earlier — which makes it all the more
interesting that such an ostensibly non-political appointment should
have been most easily attacked in those particular terms. The
politique du clocher of French village life thrived no less for being
quite inextricably attached to wider political categories. When the
new (conservative) municipality of Pierrefeu failed to celebrate 14
July in the appropriate fashion in 1884, partisans of its (republican)
predecessor felt strongly enough to get their heads broken in a public
riot over the matter. There is an element of the *Clochemerle*, here,
surely, but not just that.[6]

Conflicts between 'ins' and 'outs' in the genuinely local, apolitical
sense were more commonly confined to the smallest and most isolated villages, where real political debate was largely absent. In Plan
d'Aups, public life since 1789 had been dominated by the rivalry
between the Roubaud and the Toulon families. Of the twelve men
who had held the post of mayor in the commune between 1790 and
1897, five had been drawn from these two clans, and most of the
others had been mere ciphers for the family rivalry. There was a
limited sense of social conflict in that the Roubauds were *propriétaires*, the Toulons *cultivateurs*, but this had come to mean
little by the 1880s and in no sense did the formal content of their
'programmes' reflect any true clash of interests.

This sort of family in-fighting was a dominant characteristic of
village life in a number of areas; the commune of Correns, later
firmly socialist, was divided between the Arbaud and Paul families,
who between them furnished ten of the fifteen mayors between 1790
and 1900. But in most cases such family feuds indicated the absence of
that sort of political and social variety which in its decline would later
lead to the successful implantation of left-wing politics. It was

communes such as La Martre or La Bastide which were dominated by squabbles between competing (and prosperous) *notables*, not the more complex and larger bourgs lower down. When Sénéquier observes that all political life in late-nineteenth-century La Garde Freinet was essentially a quarrel between two unchanging clans, notwithstanding changes in the labels and issues to which they attached themselves, he is giving insufficient recognition to the reality of such labels and issues for many of the men who attached themselves to one or other party.[7]

This in fact is the principal difficulty about identifying timeless and apparently unchanging feuds, either between or within villages. As with an excessive emphasis upon religion as a context for French political disputes, or upon sociability as a basis for the politics of southern France, such an approach explains nothing — by denying the reality of that which it should be investigating, and by over-emphasising continuity at the expense of any sense of change. Even the most backward and isolated societies experience change at certain periods — and Provence was neither backward nor especially isolated, for all that it was a region of peasants and small towns and villages. The parish-pump politics could become the politics of the political pamphlet without in the least losing their local bite. But to postulate that all labels are simply window-dressing for ultimately timeless divisions, built into the very structure of the community, is to underestimate both the political intelligence of the peasantry and also of course the very crisis in the structure of the village community which was producing the adoption of political labels such as socialism.

The concept of the unchanging political division is not one imposed uniquely upon the village. Historians have used it frequently as a context for an understanding of French political life as a whole — the Party of Movement, the Party of Order, and so forth. These categories are not without their value — in a country where Clemenceau could insist that the Revolution was a bloc which you either accept or reject, men could be forgiven for taking him at his word and historians for believing that his views represented the way things actually were. But Clemenceau was a consummate politician no less than a historical moralist, and his thesis was designed to demonstrate that all republicans should identify with one another against *all* reactionaires; a theory which, at the time of its espousal, would be of most advantage to Clemenceau's own Radicals, whose programme and identity depended substantially upon the preservation of such a state of affairs. Not surprisingly, then, it was the Radicals in the Var who most faithfully incarnated and perpetuated the sort of local feuds and disputes that I have been considering. Other parties, notably the socialists, tended to move away from these issues — and the fact that they could do so and still carry their support with them tends to the conclusion that, families, feuds, traditions notwithstanding, politics in Provence had a character which went beyond that of mere camouflage for historical village schisms. We can see this a little better by turning now to a consideration of the importance of personalities in local political affairs.

The rôle of the individual

The view of rural and village life which ascribes political choice to local or traditional divisions of a largely non-political nature naturally places considerable emphasis upon the importance of individual personalities in such matters. Men are elected, one might argue, less for what they say than for who they are, and this will be no less valid for a personality of the left than for the prominent *notable* of the centre or right. Roger Price has suggested that, for the earlier years of the nineteenth century, the importance of the local bourgeois *notables* was a consequence of the difficulty of finding local men with the leisure, education and confidence to serve either as representatives or as appointed officials. Thus, he suggests, the successful politician in the countryside had of necessity to be a well-known personality, 'further evidence of the political immaturity of this newly enfranchised mass electorate'.[8]

Leaving aside the question of whether the election of prominent personalities is prima facie evidence of political immaturity, this view has much to commend it. Some forty years later, peasants were still often dependent upon the rural artisan (though no longer the rural bourgeois) for their political education; and there is no doubt that, well into the twentieth century, mere economic considerations alone would ensure that elected representatives were usually men of greater means than their electorate — as well as being somewhat older, retirement conferring the added advantage of leisure. However, the question here is not so much whether the political 'class' in France was drawn, even after the advent of universal suffrage, from a different stratum from that of its electors; of more immediate interest is to know whether individual political aspirants were supported less for their party affiliation or political ideas than for their personal status. Was it important that they be local men? Did their occupation or local function help determine electors' choices irrespective of political labels?

There is considerable evidence in support of such a view. Dupeux, in his study of the Loir-et-Cher, notes that much of the socialist organisation in that department collapsed when Rozier departed for Paris in 1898; implicit in this is the suggestion that it was the man rather than his ideas or his (very insecurely founded) organisation who had brought local electors and militants to the socialist fold. In the Var, too, the Socialist Section in St Tropez collapsed in 1904 when its secretary, Romani, had to leave the area. Nor, of course, was the importance of individual persons confined to the left; education inspectors in Ollières in 1878 remarked upon the 'immense influence' exercised in the region by the Marquis de Félix (a rare case, for the Var, of noble influence), and their successors in 1899 were at pains to insist that, in the arrondissement of Brignoles at least, too much should not be made of the 'querelles de parti qui, dans nos villages, sont le plus souvent des querelles de personnes'. However, we should be wary of accepting at face value testimony from the official representatives of the militant Republic. In this instance, for example, the context of the quotation was a paean of praise to primary-school teachers for avoiding politics, while remaining staunchly republican. Like Clemenceau, the government inspectors were at pains to deny that quarrels *between* republicans (which by 1899 meant very often differences of opinion between Radicals and socialists) could ever be issues of substance.[9]

Nevertheless, there is something here. The votes received by Vincent, the socialist candidate in the Draguignan arrondissement in 1893, were definitely in some part a function of his standing as mayor of Flayosc. He swept the board in his own commune, and also did especially well in communes where his occupation (*ouvrier cordonnier*) made him a sympathetic candidate to others of that ilk. Similarly,

Cluseret, the ex-communard who was first elected in 1888 and held on to his seat in the Toulon hinterland until his death, maintained his support in the face of concerted socialist *and* Radical opposition from 1890 onwards. Police reports characterise him as an excellent speaker, who placed much emphasis on the concerns of his electors and was actually financed by contributions from many of his rural electors.[10]

Initial electoral success, too, was a great help in later campaigns. Octave Vigne, later the Socialist deputy for the Brignoles arrondissement from 1902 until the war, first established himself by winning the *conseil général* seat for the canton of Cotignac in 1895. Collomp, too, later a Socialist candidate at national elections, first won his electoral spurs as the *conseiller général* for the canton of Le Luc. Initially, in 1898, he did well only in the leftist-inclined communes of Les Mayons and Le Luc itself. By the outbreak of the war, his status as established incumbent had secured for him overwhelming majorities at cantonal elections even in otherwise conservative Le Cannet and Vidauban. Conversely, the electoral defeats of Prosper Ferrero at the legislative elections were ascribed by the authorities to the diminution of his influence consequent upon his failure to conserve his seats on cantonal and municipal councils in the preceding years.[11]

However, this shows only that the activities and influence of one man could be very important, and that the later political success of a given politician often depended upon his initial roots in local political affairs. We have still to establish a rather different issue: how important was it that the politician in question be a *local* man? Here, surely, lies the nub of the matter. If a political party could 'parachute' a candidate into a region and establish him there, it suggests, if the operation was repeated often enough, that the electors were less concerned with *who* the stranger was than with what he was offering them. Conversely, persistent reliance on local men would suggest that it is at least probable that their very identification with the area played an important part in their success.

In this context, Radicals and socialists show very different patterns of behaviour. Many successful local Radical politicians were local men. In 1876, three of the four victorious Radicals in the legislative elections of that year were local men. Paul Cotte, then aged 51, was born in Salernes; Augustin Daumas, 50, was a native of Toulon; Vincent Allègre, 41, was from Six Fours. Nor did the pattern alter very much in later years. Auguste Maurel, who was elected on a Radical ticket in 1881, aged 40, was born in Toulon, while Jean-Baptiste Abel, elected in 1893 at the age of 30, was also a native of that city. Louis Martin, who won Cluseret's old seat for the Radicals in 1902 and 1906, was born in Puget-Ville in 1859. Of successful local Radicals, only Rousse, Clemenceau and Jourdan were born outside the Var, and Jourdan, a native of Bastia (Corsica) was in any case not properly a Radical, standing as he did against Clemenceau in 1893.

While these men undoubtedly laid emphasis upon their local origins, these were only of marginal importance in getting them elected. Thus Cotte, in 1876, received the support of 71% of the electorate of the arrondissement of Draguignan, but in his home town of Salernes he secured only 57.4% (537 votes out of 936 electors); in the other two communes of the canton, Villecroze and Tourtour, he did even worse, securing 45.7% and 24.8% of the votes respectively.

There was little enough to choose between Radical and socialist candidates at legislative elections in most respects. Socialists, like Radicals, were normally in their forties when first elected to national bodies, and in their occupations they shared the Radical propensity for the law (Allard was a lawyer, just like Maurel, Jourdan, Abel and Martin) and for journalism. But in one respect the difference leaps to the eye: socialists were not local men. Maurice Allard was born in the Indre-et-Loire, Prosper Ferrero in Marseille, Gustave Fourment, the SFIO Federation Secretary, in Montpellier, Pierre Renaudel in Normandy, Gustave Cluseret (who was first elected at the age of 55) in Paris. Even Auguste Berthon, who defeated the official SFIO candidate in Toulon on a 'renegade' socialist ticket, was not a local man, but came from Valence in the Drôme.[12]

This distinction seems rather important. Whereas the Radical electorate might plausibly be said to be backing a man they knew well, and who had well-established local connections, those who voted for a socialist were in nearly every case voting, so to speak, for the party, not the person. The exception, of course, is Cluseret, and to a lesser degree Berthon. But Cluseret was *originally* elected as an official socialist, a Parisian and ex-communard. His personal achievement in thenceforth establishing for himself a fief is beyond doubt. But he was very much an exception in this respect — aided no doubt by the peculiarities of Toulonnais politics, which also help explain the success of both Berthon and another unofficial socialist, Charlois, in defeating the official candidate, Claude, in 1914. Elsewhere in the department the SFIO candidature seems always to have withstood changes of personnel — as when Allard, for health reasons, gave way to Fourment in the arrondissement of Draguignan with no visible effect on the socialist electorate.

The weakness of the left, and in particular of the socialists, in the mountain communes confirms this view. In the upper Var as in the mountains to the north, personal political influence, of whatever provenance, was always much more important. Isolation had much to do with this, of course, as did the property structure of many high regions, which favoured the survival of a dominant landowning class in regions of tiny smallholders and widespread sharecropping and indebted tenantry. Very few individual men of the left, however personally popular and well established in their locality, were able to achieve political domination in such circumstances.[13] Even Radicals suffered, despite the virtual absence of organisational factors in their electoral victories. But in areas where such barriers had fallen, or had never really existed, the distinction between Radical personalities and socialist politicians appears to have been quite marked. There were very few men who, like Octave Vigne, were able to make the jump from the one status to the other. As for local socialists such as Vincent, they drop from prominence after 1898, evidence in itself of the growing importance of the party organisation at the expense of individual clientèles. Whatever the later success of men like Allard or Renaudel, their initial standing in the arrondissement into which they had been 'dropped' was that of representative of a particular political movement and its programme and ideals.

We are thus led to two distinct conclusions. The first concerns the general nature of political life in the countryside. It is clear that within the Var, as in French rural society generally, the importance of local traditions, local feuds, local men varied by area and over time. Communities that were more isolated, often autarkic, usually less complex in their economic structure and social relations, were much slower to adapt to modern, urban politics. Whatever labels might be attached to them from the outside, their local representatives continued to be men whose prominence came from their local standing and the influence they continued to exercise in local affairs. Consequently, their personalities, and the traditional social relationships which they and their families represented, remained the cardinal feature of local political divisions; hence the fundamentally conservative nature of the political choices, if that is the word, made by the inhabitants of such regions.

Other communities, more open to outside influence, more socially complex and thus less conditioned to respect and obey traditional authorities, were certainly not lacking in feuds and rivalries, in personal and inter-group quarrels. But these divisions had of necessity to adapt themselves to the modern images of conflict and choice which the nineteenth century was introducing into the countryside, just as, in an earlier period, they had been adapted to the divisions which centred upon the authority of the Church. It is probably true that acute interest in politics was only aroused at times of crisis — and only then during crises which directly affected the community; the Dreyfus affair caused little stir in the communes of the Var, but the association of the ruling Radical Party with the government which presided over the crisis of *vinicole* overproduction in 1907 would prove lethal to the already declining influence of the Radicals in the region.

Nevertheless, while it required a crisis (whether the prolonged economic slump of the 1880s and 1890s or the acute difficulties of 1907) to mobilise the local population, once aroused they would have little apparent difficulty in relating their own problems to the arguments of competing political factions. And in such circumstances, the influence which a popular or powerful local personality could exercise was much reduced. Whereas that influence was accepted in less troubled times, its survival in the difficult years was very much a function of the political and economic solutions which the individual could propose. Not even Clemenceau's huge popular base in the Var could withstand his association with economic disaster.

A second, more far-reaching conclusion concerns the particular circumstances in which rural society turned away from its traditional concerns and moved towards class-based political allegiance. The term 'class' is used advisedly here. Too often its use in reference to the peasantry lacks any very rigorous meaning – peasants work their holding and hold their land in such a variety of ways that, as a community, they are no more of a class – understood in either Marx's or even Dahrendorf's sense – than were the late medieval nobility. But in the Var, after 1880, the peasantry and the rural community in general were growing ever more homogeneous. The loss of bourgeois *rentiers*, landless labourers and especially the very smallest of the owner—farmers meant that the remaining smallholding peasantry shared interests as both producers and consumers which helped generate within them a strong sense of shared concerns and common enemies. The term class, then, applied in late-nineteenth-century southern France when discussing the rural community, has for once a genuine heuristic value.

One facet of this development was the collapse of vertical allegiances and their replacement by a more horizontal social structure. We have already seen this change reflected in the social composition of *chambrées* and *cercles*. An important consequence of this was the decline of clientelist relations, the sort of vertical factionalism which lined men up behind particular clans or families for many generations. Hence, in the typical bourg or village of the central Var, the sort of social division which lay behind traditional feuds and antagonisms was fast disappearing. Since these were also the communes whose economic and demographic decline was inclining the surviving population to increasingly extreme forms of protest, it follows that there was little overlap between traditional divisions and the new, overtly political affiliations which were emerging around 1890. The socialists in particular, therefore, were not simply inheriting old feuds to which they gave new form; they were expressing a new, more homogeneous but also more acute, local sentiment which had little in common with the traditional motives for intra-village divisions.

In so far as personal squabbles were not thereby dissolved, they now tended not to emerge as a factor in determining allegiance between competing factions, but would often be worked out *within* the dominant local political formation. Thus, as the social structure of a village such as Carcès became less complex, the old Provençal economy reduced to struggling peasants and a few rural artisans, so a single political force, in this instance the socialists, came to dominate *all* areas of local life. In 1901 the local cantonal election candidate, Vigne, received 270 of the 305 votes cast.[14] In such circumstances, personal differences were expressed *within* the socialist group, or at public meetings held to choose the candidate for local or legislative elections. In the twentieth century this process has become quite firmly institutionalised. In the municipal elections of 1977 in La Garde Freinet, the only list presented was that of the Union de la Gauche; the list was duly elected. But the personal feuds and the struggles to get onto the list of the various local Socialists and Communists were quite as heated as they would have been had it been a matter of competing electoral lists. This pattern was already quite well established in some cantons by 1914. In a sense, then, the peasantry of the Var came to experience a particular and precocious form of 'one-party democracy' — no doubt because of the effective disappearance, by that time, of class conflict, properly so-called, *within* the village community!

These observations are very far from resolving the questions raised at the beginning of this chapter. And in essence they are not suscep-tible of satisfactory resolution. For every instance of 'artificial' label-ling (as when the *Petit Var* attacks the municipality of Pourrières as 'reactionary' for placing a few centimes on the municipal tax)[15] there is evidence that such labels actually did mean something and were not mere camouflage for private or ancient squabbles. Sénéquier tells us that the republicans of La Garde Freinet made a martyr in 1876 of a local man because the municipality had punished him for out-raging public decency in a nearby field in the company of a lady from the cork factory. Pure Gabriel Chevallier. What Sénéquier does not say is that such issues were often a substitute for genuine political divisions and feelings which circumstances (this was still the epoch of MacMahon and the Moral Order) would not permit men to express openly. He also underestimates the significance of the social stigma attaching to the low-paid women of the *bouchonneries* — and the consequent social and political implications of defending them, especially in compromising circumstances.[16]

Nevertheless, to go from social divisions to political allegiance is a tricky manoeuvre. Historians of the social conflicts of the mid-nineteenth century are rightly wary of such leaps, and I am writing of a period no more than forty years on. But those forty years made some important changes. Universal male suffrage had the unintended effect of politicising the peasantry if only in that it obliged them constantly to go through the act, however purely formal, of making political choices. After 1877, those choices were relatively free ones, and men of differing persuasions were ever more at liberty to appeal for the peasant's allegiance. Initially such allegiance might more willingly be given to those who were known and trusted, and who spoke in terms which were familiar. Hence the early successes of the local Radicals, in the Var as elsewhere. But with the coming of an acute and disorienting economic crisis, with the disappearance of many of the constituent elements of the rural and village community, with the Radicals' consistent failure to offer convincing solutions, and finally with the propaganda effort of the socialists in the country-side, the men of the bourgs and villages came increasingly to turn a sympathetic ear to strange men — whose ideas, albeit couched in new conceits, were not particularly novel or unwelcome in the communities of the south. After a while, it was to these ideas, and not so much to the men who espoused them, that the Provençal peasantry would give their allegiance — thus giving the lie both to the urban view of a conservative countryside and to the Olympian assumption that ideas were of little import to men of a lesser kind. The evidence from the Var shows otherwise. Traditions either fused into new allegiances — or were silently jettisoned. Personalities could be laid aside, however popular they had become, in favour of an organisation or a doctrine to which they had introduced the local community.

Without this development, socialism in rural France could never have taken root. The field would have been left open to the traditional *notables* of right and left, to the Marquis de Félix and Georges Clemenceau. Unlikely as it may appear, the peasantry of the Var were converted to socialism by the very programmes and ideals espoused by the socialist movement. Support for the candidates of the extreme left was conscious, deliberate and, in the precise sense, political.

9

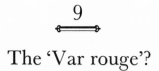

The 'Var rouge'?

There is a certain image of Mediterranean politics, and of Mediterranean society in general, which informs much writing on the subject. The picture is that of a world in which everything is somehow 'larger than life', where men say more than they think, where words and actions form part of a tradition of social behaviour which far outstrips their apparent content. Because southern France in particular has such a peculiarly lively and often radical political history, historians have sometimes felt constrained to account for its history less in terms of the specific content of the political acts of the local populace than by reference to some generic character of the region.

Thus even so level-headed and careful a scholar as Madeleine Rebérioux is at one point reduced to explaining the leftist leanings of the Midi as the consequence of a 'goût quotidien pour la politique' — which even if true is still nothing more than a description of the phenomenon, hardly an account of it.[1] Nor is this conception of southern French attitudes one born out of a retrospective attempt to understand something of the history of the area: *préfets* and *procureurs-généraux*, especially after 1851, were at great pains to produce a satisfactory explanation for the rebellious character of Provence in particular — indeed it is to them that we owe the concept, since so pervasive, of the 'red Var'.[2]

In fact, of course, lower Provence has not always been irredeemably 'red'; at best we can discuss it in these terms only from the spring of 1789, and we have even then to account for the very 'white' character of the region between 1815 and the 1840s. But it is undoubtedly true that, since the Second Republic, the department of the Var in particular has stood firmly on the left in French political life — most obviously so during the politically active years of the Third Republic. And it is this evident traditional 'leftism' of the region which has led historians to account for the various forms of that tradition in terms of the general characteristics of the region.

A second factor behind such an approach is the presumed nature of the socialist tradition in France. Since that tradition was, at least until the First World War, so heterogeneous and doctrinally vague, it has been all too easy to argue that the adoption of socialism in various parts of the country, notably the Mediterranean littoral, reflects that ideological uncertainty. Socialists were little more than Radicals, the argument runs, and hence could be all the more easily assimilated in regions where Radicalism, too, was part of a loose inheritance, as much a matter of political style as anything else. Hence the particular penchant of regions like the Var for the extreme left, itself a consequence of local tendencies to verbal extremism. Socialism in such an area had only to sound extreme, occasionally, to merit the enthusiastic and noisy support of people long conditioned to backing the most radical of the available sects; the content of political programmes was thus of minimal importance — and often in practice very similar to that of previous (and future) movements which had achieved similar popularity.

This is the view of, among others, Claude Willard, the historian of the Guesdists. It is worth quoting at length his summary of this argument, since he lays out very clearly the case which I shall be opposing in this chapter: 'le socialisme [in the Var and the Bouches-du-Rhône] constitue un magma où sont presqu'entièrement confondus guesdistes, anarchistes, allemanistes, anciens boulangistes et, exerçant une influence prépondérante, socialistes indépendants, en fait radicaux revêtus d'une tunique socialiste'. Willard, of course, is out to make a particular point — in this case, to add fuel to his argument that Guesdism, whatever its achievements in organising and educating the French proletariat and small peasantry, lacked social and ideological clarity, reflecting in this a persistent defect within old French socialism — a defect to be remedied in the postwar years. But we must treat his comments on socialism in Provence as standing in their own right.[3]

Behind Willard's conception lie two major implications. In the first place the socialist movement in Provence, in his terms, was identified not by its programme or doctrines, but by its considerable overlap with other forms of left politics — Radicalism in particular. There is thus posited a continuum over time between old and new forms of opposition politics which both enables the otherwise cloudy image of a nascent socialism to emerge the victor, and simultaneously encourages it in that nebulous character which, according to Willard, was nowhere so much in evidence as in the south-east.

So much for the nature of the political movement. The second implication concerns its supporters. These are treated as largely unconcerned with the distinctions between various forms of radical politics, interested only in pursuing their traditional allegiance to the most extreme of the available options. Hence their switch from Radicals to socialists when the former became increasingly identified with the Republic — and, after 1901, with its government.[4] Historians of French socialism who adopt this view thereby circumnavigate the problem of accounting for the peculiarly *peasant* base of French socialism in its early years in two interlocking ways: they demonstrate that, in rural areas especially, it was not really socialist, but a 'magma' of Radicals, doctrinally misinformed activists, and well-meaning individuals (among whom Jaurès). They then further argue that, following from this, the small peasant proprietors were not voting for socialism at all, at least not in the sense in which it was understood and supported in the cities. At most, their worsening situation was encouraging in them an extreme form of the politics of protest and desperation — similar to their attitude in the middle of the century, but modified by virtue of the changed political circumstances and different channels of opposition.

To contest this view of the matter, it will be necessary to treat two separate issues. Firstly, to ascertain whether in fact there *was* a continuum, a historical bridge, between Radicalism and socialism, over which tens of thousands of peasant voters passed without even noticing the chasm below (if there *was* a chasm, and not just a shallow ditch, that is). Secondly, we need to get as close as we can to knowing what exactly it was that socialism offered to the peasants, and what they saw in it. This knowledge of the relationship between ideological and political socialism is central *even if* the gap between Radicals and socialists proves as narrow as Willard, for example, suggests. In its most extreme form, my counter-argument runs that Radicals and socialists were not usually even the same people, so that the link between the two parties exists only in the grossest sense, on a small-scale map of electoral geography. But even if we do not adopt this view, the fact remains that men did change their allegiance from

Radicalism to something which called itself socialism, and we need to ask why this was. After all, Radicalism remained as verbally 'leftist' as it had always been, so that in terms of 'southern extremism' it might well have remained the vehicle for local political expression at least until 1914. But it did not.

Radicalism and socialism

Historically, Radicalism as a political animal is far easier to trace than socialism — and this is ironic, given its total lack of any doctrinal or organisational identity until the twentieth century. But Radicalism was an amalgam of negatives, an amalgam which acquired new elements with each development in French political life. It represented the defence of *le peuple* against *les grands*, later of the individual against the state. Together with the dominant characteristic of extreme anti-clericalism which it acquired in the second half of the century, these constituted the basis of Radical politics. The background to this movement is the unfinished character of much of the French Revolution — unfinished not just in some Hegelian sense but also in the eyes of the protagonists. *Notables* remained in the small towns and villages against whom new classes — shopkeepers, journalists, teachers especially — would pit themselves. Small rural property, if not enhanced by the land sales of the Revolution, at any rate survived them, leaving *in situ* a class of small proprietors and precariously-surviving sharecroppers and tenant farmers, instinctively conservative but with multiple grievances against large farmers, the tax collector, foreign competition.

Such was the peculiarly French social basis of Radicalism — a rural petit-bourgeois basis which at other times in other places has led directly to a radicalism of the far right, and which raises interesting speculation as to the importance of the French Radical Party in unwittingly barring the route to fascism in France. The varying pieces in the Radical jigsaw certainly help explain its strength in otherwise very disparate regions. Thus Bercé argues that Radical successes in the south-west, for example, were a function of its defence of small property, but more important of its negative attitude towards the state, the Church and the *fisc*, the traditional targets of resentment and anger in the marginal and impoverished countryside of eastern Aquitaine.[5]

In the Allier, the Radicals did consistently well in the central and eastern parts of the area; here the influence of large landowners, an obvious target of Radical propaganda, and the absence of any link to such centres of socialist support as Commentry, in the west, enabled Radicals consistently to outbid socialists, whereas a little to the west the reverse was true. In the Côtes-du-Nord, a vote for the Radicals was a direct snub to the Church and to the traditionally dominant local aristocracy; in the Gard, the Protestant communities were fervently Radical, attracted by its *guerre à outrance* on the Catholic Church. In each case, the specific nature of the Radical appeal enabled it to sustain its base in the face of a growing socialist movement, long after regions such as the Var had turned their back on the Radicals. And this continuity could prove very long-lived indeed: in Beaufort-en-Marche, in the Limousin, the Radicals did well in the 1880s, were the victors in 1936, and were still the best placed party, with 36% of the vote, in 1962. Where the social basis for a certain Radicalism survived, it was not the mere advent of Socialism which would displace it.[6]

Among the supporters of such Radicalism I list the teachers. The rôle of these, especially of the *instituteurs*, the primary-school teachers, is particularly illustrative of the specific nature of Radical backing. For these teachers did not at any time before the 1930s transfer their allegiance to the parties farther to the left. Radicalism mobilised them and captured their support because it emphasised the very struggles which they were themselves caught up in — notably the conflict with the Church, but also the battle in the villages between traditional *notables* and the new political cadres. The teacher was often an outsider, in every sense, usually young, and occupationally concerned with spreading the republican gospel. He or she was also, of course, very vulnerable to dismissal or transfer should the authorities grow suspicious of an excessive enthusiasm for revolutionary politics. Thus mild but committed Radicalism became the identifying characteristic of these and other *fonctionnaires* — with the result that Radicalism did very well in areas where their influence was important. And since, with the passing of time, their influence was often important in just those areas which had once seen the tutelage of older kinds of local *notables*, Radicalism did traditionally well in areas where the collectivist message of the socialists fell on

stonier ground. Indeed, the more isolated and *morcelé* the region and
its communities, the more successful the Radicals, with their emphasis
on a franchise based on the commune (the socialists favoured pro-
portional representation and departmental lists), were likely to
be — this was notably the case in departments like the Corrèze,
where the Radicals sustained their predominance until the 1950s
through their personal and local influence and prestige.[7]

This historically specific character of Radicalism, favouring its
implantation in, paradoxically, the more timeless and traditional
communities of rural France, where change was experienced as a
threat and the traditional enemies of the 1790s were still the targets
of local mistrust a century later, would lead one to expect the position
of the Radicals to be much less secure in Provence. And such was
indeed the case. Whereas in Brittany or in Aquitaine the early
socialists had little option but to throw in their lot with the Radicals,
in the Var the conflict between the historical and the collectivist left
came very quickly into the open — indeed the period of Radical
hegemony in Provence can only be said to have lasted from 1876 to
1893; in most other areas it endured at least until the election of 1910.

Even 1893 is really too late a date at which to place the ending of
Radical power, since the predominance of Radicalism in rural communities depended very much upon its being able to present itself as the
sole and legitimate inheritor of all the traditions and aspirations of
the Revolution. And in the Var it was facing challenges to this claim
from the very early 1880s. According to Derruau-Boniol, 'dès 1906,
le parti radical fait figure de parti modéré et . . . le vote radical ne
constitue plus, après 1900, une étape vers la gauche'.[8] For the Var,
we should have to antedate that statement by as much as 15—20
years.

Daylight emerged between the two movements from as early as
1882, that is to say only three years after the first signs of a socialist
presence in the department. In March of that year, the Toulon Ligue
Ouvrière, composed largely of workers at the arsenal, wrote an open
letter to the Radical-inclined *Petit Var*. In this they attacked the
Radicals for not caring about the interests of workers — 'Qu'a fait la
République pour les petits, pour les ouvriers? Fort peu de chose.' Nor
was the distinction confined to the city of Toulon. It was in August
1883 that a meeting of socialists in Cuers adopted one Bertrand as

their candidate for the forthcoming cantonal elections, thereby incurring the fury of the Radicals of neighbouring Carnoules, who waxed indignant at this breach of republican discipline — there was already a Radical candidate for the canton — which would bring joy to the reactionary party. It was from this initial breach that there would emerge the socialist slate for the legislative elections of 1885, discussed in Chapter 3.[9]

By the mid-1880s, in the south-western area of the department, the breach was complete. In April 1884 the president of the Cercle des Etudes Sociales in Toulon wrote to the *Petit Var* rejecting all notions of joint republican lists in elections: 'Il est temps de se compter une bonne fois, pour savoir si réellement le parti ouvrier . . . veut toujours servir de marchepied à la bourgeoisie.'

By 1886, Paule Minck could make a speech in La Crau in which she openly averred that even a Clemenceau ministry would change nothing, and would not benefit the small peasants and the workers of the Var. She may not yet have been preaching to the converted, but there is no doubt that she was voicing a sentiment which was gaining currency in the region. The growing divisions within what had once been thought of as the 'republican' party were a matter for open and frequent debate in many places, Besse for example, and the popular local self-image of the Var as a *foyer* of republican fervour was already marred by these rumours of the collapse of unity on the left.[10]

The most telling evidence for this comes from the Radicals themselves. Where the enemy had once been clerical reaction, there was now a new threat from the left, and the mid-1880s saw a spate of anti-socialist articles in the local Radical press. These quite correctly observed that right-wing circles in the region were deliberately backing socialist candidates in order to bring about the defeat of the Radicals or the Opportunists. When the royalist journalist Barbès spoke in Vidauban in March 1885, to an audience estimated at 450 persons, he made a number of favourable references to the 'extreme' left (by which he made it clear he meant the 'collectivists'), and each reference was received with a cheer by large sections of this audience. Similarly, the 1888 election which saw the victory of the (then) socialist Cluseret was also the occasion for conservative candidates to advise their supporters to switch their votes to Cluseret at the second round, in order to defeat the Radical, Fouroux.[11]

Significantly, 1888 was also the first occasion on which the official Radical 'party' broke with the republican discipline which it had often invoked in its attacks on socialist candidates. Fouroux withdrew at the last minute from the second round of the by-election, but gave no instructions to his supporters as to whom they should support in his place — a major breach with an important tradition in Third Republican political tactics. As a result Cluseret was elected, but it seems that no more than 15—20% of the erstwhile Radical voters gave him their support.[12] Not surprisingly, we find that by 1889 it was socialism, not the right, which was the real enemy for Radical municipalities. The Radical mayor of Ollioules fended off attacks on his administration by claiming that such criticisms merely fuelled the dangerous fires of revolution and its advocates — a strange position for a Radical to adopt so openly, but then by 1889 the Radicals in the Var were no longer the dominant and unique force on the revolutionary side.[13]

That the breach became so visible at about this time is not altogether surprising. The Boulangist crisis of the late 1880s played a part in the development. By helping produce growing cynicism with republican politics generally (an attitude much fostered by the events surrounding the Wilson affair too), the Boulangist period helped increase an already strong tendency to abstention in the villages, just at the moment when the incumbent Radicals most needed to preserve their traditional backing. The very success of the Radicals in the decade 1876—85 had produced a tendency to take their victory as assured, with the result that the Radical electorate had become very passive — whereas the socialists, quite untarred by the republican brush and largely unaffected (in this region) by Caesarist sirens, could count on their support to turn out whenever required.

That there did exist a distinction between Radical and socialist electorates was something that would become increasingly clear. In 1885 the Radicals had won in the arrondissement of Brignoles by less than one thousand votes, whereas they had been massively victorious in Toulon, and to a lesser extent in Draguignan, where Clemenceau was especially popular. Yet within a generation, the arrondissement of Brignoles would be *the* Socialist stronghold, with the cantons of Cotignac and Barjols to the fore. Draguignan became a divided region, with the hills and the coast leaning to the conservatives, the valleys voting Socialist. As for Toulon, by 1910 it was the only part of the Var still in Radical hands; indeed the elections of that year amply demonstrate that the Socialists dominated in the rural Var, while Radicalism survived as a force only in that urban coastal area where it had first acquired its base. And even here there was some doubt as to the real standing of Radicalism; whereas in the rest of the department political labelling remained quite clear, in Toulon in 1888 we find the (Radical) mayor celebrating his contribution to the success of local 'socialism', while in the very next sentence he speaks of 'nos principes de radicaux sincères'! The confusion of which Willard speaks seems often to have been a Radical, not a socialist, failing.[14]

The discontinuity between Radicals and socialists which emerges in a region such as Brignoles in these years was part of a larger break with tradition which marked the first decades of the Third Republic. Whereas the republican sentiments of the mid-nineteenth century sometimes found their echo, however faint, in the early 1870s – as when, for example, La Garde Freinet gave a notably enthusiastic welcome to the news of the declaration of the Republic in 1870 – these patterns were quite often irretrievably broken in the following years. And whereas the Radicals tended to inherit such old allegiances as survived – witness the close correlation between areas of mid-century insurgency and communes which voted Radical – the socialists would often make their most impressive breakthroughs in regions where neither the old radicalism nor the new had ever been much in evidence.

Thus a commune like Artigues, which in 1914 would give overwhelming backing to the Socialist ticket, was described by an *inspecteur d'académie* in 1878 as 'solidly reactionary'. In the 1881 municipal elections in Tourtour an extreme conservative list was victorious and in Montfort the winning list was proclaimed as 'monarchist'. Yet both villages appear on my list of later socialist strongholds, and neither would ever pass through a Radical stage. Or there was Ampus, which elected its first republican mayor for 43 years in these same municipal elections – and would later prove unrepentantly Socialist. Even Cogolin, in the Maures, was run by a municipality which in 1883 refused permission to the local musicians to perform on 14 July! And Cogolin, too, would later emerge on the

far left, described by *Le Cri* in 1910 as a 'foyer ardent du socialisme'
(although in Cogolin the enthusiasm took the form of wide syndicalisation rather than a consistently large socialist vote). Then there is
the case of Hyères, whose municipal council in 1873 was given a
dressing-down by the *sous-préfet* of Toulon for its 'communist'
tendencies — he reminded them that a black flag had been raised in
the town when the Versaillais entered Paris two years previously. Yet
this ardent centre of dissent is prominent on my list of communes
(see Chapter 4) which consistently failed to give effective support to
the Socialists in all the elections from 1902 to 1914.[15]

The point being made here is not simply that political traditions
could prove unreliable, even self-reversing, though this is not a negligible theme. More important is the clear evidence that the years
1880—1900 saw an important shift in the political behaviour in
many villages and small towns in this region. Quite often these had
been places where conservative or even reactionary local authorities
had reigned supreme for many years, but which within a few years
would become citadels of the extreme, socialist left. Areas which
gave their backing to the Radicals, however, tended to be more consistent, emerging from old traditions of republican allegiance to
which they then remained loyal throughout the last third of the
century. Radicals *did* succeed in winning some local and a few
national elections in formerly conservative communes, but their
success was usually transient, whereas the socialists who succeeded
them in the 1890s would prove durable.

Thus the distinction between Radicals and socialists in Provence
goes beyond abstract differences in their historical make-up. They
must have been perceived differently, since it is evident that they
were supported by different people in different places and in different ways. There is no doubt, it is true, that the Radical 'phenomenon' outlived the early Radicals, thereby producing a smokescreen
of verbal and formal radicalism which it is not easy to distinguish
from the original product. But we are the better able to make distinctions because the socialists themselves went out of their way to stress
them, even as some Radicals attempted the reverse.[16] What is more,
it does seem that the two movements represented traditions and
approaches which could be clearly distinguished at the time, and
which in Provence could be seen apart from a very early date. One

way of appreciating these distinctions is to compare the programmes of the two parties.

The appeal of socialism

The most obvious difference between the political programmes of Radicals and socialists, as presented to the electorate in these years, lay in the greater degree of precision and detail which informed the proposals of the latter. Radical electoral manifestos showed a marked tendency to grow vaguer with time, and they remained consistently skewed towards political, as distinct from social or economic, demands.

Thus the seven-point programme which the Radicals drew up at a meeting in Carnoules in December 1880, and which all Radical candidates at local elections were obliged to adopt, contained only one economic proposal — that there should be reform of taxation, with the introduction of an income-tax. All the other points were political in nature. The programme, which would remain the basis of Radical manifestos for the next generation, advocated a revision of the Constitution, with the abolition of the Senate; the separation of Church and state; free, *laïc* and compulsory state education; complete freedom of association and assembly; freedom of the press; and an extension of the autonomy of the commune. In later years there would be certain small changes — freedom of the press and the right of free association were eventually achieved and would be replaced by demands for a reduction in legal costs, insistence upon all *fonctionnaires* being sworn republicans, and the favouring of a reduction in the period of military service.

It would be extremely rare, however, for a Radical candidate to go beyond these measures into the advocacy of more specific social reforms — except at certain moments of crisis when a particular tariff would be condemned or government aid for a particular sector sought. Much more typical was the descent into generalities such as that which concluded both the Radical municipal manifesto of 1884 and the legislative programme of the following year, when, without specifying what they had in mind, the Radicals called for the 'émancipation intellectuelle, sociale et industrielle des travailleurs'.

What the Radicals most decidedly did not have in mind was any transformation in the relations of property. From the 1870s through to Clemenceau's first ministry and beyond, the Radicals identified themselves firmly with the interests of 'small property' — usually by reference to 'large property', which was condemned in all its forms. Inevitably, this involved the Radical spokesmen in this region as elsewhere in increasingly nebulous and vague formulations, since they were attempting not merely to defend the militant Republic at the same time as attacking certain of its workings; they were also offering bait to electors whose interests were often far from compatible. Hence the very representative stance taken by Fouroux in 1888, when he claimed that the Radical programme of that year stood for the 'protection de tous les intérêts ouvriers, industriels et paysans du département'. Magnier, the Radical candidate in the first Toulon arrondissement in 1889, summed up the position even better, when he claimed that his party stood for 'ni réaction ni révolution'; he was against the throne and the altar, but also against all 'émeutes'; his programme was the Republic, Peace, Liberty, Work, Democratic Progress, etc., etc.[17]

Just how different were the promises and claims of the socialists? Mayeur asserts that they could not afford to stray far from the traditional appeal of democratic Radicalism, for fear of alienating small peasants who feared social upheaval no less than they disliked the traditional right. Loubère goes further. According to him: 'Of course, one looks in vain for truly collectivist planks in the platforms of successful socialist candidates, especially in rural areas.'[18] In fact there was no evident distinction between the platforms of successful candidates and those who failed; nor was the absence in French socialist propaganda of what might be called *truly* collectivist planks confined to its efforts in rural areas. Guesdists, and after them the Communists, would often present very 'reformist' programmes at elections, reserving their doctrinal collectivism for domestic intra-party consumption.[19] But even within these limits, there does seem a case for distinguishing between the appeal of Radicals and socialists in rural areas, in a number of important respects.

Throughout this period, the electoral manifestos of the socialists are marked both by a distinct 'tone' and by a much greater attention to socio-economic detail. One of the very first local socialist candidates, Auguste Isnard, who stood in the 1885 legislative elections, declared on his flysheets that 1789 had only given power to the bourgeoisie, and that a new, social, revolution was urgently required. This much was common ground among all the various socialist sects. The measures which they proposed as interim palliatives (in the case of the Guesdists) or as integral stages on the road to social revolution (as in the view of the 'reformists') were spelled out in their manifestos at ensuing elections, and it is worth considering these in some detail.

In the first place, there was far less emphasis on political reforms than was to be found in Radical proposals; as Allard expressed it in a speech at Figanières in 1905, reforms such as the separation of Church and state were a 'duperie' — they did not in the least hurt or diminish the true (capitalist) exploiters. Thus although revision of the Constitution and the separation both figure dutifully on the programmes of Vincent in 1893 and Allard himself in 1898, they are not prominently placed and are quite lost in a maze of more specific and social demands.

Secondly, it is interesting to note that socialist electoral platforms varied little as between legislative and municipal campaigns. In each case the full range of socialist demands would be stated, followed by a separate list of proposals for change and reform at the local level. Hence, unlike the Radicals, the socialists presented a fundamentally unchanged image at every electoral campaign; Radical candidates at municipal elections would usually confine their concerns to a series of local issues, while at national elections they would return to the vague perspective described above. The socialists may well have gained strength from the consistent and recognisable identity of their programme — a programme which outlived changes in the person-alities representing it.

Throughout the 1890s, and well into the twentieth century, certain themes remained prominent in socialist campaigns. Among these were the following:

The need for a Ministry of Labour.
Nationalisation of the banks, mines, railways, canals, insurance, large farms, all energy sources, the slate and quarrying industries.
Minimum wages for all factory, workshop and farm workers, together with legal maximum limits on the length of the working day.
The replacement of all existing forms of taxation (especially the hated urban tolls) by a single progressive tax on all incomes over three thousand francs.
Government-financed credit facilities for farmers, together with reduced

tariffs for the transportation of fertiliser. The latter, together with essential machinery, to be made available on easy terms to poorer farmers.
Revision of the *cadastre* [land registry], with the commune to play the
major rôle in the re-apportionment of land.

Together with more passing concerns (such as demands for a
disaster fund for peasants during the phylloxera crisis and again in
the early twentieth century) these constituted the basic demands
voiced in every socialist manifesto, at legislative, cantonal and
municipal elections. There were also a number of more properly
political proposals: administrative decentralisation, a reform of the
judiciary, the election of magistrates, the requirement on deputies to
present themselves to their electors for annual *explications*, the
requirement that elected representatives be not simultaneously
directors of companies, etc. But these and other political reforms
tended not to be prominently displayed on socialist handouts and
posters. With the exception of the campaign against the three-year
conscription law during 1912–13, political reforms were not the
leading feature of the socialists' appeal.[20]

The emphasis instead was on a twin programme of general
economic change in a socialising direction (nationalisations, tax reform) and specific improvements in the situation of the hard-pressed.
In the Var it was the concerns of the stricken peasantry which were
to the fore, in the Nord it would be the conditions of miners and
textile-workers. But in both cases the reforms demanded would be
seen as dovetailing with the wider concern of socialists for a greater
measure of state intervention on behalf of the poor, and a simul-
taneous extension of the capacity of the *people* to control their own
affairs (through the encouragement of cooperatives, favourable conditions for loans and access to vital equipment).

It is the consistency of the socialists' demands, and the constant
intermix of local and national concerns, which provide the clue to an
understanding of the peculiar character of socialism, as distinct from
Radicalism, in French politics. For despite the apparently itemised
and detailed, reform-directed character of socialist manifestos, these
were in fact informed by a consistent and clear doctrinal position.

To say this is not to suggest that French socialists had a fully
resolved and resolute attitude to the thorny question of relating
present politics to future hopes. No more than the Germans or

Italians did they succeed in overcoming the problem of what reforms to advocate in the immediate future without prejudicing their commitment to the notion of inevitable but more distant upheaval. What is more, the French had a particular difficulty: in a democracy of smallholding peasants, how to reconcile belief in the impending disappearance of small property with the immediate need to acquire the political support of the peasantry? Yet in spite of the general problem of 'revolutionary' politics in non-revolutionary societies, and the specific problem of adjusting a collectivist appeal to a property-owning electorate, the French socialists, separately and later in unison, presented a remarkably firm ideological image. Whatever the particular details of their election addresses, the framework within which these were couched changed little over the years.

By this is meant that, even in Provence, the socialists never denied their primary commitment to the rejection of the 'bourgeois' Republic and its replacement by a 'social' one. We may see this as a further example of the 'verbal extremism' of southern politics — although this stress was also present in socialist propaganda elsewhere in France. But in that case we must nonetheless acknowledge that this particular variant of the Mediterranean phenomenon was peculiar to the *socialist* left — and that they were very persistent in their attachment to it. What is more, it is hard to see how they can have emphasised their ideology for reasons of electoral advantage — although the fact that they did not *lose* support thereby is significant.

The overt emphasis on that which distinguished socialists from other parties of the historical left emerged in a variety of ways. As early as 1883, the Cercle des Travailleurs in Cuers announced its abstention in the cantonal elections, in the absence of any candidate representing the 'parti ouvrier socialiste'. Making their position plain they declared, in keeping with the views of the Guesdist party to which they belonged, that 'l'émancipation des travailleurs ne pourra se résoudre que par les travailleurs eux-mêmes'.[21] This attitude persisted. When Joseph Collomp stood (successfully) as the socialist candidate for the canton of Le Luc in the cantonal elections of 1904, he reminded his audience that he was more than ever convinced that the reforms which he supported were, in themselves, inefficacious. What was required, in Le Luc as in society at large, was a salutary

revolutionary crisis, a profound alteration in the structure of bourgeois society. In the following year, at a meeting of the *conseil
général* of the Var, Fourment, arguing that contemporary economic
problems were the result of capitalist overproduction, asked that the
conseil should campaign for the complete transformation to a collectivist society as soon as possible, in order to resolve the crisis facing
the producers of wine. All other expedients were doomed to failure.
His proposal was defeated by 9 votes to 7.[22]

All public occasions were platforms for this reiteration of the
socialist position. At a meeting in Toulon on 1 August 1909 to
protest against the Czar's visit to France, Allard reminded his audience
that *all* governments, not just autocracies, were 'forcément en lutte
contre la classe ouvrière qui veut s'émanciper'. This was essentially the
position he had taken at a meeting ten years earlier when, in the
course of an attack on the effects of the Méline tariffs, he had
spoken of his dreams for a communist society, without law or governments. All socialist proposals were aimed at achieving a transitional,
collectivist, stage on the path to this ideal.[23]

A second measure of the commitment of local socialists is the
considerable attention given to the education of their supporters in
the history and doctrines of the socialist movement. At public
meetings, such as one in Toulon in 1898, Ferrero and others would
describe the nature of socialist theories, including those of Karl Marx.
Nor were the organised working class of Toulon the only target for
such lectures. The winter months, during which the peasantry of the
villages had time to attend meetings, would often see whole evenings
spent in discussion of these matters, as when Auguste Troin lectured
to an audience of 300 people in Callian in November 1882 on the
theme of the various schools of socialist thought from the Greeks to
Benoît Malon, via Babeuf, Saint Simon, Fourier, Proudhon and Cabet,
or when the Café de Commerce in Les Salles in January 1905 saw a
two-hour lecture on 'Révolte et raison' by A. Bosquet of the local
Groupe Ouvrier Révolutionnaire.[24]

From 1904 the official socialist paper, *Le Cri du Var*, used its wide
circulation in cafés and *cercles* to provide the rudiments of socialist
history and doctrine to its readers. There were regular articles on
basic socialist terms such as 'Action Internationale des Travailleurs',
'socialisation' and the like; features on foreign socialist movements

(a whole issue in 1907 devoted to Bebel and the German Socialists), detailed explanations of what it was that distinguished socialist movements from mere reformist parties, however well intentioned, and so forth. Moreover, *Le Cri* gave special prominence to doctrinal pronouncements from within the socialist movement — as when, for example, the Var Federal Committee in October 1908 instructed its delegates to the forthcoming National Congress to remind the SFIO that it was *not* a party of reform but a movement of class struggle and revolution.[25]

However much one discounts such doctrinal extremism, and doubts its relation to anything which the socialists actually did, it is impossible to ignore the extent to which it must have identified the SFIO, in the Var as elsewhere, as a party 'pas comme les autres'. And in one particular sphere, this commitment to revolutionism in doctrine ran counter not merely to traditional radicalism, but also to what might have been the supposed interests of the socialists' putative electorate. This was the question of the advocacy of a collectivist solution to the problems of the peasants.

With this issue I come to the heart of the debate surrounding the relations between peasants and the socialist movement. The SFIO after 1905 consistently avoided taking an unambiguous stand on the matter, preferring to argue that while it remained committed to the view that capitalism was tending to the destruction of all forms of small property, and that only collective property could resolve the crises which ensued from this development, it could simultaneously represent itself as the defender of the interests of the owners of small property, rural and artisanal. What was at stake here, of course, was the larger conflict within French socialism between what we might call the Proudhonist and the Marxist inheritances. While most French socialist groups adopted the basic Guesdist view, incorporating a crudely determinist Marxism, they remained vaguely wedded to the notion that small businessmen, artisans and peasants who worked in their own shops and fields were morally justified in their property, and should thus be defended against exploitation *and* expropriation. Such a view made all the more sense in France, politically, in that so many such people still survived, however marginally. But it created a tension between the line taken on industrial matters, where inevitable expropriation from the owners of the means of production was unanimously favoured, and the attitude to small artisans and peasants who were often attracted to the socialists as would-be defenders of the *petit peuple*.

Since, until 1919, the French Socialists had no fixed and nationally declared policy document or interim programme, there was much variation in the stress placed upon the various strands which had emerged out of the nineteenth-century socialisms. It is this heterogeneous quality in French socialism which has led to the view that, while the 'hard' face was turned to industrial areas, a 'softer', minimalist line was adopted in wooing the countryside; and in particular, it follows, the collectivist orientation of much of French socialism by 1900 was deliberately muted for rural consumption.[26]

In fact, the evidence from the Var tends not to support such an interpretation. Although there were occasional bursts of pure Proudhonism — as when a description of a future collectivist society in *Le Cri* asserted that there would be neither poverty nor parasites and that property, like work, would be guaranteed to all — the general tone, particularly after unification in 1905, was firmly and unapologetically collectivist. As René Cabannes, a member of the national executive, explained in a speech at Pignans in 1907, small proprietors were just as exploited as the proletariat, whose interests they thus fundamentally shared. The official view, voiced repeatedly in meetings, in newspapers and at the hustings, was that the expropriation of the means of production from private hands was not merely inevitable, but desirable. Only thus would private power be transformed into collective power in the common interest. Socialists, the editor of *Le Cri* asserted in 1908, must not be afraid of the force of their own ideas.

Whether all Socialist candidates took this line in public is not easy to ascertain, but there is no doubt whatsoever that they were under instructions to do so. At a Federal Committee meeting in June 1907, at the heart of the crisis brought about by the overproduction of wine, Allard received unanimous support for his view that a *complete* state monopoly on the growth and sale of wine was the only possible solution. What is more, he claimed that such a programme would bring much support to the Socialists, since so many wine-growers, already enthusiastic for the cooperative ideal, were now resigned to the impossibility of independent survival. 'N'est-il pas curieux de constater que le jeu même de la société capitaliste force les propriétaires eux-mêmes à réclamer, pour les protéger contre les conséquences mêmes du régime, des solutions à tendance socialiste.' The commitment to the total collectivisation of the land remained the cornerstone of the agricultural policy of the local Socialists — and it was not muted by considerations of electoral advantage. It was in September 1909, shortly before impending legislative elections, that the Federal Congress of the Socialist Federation of the Var mandated its delegates to the National Socialist Congress to demand that the SFIO spell out its *total* commitment to the socialisation of all means of production, agricultural as well as industrial. The small proprietor in France was doomed, and the Socialists should make no claim to be able or even willing to preserve his future independence. His interests had become those of the worker, artisanal, agricultural or industrial, and the Socialists should say this loud and clear.[27]

Thus not merely did the Socialists in the Var make reiterated commitments to the need for a future socialisation of the land, but they were actually in advance of some other sections of the national party in their views on the rural crisis. This rather casts doubt upon the view of them as pink-tinged Radicals, but in fact it is not without a certain logic. Small peasant proprietors had *never* been in themselves unsympathetic to talk of land reform, redistribution, and the like. Traditionally they had seen such projects as a means, perhaps the *only* means, by which their own situation might be improved — either by acquiring the land of others, or more usually by gaining access to common pasture and gleaning rights while sloughing off the shadow of wealthier and more efficient rural entrepreneurs.[28] The triple crisis of the early Third Republic (price fall, phylloxera, foreign competition) merely strengthened this inclination among the marginal small peasantry to throw in its lot with the urban collectivists, placing their future hopes in a cooperativism which was often indistinguishable from full collectivisation of their meagre resources. Hence the paradox of small-peasant backing for specifically *extreme* forms of socialism lies not in the fact of that relationship (which has in any case been chronicled elsewhere), but in its peculiar strength in the Var in particular. Hence, *pace* Claude Willard and others, it was not the diluted nature of socialism in this region which accounts for its appeal in the countryside, but on the contrary, the very revolutionary, almost apocalyptic character of its doctrine. It was the confluence of the extremes of peasant discontent and the most outspoken of the competing socialisms which created the enduring relationship between peasant and socialism in this region.

The conclusions to which I have been leading in Part Two may perhaps be most clearly summarised in the form of six theses:

(a) That the historical and economic characteristics of Provence played an important part in favouring the emergence in the region of a left-wing political tradition, but were not the sole determinants of the form of that tradition. Cash crops, which in Calabria for example produced a pattern not of militancy but of rural out-migration,[29] were not in themselves productive of a radical peasantry, even when the crop in question was wine. Nor does the presence of traditions of sociability account for the particular *occasion* of the rise of rural socialism.

(b) That what transformed these structures into fertile soil for the socialist movement in particular was the economic crisis of the last third of the nineteenth century. The form of this crisis, its extent, and the resulting changes in the social composition of the villages and small towns, created a conjuncture of which the socialist movement in particular was well placed to take advantage. The gap between the peaks of economic crisis and the establishment of socialist political hegemony in the Var results both from the natural time-lapse between economic cause and social reaction to it, and from the need for the peasantry to emerge from the traditional authority of the Radical-leaning village *notables* into a more collective and participatory say in their own affairs.

(c) That in turning to socialism in particular the rural populations of the Var were not ignoring its implicit ideological stance, but actually approving it on that account. That is not to say that the local peasantry had a complex and full grasp of the doctrinal bases of French socialism; but they were made acquainted with its salient features and saw in these a reflection of their own presumed interests.[30] To this degree the peasantry of Provence, like the working-class Guesdists of the Nord, were responding to an ideology which appealed to them in *class* terms. Given the difficulties of syndical organisation, this response took the dual form of agricultural cooperation and votes for socialist candidates — voting being the most obvious way in which the peasantry might express their political and social identity.[31] The Proudhonist undertow in French socialism made the link between distressed peasant proprietors, cooperative ideals and socialist politics all the easier to establish.

(d) That notwithstanding the frequent presence of artisans among the educated leadership of local socialist groups, it was precisely the *peasantry* which formed the basis of socialist support in this region. They were not the passive recipients of an organisation and programme prepared, as it were, for them by other social classes.[32] Nor were the peasants of the Var merely protesting in a negative, atavistic fashion against changes of which they did not grasp the import, and through a political vehicle which was foreign to them. Unlike Wolf's 'natural anarchists', the Provençal peasantry favoured the intervention of the state, even at the expense of their own independence, in order to ensure their survival.[33] To this extent they saw the 'urban socialism' of Guesde and others as truly applicable to their own situation, and responded positively.[34]

(e) That, as elsewhere in Europe and overseas, the rural communities of the Var often passed directly from pre-modern forms of protest (such as the violent insurrections of the first half of the nineteenth century) into modern anti-capitalist politics without passing through the intermediary of liberalism in its various forms. The collapse of traditional markets, privileges, common rights, which had dated from pre-industrial times and which were declining in the face of modern, capitalist competition, led the peasantry of such regions directly into the revolutionary 'post-capitalist' camp. They had no occasion to pass through a stage of Radical affiliation, since Radical hostility to the state, etc., offered them little. Their only hope lay in identification *with* the collectivity, both local and national. Hence a bridge was formed between the collectivism of the pre-modern rural community and the collectivism of the industrial proletariat's response to laissez-faire capitalism. Thus it was not, *pace* Soboul, that their very economic and social retardation made such areas amenable to movements of protest, but rather that their very social sophistication and traditionally complex economic structure enabled them both to survive into the modern period and also gave them a natural sympathy for collectively-oriented forms of protest against the threats which modernity posed to them.[35]

(f) That the new relationship established in the Var between the much diminished rural communities and the socialist movement became, in its turn, a tradition, in time as much a 'structural' feature of the region's social and political life as anti-clericalism had been in an earlier period. The conjunctural circumstances which had brought the relationship into being once past, voting for the socialists formed part of the 'historical' character of Provençal life, long after the SFIO had ceased to perform any obvious function on behalf of the local population, and had indeed lost much of its revolutionary character and impetus.[36] After the 'de-stabilising' effect of the political conflicts and economic crisis of the late nineteenth century, a new platform was reached in the life of the region, a new tradition created, whose roots became thereby not any longer a function of sociological but of historical explanation. This is not to deny the continued rôle played by the older traditions – but they continued in muted ways and through new forms. Organised left-wing politics became the new form of sociability, inheriting and transforming those older traditions of social life which had once helped provide favourable conditions for the rise of local socialist support.[37]

If, then, the Var was traditionally 'red', this fact in isolation serves rather to blur the picture than to account for it. We can now see that Willard and Mayeur were probably mistaken in feeling the need to account for the persistence of left-wing voting in this region by playing up the historical radicalism of the local population and simultaneously casting doubt upon the credentials of the socialists. An explanation which attempts to take account of the particular circumstances of the rise of socialism in the Var can assimilate the structural and historical framework of the region without being forced to diminish the voluntaristic and conscious nature of the decision to offer allegiance to the socialists after 1890. Traditions, no less than 'geographical determinants', require at least as much to be explained themselves as to be adopted as causal factors *per se*. The socialist tradition in the Var took root in the first half of the Third Republic for a variety of ascertainable reasons — among which, though not necessarily predominant, were the pre-existing conditions of Provençal society and history. In turn the emergent domination of socialism in this area for the ensuing half-century played an important, but doubtless only partial, rôle in accounting for more recent developments in Provençal political behaviour. There may well be no historical 'beginnings'; but there is more to historical explanation than the cumulative description of structures, nevertheless.

Without in any way jettisoning these structures, it is surely the central concern of the historian to locate those 'conjunctures' at which these inherited features of a given society or set of social relations undergo sharp mutation. Through the medium of the history of French socialism, and in the limited context of the department of the Var, locating and accounting for just such a conjuncture has been the object of this study.

PART THREE

POLITICS AND THE FRENCH PEASANTRY

10 From the Var to France

Regional studies hold an honoured and prominent place in the historiography of France since the late eighteenth century. In particular, and dating from André Siegfried's work on the west of France, first published in 1913, there has been a special emphasis upon the exhaustive study of a delimited region over a given period, with the avowed aim of achieving a better understanding of traditions of social and political culture which have emerged in a given place. Siegfried's own work is now largely discredited, its ecological and territorial determinism a barrier to more subtle accounts of social change, but the emphasis upon the region which it helped introduce flourishes as never before. Indeed, recent years have even seen the expression of fears that the tendency is out of hand – that the departmentalisation of French history is no longer contributing to a better grasp of the whole, but quite the reverse.[1]

This flowering of provincial studies in French history constitutes something of a paradox. For the dominant political characteristic of French life, under Bourbons, Jacobins, Bonapartists and Gaullists alike, has been the drive to centralisation in every dimension of life. The self-image of the French state since the later seventeenth century has been one of its own unity and indivisibility. In so far as the provinces remained unreconstructedly un-French, in language, affiliations or in their autonomous economic existences, these were matters which time, *préfets*, schoolteachers, railways, and, if necessary, the army could overcome. In the meantime they, the internal colonies of the imperial Parisians, were residual categories of the French whole, and their history should be seen in this light.

This may be to overstate the case so far as it concerns professional historians (though it remains a faithful description of the attitudes of governments and officials from Richelieu to Ferry), but not by so very much. It has only been since the Second World War and the rapid changes wrought in that 'bonne vieille France' of which

Pompidou was so scornful that the historical profession has begun seriously to investigate the extent to which as late as the nineteenth century (perhaps especially in the nineteenth century) France was not a unitary nation state but a complex of distinct societies, mostly rural, often economically and linguistically independent of French influence, and only very tangentially sharing the destinies of the wider national unit which unceasingly proclaimed its hegemony over them (proclamations whose strident and missionary tone may now be seen as being, in some part, mere declarations of intent).

This burgeoning of awareness of the variety, complexity and autonomy of even quite recent provincial French history may perhaps strike students of Eastern Europe or of France's Mediterranean neighbours as a rather banal matter. *They* can have been in little doubt as to the survival of unintegrated, pre-capitalist rural subsocieties within Europe up to the outbreak of World War One – but then few students of Italian or Slav history would have felt the need to free themselves from the shadow of a precocious centralised state which so dominates our understanding of the French past. If the recent trend in academic French history has been an occasionally obsessive concern with the local and the particular, this must be understood as a natural and mostly admirable reaction against the perspectives of their predecessors and the ubiquitous imperatives of Europe's most centralised and inflexible historical state. What is more, historians of provincial France are coming up with accounts of French history in general which suggest that their approach is rich in potential beyond its proclaimed boundaries.

What are those boundaries? I referred above to 'regional' studies, but the delimitations of a region remain a matter of some dispute. In the broadest sense, writing French history from below, as it were, involves selecting one of three sorts of geographical framework as well as a decision about the time-span to be covered. In the first place there is the village study. Selecting a small community and subjecting it to exhaustive analysis and discussion opens up a variety of exciting possibilities. Continuities which get lost in more wideranging surveys can be followed with greater accuracy and understanding, and the historian of such a micro-community has the inestimable advantage of actually being able to talk about the lives of identifiable individuals. No one who has read the works of Thabault or Wylie or even (for a much earlier period) Le Roy Ladurie could fail to appreciate the advantages and absorbing interest of getting to grips with history at this level. Moreover, as Higonnet and others have shown, the study of a single community can be pursued over an extended period of time without exhausting the resources of the researcher or the patience of the reader, and this cannot but increase the historical significance attaching to even the narrowest of studies.[2]

Yet the village study, or even the comparative historical survey of two or more small communities, has not been at the centre of main-stream regional history, and there are reasons for this. No single village, or group of villages, could ever be typical or representative of the experience of the wider community. In even the most autarkic and isolated rural communities there was a network of communications and interdependencies which stretched beyond the single commune and its nearest neighbours, often reaching at least to the dominant local market town and not infrequently to some regional centre of industrial and commercial importance. What is at question here is not the search for a 'typical' rural or provincial community — such a search would undermine the very premise of a study of France in its very variety — but the desire to grasp the workings of regional communities. The historian is trying to recapture the full range of links and influences within provincial France, and if there were 'natural' boundaries of social and economic life within which the French peasant and the rural artisan moved, these seem to have stretched well beyond the limits of his commune or hamlet, even if he and his family rarely travelled them.

It is on this premise that the departmental study is grounded. The department in France is not of course a natural unit; its boundaries were drawn up in 1790 and as a function of national administrative and political requirements, and, although often following the course of rivers and sometimes the contours of hills, the limits of any given department rarely describe natural frontiers. What is more, the department's very existence creates conveniences and temptations for the historian which may be full of hidden pitfalls. The organisation of historical evidence of all kinds into departmental categories can easily lead to a departmental reading of the local experience which may ignore or even distract from more 'real' or 'natural' parameters.

Nevertheless, the department as a cadre for the writing of regional history is not quite a nonsense. By the later nineteenth century at least, the political life of an area, the administration of local life and the relations between citizen and state were all departmentally determined, and in the Var at least there is little doubt but that most of the inhabitants thought of themselves as Varois. The *préfet* of the department and the local educational and police authorities were identified with the department, newspapers were published and distributed within the department, and usually gave themselves a departmental identity (*Le Cri du Var*, *Le Petit Var*, *Var Républicain*, etc.), and in a period of increased politicisation and political and economic organisation, the electoral divisions of the country, based upon departments, led to the growth of societies, federations, syndicates all organised by department and working quite separately and with very different identities from their immediate neighbours. All in all, the department had become, by the last third of the nineteenth century, a reality for most of its inhabitants, so that treating it as the basic framework of investigation is not merely a convenience, not simply the creation of a historical virtue from archival necessity.

A third approach, while not denying the reality of the department in nineteenth-century life, asserts that the older, regional groupings survived nevertheless, if not as conscious parameters to provincial identities, then at least as real frontiers between traditional ways of life. This was especially true of the most isolated and economically stagnant parts of the country, Aquitaine or the Limousin and the Marche for example, where the modern department alone is insufficient as a signpost to what was common, what different, about the history of a particular region. This seems a very valid argument, and may indeed serve as the basis for an initial distinction between certain regions of France. Where the historian is faced with an area rather obviously reluctant to accept the imprint of French national developments — in politics or in the degree of economic change, for example — then he or she is probably well advised to treat the area, initially at least, as best understood in its historical borders — as Brittany, rather than as the separate departments of Finistère, Côtes-du-Nord, Ille-et-Vilaine, etc., or as the Limousin, rather than the unhelpfully discrete units of Creuse, Corrèze and Haute-Vienne. In so doing, of course, he or she has of necessity moved some way from the village study, and lost much of the detail and insight which it can afford. Also lost is something of the tautness and internal coherence of a departmental study, and unless he or she wishes to write a very large book indeed (Corbin's study of the Limousin is nearly 1200 pages long) the regional monograph will already be forced into that selectivity and level of generality which, on the wider scale, robs national histories of much of their value.

The chronology of local studies is in essence a rather simpler matter. This may sound strange, because at first sight the historian who wishes to write the history of a province or department has somehow to overcome the difficulty imposed by the 'natural' dates of post-Revolutionary French history, dates whose character is determined by national, usually political, often military considerations. To study the Var from 1815 to 1851, or the Loir-et-Cher from 1848 to 1914 — is this not to undermine from the very outset that autonomy of regional history which its practitioner strives to achieve? Not necessarily. Whereas the choice of boundary lines is a matter of deciding what, historically, constitutes a proper community, the commencing and terminal dates of a study, where they are not determined by accident or for convenience alone, are best seen as the result of a choice concerning what questions we wish to ask. Very broadly, the provincial historian who wishes to study demographic or economic changes in his chosen region can free himself from traditional chronology and, like Corbin or Armengaud, set his study in the years between the 1840s and the 1880s, when, as he asserts, the region in question underwent profound social and economic mutation. But if, like Dupeux on the Loir-et-Cher, Agulhon on the early nineteenth-century Var, or, more modestly, in the present study, we wish to discover the answers to what are in essence questions about the political behaviour of provincial populations, then it is not just convenient but probably essential to work within dates which are themselves political. The explanations adduced to account for whatever political changes are being studied will of course flow back and forth across the selected dates, but where, as in this book, it is being argued that we are witnessing a confluence of local and national political life, then the traditional dating sequences of national politics cease to be impositions upon local history and become useful sign-posts to a fuller grasp of the latter.

Concern with the primary importance of the questions being asked, of the historian's *problématique*, requires some attention to the varying subject matter of regional studies. The regional studies discussed here are those which deal with provincial, substantially rural France in the nineteenth and early twentieth centuries. This of course excludes some of the very impressive studies of urban and industrial communities in the same period (such as the work by Pierrard on Lille during the Second Empire, or the massive study by Rolande Trempé on the miners of Carmaux), because the intention in this chapter is to set out a framework for an extension to the national community of the kinds of argument presented in Part Two of this book. For this purpose, the studies of politics and society in rural communities and their varying purposes and implications are naturally more immediately relevant.

It is possible to distinguish within the library of regional studies of modern France two kinds of approach. Many of the provincial monographs set out to present an exhaustive description of their chosen region over a limited period. Whether, like Barral on the Isère, they emphasise primary agrarian economic change and the accompanying political developments, or, like Armengaud on the Aquitaine region, their concern is largely demographic, the enterprise is basically a descriptive one. This is equally the case for those studies which fall as much within the province of historical geography as that of history — Livet on the agrarian structure of lower Provence, or Laurent on wine-growers and wine-growing in the Côte-d'Or. At its best, this sort of descriptive history, the social historian's variant of traditional narrative history, can be hugely enlightening — Thuillier's studies on the nineteenth-century Nivernais economy and family life illuminate much that was formerly in shadow. At their worst, or rather at their least imaginative, such monographs can be depressingly uninformative, except in the most obvious and literal sense. Garrier's two volumes on the Beaujolais and the Lyonnais from 1800 to 1970 leave the reader with a sense of disappointment — so much detail for so few insights.

The second kind of regional study avoids this trap, and seems to me all the richer thereby. This is the kind of social history, no less exhaustive in technique and detail, which begins by posing a question, or complex of questions. What makes Paul Bois' study of the Sarthe so path-breaking is not just his radical inversion of chronological approach, nor yet the infinite care taken in collecting material. It is quite simply that he is asking a question of his material. Why do some areas of the Sarthe vote in certain ways, others not? Where did the pattern start? Why has it endured? These are questions of the kind pioneered by Siegfried, of course, and it is his intelligent awareness of their importance and complexity which makes him so central a figure in modern French historiography, despite the rather reductionist responses he finally produced. As Bois, so Agulhon and Corbin, both striving to establish the proper relationship between the social structures and economic changes of their regions and the political traditions which emerged within these. If it seems strange to suggest that the best recent French social history is that which is primarily concerned with politics, the paradox is only apparent. In fact, until the political dimension was reintroduced into social history, the subject could not come of age.

The case for asking political questions of social data is not made merely by asserting that politics was a central domain even in the most remote rural communities, though this was probably more the case than is often supposed. What makes the tradition pioneered by Siegfried (and, in a different way, Lefebvre in his study of the peasants of the Nord),[3] and pursued with such success by the historians just named, so consistently important is that it enables the regional specialist to re-establish a link between local and national history. This cannot easily be done by the descriptive regionalist, whose emphasis upon the details and peculiarities of his region precludes him from saying very much other than of the most general kind about other areas and other times. But if a historian writes in depth of a given time and place with a view to answering questions which would be just as interesting and valid if posed of other times and other places, then what he comes up with may be of some wider heuristic significance.

A digression. Why *need* regional history purport to contribute to a wider sphere? Is it not sufficient unto itself? *Sub specie aeternitatis*, the answer must be yes; but *sub specie temporis*, in contemporary France, there *was* a national unit, as well as a multiplicity of provincial and local ones. French national history does exist. The regional specialist's proper objection to it is not that it should not be written, but that until we have paid greater attention to other matters, it cannot be written properly — a quite different proposition. And there is another dimension, too. Even the most carefully selected region and period may mislead the specialist into a reading of his or her material which wider perspectives might help correct. Indeed, if he or she has ignored the reality of an interaction between even the most isolated region and the mother country, then he or she will almost certainly have misunderstood what was happening in the former. What is more, the historian of nineteenth-century provincial France can hardly fail to be aware that within a few years the separate economic, cultural, linguistic identity of each region would be much reduced, absorbed through compulsory education, rural out-migration, industrialisation and conscription into the unitary state. Thus one is willy-nilly a contributor to the pre-history of contemporary France: in which case a conscious adoption of that rôle may be the best stance. Lest it be thought that such reflections arise from over-specialisation upon Provence, without doubt one of the more 'advanced' of France's regions, the reader should be apprised of the opinion of Alain Corbin, historian of one of the most backward areas of the country, and for an earlier period, but with preoccupations very similar to my own: '... nous n'avons jamais conçu l'histoire régionale comme une fin en soi, mais seulement comme un moyen de parfaire la connaissance que nous pouvons avoir de la société nationale globale'.[4]

Of course, significant questions do not have to be about politics, though in modern societies most questions about why people make the political choices they do are likely to be significant. The investigation I have conducted into the origins of socialist support in the Var depends for its success upon answering certain questions about the relations between social conditions and political options, with particular reference to the case of a society of peasant predominance. It is located in the Var because the socialists were successful there, and in the Var alone because it was hoped to dig out the sort of answers which might be harder to turn up in a more broadly-based study. Neither of these considerations precludes the possibility of extending the conclusions of this study to other areas, but both of them suggest the need for very careful sorting out of what is, and what emphatically is not, legitimate by way of extrapolation from the particular to the general.

To begin with what the specialised regional study (specialised by virtue both of the region chosen and the questions posed) cannot offer to the national historian, we have all those specific conclusions which depend for their force upon what is unique about an area. Thus in so far as Breton conservatism or the peculiar political divisions within Alsace depend upon what is unique to these provinces, accounts of them will not readily serve as broader contributions to the history of right-wing politics in France. In respect of the Var, Eugen Weber has suggested that the social life and political predilections of the peasantry of Provence are so unusual, in the French context, that what is of interest about their history is not any light which they may shed on peasants and politics elsewhere in France but, on the contrary, just how different and atypical they really are.[5]

However, such an approach, logically pursued, would signal the end of any useful relationship between regional and national history. For it is of course true that, in their totality, the historical experiences of the populations of Provence are unique – this is the very premise on which regional history is constructed. But it would be as true of the Bourbonnais, Flanders, Normandy, even the deathless villages of the Beauce, as of far-flung Provence. But reduced to its parts, the history of rural Provence is not consistently without application elsewhere. Take the question of the sociability, and its importance as a political variable (see Chapter 6). Undeniably, there is something unique, Mediterranean rather than French, about the pattern of social relationships in the villages of lower Provence. But it is not upon that peculiarity that I have constructed my explanation of why some villages were socialist, others not. What has seemed important is to emphasise that different traditions of social behaviour in different parts of the region could provide alternative climates in which the same later developments could take very different paths. And Mendras offers confirmation that *this* perspective does say something to other French communities: when television came to the Beauce, it helped accentuate a deep-rooted local anomie – reinforcing local inclinations to live in small, closed family units. In the Gers, on the

other hand, and not just through a shortage of private means, television helped reinvigorate the tradition of public, café life, with
clienteles of differing political persuasions gathering in different cafés
to watch and discuss the programmes.[6]

There are, however, more subtle respects in which local conclusions
may be misleading. Corbin very carefully draws our attention to the
fact that, notwithstanding received ideas on the subject, temporary
migration in the Limousin was not of itself important in introducing
the later predilection for Radical and socialist politics. But his argument is *so* dependent upon the special circumstances of village social
structure in the region, the demand pattern in the building trades,
the character of peasant farming in the Marches, the strengths and
weaknesses of an industrial sector heavily dependent on overseas
demand (porcelain and china manufacture in this instance) that one
is tempted to conclude that here, indeed, *is* something unique to this
region, and that in the Alps, the Pyrenees (as Armengaud suggests)
and the eastern Massif Central, returned temporary migrants *were*
the dominant force in the radicalisation of the countryside. This
does not detract from the study of the Limousin — the relationship
which Corbin set out to explain there between economic backwardness and perennially advanced politics was always likely to produce
some special explanation — but, as with the Breton case, it is likely
to be of limited national application.

A distinction is being drawn here, the reader will have observed,
between that which constitutes a contribution to the provincial
underpinning of French history, and that which has what might be
termed methodological application. So far as the former is concerned,
anything written about any part of France, given only that it is information and not surmise, is a contribution to our understanding of
France. But it is quite likely to be a contribution to our sense of the
infinite incomprehensibility of France, too. Thus in these pages I
have argued that there is little to be learnt from that technique which
purports to see religion as the determining variable in French
political life, not because there is not a clear negative correlation
between left-wing areas and churchgoing ones, but because that is
not really news and only describes afresh that which it purports to
explain. As a heuristic principle this must be true for every region,
but there is no doubt that in some parts of the country the Church

issue would have to figure far more prominently in any account of local political developments. Thus what we learn from the Var in this matter is not very helpful, except negatively, when it comes to similar questions being posed elsewhere.[7]

In the matter of historical method, however, the local historian can make rather more confident claims, however recherché and unrepresentative the data on which the method has been brought to bear. What has been said in this study with respect to ecological, occupational or territorial reductionism, using the unfortunate Professor Loubère as a *bouc émissaire*, could only be asserted with conviction on the basis of a detailed local study — and in principle the peculiarities of the area selected would be immaterial. It is worth focussing attention for a moment on this point, since it has often been assumed (again, since the work of Siegfried) that a prime function of local studies, in so far as they set out to explain human behaviour in some respect, is to show the links between the special features of a locality and the behaviour observed. Otherwise, the unreconstructed national historian might ask, why bother to write local history? Except, of course, for its own sake, as 'matière à pure érudition' (Soboul) — an intention which most local historians would firmly and properly deny.

In fact, the regional historian has precisely the same concerns as any other, and his material sometimes makes him better equipped to respond to them. The regional specialist can take the cyclical concerns of a Labrousse, or even the more abstruse queries of a Poulantzas, but can consider them in relation to a much more visible and complete range of information. Yet, far from producing thereby a tighter, more determined network of links between the various dimensions of people's lives, my experience, and the reading of other local studies, suggests that the more we know about a given community, the more likely we are to be impressed with the importance of conjuncture, of choice, of chance and autonomy in even the best-defined circumstances.

Thus, for example, there is nothing in the experience of the Var to confirm Loubère's view of wine-growing as *the* variable in left-wing politics in Mediterranean France. Of course, one might control for a variety of special factors: the structure of property, patterns of habitat, the rôle of the wine merchant (who can sometimes be the dominant local factor, a point hidden by his apparent standing as just another smallholding *vigneron*),[8] the accidents of phylloxera and overproduction and so forth. But it is precisely all these variables and many others which render the single-factor explanation such nonsense.

If we dismiss ecological determinism of this particular kind, what of territorial explanations? They are surely tempting – I have myself discussed the possible impact of habitat, location, etc., as determinants in the political behaviour of communities. But if we look to Spain or Italy we find that the Mediterranean population grouping is actually a result, not a promoter, of certain social and economic pressures, and that, here again, the political emerges as a disturbingly and inconveniently autonomous sphere. The grouped villages of the grain basin on the Ile de France show anything but a predilection for active social and political cooperation. Doubtless this has much to do with centuries of close surveillance, the absence of a historical leavening of politicised bourgeois and artisans, the nature of the grain market which tended to exclude the peasant from much relationship to any world but that of his most immediate neighbours. But in which case, here too, we find that even when dealing exclusively with 'fixed' structures, any method of explaining Frenchmen's political behaviour by extension from their social and environmental conditions is doomed to failure. And the problem with the study of conjunctures is that they have to be studied separately and in their uniqueness. Of course that is what makes history rather more demanding a discipline than sociology (supposing a legitimate distinction to be worth drawing), but it can tend to make the methodological lessons to be drawn from local work rather negative.

But the most negative lesson is only negative when first encountered. In fact, the news from the provinces is positive, on the whole. There are rather more applications of locally-established hypotheses than one might expect. One of these, to take a cue from the preceding paragraph, is that so far as explanations of the political history of France are concerned, the level of sophistication of the French electorate was rather high in the second half of the last century, although the precise perceptions of self-interest varied widely according to area and degree of integration into the nation. This seems a proper conclusion to draw from my own researches, and it is confirmed by the work of Vigier, Corbin and Agulhon on 1848–9, finally making clear precisely why and with what expectations the various peasantries supported Louis Napoleon. The rather harder question, regarding the tendency for certain political traditions to endure beyond the lifetime of those circumstances which first helped mould them, the question which led Siegfried and others into the search for political causality among the winds and the ploughtracks of differing fields, this is now responding to the investigations of a succeeding generation and, when applied in its turn to national affairs, may finally dispense with the dead hand of electoral geography which lies across so much of received opinion (and student texts) on the subject.

But why the obsession with politics? Is not this too a dead weight from the past, tempting the regional historian into asking questions and setting out techniques which bias his whole understanding of the society he is studying? After all, there has arisen in recent years a further refinement in the matter of grass-roots French history, that associated most notably with the school of *Annales* and the work of Theodore Zeldin, which emphasises the *quotidien*, the private, the personal, professional and other concerns of the millions of French men and women who took no active (and probably no passive) part in political life. If we wish truly to reconstruct the history of France, should we not be abandoning politics altogether and wandering off, literally no less than in metaphor, down the by-ways of past times?

It is very tempting to respond with an enthusiastic Yes! Few of us can resist the iconoclastic temptation to redraw *de novo* the lines of our professional interests, and the arguments for following in the footsteps of the *annalistes* are powerful. What is more, the difficulties of writing the political history of the provinces without slipping into a Parisian perspective are such that it would be very pleasing to be able to abandon the enterprise as not merely difficult but misconceived, and write, instead, 'history with the politics left out'. Even if such a break were felt to be a little too radical, one might settle for the example offered by Weber in his recent book on the transformation of rural France, and attend to the process by which provincial France was 'nationalised', while paying little attention to the accompanying complex of links between region and nation.[9]

I remain convinced, however, that the central experience of the French nation since the Revolution has been a political one – not in the simple and usual sense of elections and revolts, but because people's lives became ever more affected by events in the wider world. In the Var, for particular reasons, they were able and willing to respond actively; but even in less politicised areas why men voted as they did was *becoming*, by 1900, the most interesting thing to learn about them. This is because France itself was becoming, by the turn of the century, a political nation (as Weber, for example, would agree), and the attitudes and opinions with which Frenchmen would enter this nation are central to any sense we are to make of what happened thereafter.

What is more, the historian of France has the special advantage of observing the workings of a precocious universal male suffrage in a society still in many ways politically unformed; there is thus the possibility of studying how provincial Frenchmen understood and responded to the political nation even before they became an integrated part of it. It would be foolish to ignore the insights thus offered out of a justified distaste for the traditional forms of political history.

This is one reason for emphasising the political and making it the central theme of this book. Another has to do with the nature of historical questioning. To grasp the relationship (causal? linear? accidental?) between what was and what became, between the circumstances in which people found themselves and the circumstances which they proceeded to create, is not of course the only question worth asking of the past. But it is one of the more absorbing, because it is about how and why change actually happens, about who brings it about, but pinned down to a particular set of changes in a particular place at a given time. Even were there no other reason for placing a political grid across social and economic subject matter, the heuristic convenience of the device would be sufficient justification.

The final chapters of this book are thus a response to Corbin's invocation. They represent a tentative move from the particular to the general, but only in so far as the former has stood up to tests designed to eliminate the peculiar and the special instance. Chapters 11 and 12 are avowedly addressed to the political history of France – the very field whose traditional deficiencies in a particular respect were the mediate motive for this study. I have tried to include reference to some of the work done by authors mentioned in this chapter, among others, with the aim of grounding my conclusions more convincingly in the generality of the French experience. None of this has any reflective bearing on the conclusions expressed in Part Two, which stand in their own right (and fall, if they must, likewise). But if regional monographs are to command respect, they must have the courage occasionally to overreach themselves. The following chapters are accordingly something of an exercise upon the historical rack.

II

Politics in the countryside

A leading theme in this book has been the close identification, in Provence, of the socialist movement with the peasantry. There are, of course, substantial qualifying considerations – the peasantry of the Var lived in an environment more urban than rural, they were predominantly property-owners (on however small a scale) rather than tenant farmers or sharecroppers, and their historical experiences certainly helped create an environment apparently favourable to left-wing political movements. Nevertheless, I have also argued that they did not depend upon the artisanat or the small-town bourgeoisie for their political mobilisation, and that substantial redefinitions of socialist are not required in order for us to understand what it was that they were favouring. To this extent, the identification of a growing socialist movement with a discontented peasantry is an established characteristic of late-nineteenth-century Provence.

Such an identification will not come as news to students of modern political movements and revolutionary upheavals in rural societies in the non-European world (although the precise nature of the revolutionary commitment of the Chinese or, say, the Mexican peasant is both complex and only partially analogous to the European experience). But it runs counter to much received opinion concerning post-Revolutionary France, and this for two reasons. In the first place the creation of a society of conservative, small-property-holding peasants, tenaciously defending their independence and their status, is *still* held in some quarters to have been the major achievement of the French Revolution, notwithstanding the vast amount of work of recent years, much of which has served to show both how much eighteenth-century France was already changing *and* how much of pre-modern France survived the upheavals of the 1790s. And if this view is taken – that rural France in the nineteenth century was overwhelmingly peopled by a defensive and obdurate class of *petits propriétaires* – then clearly the proposition that such a category should have formed the basis of socialist success, even in a single region, must appear a little unlikely.[1]

The second reason why the hypothesis of a close relationship beween peasants and socialism cuts across traditional assumptions is because of the corollary to the first. If French peasants were obsessively concerned with defending the property they had seized, bought or been given in the Revolution, then the emphasis within socialist theory since Marx upon the eventual disappearance of such property (a necessary emphasis in an ideology committed to the proposition that class is predicated upon relations of production and that a socialist society shall be a classless one) ought to have ensured a continuing antipathy towards socialists among all but the poorest and propertyless inhabitants of the countryside. For this and other reasons, Marx and many of his followers were dismissive of the peasantry, *particularly* the French peasantry, and theirs was no extreme view. The Italian manufacturer Pirelli, commenting with misplaced confidence upon the impossibility of Italian socialist propaganda ever appealing with success to *his* employees, argued that this must be so since they were overwhelmingly 'peasant, female and ignorant'. Restated in the conventional syntax of late-twentieth century Marxism, and without the sexist connotation, this is the view of Nicos Poulantzas, who ought to know better. But then he, like many before him, is searching for an explanation for the failure of the strong tradition of leftism in France ever actually to produce a socialist *revolution*, and the peasantry are such a convenient scapegoat that the temptation to explain the failure of what, it is argued, would otherwise have been an exemplary proletarian movement, in terms of the *deus ex machina* in the fields, is irresistible.[2]

A primary purpose of this chapter is to show why it must be resisted. No one would suggest that there is some one-to-one relationship between small peasant proprietorship and socialist support, except under very special local and historical conditions, and perhaps not even then. But I shall argue that the peasantry *were* political in nineteenth-century France, that some of their political behaviour can usefully be understood in terms of the structural divisions within the peasant community, and that we ought therefore to treat the links between production relations, property-holding and political consciousness in the countryside with as much attention to discrete variations and internal differences as historians more traditionally exhibit when studying the urban community.

Rural France in the nineteenth century

In terms of property structure, division of labour, distribution and the like, there was much in nineteenth-century French agriculture which was already present long before 1789. The various categories of peasant — property-owning, leasehold tenant, sharecropper, landless labourer, and the many categories of artisan—peasant — are all to be found in the eighteenth-century community. What had altered, of course, was the balance between them. The number of small and middling proprietors had grown (although the fastest rate of growth in this group came not between 1790 and 1820, but in the following two generations); the number of very large landowners had diminished, and large properties of this kind had lost their overwhelmingly noble and aristocratic connotation, though not completely, especially in the west and north. Landless labourers had diminished in number, though less as a consequence of the Revolution (very few of them had been the beneficiaries of Revolutionary land sales) than through rural out-migration and the expansion of opportunities in the cities, to the point that the 1860s saw the onset of a crisis of labour shortage in the countryside.[3] Tenant farming and sharecropping (métayage — normally on one-yearly renewable agreements) remained, and it is the predominance in many areas of this form of land tenure and agriculture which makes any description of modern France in terms of a 'society of small peasant proprietors' something of a nonsense.

It was the condition of the métayers which accounted for the survival into even the twentieth century of certain feudal residues, and above all a real fear of the possible return of seigneurial authority. The métayer usually rented land, buildings and equipment from a landowner for the period of one year, commencing in November, after the completion of the harvest and post-harvest sales. Rent took the form of a fifty—fifty division of the annual proceeds between the tenant and his landlord. Furthermore there was normally a variety of additional requirements upon the tenant — that he provide from his home farm poultry, dung and vegetables to the landlord, that he provide at his own expense whatever labour force was required for the busy seasons, etc. Not uncommonly, the lease was unwritten, its implementation and renewal depending upon the whims of the landlord or his agent. In some regions, the landlord traditionally claimed the right to specify conditions concerning the civil status of his tenant — in the Beaujolais and Burgundy vineyards, the *vigneron—métayer had* to be married, and were his wife to die and he to remain single, the lease would not be renewed. The economic reasoning here was sound, if cruel: a tiny vineyard was only viable if no labour costs were incurred, yet extra labour was occasionally vital (as during the *vendange*). Hence the significance of a skilled, wageless slave in the form of a wife. But the implications for what amounted to a landlord's seigneurial control of the private life of his tenantry are no less significant for being economically rational.

Areas of predominant *métayage* (which were far more important in size than census returns of the numbers of *métayers* would suggest, since a tenantry would often cover very large tracts of arable land) were also those in which 'feudal' relations survived in even more obvious form. The survival of the tithe has been documented, in the Dauphiné and Aquitaine, for example, into the late nineteenth century, and it is perhaps significant that in those few areas of the Var where holdings under *métayage* prevailed we find reference to fears of a revival of seigneurial and pre-Revolutionary privileges; Radical propaganda in the upper Brignoles arrondissement in 1885 emphasised the danger of a return to *Lettres de cachet*, etc., in the event of a reactionary success. I shall return to the beholden and dependent status of the French *métayer* in the next section, in the context of a consideration of the relationship between conditions of land tenure and political affiliation.[4]

Tenant farmers paying money rents and usually owning their own equipment were also a survival of pre-Revolutionary days, although their status and economic position were vastly superior to that of the sharecropping *métayers*. They shared, of course, their membership of that residual category of non-property-owning peasants, but far from diminishing the standing of the *fermier* this often worked to his advantage. In the wealthy arable regions such as the Beauce and the Paris basin, where *fermage* predominated, it was quite common for a *fermier* to be the 'tenant' of anything up to a dozen small proprietors. The land held by these latter was, separately, often small and not very economically viable. But a tenant farmer could, by careful bringing together of contiguous small properties, create for himself a large and profitable farm. As a result, the individual small peasant proprietors would find themselves in receipt of a fixed money rent (often fixed for many years at a time), a rent insufficient for the maintenance of their families. The *fermier*, meanwhile, was now in effective charge of a large and profitable holding over which he exercised complete control. And as farm labourers he would employ the selfsame *petits propriétaires* whose separate parcels comprised the constituent parts of a large unit which would provide work for whole villages of peasant landowners, now dependent upon their own tenant for their wages![5]

It will be understood from even such brief accounts of the position of the 'landless' peasantry of post-Revolutionary France that it was not these people who would have any interest in the preservation and use of the quite considerable tracts of common and communal land which survived the enclosures and sales of the Revolution. To the *métayer*, whose consuming ambition was to save or borrow enough to acquire land of his own, common land only had value in so far as it represented a resource which might one day cease to be common and become, at least in part, his own. To the *fermier*, common land (which was in fact rare in those areas of high-intensity arable farming where *fermage* predominated) represented either a wasted resource or else a threat to his own local monopoly (although the smaller *fermier* might, like the *métayer*, see it as a possible future resource of his own). Paradoxical as it may seem, it was the small-property-owning peasant who regarded the preservation of common lands and common rights as a high priority. Such land could be used for the pasturing of animals (something impossible on a tiny property necessarily devoted totally to crop production), for the collection of gleanings, or even for the raising of crops, in agreement with other users. Thus the frequent survival in nineteenth-century France of ancient common rights and lands was nearly always associated with a local preponderance of very small peasant property (larger peasant landholders had less need of such social resources), in such a way as to create a bridge between post-Revolutionary property structures and pre-Revolutionary communal relations, a bridge which was to prove very important in linking peasant communities with later collectivist doctrines.

Yet a further important survival from earlier times was the continuing obsession with *subsistances* in rural France — more precisely with the price and supply of bread. This should not surprise us — the changes wrought by the Revolution had little direct bearing upon this problem which had so absorbed the attentions of eighteenth-century French administrators. Until the last quarter of the nineteenth century brought a wholesale change in the supply and distribution of corn, the question of controlling the availability of bread (or, more precisely, of what might happen were it to become scarce or dear) continued to absorb much of the attention of village mayors. Even in Provence, where proximity to communications made this traditionally less acute a problem than in more isolated regions, the mayor of Besse resorted to municipal decrees to control bread prices in 1884 — and there were threats of serious conflict in Cuers, when the mayor refused to oblige the bakers to reduce their prices, taking his stand in the name of economic liberties. In 1886 the municipality of Ollioules distributed bread free to day-labourers in the market gardens there when unseasonable flooding had deprived them of work. Objections to this costly undertaking were met by reminders that the responsibility of the municipality in such matters was a well-established one, dating back many years before the Revolution. The persistent survival of pre-modern problems (Corbin dates the decline in the acuteness of the subsistence problem from the 1850s at the very earliest for the Limousin) necessitated the continuing use of devices for social control and harmony whose character owed much to eighteenth-century conceptions of the community.[6]

This said, it would be wrong to infer either that rural France in the nineteenth century was substantially similar to pre-Revolutionary France, or that whatever similarities did persist were not themselves undergoing change. It is only the rapidity of change in urban France during the nineteenth century which, by contrast, tends to make the countryside appear so very static and immobile. In fact the rate of change in the French countryside from the 1840s and the onset of rural de-industrialisation (see below) was quite marked, if measured in demographic terms, for example. One has only to compare the worlds described by Balzac and Zola in their respective treatments of the countryside (and even allowing for the very different conceptions which these two authors brought to bear upon their subject matter) to see that rural France in 1890 was not the same as rural France in 1840. Even the *métayer* who is the focus of Guillemin's *Vie d'un simple*, living in isolation in deepest Bourbonnais, is a conscious witness to changes in the countryside during his own lifetime (*c*.1820—*c*.1900), changes manifest not least in his own political and social consciousness.

But it is as well to recall that the changes taking place affected different communities in varying ways, and this because so many of these communities were already so distinct in their characteristics. Not merely was the rural community in the nineteenth century manifestly heterogeneous in respect of land tenure, production, market-orientation, etc., but the extent to which these had been affected by recent national developments was also very variable. There were, too, massive differences in the physical appearance and size and location of peasant communities: the peasant might be an isolated unit in a farm hidden deep in the *bocage*, or he might be one of thousands living in an 'agro-town', all peasants and commuting daily to their work on the lands around. Such peasant cities were more commonly to be found in Spain or southern Italy, it is true, but on a smaller scale they formed the basis of the rural habitat in Mediterranean France at least, as we have seen. Such variations in habitat overlaid other variations within the rural community, and if the example of the Var is any indication, they probably had considerable importance in determining the extent of the survival of older attitudes and beliefs among the peasantry.

There was thus in nineteenth-century France a real tension between continuity and change, between that which endured from earlier years and that which had developed out of recent events, between those aspects of rural life which were determined by fixed elements in a given community and those which were influenced by outside changes. Whatever truisms one feels tempted to attach to rural France in the years which followed the Revolutionary turmoil, the description of it as a society of small-property-owning peasants, content with their lot, seems peculiarly ill-adapted. What remains to be investigated, however, is precisely *what* distinctions within rural France were significant in accounting for the varying ways in which different communities of peasants reacted to the changes they faced during the course of the century.

Property, produce and politics

It would seem to follow in principle from the above that the small peasant proprietor might be the most natural candidate for political radicalisation, if only because he was reasonably free of the sorts of social and economic constraints which made leaseholding share-croppers so vulnerable, while at the same time he lacked the wealth and security which made the larger sort of tenant farmer so natural a conservative. What is more, an initial reference to a map of French land tenure in the nineteenth century confirms this inference, since regions where small private property predominated were in most cases also regions where the political left did rather well.[7] But there are certain difficulties associated with both the logic of the argument and the conception of 'small' and 'large' property which need to be noted.

To begin with, we do well to recall Paul Bois' observation regarding the political attitudes of smallholding peasants: are the latter politically radical because they are independent and thus free of constraint, or is it that their small, marginal, often indebted and vulnerable economic standing makes them natural candidates for parties of opposition, just as a similar complex of circumstances produces revolutionary sentiments among an industrial proletariat? Or we can reverse the question: what makes the middle-ranking tenant farmer a conservative (as he so often seems to have been, in the Sarthe, in the Paris basin, in Provence)? Is it his relatively comfortable position, or is it the docility which comes from being in principle dependent upon the whims and interests of a landlord?[8] In the case of the *fermier* it seems clear that it is his economic rather than his social standing which makes him impervious to radical politics, since his 'inferior' social standing was often an illusion — within his community he often dominated the landlords whose property he leased. But for the *métayer* it may well have been the reverse: his insecure and impoverished economic status (very few *métayers* ever succeeded in establishing security of tenure, or in buying their way out of their 'class') ought to have identified him with the political radicals in the countryside, but his fear of the proprietor, that is to say his social standing or lack of it, induced in the *métayer* a well-documented passivity.

Thus we find nineteenth-century landlords disapproving of the

education of their tenants' children being given priority over the
needs of the farm: since in a *métayage* system the landlord took a
percentage of the produce, rather than a fixed cash rent, he would
take an interest in everything the tenant did − not least with his
children, who could be usefully employed on the land, at no extra
cost to the landlord. By the twentieth century the intervention in the
affairs of the tenant had often become much more overtly political,
without thereby losing its basis in economic interest: in 1905, a
proprietor in St Crépin en Mauges (in the west) wrote to his tenant
in the following terms: 'Il y a longtemps que je souffre en silence de
vos idées laïques. Si vous ne mettez pas vos enfants à l'école religieuse,
je me séparerai de vous.'9

In these circumstances it seems reasonable to argue that the
political passivity of the rural tenant was largely conditioned by his
fear of the repercussions of offending his landlord. But it is not
always easy to separate this from a further consideration. Although
métayage was commonly practised in arable areas, particularly in the
wheatlands of northern France, the tenant himself often had little
contact with the market to which his produce was directed. After the
harvest he might sell his share to the landlord's agent, or to a local
merchant, and have no occasion to take part himself in the commercial transactions which then ensued. For the remainder of the year
the isolated habitat of much of rural France north of the Loire conditioned him to an existence which kept him out of contact with the
outside world, saving only for occasional visits to the local church
and rare excursions to the nearest market town for the purchase of
the few essentials which could not be domestically produced. As a
result, *métayers* were often more remote from and unaffected by
political developments in the nation than were the *petits propriétaires*
who had much more occasion to take part in the market and who
were much more sensitive to national economic (and by extension
political) developments. And this apolitical characteristic of *métayage*
is only indirectly related to the position of social subservience
attaching to the leasehold form of tenure. It is part of a distinction
between market-oriented farming and subsistence agriculture which
can be traced well back into the seventeenth century and beyond,
and which even then often followed a line distinguishing the outward-
looking *fermier* or smallholder, and the isolated and ignorant *métayer*.

This in turn raises the question of the strategic significance of the crop or product in determining, or helping to determine, the outlook of the peasant. Until the cash market really began to impinge upon all areas of rural activity in the second half of the nineteenth century (later in some areas — exchange rather than purchase, and subsistence rather than production for sale were still important features of the rural economy in the western Massif Central, in upper Brittany and in the Pyrenees well into this century, for reasons of geography and soil among others), it was possible to distinguish between those crops which drew their producer into the market and those which kept him firmly trapped in a circle of subsistence and autarky. Thus wine, famously, forced its grower into the wider world because it tended to preclude a balanced agriculture — because it was so demanding in labour and so uniquely oriented toward sale rather than consumption. *Vignerons* had to purchase their bread, clothes, meat and often their tools; as a result they shared in the economic interests of the urban community in respect of their attitudes to prices, for example. Wood-cutters, resin-gatherers, although permanent members of a rural community, nevertheless shared little in common with the growers of corn or the raisers of cattle and sheep — not surprisingly, we find the woodcutters prominent among the rural *taxateurs* bands in the 1790s, demanding, like the *sans-culottes* of the towns, maximum prices and the enforcement of food-supply.

At the other extreme came the 'true' peasant. Either because he formed part of a large and diffuse community of like peasants, producers of corn or, in the north, beet, or else because he lived and worked in such poverty and isolation that he had little or nothing to offer for sale (and therefore little or nothing with which to purchase), such a man remained remote from that other world of markets, moneylenders, roads, later railways and the like which the cash-crop producer knew so well. There were overlaps, of course: market crops and subsistence crops could exist side by side — indeed a crop could be either (or both) depending upon the scale of its cultivation. But in such cases the autarkic community tended to prove the weaker, drawn into the dominant market centre, often to its cost (as when perfectly balanced and viable subsistence polycultures were tempted to turn over to monocultural production of a cash product such as wine, or beet, or pigs, thereby wrecking their natural balance without benefiting from a powerful and established position in the market).

That the orientation towards sale and purchase rather than subsistence was an important variable in the formation of rural political attitudes is well documented. The peasant risings in later medieval Europe nearly all took place in the most commercial regions of agriculture – the Paris basin, Flanders, Picardy, Lombardy, Catalonia and, arguably, south-eastern England. This is not to say that being drawn into a wider orbit necessarily serves to radicalise rural communities: there are well-documented instances of what might be termed 'reactionary' (as distinct from radical) peasant uprisings occurring in either the same areas, or else in other regions which are just entering a commercial economy (e.g. the centre-west of France at the end of the eighteenth century). What *can* be said, though, is that whatever other conditions obtain, peasant communities whose produce, either because of its nature or scale, brings them into frequent contact with a wider network of contacts are more likely to respond to changes in their condition by organising themselves politically. Whether this is because of a greater acquaintance with political possibilities (as in the Var) or through a violent reaction against the changes which are coming in from elsewhere (arguably the case for much of the regional discontent of the 1840s) is another matter.[10]

I have already suggested that one important factor in determining a peasantry's response to change is the scale on which they produce whatever crop it is which gives the region its economic identity. This question of scale also casts light on an issue raised earlier – the significance of property *ownership* (as distinct from the social relationships which it generates). We talk easily of 'small' and 'large' property as if these were self-evident categories. In fact there never was, in France at least, a 'norm' for distinguishing small property from medium-size holdings, or the latter from large ones. In regions where the soil was poor, or where the local crop was only profitable when grown on a large scale, holdings of less than 10 hectares might be worthless (except in status terms – their owner might have to earn his living as a labourer or in a factory, but he appears in census returns as a *propriétaire–cultivateur*), contributing to that statistical illusion which sees contemporary France as dominated by smallholding peasants, many of whom own what English statistics would record as a garden, or perhaps an allotment. At the other extreme, in areas of high-quality wine production, 2 hectares was a necessary and sufficient holding. Less than that and the *vigneron* could not produce enough to meet his costs; more, and he would be constrained to hire labour, without increasing his returns in commensurate proportion. As a result, we find that in the west 40 hectares and above was normally treated as a *grande exploitation*, with all the prestige and influence attaching thereto; in Brittany, a holding of 30 hectares qualified its owner as *un grand*. In the Beaujolais, during the nineteenth century, the owner of a 20-hectare vineyard was a major employer and dominant local figure. But in the impoverished Limousin, a holding of less than 25 hectares defined the owner as a *petit propriétaire* (although in the favoured, wine-producing micro-region around Brive, a proprietor of 6–8 hectares was doing very well – the crop conditioning both the economic and thus the social standing of its producer).[11]

Regions of predominantly large property (defined in local terms) tended to conservatism in politics. At first sight this may seem an unlikely proposition, since large property meant a high proportion of *journaliers*, agricultural labourers, of whom one might expect more radical behaviour. But in fact landless workers in rural areas were *not* noted for their political radicalism – or for political commitment or participation in general. They had little enough attachment to the area (unless they were simultaneously small owners, rounding out their incomes while their family cared for the property – as in the Seine-et-Marne, or in the Hérault where struggling *vignerons* worked on the new estates from the 1890s), and when faced with unemployment or a difficult employer would often simply depart. Furthermore, they were in short supply after about 1860, and the wages they could command often served to make them better off, particularly if they received lodging as well, than the sharecropper or tiny proprietor. Finally, they lacked common backgrounds and a base in the community, often being fairly recent arrivals, young men without families. What is more, the temporary and seasonal migration which served to introduce new and radical ideas and attitudes into the communities whence the migrants came was very rarely found in regions of large property – because work was to be had in the locality and did not have to be sought farther afield. Consequently, this too tended to preserve regions of large property from radical politicisation (although one might ask whether it was the social predominance of large landowners or the absence of radicalised migrants which made for such conservatism). The Guesdists, like the Démocrates–Socialistes of 1849, reflected this situation by concentrating their attentions elsewhere, at least until the strike of the *bûcherons* in the winter of 1891 drew their attention to the political potential of discontented rural workers.[12]

But if the scale of operations of the large landowners, and the local influence they could exercise, worked against the introduction of collectivist political ideas in regions where such forms of property predominated, did not the very smallness of small peasant property also create unfavourable conditions? More precisely, was not the individualism of the small proprietor, whatever he grew, however marginal he was, an insuperable barrier to the radicalisation of the countryside (radicalisation, that is, beyond the essentially conservative radicalism of the Radicals)? It seems not. Regions where small property predominated and which evinced a marked aversion for collectivism in theory and in practice seem commonly to have had long-standing traditions of opposition to *any* external interference with their affairs. This is certainly true of the Limousin, and it also holds for the Béarn, where the post-1945 introduction of producers' cooperatives was bitterly fought by the local peasantry, who (perhaps correctly) saw cooperatives, with their large-scale operations and bureaucratic tendencies, as the direct successors to the *négociants* and the tax-gatherers of old, traditional exploitation of the small man but in a new guise. But cooperatives and rural syndicates had a great success both in Provence and also (at a later date) in Brittany, though in rather different forms.[13]

In general, the 'individualism' of the smallholding peasant has probably been overstated: we have already seen how small property could coexist with the survival of common land (which occupied up to 50% of the farmland of some communes); but by the end of the nineteenth century the main argument against the thesis of the conservative independent peasant is quite simply that for most of the smaller units this independence was quite illusory. One assessment puts the number of indebted property-holding peasants by 1900 as high as 90% of the total. In these circumstances, the appeal of a 'collective' solution to their chronic economic difficulties may have been stronger than one might first assume. Nor do the residual anti-collectivist attitudes of certain areas of small property necessarily conflict with such an argument, since it is noteworthy that the areas in question were predominantly those which had retained their autonomous, isolated character later than most. Thus their reaction to the changes affecting them in the mid-twentieth century should be seen as a defensive response to the incursions of urban capitalism into hitherto largely unaffected regions – in this sense their attitudes mirror those of the more advanced regions a century earlier. But because state-favoured 'collectivism' (e.g. centrally-financed cooperatives) now represents the form in which the modern economy impinges upon rural society it is resented and rejected – just as liberal capitalism was in the previous century. To emphasise the importance of the property-holding features of the affected regions might suggest a continuity of structural causality at the expense of the historical conjuncture – an approach which work on the Var suggests to be empirically misguided as well as epistemologically unsound.

Urban peasants and rural workers

Thus far I have emphasised the specifically rural and agricultural characteristics of the French peasantry. But the notional homogeneity of the latter is further weakened when we recall the very considerable extent to which industry and agriculture, peasant and worker overlapped and interacted in post-Revolutionary France.

To begin with there was the confusion of geographical identity, a confusion accentuated in France by the administrative distinction between rural communities (those with less than two thousand people) and urban ones. In fact, many communities which were officially 'rural' housed a large percentage of men and women whose work and outlook was essentially urban (as in the case of the many mining villages of the centre). *Mutatis mutandis*, there were frequent instances of sizeable towns which housed a majority of people who worked in the fields. Furthermore, even a small, 'rural' community of some 1500 people, predominantly peasant in occupation, might be so distinctly urban in character as to have very little in common with the true peasant hamlet or village. Such was the case for some of the bourgs of Lorraine, and also of course for the Mediterranean region of France. Also, the complexity of a village economy might give its community a mixed, almost cosmopolitan character quite different from the purely peasant and agricultural nature of a much larger village of the type found in the Beauce or in Artois. These distinctions between peasant communities, rural communities and agricultural settlements would all have had marked effects upon the differing political traditions and allegiances which the various populations manifested.

Secondly, even the most truly rural community in nineteenth-century France was very rarely exclusively agricultural. It could not be otherwise. Those working on the land required the services of blacksmiths, tailors, bakers and the like, but they also were not infrequently in need of a second income themselves, so that many peasant communities were in fact occupationally 'mixed' — the peasant would survive only if he (or, very often, his wife) served simultaneously as a rural labour force for urban-based industry. Sailmakers, spinners and especially weavers, hatters, lace-workers, tanners, masons, all these and many others were to be found closely interwoven into the rural economy. In Cuers, for example, the local tanneries depended upon the sumac grown by the poorer peasants on the hillsides, just as they depended upon those same peasants for occasional work in the tanneries themselves.

Often enough, rural industry and peasant farming constituted a small-scale economy substantially apart from the money nexus of the national market. Thus a peasant might provide a village tailor with a given quantity of cloth in order to make up an item of clothing. The quantity provided would be in excess of that required, the difference being retained by the tailor in lieu of payment. A similar system operated for relations between pastoral farmers and butchers, or corn-growers and millers or bakers. Nor were the two forms of production complementary only at the point of consumption. Since many rural industries depended upon water power, it was not unusual in the Alps, the Massif Central and the Pyrenees for mills and their dependent workshops to function for part of the year only. During the dead season (and also, but for other reasons as well, during the harvest months) the manufacturer, himself often a local landowner, would employ his labour force on the land, a system which offered security to both sides.

Much of this characteristically pre-modern society, where industry and agriculture were in many social respects inseparable, was undergoing change during the nineteenth century, as urban-based industry increasingly undercut and outproduced its rural predecessors, benefiting from improved communications in order to send its competitive products deep into the heart of the countryside. But France offers an interesting instance of a country where this change took longer to effect than in many other industrialising countries, with a number of important consequences.

One of these was the creation, and extended survival, of two categories of employee in French society, the worker—peasant and the part-time peasant. A paradigm of the first type were the miners of the western Allier, in the Commentry region. These men, employed full-time in the local mining industry, nevertheless retained their smallholdings in the region and continued to employ their families and in-laws upon them. They themselves would often put in an evening's work on their holding after a shift in the pit, but in the harvest season the mines would close down, in order that all might give their full attention to the needs of agriculture — which suggests that the latter must have retained at least some economic significance in the community. This pattern obtained elsewhere, and in other industries. In 1870, 30% of the labour force at the Carnoules—Houlès textile factory in Castres worked only in the winter, returning to its (freehold) land in the spring. When the iron-forges of the eastern Pyrenees closed in the 1860s, many of the men who had been classified as *métallos* in the census of 1856 appeared on that of 1876 as owner—farmers. The miners of Epinac in the Saône-et-Loire fought against 12-hour shifts not because of the wages or conditions (the company offered considerable concessions in earnings, accommodation and fringe benefits in return for agreement on a 12-hour day) but, by their own admission, because they preferred a lower-paid, shorter day which allowed them to put in a few hours' work on their land after coming off. Even the steady, year-round employees in the industries of the eastern Tarn retained a piece of land, often a pig and some poultry — and went to work in the vineyards of the Hérault whenever they were laid off.[14]

The corollary of the industrial worker who retained all his links with his rural origins (often over two or three generations of industrial employment) was the peasant who looked increasingly to industry for part-time employment. This could take the form either of local seasonal work, or else temporary migration. The former was the more widespread, since it was in essence the natural development from pre-modern cottage out-work; as the small peasant (owner or tenant) found his position ever more threatened, so he would look increasingly for work which would offer a steady money income with which to help him survive in an increasingly monetarised agricultural economy. He might, if he lived within reach of a manufacturing city such as Lyon, attach himself to the industrial network of the city; failing that he would set up as a part-time shoemaker, carter, tradesman, in the hope of subsidising thereby his income from farming. The usual result was that the latter declined still further and, while the peasant himself might scrape by, his offspring would almost certainly be obliged to move away from the village.

The second category of part-time peasants was the voluntary migrants. The masons of the Creuse are the best known case, not least because they had been carrying their skills abroad for so many years (the presence of Limousin masons has been documented in Uppsala, Sweden, for as far back as 1287!). But in fact many other regions showed similar patterns: tinkers and booksellers, employees in the catering and hostelry trade, wandering teachers, not to mention the thousands of Alpine farmers who descended to the valleys in search of work every year, all of these were temporary migrants, normally from a region of small rural property. In a majority of instances they were men whose families held property in the home village, and for whom migration, with or without a particular skill, was always temporary: both in the sense that they would often return every year, and more generally in their long-term intention to settle and raise a family in their community of origin. In this sense, they remained peasants, in their outlook and expectations, if not in their acquired skills; but of course they brought back with them from Paris or Lyon, or simply from their encounters on the road, new ideas and critical attitudes which would have significant effects upon the rural commune whence they came.[15]

It is this political impact of the interaction between town and country, peasant and worker, which interests me here. Whereas the part-time peasant who remained at home never acquired the outlook of the proletarian, because his forays into the factory or the mine were temporary, unwilling and seasonal, the industrial worker who retained close links with the land seems to have developed a dual consciousness. He acquired in the mining community in particular a strong occupational, if not class, consciousness, while simultaneously rejecting the fatalistic attitude of the worker whose horizons had become firmly bound by the factory and the city street. Moreover, the worker—peasant had, in his land, an invaluable resource, however small, on which to fall back in a major industrial conflict. Thus in the strikes at the silver mines of Giromagny, in the Belfort region, in 1893, forty miners struck and held out for eleven days. The strike failed — but only five of the original strikers returned to the mine; the rest chose to stay on their fields until they could find alternative work elsewhere. A few years later, during a strike in a textile factory in Lepuix-Gy over an unpopular foreman, strikers ignored the owner's threat to sack all those who did not return. Instead they went to work on the land which most of them had retained, through their families. The owner eventually gave in, sacked the foreman and raised wages in a (successful) attempt to induce the striking weavers to return. A final example might be the striking brickmakers of St Zacharie, in the Var, in January 1924, who found work in the fields even in midwinter and held out until their claims were met. The contrast with the fully industrialised and landless, hence vulnerable, industrial proletariat of contemporary England, or Belgium, is very marked.[16]

The foregoing suggests the importance of the rural connection in any account of the occupational militancy of certain categories of French worker before World War One. It is rather harder to assess its impact upon the countryside itself. Did the enduring contact between industrial worker and rural peasant in modern France result in the precocious introduction of political consciousness, acquired in the cities, into the countryside? It would appear unlikely, except in the special case of rural communities heavily dependent upon a unique class of migrants — yet even there Corbin warns us against facile assumptions: the events of Paris in 1848 appear to have left unhappy memories in the migrant villages of the Limousin, and Corbin has demonstrated beyond reasonable doubt the absence of any neat correlation between migrant populations and political leftism (although his evidence suggests above all that it was the sedentary, urban Limousin which was sympathetic to the left, not the migrant, rural regions; but what made the former left-wing – its sedentary character or the fact that it was urban?).

The answer appears perhaps a little more complex. The truly important result of such a long period of changeover, during which industrial and agricultural France shared an often interchangeable labour force, was that the rural community was given an extra lease of life – there remained in France a huge peasant sector long after the bases of an industrial society had been established. Consequently, the political organisations and doctrines which responded to the growth of an industrial and capitalist economy had a large and increasingly discontented rural population to whom they could also appeal (indeed, in conditions of a precociously established universal male suffrage, to whom they *had* to appeal). Moreover, the specific forms of discontent emerging in the countryside lent themselves rather well to expression within modern political categories, particularly those of the socialist movement.

The major factors here were the twin emergence of monoculture and rural de-industrialisation. Both of these were induced by industrialisation in the wider community, both had de-stabilising effects upon the rural community, and both led, in a country where there remained strong cultural as well as economic grounds for resisting emigration (whether to the city or overseas – in the former instance because of the *relatively* slow growth of the urban demand for labour), to an increased politicisation of the affected peasant populations.

The impact of a switch from a balanced polyculture to a single-crop economy is something I have documented for the Var. But the conclusions to be drawn from the Provençal experience seem generally applicable. Initially the result of a transfer of resources to a single cash-crop such as wine was a marked increase in profits and living standards. But within a very short while the vulnerability to disease, market fluctuation and climate of any single crop would produce growing debts, bankruptcies, sales of smallholdings and an increased concentration of land in the hands of a few large landholders, men who could afford the investment and reserves necessary to grow wine or raise sheep on an economic scale. Very often such men, as in the case of the transformation of the vineyards of the Hérault after the phylloxera, would be former *rentiers* or even industrialists, attracted by the potential profits to be had (the only major capital outlay being the initial land purchase).

This fairly standard pattern of events is documented for colonial economies as well as for the agricultural lands of Europe. The balanced and self-sustaining polyculture of Ceylon was destroyed by the introduction of tea as a unique crop, and it may be fruitful to think of the recent history of rural communities in France (as in Italy) as closely analogous to the experience of the colonised societies of the Third World (such an analogy, pursued within reason, would twin with Eugen Weber's view of the 'national' colonisation of provincial France in cultural terms — and it would also remind us of the similarly radicalised peasantry of the ex-colonies). If we add to the list of disadvantages incurred by villages which had switched to monoculture the fact that many single-crop economies were destructive of the soil, at least until modern developments in chemical fertiliser, we have the beginnings of an understanding of the link between economic change and political radicalisation. It was not difficult for the indebted peasant to see the large individual entrepreneur as the cause of his troubles, and the collectivity (or even the state?) as the only source of salvation.

Rural de-industrialisation was the corollary of the ending of a polycultural subsistence economy. Artisans, retired bourgeois *rentiers*, small rural industries (especially those in direct competition with urban manufacturers), all depended in large part upon the viability of the peasantry, upon a thriving agriculture, for their survival. For a generation or so they might survive through partial and temporary migration, or by switching their own resources back into agriculture. But the former led logically to departure, while the latter was precluded by the very crisis which had induced it. Once the rural economy became both simplified and integrated into the national one, once, that is, the peasants became effectively a service sector for the towns rather than a community in their own right, it was the non-agricultural population which was the first to leave — a process which is as well documented for the Limousin or Picardy as it is for the Var. From the 1870s onwards, the rural community in France was becoming increasingly a purely agricultural one. The fact that this process was slower and more delayed in France than in most industrial countries does not detract from its implications for French politics.[17]

Quite the reverse, in fact. This is because the de-industrialisation of the countryside, leaving behind a rural population more purely peasant than it had ever been, was followed in France by a *décalage*, a time lag before the onset of the transformation of agriculture and the departure of the peasantry. It is this time lag, which endured for roughly the same period as the Third Republic (a coincidence pregnant with significance for a proper understanding of that régime), which created a peculiarly peasant community, in many respects especially receptive to rapid politicisation.

Most of the reasons for this have been considered above and in Part Two. It remains to note, however, that the increase in political activity in France in the freer air of the Republic coincided with a period when political and economic authority in the villages often came very close to being synonymous. As the previously dominant artisans, small entrepreneurs and the like departed, so the municipal councils came increasingly to be dominated by the agricultural peasantry. These were, moreover, frequently the selfsame men who appear on the committees of agricultural cooperatives, rural syndicates and the like. In consequence the municipality often ended up as a sort of economic council, administering the purchase and distribution of fertiliser, seeking out buyers for the cooperative, etc. In short, economic and social homogeneity led to political unity, the latter reflecting very precisely the interests and character of the former. I have documented this pattern for the Var, where traditions of communal collectivism might be thought to have overdetermined such a development; but Mendras suggests quite convincingly that it was something common to many different regions of the country in the years after 1890.[18] The rural community drew closer together, both through adversity and through the absence of competing interests (the capitalist interests, urban and rural, which threatened the community were very rarely based in it), and was thus all the better able to manifest a collective political attitude. From this to the adoption of collectivist ideas was but a small step, in view of the nature of the crises faced and the contingently relevant appeal of collectivist theories.

A class of peasants?

Much of the foregoing is highly germane to a debate which has been conducted through the literature on recent French rural history concerning the precise identity of political conflicts in the countryside. What has been at issue is the extent to which political divisions in rural communities correspond to the categories of social division usually subsumed under the heading of class conflicts. Those who deny such a correspondence tend to treat the countryside as, if not economically homogeneous, then at any rate so heavily dependent upon traditional forms of social relations (clientelist politics, powerful village *notables*, etc.) as to stand quite outside of the usual divisions between employers and employees, owners of the means of production and propertyless workers, etc. The peculiar character of rural society then manifests itself through political allegiances which have more in common with one another than they do with any analogous strata in urban communities. The politics of rural protest are thus, it is argued, a sub-category of *agrarisme*, that general attitude of mistrust and separation which characterises *all* peasants in their dealings with the rest of society.[19]

Enough has been said here for it to be clear that I do not share this view. But it does not follow from this that a 'class'-based view of peasant political behaviour is the correct one in every instance. The very nature of the countryside — physical separation from other peasants, the absence of regular human contacts, the predominantly private and individual character of the annual work routine, except for particular crops and at particular seasons — all this cannot but accentuate the 'low-classness' of peasants.[20] Only under the rather special circumstances of the Mediterranean habitat, and even there only in very particular historical circumstances, could peasants acquire a consciousness of their common identity, and the opportunity to act upon that awareness.

Notwithstanding this, we do well to remind ourselves that the usual condition of most peasants, in France as elsewhere, is one which conforms in a variety of ways to certain common denominators of a social class. In so far as they are neither nomadic, *rentiers* nor regular wage-earners, the bulk of the peasantry who *work* the land in fact constitute a common unit. This fact is disguised by complicated variations in land tenure, which, as in the case of the large multiple-tenancy *fermier* and the marginal small proprietor, can be extremely misleading. In many instances, tenants, sharecroppers and small-holders suffered at the hands of moneylenders, middlemen, absentee landowners, *négociants* and the like. The *vigneron—métayer* of the Beaujolais provides the paradigm: year in, year out, he would deliver his wine at the *vendange* to his landlord (who was often himself a wine merchant), receiving the lowest possible price for it. The landlord would then store the wine in his cellars until the price rose after a couple of years, selling it at the most advantageous point. The *vigneron*, who had no storage resources and in any case could not afford to wait until prices rose (even if this was a matter of months rather than years), would thus be a consistent victim of any price rises in cereals, for example, since his own income was not susceptible of increase to match. It made little difference whether the *vigneron* was a leaseholder or freeholder, since in either event it was the small scale of his operation which made him a victim of the market both as producer and consumer. In effect, the landlord—*négociant* was extracting a form of surplus value from the small wine-growers, and the notional independence of some of the latter is irrelevant to the fact.[21]

Thus although one cannot speak of a neat relationship between ownership of the means of production and social class, the more subtle but no less effective control exercised by *some* producers over the condition of *everyone* created relations of production which come very close to being the same thing. Now such a set of relationships in the countryside *cannot* reproduce the urban experience – thus share-croppers cannot strike, however oppressed and exploited, because they have a share in the crop whose production they would prejudice, a share in more precise a sense than that applicable to the factory worker who 'prejudices' the thing he produces for an employer by ceasing, temporarily, to produce it. What is more, this complicating element in rural life, a result of the conditions of rural production and of social relations inherited from feudal economies, accentuates a phenomenon which can be observed in urban politics. To put it at its most simple, it is not the poorest and most downtrodden who are necessarily best placed to recognise their predicament and act upon it. As for those who can and do respond to their condition – in this instance the small and independent peasantry – their response *has* to be a political rather than an economic one. That is to say that the opportunity and propensity for joining a union is lower in the countryside than in the city, for obvious reasons of convenience and organisation. But the consciousness of their position and the desire to alter it expresses itself instead through political allegiance, which poses fewer difficulties of access and action than does trade-union activity. This may be one reason for the absence of that 'trade-union consciousness' which is supposed to have plagued some sectors of the working class and blunted their capacity for revolutionary action. Such a problem, if it is one, would be unlikely to arise in the country-side. On the other hand of course, it is trade-union activity which most clearly articulates a certain class consciousness – hence the apparent absence of the latter in even the most politically radical rural community.[22]

If we accept the notion that the French peasantry may be seen as exhibiting some of the characteristics of a class – or at any rate, that the notion of a class conflict in the countryside is a heuristically useful device, in the way that theories of 'agrarian' society are clearly not – can we advance from this to some conception of class-based politics in rural France? Can we, that is, link the politicisation of the French peasantry in the second half of the nineteenth century to some broader view of the relationship between social class and political behaviour?

One insuperable difficulty in the path of such a procedure is the immense variation in the chronology of political development in rural France, as in the rest of the country. If 'politicisation' merely means the introduction of formal political divisions and consistent party or group allegiances into every level of French life, then of course one can date it in the first half of the Third Republic, because that is when France became a modern political nation, largely through the conscious efforts of her administrators to make her one. But if we go further than this, and try to identify the moment when the rural community began to express its internal conflicts and discontents in modern political terms, or even in political terms *tout court*, then of course we shall meet not merely the extraordinary range of regional differences, but also the phenomenon of the *autonomy* of political life in France. In a society whose political development, at the national level, so outstripped and outran her rate of social change, it is not surprising that we find memories of the Revolution, and the ideas and aspirations it produced, occasionally surfacing in regions whose own historical experience and economic development would have been otherwise most unlikely to generate such things.

As a result, even the most careful and sophisticated attempts to 'date' the end of the 'old' politics of violent atavism born of economic backwardness, and the beginnings of the 'new' politics of integration and acceptance of change seem misconceived. The Var was politicised, in most senses of that word, well before the mid-1850s where Charles Tilly and others place the changeover, just as the Limousin, Brittany and perhaps the Cevennes were still not so politicised a generation and more after that date. As for the argument that there is a coincidence which goes beyond mere chance between the ending of fears of a subsistence crisis, around 1857, and the ending of violent rural upheavals in the same decade, this is weak on both economic grounds (*fears* of a *crise de subsistances* — and it was the fear, not the reality, which mattered — can be found as late as 1888 in Toulon) and political ones (the ending of violent rural upheaval has something to do with the scale of repression, quite unparalleled, in 1851–2; social historians ignore the history of authority and repression, and its impact upon the repressed, at their own risk).[23]

On the other hand, if we abandon the rather barren obsession with the dating of 'modernisation' in France, and concern ourselves with the modality of the process, the outlook is more positive. It does seem that the higher the 'classness' of a given rural community, the greater its propensity to adopt left-wing political allegiances at the point that the community in question entered the national political world. Thus the hamlets and bourgs of the west, whatever the condition of the local population, were mobilised politically behind Church and noble, or at least *notable*, and thus integrated into the nation as part of the conservative France. The presence of a powerful local bourgeoisie, or the economic preponderance of one or more large landowners, overlay whatever sense of identity might have been achieved by the local peasantry — the more so in that these were regions where the sense of identity was undermined by geographical dispersion and economic isolation. But where there *was* no such leavening of social superiors, no filter through which the outside world entered the peasants' consciousness, then the latter's capacity to manifest itself directly through that political ideology most closely reflecting its own interests comes across strongly.

It is important to be clear that the difference between left- and right-wing areas was not just a matter of shifting styles of clientèle politics. That is, the socialists at least were not merely taking up where the previous generation of *notables* had, as it were, left off. If we adopt Halévy's definition of the local *notable* in Third Republican politics, we can see this clearly: the local *notable* at the village level, he suggested, had three consistent characteristics. He mixed social and economic and political power, rendering them indistinguishable; he occupied positions of both local and external (or national) authority, thus conveying in both directions a sense of political legitimacy; and he was heavily dependent upon a network of local and personal relations for his success. None of these applies to the socialists in the Var — but all of it, of course, fits neatly the pattern of *Radical* success in the countryside. What is more, the Radicals consistently did better, as we have seen, in the cantonal capitals, where such power-broking took place, whereas socialists won their victories in the communes. From this we may conclude that the Radicals came close to inheriting and practising the politics of local influence and notability, mirroring thereby the conservatives with whom they competed for such authority. But the Socialists (and later the Communists) were an altogether different phenomenon, representing as they did a much more modern style of political mobilisation. In this, at least, the Socialists were showing the way to a more urban pattern of political allegiance, breaking clear of the more complex and refracted forms of political relations which had dominated until then. *Pace* Tilly, the real break between the old and the new politics in France comes not in the middle of the régime of Napoleon III (always an unlikely proposition, if only because of the effective absence of any political life for the greater part of that régime), but at the end of the first generation of the Third Republic.

In the light of what has been suggested in this chapter, it seems not merely unsurprising that the peasantry should have provided, under certain conditions, a favourable soil for the socialist movement, but actually a rather obvious proposition. Whatever their status as a class, and I have argued that such a status has some claims to recognition, the peasantry have *always* exhibited a greater propensity for revolutionary fervour than have the other constituent groups of modern societies — and the fact that the very structure of peasant society prevents this fervour from carrying through into organised, self-interested and successful action in most cases is neither here nor there. In the absence of an organised and directed channel for such fervour, it has traditionally taken 'negative' forms — *jacqueries*, rick-burning, lease-burning, grain-seizing, even assaults on towns. But with the coming of modern political movements of the left — and given that the latter have been constrained to take notice of the peasant, something they have been ideologically disinclined to do — the political force represented by the peasantry, particularly in the special circumstances of their decline and delayed disappearance in France, has provided a vital platform for the initial success and implantation of such movements.

But this fact prompts a further question: what has been the long-term effect upon socialism in France (the question would be no less interesting for Italy) of its support from within the rural community? It is sometimes said that the inadvertent achievement of socialist movements, indeed their very historical function, has been to integrate the working class into capitalist society, via the political opportunities created by the liberal ideals of such societies. But what of the view that the socialist movements, in their turn, have been integrated harmlessly into the very society whose overthrow constituted their initial *raison d'être*? It would be difficult to deny that this has happened — and is happening to their successor movements further to the left. But unless we adopt the attitude which sees the socialist parties of industrial societies as flawed from the outset we have still to explain why political socialism in western Europe did not achieve any of its initially-stated ends. Is the answer not perhaps to be found in the unexpectedly *rural* character of much of socialist support in its formative years? The frustratingly barren nature of recent attempts to account for the absence of revolution in industrial societies, so often centred around discussions of the presence or absence of innate and immanent revolutionary consciousness in a proletariat which has balked at the last fence, makes some redefinition of the question in other terms at least worth attempting. The final chapter of this book is accordingly devoted to an assessment of the impact of rural society upon the chequered recent history of the revolutionary tradition in France.

12

The roots of socialism

The history of socialism in France is normally conceived in terms of a study in failure. The theme lends itself to variations: political incompetence, intellectual inadequacy, moral turpitude, a failure of the will. The perspective adopted rather depends upon the location of the observer, of course, but it is fairly common to most students of the subject that they see the history of the left in France as uniquely unsuccessful in view of the advantages which are taken to have been conferred upon it by its inheritance of the mantle of revolutionary tradition, stretching from the Bastille to the Commune. With everything going for them, so to speak, French Socialists still failed in their historic mission.

Describing the matter in those terms, of course, is loading the dice quite heavily. Only if one takes a very particular view of the historical process is it possible to assert that the Socialists failed to achieve certain ends whose attainment was their historical function. More precisely, the Socialists failed to bring about that proletarian revolution which was their *raison d'être* and the logical as well as the moral basis for their doctrine. Now to say this is to admit that there was nothing very peculiar to the French about this particular defect in the historical performance of the left; their British and German colleagues have done no better, *sub specie temporis*. But whereas even the most mechanistic followers of Marx have been constrained to admit that certain peculiar and autonomous characteristics of British politics and culture are an important aid to the understanding of the reformist character of much labour history in this country, such an explanation hardly applies in the French case. Quite the reverse: in so far as national political traditions play a rôle in complicating the forms of social conflict in industrial societies, the left in France, as the legitimate heir to the unique traditions of upheaval in that country, ought to have been especially well placed to channel the immanent revolutionary consciousness of the masses into successful organised action.

The fact that the left in France has failed to achieve its aims apparently despite such a favourable inheritance could of course be ascribed to the incomplete and peculiar development of those forces within French society whose historical 'rôle' it was to support the Socialists in their aspirations. But while this is on the face of it an attractive notion, it soon meets two difficult objections. In the first place it merely postpones the real problem, since it implies that once the disadvantages resulting from belated industrialisation and a fragmented proletariat have been overcome, the revolutionary tradition in France will come into its own. It is not clear, on the basis of the post-war experience of rapid industrialisation in France, that this need be the case. And in any case, such a perspective encounters the second major objection — that other countries with large and well-organised industrial proletariats have come no nearer to experiencing a socialist revolution (except, as might be argued in the Czechoslovak case, where the change has been imposed from the outside). This is not the place to enter into the debate concerning the putative revolutionary characteristics of the industrial working class — except to say that the inadequacies and ideological presuppositions of sociological theories of 'bourgeoisification', a 'new' working class and the like do not weaken the force of their common theme — the historically *un*revolutionary nature of the industrial proletariat in mature or late capitalist societies.

However, to speak of the historical weakness of the French left is not necessarily to locate oneself within the Marxist tradition. It is true that the failings of socialists in recent French history appear particularly marked if set in the context of certain determined expectations, but there are other perspectives from which it is no less reasonable to speak of failure. One might argue that the French left has consistently failed even to take such opportunities as history has offered it to better its own political standing and perhaps thereby contribute to the improvement of the condition of those whom it purported to represent. On those rare occasions when it has attained power in the state, the left in France has apparently exhibited a degree of political incompetence and moral inadequacy almost unrivalled in the history of social democracy. Without entering into the details of each instance, one has only to refer to the sad decline of the Popular Front, the unwillingness to capitalise upon the opportunities and hopes of the years 1944–7, the Algerian policies of Guy Mollet in the mid-1950s, to see that the history of the left governments in France is not a happy one. The achievements of the left in opposition are a different matter – perhaps the most remarkable being the capacity to survive an almost unbroken period in the political wilderness from 1871 to 1924, and again from 1958 to 1977, without disappearing altogether. Otherwise, the chronic inability of the socialist left in France to remain united and coherent even in opposition has been paid for heavily in the failure to capitalise upon social discontent and the inability to establish itself firmly in office when the opportunity arose.

One might perhaps argue that this fragmented characteristic of the modern French left is in fact one of the ways in which it has most diligently inherited and continued the revolutionary tradition in the nation's past. The history of the left (a convenient anachronism) in the years from 1796 to 1871 was nothing if not one of failure, even of despair. But such an argument has its limitations – after all, the experiences of the later Jacobins, of the Babouvistes, of Blanqui and the Quarante-huitards, even of the communards, were of reformers and revolutionaries whom even their contemporaries understood to have little hope of lasting success. But that sort of failure might be thought to be of real benefit to later, better-organised generations, offering them a myth and a legitimating martyrology, without prejudicing their own chances of reaching their goals.

There is common agreement, then, that the history of the left in modern France has not been a very glorious one. Some believe that it has failed in a world-historical sense, others that it has merely missed opportunities, others still that it has simply been unable to fulfil even its most moderate ends, when the opportunities were there. And most agree that there was some reason in contemporary French history to suppose that such need not have been the case – France had an early and important Revolution, whatever particular or historical character we give it, there was a long-standing and well-developed movement of social protest and reform, a more or less liberal society survived longer than in any other major continental European country (Spanish, Italian and German socialists faced difficulties of which their French counterparts had no experience until 1940), and a large number of French people consistently voted for the Marxist left. Why has the latter been so unsuccessful in attaining either its long-term or even its medium-term ends?

On the weaknesses of the left in France

Views from within

A dominant theme of critics taking their stance within the Marxist tradition in France has been that of the failure of leadership. The evident inability of the SFIO to take advantage of the opportunity for revolution offered by the crises of 1917–21 and again of 1936 is held to result from that party's historical inertia in the face of revolutionary praxis. It could organise the industrial masses behind a party whose theoretical basis was revolutionary, but it offered neither firm leadership in the matter of tactics and political strategy, nor any sure grasp of the proper relations between theory and practice on the one hand, and party and class on the other.

Not surprisingly, such a description of the state of French socialism before 1920 is peculiarly well adapted to the needs of the PCF, whose own historians have been to the fore in presenting it. In the first place, it locates the SFIO firmly in a particular historical context and rôle, while simultaneously asserting that the context ended with the First World War and the rôle ceased once the industrial proletariat had completed the first stage of its mobilisation and organisation as a class. Secondly, it justifies the entry of a Leninist party on to the French scene after 1920 by arguing that the previous defects of organised protest in France arose from the absence, in effect, of a *revolutionary* party (which the old SFIO was not and could not become) – a defect to be made good by a new party modelled on the Russian one (while, it is claimed, simultaneously capitalising on the élan and revolutionary praxis of the old French revolutionary tradition which the SFIO had squandered in its search for a wide membership and electoral success).[1]

Such a view of things might have appeared reasonable until 1936, perhaps even until 1945. Indeed, in so far as it serves as a commentary upon the apparent tendency of socialist parties to lose their revolutionary character in their efforts to achieve successes in the short term, it is an interpretation which could be found in the writings of men and women who would be quite shocked to find themselves in such company. But as a description which purports to explain weaknesses in pre-1914 socialism *which would disappear* with the coming of Communist parties, it loses most of its force when we realise that, in the half-century which has elapsed since their birth, Leninist parties in industrial societies have followed much the same route, in their political *practice*. And if they would maintain that they have retained their revolutionary character in theory, then this was the defence which the old Socialists used to make as well, in their own instance, so that the charge of separating theory from practice, which was so much a part of the original Communist case against the SFIO, might well be turned back upon the Communists themselves.

Thus the argument from failure of leadership, that what was missing was a revolutionary party, applies so broadly, both within France and elsewhere, that it hardly serves as an answer to the particular problem of French socialism. It is, after all, the basis of the political critique levelled at the PCF in the aftermath of May 1968 by the New Left. This does not make it wrong, of course. It merely reduces it to the level of other, equally interesting, statements concerning the character of mass parties of the left in pre- or non-revolutionary situations.

A second theme commonly found in the writings of sympathetic critics of French socialism is the importance of the split between syndicalism and political socialism. This schism, it is argued, weakened the latter in two respects. It reduced its potential base in the industrial masses, not just in terms of numbers but in quality, since the most militant and class-conscious workers were precisely those who showed the strongest syndical sympathies. Furthermore, by making parliamentary socialism so obviously a *political* movement, it undermined its claim both to represent the working class and to be a party born from and heir to the revolutionary character of an exploited work-force.

There is much to be said for this view. Syndicalism existed in other countries, of course, in a variety of guises, but nowhere was it so well developed, both as a movement and as a doctrine, as in France. The historical explanations for this are diverse, but revert in essence to a single theme, that of the peculiar character of industrialisation in France. With the process of industrialisation spread over so long a period, the work-force had the time to organise in a cooperative defence of its independence. What is more, the survival of many small industries and artisanal enterprises into the late nineteenth century made it plausible for syndical theorists to argue that their disappearance was not inevitable — indeed that the survival of small units and an artisanal labour-force was both desirable and might even serve as the basis for a future socialist organisation of society. This economic rationale for syndicalism was coupled with a very powerful political argument: the experience of the revolutions of 1848 and especially 1871 showed the hopelessness of attempting to transform society from above, or via national political means. The aim of a revolutionary proletariat and its fellows should be to organise themselves from below, avoiding direct conflict with authority (and also keeping clear of the temptations of parliamentary politics) until the single, final clash with the state — a clash which would be essentially economic in character but which would have the political effect of overthrowing the existing order and replacing it with a syndically-organised society.

The anti-political character of such an argument reflected, rather than caused, the weaknesses in French socialism in the aftermath of the Commune; there is an analogy with the growing interest in *autogestion*, workers' self-management, which has characterised the far left in France since the late 1960s, disenchanted with the failure of the left-wing parties to unseat the Gaullist régime, and disillusioned with politics in the light of the events of 1968. In neither event, it seems to me, can we find an explanation of the weaknesses by focussing on the attitudes to which they gave rise. Syndicalism certainly divided the French left up to 1906; but the split was already mending by 1914, and the success of the Communists in establishing an unabashed hegemony over the CGT in recent years suggests that the split has long since healed. In large part this is because the old skilled unions of earlier days no longer dominate syndical life — their place has been taken by the large mass unions, for whom a revolutionary perspective based upon a utopia of small concerns and autonomous producers has little appeal. But this merely returns us to the point of departure — revolutionary syndicalism was the ideology of a declining class of artisans and partially-proletarianised workers which endured in France because its social base took longer to melt away than was the case elsewhere. In other words, the line of reasoning which blames the failings of the French socialists on the divisions caused by the impact of an autonomous syndical movement is in essence the same as that which says that socialism in France suffered from the absence of a large and fully industrialised factory proletariat.

We are thus brought to the third of the 'internal' critiques of French socialism, from those whose basic sympathy with the ideology and aspirations of Marxist socialists leads them to search for explanations of the latter's failures in terms of specific historical conditions which barred them from achieving aims which were otherwise both legitimate and susceptible of attainment. If the view is taken that there is some normative relationship between an industrial proletariat in a capitalist system and the socialist parties who represent their interests and embody their historical aspirations, then the fact that the working class in France was smaller than in other major western countries, and that it was less concentrated and represented a lower percentage of the work-force than in Germany, Belgium or Britain, will naturally loom large in any account of the consequent inadequacies of French socialism.

What is more, there will often be a corollary to such a view which states that the large number of peasants in the French population was a further block on the development of a successful revolutionary movement of the left. We have already seen (in Chapter 11, note 2) that this is the view of at least one of France's leading contemporary Marxists, and he is not alone in his opinions. Yet such an interpretation of the recent French past depends more upon deduction than on evidence. It is *not* clear that a large and concentrated proletariat is the best base for a revolutionary movement (small concentrated work-forces have a better track record in this respect, but they are usually to be found in societies where the peasantry is still the dominant social unit). But even if it were so, then the fact that such a proletariat is absent in a given society is *of itself* the major factor explaining the absence of revolutionary class consciousness. That is to say that the explanation is essentially a negative one – the major revolutionary component is absent, or incomplete. The presence of a large peasant sector *may* be a significant additional factor or it may not – in either case that would remain to be demonstrated.

Unfortunately, it is all too commonly asserted as self-evidently relevant to explanations of conservative predominance.

Lacking in rigour, the argument from 'backwardness' nevertheless offers certain advantages. It simultaneously explains the failures of the French left in the Third Republic, while offering renewed hope to left-wing opponents of the Fifth. For it is beyond dispute that France has seen, since 1945, a rapid drop in the number of peasants, a growing industrial concentration and the disappearance of many of the small businesses and workshops which had managed to endure into the 1950s. Any history of the labour and socialist movements in France which takes as its starting point the problems caused by the retarded development of French capitalism will thus be tempted to end upon a hopeful note — the theoretical premises remain intact and the practice is now, at last, becoming possible. Those social groups which had presented major stumbling blocks on the path of revolution, because of their natural commitment to the past, or at best to atavistic and negative forms of protest, are disappearing, and with them that middle ground which stood between the industrial proletariat and its historical rôle. Those who believe this see the future of politics in France as one of direct and definitive conflict between the revolutionary party of the left and the defenders of 'state monopoly capitalism'. Like André Malraux, they see a coming polarity between the 'party of the working class' and the 'majority', between Communists and Gaullists.

Unfortunately, such a view does not throw much light on the development of French politics in the 1970s, nor does it appear very accurately to describe the social divisions within the nation. And if it fails to make much sense of contemporary French life, we may be forgiven for questioning its accuracy when applied to the past, the more so because in respect of the putative conservative predilections of the peasantry it is quite misleading, as we have seen. More seriously, it makes assumptions regarding the revolutionary potential of the industrial proletariat, and the imminent, or at least immanent overthrow of capitalist society which take rather too much for granted, in the light of the experience of the last half-century. This will be clear if we now turn our attention briefly to interpretations of socialist history which, while not necessarily unsympathetic to socialist ideals, stand outside the Socialists' own frame of reference, and make their observations from a critical distance.[2]

Views from without

None of the arguments considered so far is of itself dependent upon some prior commitment to the socialists' own view of the world and their tasks within it. It is possible to believe that a generation of Socialist/syndicalist conflict prejudiced the chances of the former without believing that things *ought* to have been very different and would have been in a 'controlled' situation. But most of the arguments so far noted depend for their force upon certain presuppositions regarding the fate of capitalist societies, the character of working-class consciousness, or the relationship between social class and political behaviour; and these presuppositions are essentially the selfsame ones upon which the original socialist enterprise was founded. There are however certain alternative arguments which do not share these premises, and a brief consideration of them is necessary if we are to do justice to the problems at issue.

One alternative perspective takes as its starting point the denial of just those features of a capitalist society which are held by Marxists to be central to it. The idea of class conflict as the fulcrum of social relations in such a society, the argument goes, is misconceived. Not merely are social classes tending to merge, but such conflicts as they generate are no longer the result of deep divisions of interest over control of the means of production, and the exploitation by those who possess them of those who do not. In so far as the conflict between classes was *ever* the dominant feature of capitalist society, this was a passing feature characterising an early and unstable stage of its development. Once the mechanism became fully developed, its integrative capacities replaced those which had promoted conflict.

It follows from this argument that the term 'capitalist' is redundant, since the important feature of modern societies is not the form in which wealth is mobilised — such forms in any case tending to a common pattern — but the scale of industrial development which in turn determines the capacity of the society to meet the needs of its members and thereby integrate them within itself. In other words, the history of the world since the later eighteenth century is the history of the emergence on the scene of *industrial* societies; nor is this a mere staging post in the history of the world — industrial societies are permanent and have become the norm.[3]

All of this is the stuff of much modern thinking about the effects of industrialisation upon society, and will be familiar in far more sophisticated a form to those acquainted with sociological theory as it has emerged since the 1950s, particularly in the United States. Its relevance to my theme is this: in such a perspective as just described, the socialist parties of the nineteenth century in Europe could serve two overlapping functions. They voiced the discontents of a work-force newly mobilised for factory work in the cities, discontents which were not infrequently expressed in the optimistic, utopian terms to which the apparently infinite potential of the new industrial world had given rise (everything was now possible, vastly increased output, the final liberation of humankind, and, why not, the latter through the former). But they simultaneously served to integrate the new proletariat into the industrial society by providing it, however indirectly and illusively, with a political stake in its own future. In short, the socialist movements were the unconscious vehicle through which the otherwise rebellious and refractory elements in the new societies were encouraged to accept the new situation. In so far as that acceptance is still incomplete, in countries like France, or *a fortiori* in newly-industrialised nations, the socialist parties and their successors can still pursue this rôle. Where the need no longer exists their ideological identity is redundant, and its continued survival a matter of regret.

For those who argue this view, the history of socialism in the West is essentially a success story, and the fact that it is not seen as such by the socialists themselves merely confirms the fact. If we accept such an account, then the history of socialism is not much more than the story of a dramatically false consciousness at the service of a history no less teleological than that of the Marxists, but with a radically different end in view. In so far as the French Socialists have been more or less successful as an integrative force in modern French society, this has depended primarily upon factors over which the Socialists have little control, and thus the relation of their theory to their practice, or of their class analysis to their actual social base, is essentially a secondary consideration.

The defects of such a view are well known and do not need to be listed here. It trails its coat rather blatantly, and is as firmly rooted in the era which produced it as is the nineteenth-century Marxism to which it was a response. The resurgence of social conflicts which have their base in subjectively perceived class differences in industrial Western Europe since the mid-1960s rather cuts the ground from under the (ironically) positivist notions of an ideology-free industrial society; moreover, such notions have little to say concerning *Communist* movements, particularly once the latter have loosened their links with the Soviet Union, since these links were essential to an interpretation of communism which could hardly see it as constituting a uniquely 'integrative' force in the industrial West. But the most serious defect for the student of the French left is that this sort of sociological theory offers no framework for explaining the *enduring* relationship between the Marxist left and non-industrial groups — notably the small peasant.

There is an alternative and considerably more subtle, as well as empirically grounded, thesis concerning the relationship between industrial societies and the movements of opposition within them. This argues that the notion of class *is* central to any understanding of the structure of modern societies, and that the concept of class conflict as a central feature of the latter retains its importance. Where it differs from the Marxist analysis is in seeing *revolutionary* consciousness as not necessarily inherent in the class consciousness which capitalist societies help create. Or, to be more precise, revolution does not appear as the necessary end-product of the conflicts which industrialisation generates.

On the contrary, it is argued that the potential for revolution, if one can speak of it thus, exists much more strongly in the early years of capitalist development, when the strains of a more or less rapid transformation of a feudal and agricultural society into one based on industrial production create discontents which the new structure may not be in a position to resist. This would certainly make sense of the fact that the great social upheavals in the West occurred in the period from 1780 to 1850, and it would have something to say to the Russian experience too. Once the capitalist forms of production are firmly established, the proletariat which appeared likely to threaten the very foundations of the system tends increasingly to become drawn into it — *not* losing its identity as a class, nor even its propensity for *economic* discontent, but losing both the will and the ability to replace the political realm with something different.

At this point this argument meets the earlier one, in asserting that the socialist movements which were born out of the revolutionary hopes of the earlier period become the channel through which the proletariat enters the mature capitalist society — and as the proletariat loses its revolutionary identity, so does the socialist movement, becoming instead that social democracy which, as Giddens has it, was 'the normal form taken by the systematic political inclusion of the working-class within capitalist society'.[4]

The trouble with such a view, as Giddens acknowledges, is that it leaves something out. What remain to be accounted for, as he says, are 'those cases [France] where a revolutionary orientation has in fact become strongly marked'.[5] And one could add Italy and Spain to that requirement. What appears to have been left out, in an argument which otherwise has much to recommend it, is any consideration of the identity of socialist theory, as distinct from a discussion of the historical *function* of socialist parties. Moreover, we are still left with a question mark hanging over the precise rôle, in such an account, of the thriving Communist parties of Latin Europe. There is a lot to be said for Annie Kriegel's case for seeing the birth of the French Communist Party as something of a historical accident, and the survival of both the Italian and Spanish CPs doubtless owes something to their preservation in exile.[6] Nevertheless, Mme Kriegel would be the first to admit that the accidental circumstances of a movement's birth (in the sense that it was neither logically nor historically *required*) do not preclude a more *social* account of its survival and basis in popular support. Finally, although the second 'outside' account of the function of socialist parties in industrial societies does address itself to the social base of such parties, it too leaves out of account the survival of non-industrial groups, a fact of some importance in the political life of some of the industrial and capitalist societies which it analyses.

Some unresolved problems

Since the only critique of the French left which addresses itself to the *ideology* of the latter is that which takes as its starting point the fundamental inadequacy of earlier socialist thought, there remains something of a gap in the usual histories of the movement when they come to deal with the socialist doctrines espoused by the first generation of French Marxists. One solution has been to treat the Marxism of the Second International as an alien growth which perverted the 'indigenous' (and natural) development of the domestic product.[7] Since the domestic product consisted of a rich but socially marginal assortment of utopians and insurrectionaries, it is difficult to see where an unaffected development might have led. Proudhonism and its ancillary theories depended heavily upon the essentially illogical ideal of a community consisting *exclusively* of small owners of agricultural and artisanal property — hence the appeal in a country such as France, but an appeal necessarily declining as industrialisation rendered it ever more unrealistic. The utopians had ceased to matter outside certain very narrow circles well before Marx wrote his most influential works, and as for Blanqui and his ilk, it was their very failure which paved the way for the introduction of a doctrine more firmly grounded in political reality. In short, Marxism, in so far as it *was* a foreign commodity (uncertain — not merely was much of Marx's politics grounded in the French experience, but his and Engels' conceptions of the political tactics of a socialist party were most directly applicable to the sort of régime which obtained in France — but not Germany or Italy — after 1875), was entering on a market where an expanding demand was otherwise starved of supply. There was nothing very strange about what the Marxists had to say about exploitation, class, the need for organisation and the like. Only the emphasis on a closely-articulated political party was new in the French experience — though well within the Jacobin tradition — and the eventual establishment of a Guesdist hegemony suggests that it had little enough difficulty in setting down roots.

An alternative view has been that which denies the importance of socialist theory in the years from 1880 to 1914. It could not have been important to socialist supporters, the argument runs, or else they would have noticed the contradictions between what was said and what was done. What is more, if they *had* listened to it, most of them would have kept clear, since its collectivist and chiliastic emphasis would have run counter to their instincts and interests. But the fact is, as we have seen, that it *was* central to socialist propaganda, and that if the Socialists gained support it was not because their voters ignored the character of the party they were electing, but precisely because of that character. One might argue that, as with the Communists today, their supporters did not *really* believe in an imminent revolution or really desire it; they merely wished to express outright opposition to the *status quo*. As it happens, this was probably not the case. Recent French history was sufficiently unstable for men to have genuine expectations of imminent change. Hence, paradoxically, the real coherence in French socialist doctrine – it could afford to speak of a future revolution while practising in a reformist present because the assumption that the one might not be a natural outgrowth of the other was not yet commonly made.

In other words, the ideology of the socialist left in France was not merely an excrescence upon its functionalist character; it played a central part in its success. Without a peculiarly rigid doctrinal stance concerning their own relationship to contemporary French society and the state, the Guesdists, and later the SFIO, would have lacked that ability to distinguish themselves from the Radicals which was so important in their early successes – not just in the Var, but elsewhere too. What is more, a doctrinal stance was central to their organisational coherence – in fact in France it was *particularly* vital for a party of the extreme left to have a firm and constant intellectual identity, and one which it was willing to impose upon its members, if it wished to avoid the largely negative inheritance of the French revolutionary tradition – the tendency to schism and dispersion. The 'democratic centralism' of the modern Communist Party has tended to obscure our view of its roots in a French rather than a Russian tradition – the SFIO was no less rigid and unmoving in its doctrinal assertions and its disciplining of those who transgressed.

None of the accounts of French socialism described above makes due allowance for the centrality of ideology in the history of the modern French left. As a consequence, none of them really captures the special complexity of that history. The constituent parts of that complexity might be listed thus: a socialist movement both pre-cocious and enduring which remained committed, until the mid-1960s, to a socialist revolution as its end; a mass base in both the city and the countryside; a political and cultural inheritance unequivocally insurrectionary but ambiguously political; a society where the political theories of socialist revolution antedated the emergence, much less the fruition, of a fully industrialised capitalism; a deeply conservative political practice, not only on the part of the (predominant) parties of the centre and right, but also on that of the parties of the extreme left on their rare incursions into power; the absence, despite the foregoing, of any organised assault on the state since 1871.

Nothing short of a full-length analytical history of the socialist and communist movements in France since the mid-nineteenth century could do justice to these themes. The purpose of raising them here is to illustrate the distance that still needs to be covered if we are to achieve a satisfactory understanding of this central area of recent French history. However, in the context of the present book, it ought to be possible to make a dent in the armour plating of our ignorance. Whereas the sympathetic critique of French socialism relies too heavily upon suppositions regarding the revolutionary character of the industrial proletariat, and builds too ambitious an edifice upon the failure of the socialists to forge real links with the workers, or the failure of the workers to reproduce themselves in sufficient numbers, such an approach has one important virtue. It treats the history of socialism in France as essentially a problem in *social* history.

This is not to deny the importance of socialist ideology — quite the reverse. Any social history which diminishes the significance for men and women of the ideas and ideals which they encountered does them an injustice and impoverishes itself. But the history of these ideas has to be written *socially*, not treated as a dimension unto itself. Thus the most promising approach to the history of a political movement such as socialism is through an awareness of who its supporters were and what it had to say to them. This, however, involves a proper investigation of just who those supporters *really* were, rather than prior assumptions about who they ought to have been, in the light of the investigator's prejudices, received ideas, or even the party's own self-image. Nor can we rely on the nature of the party's published propaganda to give us an indication of the *likely* source of its support — a warning as valid for the votes culled among the professional classes today as it is for the rural socialist votes of the 1890s.

In practice, as regards the history of the Marxist left in Latin

Europe, this means that we must replace the peasantry, and the problems they pose, firmly back at the centre of that history. It may be that we shall find that what emerges is something very close to the second of our 'external' critiques – that socialism does well in Latin Europe because that is the least industrial region of the capitalist West. But even so, it will not do to treat the phenomenon of peasant socialism as transitory, and the existence of the peasantry and their needs as a residual category of industrial society, soon to be resolved out of existence. And this is because they continue to exist, continue to influence the politics of their countries, and continue in particular to support the parties of the far left. The historical relationship between socialism and the peasantry is thus a matter of continued interest. But I shall argue that this interest goes beyond a mere phenomenon of passing or past importance, that in fact the rôle played by the peasantry in the history of modern socialism in France at least has been central in determining both the strengths and weaknesses of the French left. What is more, although the close relationship between socialism and the peasantry in France may be coming to an end, the patterns of behaviour and the attitudes which that relationship has brought about are now so firmly a part of French socialist practice as perhaps to influence the latter for some time to come.

The socialist heritage

It is not my intention here to assert that socialism, much less communism, in France has been dominated by its support amongst the peasants. From the early years of the present century the working class has been an increasingly important element in the membership and electorate of the left. By 1973 the electorate of the PCF was 52% working-class, while 57% of the party's membership was composed of industrial workers. Even the Socialists, whose support amongst the workers had much diminished by the 1970s, could claim an electorate of which 35% were *ouvriers*, although only 16% of their *members* fell into that category.

However, it is no less significant that 14% of the electorate of the SFIO in 1952 earned their living on the land, and that this figure had actually increased (to 15%) by 1965. Even in 1972, the true peasant element in the electorate of the new Parti Socialiste had not fallen below 11%. When we recall that the percentage of the French working population which earned its living from agriculture had fallen from 26.7% in 1954 to 14.9% in 1968, it is clear that the peasant base within the French left was declining much less rapidly than the overall disappearance of the peasantry in the nation might lead one to expect. And while it is true that neither Socialists nor Communists ever achieved a very large rural *membership*, this should be interpreted in the light of the absence of any traditions of *participation* of this kind in the countryside (as well as the more general disinclination of French men and women, urban and rural, to join unions, political parties and even non-political voluntary associations).[8]

If the link between Socialists and the countryside has lingered on (in 1965, 34% of the Socialist electorate lived in communes of under 2000 inhabitants) this is in part a consequence of the importance of that link in the early years of the modern French left. Not merely was pre-1914 socialism strongest in departments which were predominantly rural, but its successes came in precisely the most agricultural regions of these departments. It was in the small rural mining villages around Commentry, not in the big mining towns around Montluçon, that the Socialists of the Allier had their earliest successes. In the Gard, 43.5% of the members of the POF Federation in the years 1900—2 were peasants, while in the Isère the proportion of peasants in the Guesdist Federation grew from 7% in the mid-1890s to 24% in this century. In the autonomous Socialist Federation of the Drôme the percentage of peasants rose from 15% in 1904 to 22% for the years 1906—14 (while the percentage of proletarian members fell from 45% to 34%). In the Aube, the Socialists drew their strength from the smallholders in the wine-growing regions around Bar. In the Côte-d'Or it was the small *vignerons* who provided the majority of Socialist votes.[9]

Thus the rural element in the implantation of Marxist socialism in France was a significant one. And although alterations in the social structure of the nation produced a growing predominance of urban workers among the voters of the left, the identity of interest between socialism and the peasantry established at an earlier stage remained important, increasingly disproportionate to the actual balance of forces in country and party alike.

The appeal of the Socialists to the peasantry in certain regions seems, as in the Var, to have been directly linked to the specific nature and promises of socialism, rather than to a lingering local tradition of revolutionary sympathies. This makes sense. The old and the new forms of political leftism were quite different from one another. Modern socialism offered an acceptance of the authority of the state, an emphasis upon the need to work within the framework of the changes wrought by political and industrial revolutions. Much of the *old* tradition of insurrection in the countryside involved a rejection of the state and its servants, a refusal to integrate into a wider community which offered nothing and threatened much. Moreover, a map of political allegiance in France confirms such a view: some of the old bastions of revolution – such as Paris itself – were much less accessible to the new socialism than were certain previously quiescent provinces. The older revolutionary tradition survived in other forms – Blanquism, the Possibilists, anti-political syndicalism and also, of course, Radicalism – before merging with the new, in the inter-war years, through the conscious efforts of the *Communists* to root themselves in the insurrectionary and Jacobin mould. These various paths to the present help explain certain differences in the geography of Socialist and Communist support in France which are otherwise hard to understand, such as the continuing Socialist base in the Calais region, or the Communist bastion in the south-western Limousin (until the recent local successes of M. Chirac).

At this point it may be useful to distinguish between the effect of this early successs in the countryside upon the peasantry and upon the socialist movement which they supported. The peasants, like the industrial artisans, found in the French socialist movement a vehicle for the expression of their discontents at the effects of industrialisation. Because of the relatively sluggish development of capitalism in France, the small producer, rural or urban, had both the time and the means to organise his reaction against the changes which were engulfing him. Hence the emergence and survival of a widespread enthusiasm for producer cooperatives, whether so described or in the form of syndical organisations which emphasised local organisation and economic autonomy. Both in the town and in the country the possibility of such cooperatives, and the critique which they implicitly directed at larger economic units, created a favourable climate for political socialism, although it was only in the villages that this took the form of a large Socialist electorate — no doubt because the opportunities for properly economic organisation were rather reduced, and voting played a commensurately more important part as an expression of social discontent.[10]

In the longer term, however, the socialist movement in the villages, no less than in the cities, played an important part in integrating the peasantry into the modern French nation. The chronological coincidence between the impact of compulsory education, the destruction of the isolation of the rural communities, the increased use of French in place of patois, the social effects of conscription, and the advent of a socialist movement in the villages is clearly more than a chance occurrence. Socialism served simultaneously as a vehicle for the expression of fears and protests in the affected provinces, *and* as a means of channelling that protest into, rather than against, the Republic. The fact that the Socialists' own ideology was itself directed against the bourgeois Republic only served to make their integrative rôle more effective. The Radicals could not have achieved such a successful politicisation of the erstwhile outcast populations of town and village precisely because of their rather too obvious association, particularly after 1898, with the *status quo*.

The integration of the peasantry once achieved, what was thereby created was a particular political tradition, dating not from 1789 but specifically from the experiences of the years 1880–1910. It has been observed elsewhere that this period in France, and equivalent periods in other modern nations, saw much 'invention' of tradition, as the new political community sought consciously as well as instinctively to set down roots.[11] Nor was this just a matter of generating instant nostalgia for the world which was disappearing under their noses — although the 'folklorisme' of this same era, with its manifestations in back-to-nature clubs, cycling societies, and the passion for old wives' tales, is itself revealing, not least in the extent of its ties, especially in England, with the socialist movements themselves. For the creation of traditions, whether invented or self-generating, meant that this period, the second stage of industrialisation, marked out a path for future generations.

In the case of the French peasantry, this produced in those regions where support for socialism had been strong before the First World War a lasting relationship with the Socialists. The Marxist left became, in effect, the mediating factor between the declining peasantry and the state. Voting for the candidate of the SFIO became as much a part of local culture as attending church and dutifully marching to the polls to elect the local *notable* was for the *métayers* of the south-west and the *fermiers* of Brittany. By the 1930s such electoral comportment had largely ceased to be related to the specific content of the Socialist programme, any more than the bedrock areas of Communist support in contemporary France vote for the PCF because they have carefully noted the content of its electoral manifesto. Thus a tradition of political allegiance was created in the crisis years of the later nineteenth century which gave certain parts of rural France an identity within the French political system *through* their consistently antagonistic attitude towards it, faithfully mirrored in the opposition of the SFIO. The decline of the SFIO in the 1950s and 1960s was the result of a multiplicity of causes, but one of these was undoubtedly the contemporary shrinking of the rural sector in France. The ambivalent political stance of the SFIO in these years, occasioned by its rejection of the Communists and its failure to establish a rôle for itself in the Fourth Republic, and capped by its unhappy experiences in office, no doubt helped diminish its support, particularly in areas where its previously intransigent leftism had been part of its appeal. But the fact that the party lacked any very clear social base was important too – not least in confusing the leadership, who were unsure whether their supporters saw them as a party of government or one of uncompromising opposition.[12]

The decline and disappearance of the SFIO in recent years brings me back to the second consideration raised above. If the effect of a rural socialist electorate was simultaneously to mobilise and integrate an important segment of the French peasantry, what was the effect of this process upon the Socialist Party itself? Initially, of course, it gave the Guesdists, and later the SFIO, a social base of which they might otherwise have been deprived for some years in a society whose rate of industrialisation delayed the formation of a large and concentrated industrial proletariat. Given that French conditions obliged even the most intransigent Marxists to accept the case for gradualism in the medium term, and the need to work within a parliamentary framework, a large electorate was a necessary precondition for the growth of a stable socialist movement in France. Hence the rejection of Blanquism on the one hand and, later, Leninism on the other. But a large electoral following in France meant, willy-nilly, one with a predominance of peasants.

It is sometimes argued that this was *the* stumbling block to the development of Marxism in France. Since most of the peasants were property-owners, or aspired so to become, and since the ideology of Second International Marxism held that 'small' property was doomed, the French Socialists had, on the face of it, a difficult choice: they could either abandon or at least camouflage their doctrinal premises and campaign in the countryside, or else they might retain their ideological purity but resign themselves to political impotence for many years to come. Such was certainly the view of many contemporary observers, and it was implicitly the opinion of Engels, when he attacked the Guesdists for compromising their theory in the search for votes. In fact, though, as we have seen, the Guesdists were for the most part loyal to their thinking, publicly no less than in private, and yet managed to attract considerable rural support, including that of the smallholding peasantry.

The true contradiction is to be sought elsewhere. Although French Socialist leaders and theorists agonised over their political dependence upon the peasantry, and made great play with such working-class support as they acquired, they came increasingly to rely on their popular base south of the Loire (in the main) for their survival as a political force. In consequence, what had begun as a relationship born of a meeting between the revolutionary doctrines of the Socialists and the social discontent of the peasantry ossified into a common conservatism. This is not what caused the peculiarly long life of early Marxist perspectives in the SFIO — there were good reasons for such a survival, notably the need to avoid giving hostages to Communist accusations of 'reformism'.[13] But the very success of the SFIO in establishing itself at the centre of French politics in the years between 1924 and 1958 militated against any inclination to make major alterations in its doctrine and organisation.

Nor was this immobility of the SFIO merely a function of its political success. The peasantry by the mid-twentieth century had ceased in France to be a force for change. In some sense of course they had never been a force for change. But at the end of the nineteenth century, as on certain previous occasions, the very extent of their reaction against the society around them had projected them into the vanguard of the progressive forces. But by the Second World War they had subsided again (not least through the efforts of Socialists and syndicalists to organise their discontents within the existing framework), so that the SFIO had come to depend upon a class which was now truly conservative rather than just 'objectively' so. With more than half an eye on their electors, SFIO candidates found themselves consistently opposing any moves likely to result in a further diminution of the rural sector, and simultaneously defending a small peasantry whose economic survival came increasingly to depend upon overt and hidden subsidy. Whereas the Guesdists had appealed to small-property-owning peasants in the name of a collective future, the modern SFIO found itself calling upon their support in the name of an individualist past. And while this could be squared with the socialists' moral opposition to the growth of monopolies and agri-business, it hardly made sense in terms of the polarisation of economic forces and the disappearance of small property which official Socialist theory continued to hold as imminent, necessary and, *sub specie aeternitatis*, desirable.

The French Socialists were thus the victims of their own origins. Committed to and dependent upon an electorate which was both shrinking and conservative, but which identified paradoxically with the very revolutionary character of socialism, in its negative incarnation, they came truly to follow a practice which had lost touch with its theoretical base. They could neither revise the first nor abandon the second; as a result the very features of French society which had ensured the rise of Marxist socialism in France also served to orchestrate its decline.

It therefore follows that what accounts for the weakness of the left in France is not at all the belated industrial development of the country, any more than the precocity of the industrial revolution in England has brought about a successful socialist movement there. On the contrary, socialism in France drew such strength as it had from two circumstances peculiar to France: the advent of universal male suffrage at an early date, and the existence of a large number of smallholding peasants. In the sense that both of these are benefits conferred upon France by the Great Revolution (and that is only partially the case), the French Socialists are indeed the inheritors of the revolutionary tradition. Furthermore, it was the transformation of France in the years after 1945 which sounded the death knell for the old SFIO. What has replaced it is a party which owes its success to a confluence of different factors (not least the personality of François Mitterand), but has broken away from the social as well as the ideological inheritance of its predecessor.

A number of questions remain. To begin with, a perspective such as that outlined here, even if it gives due emphasis to the integrative function of the socialist movement in the years before 1914, still leaves open the problem of the failure of revolution in France. If a socialist party firmly committed to the overthrow of capitalism was fortunate enough to establish itself so securely in a country where industrialisation was far from complete, why was it unable to achieve its ends? In the Italian context it is possible to argue that fascism served both to cut short a genuine prospect of revolution *and* to tide Italian capitalism over its formative years, notably the difficult period during which resources were shifted quite massively from the rural south to the industrial north. In England, the absence of a revolutionary ideology and a historically conscious movement in the early and vulnerable years of capitalist accumulation meant that the considerable potential for social revolution in the years before 1850 went for nought. But neither consideration applied in France. Whence, then, the failure, not in the later years of the SFIO, but precisely in its earlier period?

Part of the answer lies, again, in the rural character of France, but for a different reason. We may reasonably infer from the foregoing that nations whose experience of industrialisation involved the *rapid* disappearance of the peasantry would show less propensity for social revolution. This is true both in the sense that they do not undergo that extensive interim period of industrialisation during which the incidence of social discontent is at its highest, and in the fact that the political parties of opposition tend very quickly to adjust to their social-democratic rôle in these circumstances. This, after all, is what has distinguished the history of the Labour Party, the Parti Ouvrier Belge and the German SPD from the Marxist parties of France, Italy and Spain. At the very most the socialist movements in countries which have undergone rapid and complete industrialisation adapt themselves to their circumstances in the form of 'negative integration',[14] finding a place in the capitalist world precisely through their assertion of complete (but passive) rejection of it.

However, the fact that a large peasant base is a necessary condition of socialist (or any other popular) revolutions does not make it a sufficient one. Even in countries less centralised and far less urbanised than modern France, the seizure of power has been effected not in the countryside but in the city, where power is to be seized. The significance of the peasantry as a revolutionary force lies in their pre-revolutionary discontent and their willingness in post-revolutionary years to accept the authority and acts of a new régime. But there is only one modern instance where the success of a revolutionary transfer of power depended almost exclusively upon the balance of forces in the countryside, and few today would offer China as the paradigm for recent European history.

What was lacking in France, then, was the capacity to seize and retain power in Paris and the industrial regions. This seems a paradox in view of the long history of attempts to do just that — although the consistent and finally bloody failure of the urban revolutionary tradition in France, despite offering a myth, may also have been a strong disincentive, for those who either remembered the Paris Commune or were steeped in its history. In order to become a major political force in France, the SFIO needed its rural electorate — and the radical character of the latter helped accentuate the 'revolutionary' image of the party. But to effect the sort of changes it envisaged, the party needed a much closer relationship with the industrial unions, and they in turn needed deeper roots in the major proletarian concentrations.

To this extent, the Communists' analysis of the events of 1919—21, probably the last truly 'revolutionary' situation in recent French history, makes good sense. In 1919 a spontaneous series of strikes failed for lack of leadership and direction; in 1920 a carefully-orchestrated strike wave, overtly political in its aims, failed for lack of mass backing. But by the time a party notionally equipped to exploit such opportunities had been created, the occasion had passed. And when there have been partial recurrences of such opportunities in more recent years, that party has found good reasons of its own for not attempting to convert discontent and disorder into revolution.

Shifting the emphasis to the PCF serves finally to emphasise my theme. The Communists have proved no more successful at overthrowing capitalism than did the much-maligned SFIO. If we adopt the view that the potential for such an overthrow was at its height in the *early* years of industrial capitalism, then this comes as no surprise.[15] But it is also the case that the Communists, like the Socialists, have been deeply marked by the historical moment of their emergence. Just as the Socialists developed their strengths at a time of much rural discontent and disaffection, becoming thereby closely bound up with the support which they derived from the discontented, so the PCF's early years coincided with the emergence into full maturity of an industrial proletariat in France. Of course the Communists' advantage was that *their* social base faithfully reflected their own self-image, but in other ways the result has been similar. Not merely has the PCF been unable to conceive of social change except in terms of a proletarian revolution, but the party has come to reflect in many ways the basically unrevolutionary, though militantly class-conscious, character of the French working class.

Some interim conclusions

The themes treated in this book prompt a number of concluding reflections. The first of these is that the emphasis upon timeless regional or social traditions in accounts of recent French history is often exaggerated. In setting out to investigate the support offered to socialism since the late nineteenth century in Mediterranean France, I have been led to stress the importance of change, at a particular historical moment, in creating *new* political traditions. Such an argument could no doubt be extended to cover other traditions, other places, other conjunctures. It seems clear that electoral geography, for example, in its more naïve guise serves rather to blur the significance of change, placing the emphasis instead upon those continuities which it seeks to discover. Such an approach, and others of its kind, are fundamentally inimical to a properly *historical* account of the origins of the present. My own attempt to bring *both* structural *and* circumstantial elements into play, to explain something in terms both of what was and of what became, is of necessity less attractively precise. But it offers the possibility of explaining something (in this case socialist roots in the Var) which has occasionally mystified observers; in passing it helps increase our awareness of the variety of French history.

In the second place, I have consciously placed myself *within* the sympathetic historiography of the French left. That is to say that the absence of a revolutionary upheaval in recent French history is seen as something which requires an explanation. Part of such an explanation must be the 'functionalist' theory of socialist parties — their integrative rôle in the early years of industrialisation. But this view need not preclude the possibility that a sufficiently aggressive socialist movement in a fragile capitalist system could have achieved its ideological, as distinct from its 'functional', ends. *Pace* Marx, such a possibility existed much more realistically in early capitalism than in its later variant, if only because the latter is much better defended by the state and its resources. The French Socialists therefore 'missed' their chance in their early years, not through the lack of a large social base, in the countryside especially, but through their *political* failure to seize power at the centre. Just as a successful revolution is above all a well-orchestrated seizure and retention of power, so its absence denotes primarily the failure to seize and control the state, tautology or no.

In this perspective, the French left, like its Italian and Spanish counterparts, had a better opportunity to achieve its aims than was the case for the Germans or the English. This is because the period between the disappearance of a feudal or seigneurial society and the full emergence of a capitalist one was so prolonged. But a particular difficulty for the nations of Latin Europe, especially France, has been the historical importance of the centralised state, which emerged and developed long before the industrialising process which it would thus oversee. As a result, the historical advantages conferred upon the relatively 'backward' societies of southern Europe, so far as revolutionary potential was concerned, were nullified (and nowhere more so than in France) by the survival and repressive capacities of the pre-modern state. It follows from this that we should not be surprised that the only socialist revolution to succeed in recent European history was one where the tensions created by the early stages of industrialisation and a discontented peasantry were not held under by a well-established and self-confident state apparatus. Far from constituting an aberration, Lenin's success in overthrowing the Russian autocracy in the name of socialism thus makes considerable historical sense. As to France, the successive failures of more or less determined assaults on the state between 1830 and 1968 can be seen to owe relatively little to the ideological and strategic failings of the revolutionaries. And this became more rather than less the case as time went on. The chances of repeating the experiences of the Great Revolution were ever diminishing — in large part thanks to the innovations and institutions to which the Revolution gave birth.

Such considerations suggest a further reflection. Few today share the enthusiasms for the theory and practice of revolution as conceived by Mao or Che or Fanon which were felt by the New Left of the 1960s. But we should avoid the easy temptation to mock the popularity of 'Marxism' in Africa, Asia or central and southern America. The concept of a socialist revolution was indeed born of the nineteenth-century experience of industrial capitalism in Europe. But it can seem an irrelevance in non-European contexts only if we persist in understanding it exclusively on its own terms. That is, if we describe the socialist revolution as the solution to the problems of 'late' capitalism, based on the class consciousness of an industrial proletariat and dependent upon a high level of industrial progress and production, then clearly it will have little to say to most of the non-European world for many years to come. But if we adopt instead the perspective tentatively suggested above, then the recent European past may indeed have thrown up a political model very germane to the contemporary Third World.

If it *is* the case that the revolutionary left in Europe acquired much of its later character from the historical moment of its encounter with a rapidly transforming rural society, then the proper time for a socialist movement to seize its opportunities is at the onset of industrialisation, not at some putative future stage of maturity. And the proper social base — indeed of necessity the *only* social base in many places — for such a movement is the advanced and therefore the most disaffected and radical sector of the peasantry. And to the degree that Marxism, locally understood, is the most effective mobilising ideology for such a movement, precisely *because* it was born of a period when Europe was undergoing analogous changes, it becomes very properly the basis for revolutionary movements in the non-European world.

This is not to argue directly from the European experience to that of Mexico, or India, or even Chile. For a start, the very fact of colonial and post-colonial intervention in the Third World means that the industrialising process there has been 'aborted' — assuming that its birth might otherwise have followed paths similar to those of the colonising nations themselves. And from this fact, and from the very presence of industrial nations with interests of their own, it follows that the autonomy of both the industrial and political development of any nation today is very constricted. Not merely does the success or failure of a revolution depend upon the relative strengths of local protagonists, it depends also on the strengths, interests and intentions of other states as well.

Furthermore, any socialist revolution which *does* seize power and succeed in retaining it in a pre-industrial society, or one where the industrial process has only recently begun, faces a hitherto insuperable difficulty. It *must* strive to achieve as high a level of industrial maturity as quickly as possible, for a variety of obvious reasons — not least among them the ideological imperative. But in order to do so it may very soon have to employ coercion upon that very sector on whose willing back it rode to power — the peasantry. And this in turn necessitates the construction of a bureaucratic and often totalitarian régime. The only known alternative to such a tendency is the encouragement of the 'free play of market forces' — the process of capitalist accumulation. It may be retorted that China once again gives the lie to this cruel dichotomy; but neither the recent history of China nor the acknowledged problems it currently faces suggests that it has so much overcome the difficulty of constructing socialism in a backward country as postponed it.

These rather unoriginal reflections upon the emigration of socialism to the non-European world are made in order to remind the reader of the indivisibility of the historical experience. Just as European history in the past two centuries serves to underline the crucial importance of the *form* of transformation from feudal to capitalist society in determining the possibilities and character of any further social upheavals, so the recent history of much of the rest of the world is a salutary reminder of the central importance of a question which we tend to ignore when writing of Europe: the question of what happens to the peasants during the creation of an industrial society. It is tempting to write history in terms of the winners, or as Labrousse has it, to overemphasise the 'histoire des mouvements'; in fact we are well advised to pay close attention to the losers, the 'histoire des résistances', since they too share responsibility for the final score. Nor, at the time, did they always know that they would ultimately be defeated.

A book which has taken as its subject one small department of France ventures into broader reflections at considerable risk. However, in moving from the Var to France, and thence further afield, I have rather broken with the established canons of local history, so that there may be some justification for ending with a reflection upon the nature of the undertaking.

Anyone who has read the works of an earlier generation of self-consciously *social* historians will appreciate that the label is not always a desirable one by which to be identified. It has too long been supposed that social history, being a residual category of economic history, could only be written in the form of an appendix to an exhaustive listing of economic and social data concerning a given place or period. Such a technique assumed rather than argued the primacy of the economic, and proceeded accordingly. Strangely, for a sub-discipline born of the desire to escape the empirical and narrative tradition, it usually resulted in a book which recounted an immense volume of details and explained very little.

The present work is grounded in a more recent and altogether more promising approach. The aim is to reflect upon a particular question or cluster of questions which seem interesting, or important, or commonly misconceived, and to ask them of a time or place which is likely to offer some hope of a fruitful response. Of course, this sort of history is more explicitly 'ideological' − if only in the sense that what one historian may regard as interesting or important may seem to another ineffably dull and of little consequence. Similar differences of opinion must arise over the selection of subject matter, method of enquiry, and especially over the conclusions reached. In the present case, the two questions which have been pursued above all are those which deal with the nature of political allegiances and traditions in general, and the peculiar trajectory of Marxism in France in particular. Neither has been answered to the full, by any means. The second especially demands both a broader and a rather different treatment if it is to receive justice, and it is a theme to which I hope to return at greater length in the future. Both questions thus arise from a concern with the history of socialism which many may find misplaced. But it is their presence which provides the present work with such shape as it has.

As a consequence, this is a very political kind of social history, notwithstanding the fact that many of the Var peasants with whom it deals actually took no part in politics. The justification for this must be that much of recent history *is* past politics. This is not to detract from the virtues of the sort of history which concerns itself exclusively with the daily affairs of the non-political majority. Without knowledge of these we are handicapped in our understanding of the minority. But this applies both ways: social history which ignores the state, or unduly diminishes the importance of the way it was ruled and the struggles for control of it, necessarily ignores an important dimension of the life of even the most ordinary of ordinary men and women. Political history and social history simply do not have independent existences, except at the cost of their mutual impoverishment and to the detriment of our understanding of the past.

Furthermore, a properly conceived *social* history of political thought and action is one of the ways in which the study of the past can recapture its intellectual confidence and self-respect. It is not without significance that European, particularly French, historiography has for some time now been assured of its proper place in the pantheon of the social sciences, not least because of its evident ability to mobilise the insights and methods of the sociologists among others, while simultaneously asserting the importance of the dimension of time which is the special feature of the historical understanding. They order these things better in Paris! It would be gratifying to think that the present work has made some small domestic contribution to the reassertion of the centrality, the indispensability of a historical understanding of society, including the world of the present. If some light has been cast in the meantime upon a small corner of recent French history, then author and reader alike may feel that the effort has been worthwhile.

Notes

Chapter One

1. Draguignan was centrally placed, but it secured the privilege of becoming departmental capital because of the 'treasonable' behaviour of Toulon during the French Revolution. Under the Fifth Republic Toulon has returned to favour and in the 1970s was made departmental capital as befits its overwhelming demographic and economic importance in the region. The *sous-préfecture* of Brignoles has been abolished and its territory divided between the arrondissements of Draguignan and Toulon.
2. The Var is in fact possibly the most topographically uneven of all the departments in France.
3. For a more detailed description of the geology and geography of this region see *Atlas historique de Provence* (Paris, 1969), and R. Livet, *Habitat rural et structures agraires en Basse-Provence* (Aix, 1962).
4. Arthur Young gives an extremely interesting and perceptive description of the area in his *Travels in France* (New York, 1969).
5. See E. Baratier, *La démographie provençale du 13ᵉ au 16ᵉ siècle* (Paris, 1961), p.110.
6. Details of eighteenth-century communications in the region are in *Atlas historique de Provence*, plate 125.
7. Nineteenth-century maps of regional communications are preserved in the *Archives départementales du Var* in Draguignan (henceforward *AD Var*).
8. See M. Agulhon, *La vie sociale en Provence intérieure au lendemain de la Révolution* (Paris, 1970), p.61. The Var 'est un pays de campagnards minoritaires, un pays de gros villages et de petites villes, un pays dont le cadre normal de vie est citadin'. See also Livet, *Habitat rural*, p. 223. On fifteenth-century Provence, see Baratier, *La démographie provençale*, p.115.
9. On the whole question of Provençal sociability, see M. Agulhon, *La sociabilité méridionale* (Aix, 1966, publications de la Faculté des Lettres, 2 vols).
10. See *Le Petit Var*, 14 April 1882, 11 March 1883.
11. See F. Braudel, *The Mediterranean and the Mediterranean World in the Age of Philip II* (London, 1972), esp. part 1; also Baratier, *Démographie provençale*, p.111; Y. Masurel, *La vigne dans la Basse-Provence orientale* (Thèse Complémentaire, Aix, 1964), p.17; L. Stouff, *Ravitaillement et alimentation en Provence aux 14ᵉ et 15ᵉ siècles* (Paris, 1971), pp.83–9.
12. On Languedoc see E. Le Roy Ladurie, *Les paysans du Languedoc* (Paris, 1966).

13. *Atlas historique de Provence*, plate 122.
14. On eighteenth-century dechristianisation in Provence, see M. Vovelle,
    Piété baroque et déchristianisation en Provence au 18ᵉ siècle (Paris, 1973),
    esp. pp.171ff.
15. See M. Bloch, *French Rural History* (Berkeley, Calif., 1966), Chapter 5,
    n. 25.
16. The nature and rôle of the *chambrées* will be discussed more fully in
    Chapter 6. But see also M. Agulhon, Les chambrées de Provence: histoire
    et ethnologie, *R.H.* 1971, 498, and L. Roubin, *Chambrettes des
    Provençaux: une maison des hommes en Méditerranée septentrionale* (Paris,
    1970).
17. See the article devoted to the history of Bagnols in *Le Petit Var*, 28 August
    1888.
18. On the geography of the Grande Peur, the anti-noble revolts of 1789,
    eighteenth-century *confréries* and the Federalist movement of 1793, see
    Atlas historique de Provence, plates 114, 154, 157.
19. See Agulhon, *La vie sociale*, p.216, n. 37.
20. M. Vovelle, in *Atlas historique de Provence*, p. 64.
21. See Agulhon, *La vie sociale*, p.462; also *Atlas historique de Provence*, plates
    197−8.
22. Anyone interested in the history of France in the nineteenth century must
    read all three volumes of Agulhon's study of Provence from the 1790s
    to the *coup d'état* of 1851: *La vie sociale*; *Une ville ouvrière au temps
    du socialisme utopique: Toulon de 1815 à 1851* (Paris, 1970); *La
    République au village* (Paris, 1970).
23. Details of the French population in the early nineteenth century in
    C.-H. Pouthas, *La population française pendant la première moitié du 19ᵉ
    siècle* (Paris, 1956). The unsatisfactory and arbitrary nature of the
    distinction between rural and urban communities, officially given as having
    populations respectively less and more than 2000 persons, is discussed later
    in this book, and in the Note on Sources, pp. 337−42.
24. For an excellent study of the masons of the Limousin, see A. Corbin,
    Archaïsme et modernité en Limousin au 19ᵉ siècle (1845−1880) (Paris,
    1974, 2 vols), esp. pp.177−225.
25. Figures for the elections of 1849 in *AD Var* II M 3 (15).
26. Full details (name, occupation, age, dwelling-place) of the Condamnés
    politiques of 1851 in the Var are in *AD Var* IV M 24 (2/3).
27. On the Var in 1851 see Agulhon, *La République au village*; on the repression
    of 1851 see V. Wright, Repression and the limits to repression, in R. Price
    (ed.), *Revolution and Reaction: 1848 and the Second French Republic*
    (London, 1975), pp. 303−33. There is also an important forthcoming study
    of the 1851 insurrection by Ted Margadant.
28. Thus the *préfet* of the Var in 1913: 'Depuis 1851 surtout, le département
    du Var a une réputation bien établie d' "extrémisme". C'est un département
    d'avant garde, où les théories antimilitaristes et antipatriotiques ont fait de
    grands progrès . . . ' Quoted in Y. Rinaudo, L'opposition à la loi de trois ans
    dans le Var (printemps−été 1913), in *P.H.* 80, 1970, p.162.

29. Apart from Agulhon's work there is an article by Jean Masse, considerable detail in Willard's study on the Guesdists, and work in progress by Jacques Girault (see bibliography for details).

Chapter Two

1. See Masurel, *La vigne*, p.21.
2. This includes the area of olive-growing around Grasse; this area was later transferred to the Alpes-Maritimes.
3. The olive remained a profitable crop in the favoured Gapeau valley, where it was grown almost exclusively for the manufacture of oil. It continued to be grown in the lower and middle Var in lesser quantity, but could not be harvested north of a line substantially similar to that which marks the limits of the vine. On the decline of the olive, the destructive impact of spring frosts, etc., see *Le Petit Var* for e.g. 3 and 4 December 1880. Also *AD Var* XIV M 19 (4) (statistique agricole), for details of the geography of local *oléiculture*. In 1882, 90% of the olive harvest of St Zacharie was lost through a frost in March of that year (see *Le Petit Var*, 8 February 1883).
4. See the observations on fruit production in early-nineteenth-century Provence in J. Vidalenc, *La société française de 1815 à 1848: le peuple des campagnes* (Paris, 1970), pp.206–7.
5. The four communes of Solliès Pont, Solliès Ville, Solliès Toucas and La Farlède alone sent to Paris, Lyon, Toulon, Marseille and further afield 15 000– 20 000 kilos of strawberries, raspberries, peas, etc. *every day* during May 1885. In this one canton, in this period, there were thirty-five different Parisian wholesale houses represented. See *Le Petit Var*, 17 May 1885, 20 June 1885.
6. *Annuaire statistique* 1901; *Le Petit Var*, 17 September 1889.
7. I owe this calculation to Livet, *Habitat rural*, esp. pp.395–407.
8. Figures on mushroom production quoted in *Le Petit Var*, 22 October 1882, 3 October 1884. For Tanneron, see Masurel, *La vigne*, p.6.
9. Even the lesser crop of rye, which covered a mere 750 hectares in 1878, had disappeared by the outbreak of war in 1914. See M. Rozycka-Glassova, Modifications de structure du système de culture dans le département du Var au 19e siècle et au cours de la première moitié du 20e siècle, in *Cahiers du Centre d'Etudes des Sociétés méditerranéennes* no.2, 1968, pp. 248–68. See also *Annuaires statistiques* for the years 1878–1921.
10. For the number of threshers in the department see Rollet, *La vie quotidienne*, p.72; wheat production is given in the *Annuaires statistiques*. A special statistical survey (see sources) for the years 1882–1929 contains inter-departmental comparative data. On the question of cereal-growing in unsuited soils, see comments by Corbin, *Archaïsme et modernité*, p.27.
11. There were 4240 sheep in Comps in 1886, 3675 in Ampus, 3592 in Mazaugues. For the same communes, in 1913, the figures were, respectively, 2750, 3500, 800, and this was the general tendency. Note, too, that the old transhumance routes hardly touched the Var, cutting across the north-western corner of the department. Figures for animal population by commune in *AD Var* XIV M 19 (11/12) for the years 1886 and 1913. For

transhumance routes, see Braudel, *The Mediterranean*, vol. I, part i, figure 5. The communes of the hills still kept a few sheep as recently as 1977 — the herd of La Garde Freinet is grazing noisily below my window as I write this!

12. On the growth of the Provençal vineyard in the nineteenth century, see comments by J. Harvey Smith, Work routine and social structure in a French village: Cruzy in the nineteenth century, in *J.I.H.* V, iii, pp.363–4; also L.-A. Loubère, *Radicalism in Mediterranean France 1848–1914* (New York, 1974), p.23; Masurel, *La vigne*, p.21.

13. Data on wine production in *AD Var* XIV M 29 (1). See also *Le Petit Var*, 9 September 1882, 1 February 1888, 9 January 1889. On American vines, see Masurel, *La vigne*, p.54 (also p.70 for the crisis of 1907). In general on the impact of overproduction and fraud in 1907, see F. Napo, *1907, la révolte des vignerons* (Toulouse, 1971).

14. Information on local silk production in *Annuaire statistique* for the year 1900. See also *Le Petit Var*, 31 October 1883, 24 June 1885, 10 June 1891.

15. It is worth commenting on the scale of the fishing 'industry' in this region. In an average year, some 1 750 000 kilograms of fish were caught off the Var littoral, and this steady and distinctive coastal activity helped accentuate a division I have already suggested between the peasants of the interior and the residents of the coast. Unlike much else farmed in the region, however, the fish, except those caught in bulk off Toulon, were largely for local consumption, even after the railways had made their despatch further afield a possibility.

16. Details of property holdings and agricultural occupations by department in *Atlas historique de la France contemporaine* (Paris, 1966), maps 62–6; *AD Var* XIV M 19 (4) which contains a breakdown of all occupations by commune for the year 1885; *AD Var* XI M 2 (6/7) and XIV M 19 (8) for the structure of agricultural property holdings by commune for the years 1872 and 1891 respectively. See also *Atlas historique de Provence*, pp.79–80.

17. See Loubère, *Radicalism in Mediterranean France*, pp.74–90; also Rollet, *La vie quotidienne*, p.28. During the depression the very smallest proprietors were forced to sell out, often at absurdly low prices. Slightly better-off peasants were thereby enabled to round out their land at little cost and thus to sit out the depression, albeit with difficulty.

18. A good example of the 'de-industrialising' of the countryside is given in the article by A. Rodgers, Migration and industrial development: the southern Italian experience, in *E.G.* 46, ii, pp.118ff.

19. For details of local industrial production and the variety of local industry see *AD Var* XIV M 1 (11) and XIV M 19 (4); *Annuaires statistiques* for the period 1878–1911; J. Girard, *Nomenclature des richesses minières du département du Var* (Draguignan, 1919), *passim*; *Atlas historique de Provence*, pp.79–80.

20. For the numbers of men and women employed by industry, see especially the *Recensement* of 1911.

21. Details of the declining cork industry are given in some interesting articles in *Le Petit Var*, 14 February 1882, 7 October 1886. The cork-workers will receive fuller attention in Part Two. In 1911, the total number employed in

cork extraction and manufacture was 3273 people; it was the fourth largest
non-agricultural work-force in the area after metal-workers (4914 employees),
seamstresses (4755) and masons (3311).

22. There were 2721 bakers, masters and workers together, in 1911. See sources
quoted in notes 19, 20.

23. For a fine study of the old bourgs of Provence in the nineteenth century,
see M. Agulhon, La fin des petites villes dans le Var intérieur au 19^e
siècle, in *Villes de l'Europe méditerranéenne et de l'Europe occidentale*
(Actes du Colloque de Nice, 1969), esp. p.323. For the percentage of
rentiers in the 1891 population, see the *Recensement* for that year.

24. It was also in communities such as Carcès, rather than St Julien, that one
found the peasant—worker described in the enquiry of 1873: men and
women who worked in Draguignan or even Toulon until their mid-fifties,
while periodically returning to their plot of land in their village of origin, land
which the family continued to own and work and to which the erstwhile
worker would eventually retire. For the distribution of population, see
ADVar XI M 3 (37). On the percentage of *rentes* in private fortunes, see
P. Cornut, *Répartition de la fortune privée en France au cours de la
première moitié du XXe siècle* (Paris, 1963), pp.85—6. For some
interesting details concerning the pattern of local working life, see Archives
Nationales (henceforward *AN*) C3021 Enquête sur les classes ouvrières
1872—1875 (grouped by department).

25. Other communes to lose up to (or even more than) one-third of their
population in these years were Bras, Cabasse, Correns, Cotignac, Aups,
Tavernes and many more. All of them had been communities of 1500 or
more in the 1860s and most of them were active (and demographically
agglomerated) centres of rural marketing and artisanal industry. For extensive data on the population of every commune in the department, from
1846 to 1906, see *ADVar* XI M 2 (1).

26. See source quoted in note 25. For national data, see the censuses for the
period 1886—1911.

27. On details of local elections and the membership of municipal councils in
these years, see *ADVar* II M 7 (21).

28. The traditional summer exodus from the Alpine plateaux began around 10
June, lasting until early August. By 1875 it was already being made by train,
rather than on foot. See R. Blanchard, *Les Alpes occidentales*, vol. IV,
Les préalpes françaises du Sud (Grenoble, 1945), p.505.

29. On the place of birth of Frenchmen, see the census of 1906, which also
contains comparative data for 1872. In 1901, 13% of the population of the
town of Aups were born outside of the Midi region (see *ADVar* XI M
2(19)). For details of Italian immigration, see the local press for the 1880s
in particular, full of expressions of concern as well as interesting details.
Many of the Italians in the Var were employed in the construction and
maintenance of local railway lines.

30. Details of the expansion of the railway network in *Annuaires statistiques*
for the years 1878—1910, and H. Lartilleux, *Géographie des chemins de
fer français* (Paris, n.d.), *passim*.

31. See *Le Petit Var*, 28 January 1888.

32. For disputes between inland and coastal communes, and pleas for and
    against new railway lines in the department, see *Le Petit Var*, especially
    for 2 December 1880, 1 May 1889, 16 December 1889. In 1883 the
    peasants of St Paul refused to replace their diseased vines by other crops
    unless assured of access to markets via a railway link. See *Le Petit Var*,
    29 December 1883. For the costs of the Draguignan line, see the official
    reports quoted in *Le Petit Var*, 13 May 1882.

33. The price of olive oil also fell in these years. Fetching 145 francs for 100
    litres in the Var in 1884, it could only sell at 90 francs the following year,
    and continued to fall thereafter. On prices in this period, see: *AD Var* I Z 4
    (1) (sub-prefectoral reports on the Brignoles arrondissement); *AN* F^{11} 2678
    (Prix des grains 1889–1895); C. E. Labrousse, *Le prix du froment en France
    1726–1913* (Paris, 1970); J.-M. Mayeur, *Les débuts de la Troisième Répub-
    lique* (Paris, 1973), p.82. The *Petit Var* also published monthly the market
    prices for selected local produce (beef, mutton, olives, wine, fruits).

34. It is perhaps significant that the socialist movement received its first real
    impulsion from the price fall, whereas the conflicts over inadequate wages, a
    decade later, benefited the syndicalists. For data on wages, see in particular
    AD Var XVI M 15 (1) for wage rates in the Var from 1882 to 1912. Also
    D. Vasseur, *Les débuts du mouvement ouvrier dans la région de Belfort-
    Montbéliard 1870–1914* (Paris, 1967) who quotes (p.76) some national
    wage rates for the 1870s. Also *AD Var* IV M 56 (1–6) which gives details
    of wage demands – and existing rates of pay – in local strikes for the
    whole period 1871–1914. Further details in *Le Petit Var*, especially for
    19 May 1881, 2 March 1882, 14 July 1883, 26 March 1886. By 1910, the
    cost of living in Draguignan was estimated at 3 fr. 95 per day – higher
    than the average daily wage in the town. See *Le Cri du Var*, 30 October
    1910.

35. For what follows, see sources quoted in note 13, together with Livet,
    Habitat rural, p.101; Masurel, *La vigne*, pp.43ff; and *Le Petit Var* through-
    out the 1880s.

36. Agulhon, La fin des petites villes, p.326.

37. Eugen Weber, *Peasants into Frenchmen. The Modernisation of Rural France
    1870–1914* (London, 1977).

38. Writing in 1836 of the population of the Verdon region, the *sous-préfet* of
    Castellane (Basses-Alpes) described them as 'plus éloignées de l'influence
    française que les Iles Marquises . . . les communications ne sont ni grandes ni
    petites. Elles n'existent pas.' Quoted in Blanchard, *Les Alpes occidentales*,
    vol. IV, p.415.

39. The phrase is Raoul Blanchard's.

Chapter Three

1. For electoral abstentions in the Var, my calculations are based upon the
   election results in *AD Var* II M 3 (15–46). For an excellent study of the
   phenomenon of electoral abstentionism, see A. Lancelot, *L'abstentionnisme électoral en France* (Paris, 1968).

2. See *AD Var* II M 7 (Municipal elections) and *Le Petit Var*, 24 January
   1883, 7 August 1883.

3. See the example of the Toulon *conseil d'arrondissement* at its meeting on 25 September 1882. Details in a report in *Le Petit Var*, 26 September 1882.

4. Report of the Brignoles *sous-préfet* on political activity in his arrondissement in *AD Var* I Z 4 (1).

5. See *AN* F[7] 12723 (Agitation révolutionnaire par département 1893– 1914), report for 1909. Also *Le Petit Var*, 18 December 1880, 5 January 1881.

6. Data in this section drawn from material in *AD Var* II M 3 unless otherwise stated.

7. A red flag tied to a tree near Le Beausset was still considered worthy of a police report – in 1883! See *AD Var* IV M 41 (Rapports sur l'esprit publique 1877–1909).

8. On the First International in the Var, see references in A. Olivési, *La commune de 1871 à Marseille* (Paris, 1950); also J. Maîtron (ed.), *Dictionnaire biographique du mouvement ouvrier* (Paris, 1964–), vols covering the period 1864–1871. For the events in Entrecasteaux, see *AN* BB[30] 486– 90 (Aix Cour d'Appel 1871–1877).

9. See *AD Var* IV M 40 (Rapports sur l'esprit publique 1870–1873). In the early 1870s there was much sporting of phrygian bonnets, a form of sartorial politics still banned by the government of the Moral Order.

10. See *AD Var* IV M 41 for details of the events of 1877.

11. For these and other episodes, see *Le Petit Var*, esp. 8 December 1880, 11 February 1881 (reports on the burial of Blanc), 22 March 1881, 31 July 1881, 19 March 1882.

12. See for this period the daily reports in *Le Petit Var*, and the monthly summary of political events in *AD Var* IV M 41. The 1881 municipal elections appear in full in *Le Petit Var*, 11 January 1881, as well as in *AD Var* II M 7.

13. Quoted in *Le Petit Var*, 6 November 1881.

14. A departmental committee, composed mainly of Radicals, was formed on 13 February 1884 with the purpose of pressing for a revised constitution.

15. See the St Tropez election results in *AD Var* II M 3 (35).

16. On the foregoing, and much else, see the very full political coverage in the local press during the 1880s and 1890s.

17. See Agulhon, *Une ville ouvrière, passim*, and Dominique Desanti, *Les socialistes de l'utopie* (Paris, 1970). Also C. Johnson, *Utopian Communism in France: Cabet and the Icarians 1839–1851* (Cornell, N.Y., 1974). Bastelica in 1869 had been 'émerveillé par la perméabilité aux idées socialistes de ces masses rurales, mi-ouvrières, mi-paysannes'. Quoted in Maîtron (ed.), *Dictionnaire biographique*, 1864–71, p.433.

18. On developments in Cuers during the 1870s, see *AD Var* III Z 6 (15) (Police Générale, Toulon arrondissement); *Historique et vie de la Fédération Socialiste du Var* (Toulon, 1936), pp.7ff; A. Compère-Morel, *Encylopédie socialiste* (Paris, 1921), vol. 3, *passim*; C. Willard, *Les guesdistes* (Paris, 1965), pp.105ff; on data concerning the town of Cuers, see *AD Var* XI M 2 (1) for population figures, and *AD Var* XIV M 19 (4) for economic and occupational information.

19. *Le Petit Var*, 13 November 1881.

20. See reports in *Le Petit Var*, 19 October 1888, 21 October 1888, 30 October 1888.
21. See *Le Petit Var*, 8 and 24 November 1888, 4 October 1889.
22. *Le Petit Var*, 16 November 1888.
23. Voting figures in *AD Var* II M 3, and in Compère-Morel, *Encyclopédie*.
24. *Le Petit Var*, 12 to 16 April 1889.
25. Details of the elections of 1889 in *AD Var* II M 3 (35), also in *Le Petit Var*, 24 August 1889.
26. Quote from an interview in *Le Petit Var*, 7 November 1889.
27. Quoted in a report in *AD Var* IV M 41, for March 1895.
28. References to Guesde's followers as 'marxistes' begin to appear in 1889.
29. See Willard, *Guesdistes*, p.108.
30. Details of the committee appear in the electoral material preserved in the departmental archives – *AD Var* II M 3 (37).
31. Reference to these socialist groups is scattered through official reports and news items which appeared in the 1890s.
32. *AD Var* IV M 55, reports on activity on 1 May for the years 1892–1914.
33. See reports in *AD Var* IV M 41; details in *Historique et vie*, and in *Le Petit Var* for these years.
34. Details of these and all other legislative elections in *AD Var* II M 3.
35. Cluseret's support remained consistently steady throughout the period, hovering between 5400 and 6300 votes.
36. Copious details of the establishment and brief lives of the two socialist Federations in the Var before unification may be found in the following sources: *AD Var* IV M 41 (reports on congresses 1902–4); *AN* F[7] 12503 (details of relations between the Var Revolutionary Federation and the Parti Socialiste de France); Compère-Morel, *Encyclopédie* (section on Var); *Historique et vie*, pp.7–12; Willard, *Guesdistes*, pp.444–512.
37. *Le Cri du Var*, 4 September 1904.
38. On the process of unification, see the archival sources quoted in note 36. Also Willard, *Guesdistes*, p.585; *Le Cri du Var*, 2 April 1905, 10 September 1905. Details of the national developments in Georges Lefranc, *Le mouvement socialiste sous la Troisième République 1875–1940* (Paris, 1963), and Aaron Noland, *The Founding of the French Socialist Party 1893–1905* (Cambridge, Mass., 1956).
39. *SFIO Congrès Nationaux; comptes rendus sténographiques. Rapports 1905–1906*. For the *préfet*'s enduring interest in socialist affairs, see *AD Var* IV M 41 for the years 1905–9.
40. Membership figures were published at every Federal Congress, as well as in the annual report of the SFIO.
41. On the enduring problem of establishing a disciplined Marxist party in France, see many of the works in section (ii) of the bibliography. The question is considered in detail in T. Judt, *La reconstruction du Parti Socialiste 1921–1926* (Paris, 1976). The Communists faced similar initial difficulties – see the excellent study by R. Wohl, *French Communism in the Making 1914–1924* (Stanford, Calif., 1966), and of course the seminal works of Annie Kriegel (see bibliography).
42. See e.g. *Le Cri du Var*, 2 October 1904.

43. See *Le Cri du Var*, 25 March 1906, 10 and 24 June 1906, 1 and 8 July 1906. Also *Historique et vie*, section one.
44. *Historique et vie*; also *Le Cri du Var*, 4 August 1907.
45. *Le Cri du Var*, 23 February 1908, 16 August 1908.
46. Quoted in *Le Cri du Var*, 24 January 1909.
47. See *AN* F[7] 12503 for 1905. Also *AD Var* IV M 41 and *Le Cri du Var* for the whole period 1905–9. Police and newspapers alike gave the Toulon quarrels very full coverage.
48. Comments on the weakened and divided condition of Toulonnais socialism abound in the local press. See also the observations of the local police reports in *AD Var* IV M 42 (Rapports sur l'esprit publique 1909–13) and *AD Var* III Z 4 (3) reports for 1910.
49. See *Le Cri du Var* for 18 December 1910, 30 March 1913, 6 April 1913. In the local elections of 1913, where there was no Socialist list, voters were urged to support the most revolutionary anti-militarist candidates, of whatever political label. See also Rinaudo, L'opposition, esp. pp.174–7.
50. *Le Cri du Var*, 28 June 1908.
51. *Le Cri du Var*, 8 July 1906, 19 May 1907, 24 October 1909.
52. See *Le Cri du Var*, 8 October 1905.
53. Reports on Congress debates, and publication of their rulings, were an important part of the function of the Federation's paper, *Le Cri du Var*. Unlike the national party, of course, the local Federation could ill afford to publish and circulate its congress minutes. For the discussions on freemasonry, syndical membership, etc., see *Le Cri du Var* for 27 August 1911, 4 February 1912, 11 January 1914.
54. See *Le Cri du Var*, 14 October 1906, 29 December 1907, 23 August 1908, 28 May 1910.
55. See *Le Cri du Var*, 10 July 1910, 9 July 1911, 26 March 1913. Also *AD Var* IV M 42 (Rapports sur l'esprit publique 1913), where there is a unique reference to a criticism levelled at *all* the Socialist parliamentarians by some Hyères militants at the 1913 Congress.
56. On the depth of feeling between Toulon militants and socialists in the rest of the department, see comments in *AD Var* IV M 42, and also the speeches at the Federal Congress held in 1906 (*Le Cri du Var*, 11 March 1906).
57. See the numerous references to the presence of militant Italian socialists from the 1880s onward in *AD Var* IV M 40–43; *Le Petit Var*, 18 March 1885, 24 July 1888, and *Le Cri du Var*, especially during 1907 and 1908. The Italians were organised into groups of their own, but they took part in local (French) Federal Congresses, and joined in meetings and demonstrations organised by the departmental Federation.
58. On the general presence of Italian workers in the Var see above in Chapter 2, p.46.
59. Details of lists presented at cantonal elections are in *AD Var* II M 5 (165–231) for the years 1876–1913. See also *Le Cri du Var*, 7 August 1910, 15 January 1911.
60. The Brignoles Groupe d'Union Socialiste only met during the winter months and there were many sections and groups which did likewise. See *Le Cri du Var*, 15 October 1905 for details of the Brignoles Groupe's activities.

61. This raises other questions. Annie Kriegel wisely warns us that membership and votes are figures of two different orders – the one a matter of organisation, the other an expression of opinions. They cannot easily be compared. See A. Kriegel, *La croissance de la CGT (1918–21)* (Paris, 1966), p.166. But in the tiny bourgs of lower Provence, there *may* be some value in comparing the two. Not in any statistical sense, of course, but in order to establish precisely whether there was any relationship between organisation and opinion. It would be quite reasonable to advance, as a hypothesis, that a well-organised and lively local Socialist section was often the basis for a high turnout at the polls, in favour of the Socialist candidate. For reasons to be discussed later, such a hypothesis would not be very tenable with respect to the presence of a *syndical* organisation, except in certain kinds of rural industry (e.g. shoemaking).

62. See *AD Var* IV M 52 (Manifestations syndicales 1871–1914) reports for 1871–4.

63. On the Carqueiranne rural federation, see *Le Petit Var*, 7 April 1881. General details on the growth of the labour movement in the Var may be found in the *Annuaire statistique* in each year for the period 1878 to 1913.

64. On the strike of cork-workers in La Garde Freinet, see *ADVar* IV M 56 (1–6), also *AN* F^{12} 4664 (Grèves 1880–1889), and *Le Petit Var* during December 1881 and January 1882. The details of the local population are taken from *ADVar* XI M 2 (population by commune 1846–1906).

65. See *ADVar* IV M 56. Between 1906 and 1914 the farm labourers in Ollioules, Hyères, La Valette and elsewhere in this region of intensive farming struck on many occasions, usually over wages, and often with the women workers to the fore. In most other respects, the pattern of strike activity in this region reflected national trends: 1906 saw the peak of labour unrest in this period, in the Var as in France. In that year there were 4325 strikers taking part in stoppages affecting 725 establishments. In general, strikes after 1900 were more numerous, shorter, and involved more people. See France: *Statistique des grèves*, for the years 1890–1908. These developments also reflect national patterns, as described in the work by E. Shorter and C. Tilly, *Strikes in France 1830–1968* (Cambridge, 1974) and especially in the study by Michèle Perrot, *Les ouvriers en grève* (Paris, 1974, 2 vols).

66. In 1906, the Syndicat International des Ouvriers en Chaussures was well established in the region, with its centre at Bargemon, with 150 members. Of these, 32 at most can have been members of the SFIO in that year, but these 30 or so men appear to have been the leaders and driving force behind the activities of the syndicat. See *AN* F^{22} 150 (Syndicats ouvriers), and congress reports in *Le Cri du Var* for details of the socialist membership of the Bargemon Section.

67. *Le Petit Var*, 22 November 1884.

68. The Coopérative Agricole in Trans in 1896, for example, existed in order to purchase fertiliser and to 'facilitate commerce'. See *AN* F^{12} 4702 (Syndicats agricoles dissous).

69. See *AD Var* IV M 41 (Rapports sur l'esprit publique 1877–1909); also *Le Petit Var*, 7 July 1887. Occasional later attempts by Toulon anarchist leaders to 'break out' into the rural department met with no greater success.

70. Details in reports in *AD Var* IV M 41. Although the police kept a very close eye on Toulon anarchists, especially in the 1890s, they never successfully established just how many there were. The number seems to have wavered from 60 to upwards of 300. Anti-militarist meetings or visits by such leading figures as Sébastien Faure produced the largest audiences. See *Le Petit Var*, 15 August 1891, and *AD Var* IV M 41. When Faure visited the Var, he confined all his speeches to the Toulon area, saving only a rare visit to a nearby town or one of the neighbouring coastal communities.

Chapter Four

1. The basic work of reference for all students of electoral geography is that of François Goguel, *Géographie des élections françaises sous la Troisième et la Quatrième Républiques* (Paris, 1951), which uses calculations at a departmental level.
2. On 10 January 1905, the Groupe Ouvrier Révolutionnaire in Les Salles spent two hours in the Café de Commerce discussing a talk given by A. Bosquet, one of their number, on 'Révolte et raison'. None of the surrounding villages had a socialist group, in 1905 or for many years to come. See *Le Cri du Var*, 15 January 1905.
3. Here, as for the remainder of this chapter, my calculations are based upon the complete returns for all legislative elections for the period 1876–1914, as given in *AD Var* II M 3 (29–46).
4. The communes, ordered by region, were the following:
   Les Salles, Baudinard, Artignosc, Montmeyan, St Julien, Ginasservis, Vinon; Varages, Pontèves, Sillans, Salernes, Cotignac, Entrecasteaux, Seillons, Châteauvert, Correns, Montfort; Tourtour, Flayosc, Ampus, Figanières, Bargemon, Claviers, Fayence, St Paul; Roquebrune, Le Muy, Le Luc, Les Mayons, Collobrières, La Garde Freinet, Plan de la Tour, Bormes, Grimaud; La Cadière, Bandol, Ollioules, La Crau; Besse, to the south of Brignoles, and Camps, on the Issole river just off the N7 highway, were the remaining two.
5. For details of the elevation of each commune in the Var, see the data in the *Indicateur du Var* (Toulon, 1937). The height given is that of the communal *chef-lieu*, rather than that of the outlying hamlets or isolated farms. On grouped and dispersed habitat, see *AD Var* XI M 3 (37) for the year 1893.
6. Details of the size of population by commune are given for each decade of the period 1846–1906 in *AD Var* XI M 2 (1). These figures are from the decennial 'dénombrement de la population'. Only four of the socialist-leaning communes had populations of less than 300 people in 1896 (in that year the department numbered twenty communes of that size or below).
7. See *AD Var* XIV M 19 (4).
8. Communes without any reported industrial activity in the mid-1880s were Les Salles, Baudinard, Artignosc, Montmeyan and St Julien in the north-west, Tourtour, Sillans, Entrecasteaux and Châteauvert in the centre and Besse to the south. A further four communes – Vinon, Ginasservis, Seillons and Montfort, all in the north-central part of the Brignoles arrondissement – were reported as having a small number of people (18 in Montfort, 5 in Vinon) engaged in the milling of olives.

9. The population of Flayosc in 1886 was 2624 people.

10. In 1886, the populations of Cotignac, Le Luc and Le Muy were, respectively, 2529, 2929 and 2789.

11. *AD Var* XI M 2 (6/7) and *AD Var* XIV M 19 (8). The first enquiry is more detailed but very incomplete, the second decidedly overstates the number of *petits propriétaires*, doubtless through the inclusion of many plots of less than two hectares owned by workers and tradesmen, recorded as landed property but hardly constituting genuine 'peasant' property.

12. Details of hectarage of vines, and of the volume of wine production are in *AD Var* XIV M 29 (1), and Masurel, *La vigne*.

13. Only Besse was a substantial producer of grain — 2000 hectares in 1895. In contrast, there were a mere 200 hectares devoted to grain in Varages, 230 hectares in Entrecasteaux, 200 hectares in Le Muy, and a mere 32 hectares of wheat in Bargemon. See source quoted in note 7.

14. Full data on the animal population of the Var for the years 1886 and 1913 are in *AD Var* XIV M 19 (11/12).

15. In La Bastide, a tiny commune on the plateau east of Comps, the entire economy in 1885 consisted of 442 hectares of arable land (of which 180 hectares were under wheat, the rest barley, rye and potatoes), together with 34 horses, a dozen donkeys, one cow — but with a herd of 770 sheep, on which the community's livelihood depended.

16. See *AD Var* II M 3 (15).

17. The link with 1849 is stronger among those areas of high socialist voting in 1893 than it was with the socialist strongholds of the years after 1898. This suggests perhaps that the initial socialist advances benefited from traditional allegiances, but that later support requires a more circumstantial explanation.

18. The seven in question were Châteauvert, Correns, Montfort, St Julien, Sillans, Ampus and Tourtour.

19. Plan d'Aups, Riboux, Vérignon and La Martre all had less than 500 inhabitants in the 1890s, while Fréjus, St Tropez, St Nazaire and of course Hyères all had well over 3500 inhabitants by this time.

20. Fréjus grew by 20% in the years 1876–1906, Hyères by 44% over the same period, reaching 17 790 people by the latter year. Even tiny Plan d'Aups was a growing village: from a population of 112 in 1876, it had reached 123 people by 1906, a population increase of 10%, unique in the otherwise depopulating arrondissement of Brignoles!

21. Sources used in compiling the information in this chapter on socialist groups in the Var include:
Rapports of SFIO Congresses 1905–14; *AD Var* II M 3 (Elections 1876–1914); *AD Var* VIII M 16 (1–28) (Cercles); *AD Var* IV M 41 (Rapports sur l'esprit publique 1877–1909); *AN* F[7] 12489 (Congrès socialistes 1880–2); *AN* F[7] 12494 (Congrès divers 1899, 1900); *AN* F[7] 12723 (Agitation révolutionnaire par départements 1893–1914); *AN* F[7] 12886 (Parti Ouvrier Français 1896–9); *Historique et vie*; Compère-Morel, *Encyclopédie*; Maîtron (ed.), *Dictionnaire biographique*; Willard, *Guesdistes*; *Le Petit Var* (1880–1905); *Le Cri du Var* (1904–14).

22. Among evidence which I have used to construct this map are details of sales

of the socialist newspaper *Le Cri du Var*. The number of copies sold is irrelevant — readership vastly exceeded copies bought. But the presence or absence of a few subscribers to *Le Cri* was a very strong indication of the presence or otherwise of a socialist group — though it has only been given credence when supported by other evidence — e.g. police reports, etc. *Le Cri* was on sale in 1906 on the streets of the following towns and villages: Draguignan, Brignoles, Collobrières, Gonfaron, Pierrefeu, St Raphael, Solliès Pont. By 1909. the paper was available in the following places: Toulon, Draguignan, Brignoles, Aups, Barjols, Besse, Cogolin, Collobrières, Correns, Cotignac, Cuers, Fayence, Flayosc, Fréjus, Gonfaron, La Garde Freinet, Le Luc, Pierrefeu, Solliès Pont, Ste Maxime, St Raphael, St Tropez.

23. Of the 64 communes being considered, 32 had populations of over 2000 people in 1896, and of these 32, 9 were large towns, of 3500 people or more. Conversely, socialist groups did not flourish in the smallest bourgs and tiny villages — only 12 of the 64 communes with a socialist group had less than 1000 inhabitants in 1896.

24. Five of them (Seillons, Pontèves, Artignosc, Montmeyan and Sillans) had less than 500 inhabitants in 1896. Indeed, of all 17 communes where socialists won elections but established no militant base, only La Cadière, near Toulon, had a population of average size (1700 in 1896).

25. See sources cited in note 21, together with the following: *AD Var* XIV M 7 (2) (Syndicats agricoles 1900–1909); *AD Var* XIV M 7 (6) (Coopératives); *AD Var* IV M 52 (Manifestations syndicales 1871–1914); *AN* F²² 150 (Syndicats ouvriers).

26. See *ADVar* VIII M 16 (1–28), and *Le Cri du Var*, 23 December 1906.

27. *Le Cri du Var*, 13 June 1909, 2 January 1910.

28. Thus in the Var as elsewhere, the schoolteachers, pathfinders for the Radical republic and its ideals, did not switch their allegiance over to the extreme left before World War One — understandably, perhaps, given the treatment by republican governments of men and women whose politics became too openly socialist. See also *Le Cri du Var*, 1 January 1907.

29. It was Comps, for example, which had a series of bourgeois mayors from 1860–1900, just as it was Plan d'Aups where two families, both of them well established and reasonably wealthy, had dominated local politics since 1790. See J. Salvarelli, *Les administrateurs du département du Var 1790–1897* (Draguignan, 1897).

30. *Le Cri du Var*, 20 March 1910.

31. *Le Cri du Var*, 3 May, 10 May and 17 May 1908. In 1906 the population of Draguignan stood at 9770 inhabitants.

Chapter Five

1. J.-P. Aron, P. Dumont and E. Le Roy Ladurie, *Anthropologie du conscrit français* (Paris, 1972), p.29.

2. Corbin, *Archaïsme et modernité*, p.330.

3. P. Gratton, *Les paysans français contre l'agrarisme* (Paris, 1972), p.39.

4. Loubère, *Radicalism in Mediterranean France*, p.1. See also pp.4, 22, 206.

5. See J. J. Linz, Patterns of land tenure, division of labor and voting behavior

in Europe, in *Comparative Politics*, VIII, iii, pp.390–1.

6. For these details, see *Le Petit Var*, 9 November 1880, 6 March 1881, 31 August 1884, 8 February 1885. These fairs had other, social, functions of course, but here we are concerned with their rôle as channels for the dissemination of goods and (indirectly) ideas among the villages which depended upon them.

7. Armengaud notes a similar phenomenon in Aquitaine, and quotes an official comment on the subject from the 1840s: 'les cultivateurs venus à Toulouse pour le marché y achètent un journal démocrate et deviennent ensuite dans leurs campagnes d'actifs agents de propagande anarchique'. See A. Armengaud, *Les populations de l'Est-Aquitain 1845–1871* (Paris, 1961), p.382.

8. See E. Wolf, *Peasant Wars of the Twentieth Century* (London, 1969), esp. pp.282–95.

9. See P. Bois, *Paysans de l'Ouest* (Paris, 1971, abridged edn), p. 15; and E. Malefakis' article in R.J. Bezucha (ed.), *Modern European Social History* (Lexington, Mass., 1972) esp. p.198.

10. See an analysis of Socialist voting support in the region, published in the Federation's own newspaper, *Le Cri du Var*, 7 September 1913.

11. See R. Bezucha in Bezucha (ed.), *Modern European Social History*, p.111.

12. For details of the numbers employed in various rural industries, see the very detailed breakdown given in the *Annuaire statistique* for 1911. This argument tends to confirm the Weberian (Max, not Eugen) conception of the importance of organisation. Where a highly articulated organisational framework exists, it will tend to gather affiliation which then ceases to be 'available' for alternative and competing ideologies. This is an overly functionalist view of the matter, but as a corrective to the determinist model of economic causality it is relevant here. It is also the case that certain industries – shoemaking, for example – have a strong tradition of organisation and militancy in other places and at other times. (See Agulhon, *Une ville ouvrière*, p.292; L. Tilly in Bezucha (ed.), *Modern European Social History*, p.145, on the shoemakers of Milan in the 1890s.) This makes their presence in such force in the midst of rural Provence all the more important.

13. See *Le Petit Var*, 24 April 1886, 16 April 1891. Also *Le Petit Var* for 4 March 1885, where the *bouchonniers* of La Crau are reported as voting to support their bosses against Parisian merchants over the issue of tariffs on imported Spanish corks.

14. On the Beaujolais, see G. Garrier, *Paysans du Beaujolais et du Lyonnais 1800–1970* (Grenoble, 1973, 2 vols), esp. vol. I, pp.438–9.

15. At a Federal committee meeting in Draguignan on 2 June 1907, Maurice Allard explained that the Socialist remedy for the wine crisis and the fraudulent production of 'ersatz' wine was a state monopoly on the production and sale of all wine. On other occasions, the Socialists lent their backing to the Fédération Viticole Varoise, with its programme of producer cooperatives, *vigneron* syndicates, and subsidised credit. See *Le Cri du Var*, 9 June 1907, 27 October 1907. There was an implicit conflict between the cooperative solution and the response which invoked a nationalisation

of the vine. But the implications of this important distinction only became clear in the post-war years.

16. See Harvey Smith, Work routine and social structure, *passim*.

17. Rumours of a coming series of protectionist tariffs on imported wheat produced protest meetings in the Var from as early as 1887. One of the most actively anti-protectionist communes was Montfort in the Argens valley, always a stronghold of local socialism, and whose population was predominantly peasant, smallholding and wine-producing. By 1891 there were angry meetings all over the central and southern Var protesting against the effects of protection. See *Le Petit Var*, 31 March 1887, 7 April 1887, and throughout the spring of 1891.This is one of many instances revealing the sensitivity of the local peasantry to changes in the *price* of goods, an issue which played a far greater part in mobilising them politically than did disputes over *wages*, which were the basis of social protest and political action in the towns.

18. For membership of municipal councils see *AD Var* II M 7 (21) (Municipal elections 1896–1908). For the occupations of mayors in the department, see Salvarelli, *Les administrateurs, passim*. The population of each commune, with details of occupation and place of birth, is given in *AD Var* XI M 2 (Dénombrement de la population).

19. Details in *AD Var* IV M 24 (2/3).

20. See *Le Petit Var*, 7 January 1882. The significant fall in population of La Garde Freinet, from 2331 to 1872, came in the years 1886–96. Between 1846 and 1886 the population had fallen by only 102 people, although there had of course been rather steeper interim fluctuations.

21. This is a view offered tentatively, by Bois, in *Paysans de l'Ouest*, abridged edn, pp.40ff.

Chapter Six

1. See Braudel, *The Mediterranean*; also J. Peristiany (ed.), *Contributions to Mediterranean Sociology* (Paris, 1968), and J. Davis, *People of the Mediterranean* (London, 1977), esp. pp.1–5, 55–64, 127–32.

2. Among the many invaluable historical studies of Provence, see in particular Vovelle, *Piété baroque*; Agulhon, *La sociabilité méridionale;* Agulhon, *La vie sociale;* R. Baehrel, *Une croissance: la Basse-Provence rurale fin 16ᵉ siècle–1789* (Paris, 1961).

3. See *Atlas historique de Provence*, p.51 and plate 114.

4. On the foregoing, see Agulhon, *La vie sociale, passim*; Agulhon, Les chambrées de Provence, pp. 342–50; Agulhon, Un problème d'ethnologie historique: les 'chambrées' en Basse-Provence au XIXᵉ siècle, in M. Agulhon et al., *Ethnologie et histoire: forces productives et problèmes de transition* (Paris, 1975).

5. See Agulhon, *La République au village*. Also, for a description of eighteenth-century Jansenism in this area, the works by Vovelle and plate 118 in *Atlas historique de Provence*.

6. *Le Petit Var*, 30 November 1881, 24 March 1887.

7. M. Agulhon, Les chambrées de Provence, p.250.

8. With Agulhon, I feel that L. Roubin overstresses the exclusively masculine character of Provençal social life in her book *Chambrettes des Provençaux: une maison des hommes en Méditerranée septentrionale.* This is in large measure a result of her rather static and functionalist approach to the study of the region and its social formations, making little allowance for changes brought about over time.

9. See *Le Petit Var,* 3 June 1881.

10. See *Le Petit Var,* 10 May 1882, 16 June 1882, 15 January 1883, 10 March 1883, 13 May 1883, 26 August 1883.

11. See *Le Petit Var,* 27 August 1882, 9 December 1882.

12. See *Le Petit Var,* 9 February 1887, 27 February 1891. Also *AD Var* IV M 40 (Rapports sur l'esprit publique 1870–3). An editorial in *Le Petit Var* in June 1885 correctly observed that the disappearance of communal holidays and local saints' days meant a greater routinisation of agricultural work, the year no longer being broken up by ancient and popular festivals which afforded time for relaxation. One particular form of common activity survived into this period, though in muted form: the charivari. It surfaced occasionally, as an informal social and moral sanction as well as an occasion for public singing, dancing and revelry, as in Figanières where nocturnal disturbances to 'chasser la carême' were banned after 1882, or in La Seyne, where a full-blown charivari took place on the Place de l'Eglise in January 1885 for the expression of public (mostly youthful) disapproval at the over-hasty remarriage of a recently widowed lady. See *Le Petit Var,* 6 April 1882, 19 January 1885. From around 1890, these classic forms of pre-modern sociability were no more to be found.

13. See *Le Petit Var,* 28 May 1886. Competing orchestras of this kind were a common feature of the area.

14. See *Le Petit Var,* 29 September 1880, 13 April 1882. Also *AD Var* IV M 41 (report for August 1886).

15. On the absence of organised sub-communities in Castilian villages, see the contribution by M. Kenny in Peristiany (ed.), *Contributions to Mediterranean Sociology,* p.157.

16. *Le Petit Var,* 3 June 1882.

17. See P. Sorlin, *La société française 1840–1914* (Paris, 1969), p.57.

18. On the growth of the 'café-bank' west of the Rhône, see D. Fabre and J. Lacroix, *La vie quotidienne des paysans du Languedoc au 19ᵉ siècle* (Paris, 1973), p.177.

19. See *Le Petit Var,* 9 June 1883; *AD Var* IV M 40 (report dated December 1873).

20. *AN* C3021 (Enquête sur les classes ouvrières (1872–5 (dossier Var)).

21. See Shorter and Tilly, *Strikes in France,* p.156.

22. Fabre and Lacroix, *La vie quotidienne,* p.247. Also Le Roy Ladurie, *Les paysans du Languedoc, passim.*

23. On Brittany see S. Berger, *Peasants against Politics: Rural Organisation in Brittany 1911–1967* (Cambridge, Mass., 1972).

24. See J. Masse, Les anarchistes varois 1879–1920, in *M.S.* no. 69, 1969. Also *AD Var* XIV M 7 (2) (Syndicats agricoles 1900–1909).

25. See *Atlas historique de Provence*, plate 122 (eighteenth-century fairs); *AD Var* IV M 24 (2/3) for the insurrection of 1851. Communications played a vital rôle in fuelling organised resistance. In 1851 the Dijon–Grenoble coach, a veritable 'société secrète roulante', got news of the December-2nd insurrection to Besançon by 8 a.m. on the following day. See R. Laurent, *Les vignerons de la Côte d'Or au 19ᵉ siècle* (Paris, 1957), p.471, n.5.

26. List given in *AD Var* IV M 41. It is noteworthy that Camps, with a population of 1019, had *four cercles* in 1877, all of them banned by the authorities during that summer. The hat-makers of this commune and its environs were clearly at the centre of this active social and political existence, but it is significant that even after the hatting industry had gone into a steep decline, Camps remained a stronghold of (increasingly peasant) socialism.

27. See B. Barbier, *Villes et centres des Alpes du Sud* (Gap, 1969), p.28.

28. *Le Petit Var*, 12 October 1880.

29. Barbier, *Villes et centres*, pp.30–1.

30. On the population of these communes, see *AD Var* XI M 2 (1). For the numbers living outside of the communal *chef-lieu*, see *AD Var* XI M 3 (37).

31. See Baratier, *La démographie provençale*, pp.110–15.

32. M. Agulhon, La diffusion d'un journal montagnard, 'le Démocrate du Var', sous la 2ᵉ République, in *P.H.* no.39, 1960, pp.14–18; also Corbin, *Archaïsme et modernité*, p.839.

33. See *Le Cri du Var*, 17 April 1910, 6 June 1909. Election details in *AD Var* II M 3 (44).

34. Bois, *Paysans de l'Ouest*, abridged edn, pp.119, 308.

35. On this question, see the following chapter.

Chapter Seven

1. Among the best examples of their kind, see F. Boulard, *Introduction to Religious Sociology* (London, 1960); F. Boulard and J. Rémy, *Pratique religieuse urbaine et régions culturelles* (Paris, 1968); G. le Bras, *Etudes de sociologie religieuse* (Paris, 1955), vol.1; G. Cholvy, *Géographie religieuse de l'Hérault contemporain* (Paris, 1968); J. Gadille, *La pensée et l'action politiques des évêques français au début de la Troisième République* (Paris, 1967, 2 vols); C. Marcilhacy, *Le diocèse d'Orléans au milieu du 19ᵉ siècle. Les hommes et leurs mentalités* (Paris, 1964).

2. See *Le Petit Var*, 12 and 17 July 1882.

3. See *AD Var* III Z 6 (15) (Rapports police générale for October 1877); *AD Var* III Z 4 (3) (Police politique Toulon — le mouvement ouvrier 1886–1910, report dated February 1901); *Le Petit Var*, 19 August 1884.

4. See Gadille, *La pensée et l'action*, p.152. Also N. Belmont, *Mythes et croyances dans l'ancienne France* (Paris, 1973), p.39; Y. Brékilien, *La vie quotidienne des paysans bretons au 19ᵉ siècle* (Paris, 1966), esp. pp.243–50.

5. *AD Var* VII U 29 (3); AN F¹⁷ 14295; *Le Petit Var*, 8 October 1881.

6. Quoted in Fabre and Lacroix, *La vie quotidienne*, p.368; see also *AD Var* I Z 4 (1) (report dated 1869) and *AN* C3021 (Enquête sur les classes ouvrières 1872—5).

7. See *Le Cri du Var*, 20 November 1904, 11 December 1904, 10 December 1905. According to police reports, much of the renewed anti-clerical agitation of 1904 in Draguignan was the work of the ex-*abbé* Taillefer, like Emile Combes a former seminarist. See *AD Var* IV M 41.

8. *Le Petit Var*, 20 December 1882.

9. Vovelle, *Piété baroque*, pp.120—1; Gadille, *La pensée et l'action*, *passim*.

10. *Le Petit Var*, 10 and 31 October 1880, 21 October 1885. Also *AD Var* XI M 1 (119), where Lorgues is reported as having fifteen priests and novices in residence in 1872. In the same year, there were nine in Le Luc and two in Vidauban, both communes only a little smaller in population than Lorgues. In July 1906, a socialist in St Maximin, reporting on the meagre local attendance at a Bastille Day celebration, noted with a certain exaggeration: 'Il est vrai que nous sommes ici dans le pays le plus clérical de France, et réactionnaire tout plein encore.' See *Le Cri du Var*, 22 July 1906.

11. See *Atlas historique de Provence*, plates 118—19; *Annuaire statistique* 1901. According to the Toulon police records, the only significant concentration of Protestants in the department by the 1890s was in the coastal strip between Le Beausset and Hyères. See *AD Var* III Z 26 (1) (Culte protestant).

12. See *Le Cri du Var*, 20 August 1904, 24 April 1910, 18 May 1913. Maurice Allard wanted to dechristianise France, to rid it of the 'judeo-christian phantasmagoria' which cloaked the witch-doctor rôle of all priests. A group of his supporters in Vidauban, campaigning in 1910, attacked Schneider and Krupp as Jewish (!) capitalists, and accused the Radicals of facilitating the interests of international Jewish finance. They were not publicly disavowed.

13. *AD Var* III T 1 (5) (Instruction publique).

14. *AD Var* III T 1 (5) (2). Also *Le Petit Var*, 15 April 1881, 12 March 1883.

15. *Le Petit Var*, 7 May 1882.

16. See *Le Petit Var*, 15 May 1882, 29 October 1889.

17. Vovelle in *Atlas historique de Provence*, pp.63—4; Bois, *Paysans de l'Ouest*, abridged edn, p.65; Malefakis in Bezucha (ed.), *Modern European Social History*, p.202; Garrier, *Paysans du Beaujolais*, p.320, n.52, quoting P. Goujon on the Mâconnais. See also Vovelle, *Piété baroque*, p.455, on literacy and schoolteachers in the eighteenth-century Alps.

18. *AN* F[17] 14270 (Degré d'instruction des conscrits 1899). National figures for 1901 quoted in M. Rebérioux, *La République radicale?* (Paris, 1975), p.202. By 1914, the national average was 4% — about that of the Var in 1899.

19. *AD Var* XI M 2 (64 — Comps), (119 — Lorgues), (121 — Le Luc), (181 — Les Salles), (206 — Tanneron).

20. See *AN* F[17] 14269 (Instruction publique 1900); *Le Petit Var*, 6 November 1882, 25 February 1887.

21. On the language question at this time, see the perceptive comments in

E. Weber, *Peasants into Frenchmen*, esp. pp.67–95, 303–39; also
Le Cri du Var, 19 November 1911, where the Aups Section of the Socialist
Federation requested that minor business be discussed in the local
sections, prior to the taking of decisions at Federal Congresses. That way,
local militants would have the chance to express their views on the matters
in question – in Provençal.

22. See Corbin, *Archaïsme et modernité*, p.991; *AD Var* VIII M 16, for the
membership of the Cercle de la Liberté in Le Luc; Price (ed.), *Revolution
and Reaction*, p.51; C. Cippola, *Literacy and Development in the West*
(London, 1969), lists the Var 24th in a ranking of French departments for
the years 1786–1790 according to the percentage of newly-weds who
signed the register with their mark. Provence, the Midi generally and the
western Massif Central all appear as particularly illiterate regions – and
would all become strongholds of the left. Karl Deutsch suggests that, while
literacy and economic progress do not necessarily correlate, there may be a
relationship between growing literacy and political instability. But, as with
the geography of dechristianisation, are we not here dealing with parallel
effects, rather than a causal link? See K. Deutsch, Social mobilisation and
political development, in *A.P.S.R.* LV, 1961.

23. *Le Petit Var*, 1 December 1880.

24. See J.-J. Darmon, *Le colportage de librairie en France sous le Second
Empire* (Paris, 1972), esp. parts I, IV, V.

25. See Agulhon, La diffusion d'un journal montagnard, pp.18, 27.

26. Agulhon, *La vie sociale*, p. 305; on artisan tailors, see the interesting
contribution by Christopher Johnson in Price (ed.), *Revolution and
Reaction*, pp.87–115.

27. Y.-M. Bercé, *Croquants et nu-pieds. Les soulèvements paysans en France
du 16ᵉ au 19ᵉ siècle* (Paris, 1974), p. 204; *AD Var* IV M 24 (2–3). See also
Bezucha (ed.), *Modern European Social History*, p.107.

28. On the diffusion of anarchist propaganda among Andalusian *braceros*, see
the contribution by Waggoner in Bezucha (ed.), *Modern European Social
History*, esp. p.161. On the Limousin, see Corbin, *Archaïsme et modernité*,
p. 794. On the social rôle of the blacksmith's forge in the Lyonnais
countryside, see Garrier, *Paysans du Beaujolais*, p.198. Demographic and
occupational data concerning Lorgues in *AD Var* XI M 2 (119) and
AD Var XIV M 19 (4). Membership of the Cercle des Travailleurs in
Cuers in *AD Var* VIII M 16.

29. Corbin, *Archaïsme et modernité*, p.308.

30. For Flayosc see *AD Var* VIII M 16.

Chapter Eight

1. Agulhon, *La vie sociale*, p.229, where he notes that a similar antagonism
existed between Jacobin Grasse and moderate Antibes. Also *Le Petit Var*,
10 March 1886.

2. See an interesting article on the conflict in *Le Petit Var*, 8 February 1887.

3. See *Le Petit Var*, 25 April 1881, 10 August 1883. Population statistics in
AD Var XI M 2 (1).

4. See *Le Petit Var*, 30 May 1891. Also *AD Var* XI M 2 (1) and *AD Var* II M 3 (Elections); *AD Var* IV M 24 (2/3) (Condamnés politiques 1851).
5. See *Le Petit Var* for the month of December 1881.
6. Livet, *Habitat rural*, p.204; *Le Petit Var*, 17 July 1884, 26 August 1891.
7. See Salvarelli, *Les administrateurs, passim*; L. Sénéquier, *Connaissances de la Garde Freinet* (Draguignan, 1965), pp.100–1.
8. Price (ed.), *Revolution and Reaction*, pp.26, 36.
9. G. Dupeux, *Aspects de l'histoire sociale et politique du Loir-et-Cher 1848– 1914* (Paris, 1962), p.533; *Historique et vie*, p.10; *AD Var* III T 15 (1/2).
10. *AD Var* II M 3 (37) (Elections législatives 1893); *AD Var* II M 3 (38) (police notes on Cluseret, 1898).
11. *AD Var* 11 M 5 (169–175) (Conseil général, elections); *AD Var* II M 3 (38) (police notes on Prosper Ferrero).
12. Even among the Radicals, only Louis Martin appears ever successfully to have capitalised upon his origins; in 1902 he received 41.5% of the electorate's support in the second arrondissement of Toulon. But in his home village of Puget-Ville he got 425 votes out of a possible 561 — 76% in all. For these and many other biographical details, see J. Jolly, *Dictionnaire des parlementaires français* (Paris, 1960–), and Maître (ed.), *Dictionnaire biographique*. Election results in *AD Var* II M 3.
13. See Barral on the political relationships in mountain communites of the Isère, in Pierre Barral, *Le département de l'Isère sous la Troisième République 1870–1940* (Paris, 1962), p.450.
14. *AD Var* II M 5 (Conseil général, elections).
15. *Le Petit Var*, 1 July 1881.
16. See Sénéquier, *Connaissances*, pp.108–16.

Chapter Nine

1. Rebérioux, *La République radicale?*, p.62.
2. On the 'red Var', see the interesting article by Jacques Girault, A la recherche du 'Var Rouge', de l'insurrection de décembre 1851 au Front Populaire, in *Cahiers de la Méditerranée*, déc. 1973.
3. Willard, *Guesdistes*, p.100.
4. This is also the view of Loubère, *Radicalism in Mediterranean France*, pp.106ff.
5. See Bercé, *Croquants et nu-pieds*, p.230. On this region see also André Armengaud, *Les populations de l'Est-Aquitain, 1845–1871* (Paris, 1961).
6. S. Derruau-Boniol, Le socialisme dans l'Allier de 1848 à 1914, in *C.H.* no.2, 1957; Linz, Patterns of land tenure, etc., in *Comparative Politics*, VIII, iii, 1976; Loubère, *Radicalism in Mediterranean France*, p.137; M. Jollivet and H. Mendras, *Les collectivités rurales françaises* (Paris, 1971), vol.I, p.116.
7. See Corbin, *Archaïsme et modernité*, p.729, n.67; also A. Prost, *L'enseignement en France 1800–1967* (Paris, 1968) and J. Ozouf, *Nous, les maîtres d'école* (Paris, 1967).
8. Derruau-Boniol, Le socialisme dans l'Allier, pp.152–3.
9. *Le Petit Var*, 4 March 1882, 5 August 1883.

10. *Le Petit Var*, 24 April 1884, 9 December 1886.
11. *Le Petit Var*, 3 March 1885, 24 November 1888. Once the Socialists were firmly established as the leading party of the left, however, it was to the Radicals that the local conservatives would turn, still with the aim of abetting the division of the left-wing vote.
12. Calculation based on figures in *AD Var* II M 3 (34/35).
13. *Le Petit Var*, 29 January 1889.
14. *Le Petit Var*, 23 May 1888. Philippe Gratton suggests that economic changes in the departments of the Cher and the Nièvre were creating there too a rural socialist electorate quite distinct from the old Radical clientèle. See P. Gratton, *La lutte des classes dans les campagnes* (Paris, 1971), p. 106.
15. *AD Var* III T 1 (5) (Instruction publique 1878); *AD Var* IV M 40 (Rapports sur l'esprit publique 1870–3); *Le Petit Var*, 11 January 1881, 12 January 1881, 25 May 1881, 5 July 1883; *Le Cri du Var*, 17 April 1910.
16. Standing as a Radical candidate in Toulon East in May 1891, Abel urged his electors: 'soyons socialistes'. Rather more presciently he observed that the old quarrels were dead — 'we are all republicans now' (!). See *Le Petit Var*, 26 May 1891.
17. Details in *AD Var* II M 3 (15–46); see also *Le Petit Var*, 25 December 1880, 3 May 1884, 23 November 1888, 6 October 1889.
18. Mayeur, *Les débuts de la Troisième République*, p.79; Loubère, *Radicalism in Mediterranean France*, p.205. Of course Mayeur is clearly correct to argue that the peasantry was not in any real sense enthusiastic for a social revolution — but then nor were the Socialists. This did not prevent both peasants and Socialists from being committed to a degree of social change qualitatively different from that advocated by the Radicals.
19. As we shall see, the commitment to the immediate collectivisation of various economic resources, including land, *was* part of the Socialist platform. It is difficult to see what Loubère means, unless he is looking in election manifestos for incitements to the immediate application of the revolutionary *loi agraire*.
20. See election bills, posters, pamphlets, preserved in *AD Var* II M 3. Cantonal election manifestos (with prefectoral comments on occasion) in *AD Var* II M 5; see also *Le Cri du Var*, 27 August 1905.
21. *Le Petit Var*, 10 August 1883.
22. *AD Var* II M 5 (207–213); *Le Cri du Var*, 5 March 1905.
23. *AD Var* IV M 52 (Manifestations syndicales 1871–1914); *AD Var* IV M 41 (Rapports sur l'esprit publique 1877–1909).
24. *AD Var* IV M 41; *Le Petit Var*, 17 November 1882; *Le Cri du Var*, 15 January 1905. Les Salles, at this date, had a population of just 407 persons, exclusively peasant (see *AD Var* XI M 2 (1)).
25. See *Le Cri du Var*, 13 August 1905, 27 August 1905, 6 January 1907, 18 October 1908. An article by Charles Guieysse in 1904 criticised the reformist socialism which had emerged out of the Dreyfusard alliances, camouflaging the 'true' conflict. 'We must *avoid*', he wrote, 'a return to the spirit of '48.' That such a statement could be made in the pages of the official local Socialist paper suggests that the breach with the radical past ('the spirit of '48') was very real — and that the Socialists were not afraid to say as much, nor lost support by so doing.

26. See on this H. Goldberg, Jaurès and the formation of a socialist peasant policy, in *I.R.S.H.* 1957; C. Landauer, The Guesdists and the small farmer, in *I.R.S.H.* 1961; A. Compère-Morel, *Le programme socialiste de réformes agraires* (Paris, 1919); A. Compère-Morel, *Le socialisme et la terre* (Paris, 1921); M. Augé-Laribé, *Le problème agraire du socialisme* (Paris, 1907).

27. *Le Cri du Var*, 19 May 1907, 9 June 1907, 10 May 1908, 29 November 1908, 3 October 1909, 11 December 1910.

28. See an interesting discussion of this point in Gratton, *Les paysans français contre l'agrarisme*, p.23 and n.19. I cannot agree with Gratton, however, when he writes (*La lutte des classes*, p.371) that until 1921 the SFIO was 'openly uninterested' in its agrarian programme. It was certainly embarrassed by what it saw as the need to appeal for the support of 'doomed' classes such as the uneconomic smallholder; but the extent to which its support actually came from this sector gave the party little option but to show an interest in the small peasantry's concerns — as witness Compère-Morel's frequent writings on the subject and his prominence in the party on this account. P. Barral (Aspects régionaux de l'agrarisme français avant 1930, in *M.S.* no.67, 1969, p.198) rightly observes that Compère-Morel's propaganda to the peasants before 1914 was considerably 'firmer', doctrinally speaking, than that of the Communists in the early 1920s. And Compère-Morel's pamphlets were in circulation in the countryside: the secretary of the Aups Socialist group distributed copies to all his members in 1909 (see *Le Cri du Var*, 11 July 1909).

29. J.S. Macdonald, Agrarian organisations, migration and labour militancy in rural Italy, in *Ec.H.R.* 1963—4.

30. D. Vasseur notes this basic but profound grasp of the character of socialist ideas in the militants of the Belfort region too (see Vasseur, *Les débuts du mouvement ouvrier dans la région de Belfort-Montbéliard 1870—1914*, p.51).

31. On the various forms of indirect political participation available to rural populations, see the comments by Deutsch, *Social Mobilisation*.

32. As Lucien Febvre suggests, radical doctrines (of a religious or political nature) were sometimes *born* in the countryside, rather than merely exported there from the town. See. L. Febvre in G. Friedmann (ed.), *Villes et campagnes* (Paris, 1970), p.35.

33. Wolf, *Peasant Wars*, p.295.

34. Or, to quote Maurice Agulhon, 'On s'étonnera au temps de la Troisième République de la facilité paradoxale avec laquelle le paysan propriétaire du Var adoptera les idées parfois *les plus extrêmes* du socialisme ouvrier.' Agulhon, *La vie sociale*, p.179 (my italics).

35. See Derruau-Boniol, Le socialisme dans l'Allier, p. 147, where she describes how the rural area around Commentry and Montluçon passed from conservatism to socialism without ever turning to the Radicals. See also A. Soboul, Les troubles agraires de 1848, in *Paysans, sans-culottes et jacobins* (Paris, 1967), p.248; Wolf, *Peasant Wars*, p.292. It is interesting to compare the politics of the late-nineteenth-century peasantry in the Var with the attitudes described by Margadant for an earlier period. What seems above all to have shifted is the small peasant's conception of the state, and his sense

of its responsibilities. By 1900, I would argue, the small farmers constituted a *class*, in economic conflict with other social classes and interests, but via the intermediary of the state, to which they thus attached very considerable importance. On the earlier nineteenth century, see T. W. Margadant, Peasant protest in the Second Republic, in *J.I.H.* 1974, and also Margadant's contribution to Price (ed.), *Revolution and Reaction*, pp.254–80.

36. Suzanne Berger argues similarly that in Brittany the 'political coordinates laid down in the first decade of the century' determine the subsequent pattern — although I believe she overemphasises the influence of the clerical *issue* (as distinct from the clergy) in shaping *all* future political divisions, even in Brittany *(Peasants against Politics*, pp.4, 52).

37. Thus whereas Agulhon *(La vie sociale*, pp.358–60) suggests that it was the 'openness' of the ruling groups in the villages, and the diversity of the economy, which accounted for an earlier radicalism, in later years it was, surely, the very 'closing-up' of local society, the loss of heterogeneity and economic strength which produced the decisive swing to a *socialist* left.

Chapter Ten

1. See J. Rougerie, Faut-il départementaliser l'histoire de France? in *Annales*, jan.–fév. 1966.

2. Details of all the works referred to in this chapter are to be found in the bibliography, notably section (iii).

3. G. Lefebvre, *Les paysans du Nord pendant la Révolution française* (Lille, 1924).

4. A. Corbin, Limousins migrants, Limousins sédentaires, in *M.S.* no.88, 1974, p.113.

5. Personal communication.

6. Henri Mendras, *Sociétés paysannes* (Paris, 1976), p.186.

7. Even Suzanne Berger, in *Peasants against Politics*, adds little to our understanding of the rôle of the Church–politics axis in French society. Her view of the matter appears to be that political traditions in Brittany were both formed in the image of national religious cleavages and received in the villages *de haut en bas*. Certainly the residual strength of the Catholic tradition in the area — the same twelve departments which protested most strongly at the separation in 1906 still had the highest percentage of children in Catholic schools at the end of the 1950s — appears to confirm her thesis. Yet with no apparent diminution of practising faith, many of these areas elected Socialist municipalities in the 1970s. Nothing in Ms Berger's mode of explanation can be adduced to explain this. See *Peasants against Politics*, pp.8, 39. Also J.-M. Mayeur, Géographie de la résistance aux Inventaires (février–mars 1906), in *Annales*, nov.–déc. 1966, p.1272, n.2.

8. See P. Barral, Aspects régionaux de l'agrarisme français avant 1930, in *M.S.* no. 67, 1969, p.6.

9. See Weber, *Peasants into Frenchmen*. I have tried to do justice to this important work, both in respect of its many qualities and its underlying weaknesses, in a review published in *Social History*, 1978.

Chapter Eleven

1. Anyone who doubts that such beliefs concerning recent French history still exist has only to question a cross-section of history students on the matter. They presumably acquire their views from books and lectures devoted to France and her recent past.

2. Marx's own views are summarised in the *Eighteenth Brumaire*, notably in the conclusion, where he makes some very perceptive observations concerning the French rural economy, but overemphasises the extent and significance of small property. Pirelli is quoted by Louise Tilly in Bezucha (ed.), *Modern European Social History*, p.157, n.22. Poulantzas summarises his views as follows: 'La paysannerie française, y compris la petite paysannerie parcellaire, fut un des principaux remparts de l'ordre bourgeois, et un des principaux obstacles à la révolution socialiste dans un pays marqué par la combativité exceptionnelle et exemplaire de la classe ouvrière.' (N. Poulantzas, *Les classes sociales dans le capitalisme d'aujourd'hui* (Paris, 1974), pp.355—6).

3. See R. Price, The change from labour abundance to labour shortage in French agriculture in the nineteenth century, in *Ec.H.R.* 1975.

4. See, among much writing on this important theme, the articles by Soboul now brought together in the collection *Problèmes paysans de la Révolution 1789—1848* (Paris, 1976), notably part II; Armengaud, *Les populations de l'Est-Aquitain*, p.86; T. Zeldin (ed.), *Conflicts in French Society* (London, 1970), notably the contribution by Roger McGraw, pp.169—227; Garrier, *Paysans du Beaujolais*, vol.I, p.73, n.61; *Le Petit Var*, 23 May 1885.

5. There is an extended discussion of this form of agriculture in P. Bernard, *Economie et sociologie de la Seine-et-Marne 1850—1950* (Paris, 1953).

6. See *Le Petit Var*, 31 May 1884, 13 October 1884, 21 November 1886. Also Corbin, *Archaïsme et modernité*, p.514.

7. The reader is referred both to the useful maps in the *Atlas de la France rurale*, and more particularly to vol. 3 of the invaluable *Histoire de la France rurale* (Paris, 1976), which contains a wealth of maps, statistics and photographs and incisive chapters on particular themes by Maurice Agulhon and Gabriel Desert.

8. Bois, *Paysans de l'Ouest*, abridged edn, p.32.

9. Quoted in M. Jollivet and H. Mendras, *Les collectivités rurales françaises* (Paris, 1971), vol. I, p.63. See also Armengaud, *Les populations de l'Est-Aquitain*, p.329.

10. See R. Hilton, *Bond Men Made Free* (London, 1977), pp.174—5. There is a useful discussion of the impact of the market upon peasant attitudes in D. Chirot, The growth of the market and servile labor systems in agriculture, *J.S.H.* 1974.

11. See Bois, *Paysans de l'Ouest*, abridged edn, pp.42—54; Brékilien, *La vie quotidienne*, p.31; Garrier, *Paysans du Beaujolais*, vol.I, p.131; Corbin, *Archaïsme et modernité*, p.242, n.59.

12. See Gratton, *Les paysans français contre l'agrarisme*, pp.90—1.

13. See Corbin, *Archaïsme et modernité*, p.116, n.83; H. Mendras, *The Vanishing Peasant — Innovation and Change in French Agriculture* (Boston, Mass., 1970), pp.180—1; Berger, *Peasants against Politics*, *passim*.

14. Derruau-Boniol, Le socialisme dans l'Allier; A. Armengaud, La population française au XIXe siècle (Paris, 1971), p.26; Corbin, Archaïsme et modernité, pp.46, 163 n.63; E. L'Huillier, La lutte ouvrière à la fin du Second Empire (Paris, 1957), p.15; Armengaud, Les populations de l'Est-Aquitain, pp.242–67.
15. See Jollivet and Mendras, Les collectivités, vol. I, p.111; also the various books and articles by Corbin, Châtelain and Hohenberg listed in the bibliography.
16. See Vasseur, Les débuts du mouvement ouvrier, pp.72, 145. Also AD Var IV M 56 (8) (Grèves, 1924).
17. Derruau-Boniol, Le département de la Creuse, R.F.S.P. VII, 1957; Fabre and Lacroix, La vie quotidienne des paysans du Languedoc, pp.21, 79; Harvey Smith, Work routine and social structure, pp.368–71; Mendras, Sociétés paysannes, p.148.
18. Mendras, Sociétés paysannes, pp.165–6.
19. For studies centred around these issues, see the works listed in sections (v) and (vi) of the bibliography, notably the contributions of Barral, Gratton, Jollivet, Mendras (separately and together) and, for an earlier period, Mousnier, Soboul and Porchnev, Les soulèvements populaires en France de 1623 à 1648 (Paris, 1972).
20. On the 'low-classness' of peasants in general, see the comments by E.J. Hobsbawm on the subject in the Journal of Peasant Studies, vol. I, no. i, 1973. His observation that much of their politics 'cannot be directly derived from [their] specific relations to the means of production' applies very well to France — unfortunately the same might be said all too often of the urban proletariat as well.
21. See Garrier, Paysans du Beaujolais, pp.264–7. These excellent pages are the best part of an otherwise rather disappointing book.
22. Philippe Gratton has reminded us that there were militant syndicates in rural France during the Third Republic; but these were primarily active among the marginal producers — resin-gatherers, forestry workers and the like. What is more, with the special exception of the vignerons' revolt of 1907, the unionised peasant was a phenomenon of the years following World War One — by which time the syndicates could benefit from the mobilisation of certain regions, through political socialism, in the previous generation.
23. Le Petit Var, 18 and 19 September 1888; C. Tilly, How protest modernised in France, in Aydelotte, Bogue and Fogel (eds), The Dimensions of Quantitative Research in History (Princeton, N.J., 1972); V. Wright, The coup d'état of 1851: Repression and the limits to repression, in Price (ed.), Revolution and Reaction; H.C. Payne, The Police State of Louis-Napoleon Bonaparte (Seattle, Wa., 1966). In so far as the mid-nineteenth century did see a significant shift in the nature of political opposition in the country-side, this probably had a lot to do with the disastrous and enduring impact of the economic crisis of the 1840s upon rural industry.

Chapter Twelve

1. See e.g. the much reprinted book by Jean Fréville, La nuit finit à Tours (Paris, 1959, etc.).
2. The major works on the history of French socialism are listed in section (ii) of the bibliography. The best of them is the book by Georges Lefranc,

Le mouvement socialiste sous la Troisième République (Paris, 1968), but it only deals with the period up to 1940, and is written from a 'planiste' perspective; that is to say that Lefranc was a strong supporter of the tendency within the SFIO which wanted to move away from rigid dogmatism concerning the possibilities for reform in a capitalist system. As a result the book is occasionally unfairly dismissive of the 'old guard' and underestimates the importance of the Marxist element in the Party.

3. See of course Daniel Bell, *The End of Ideology* (New York, 1961); also R. Bendix and S.M. Lipset, *Class, Status and Power* (London, 1967), R. Dahrendorf, *Class and Class Conflict in an Industrial Society* (London, 1972), and Alain Touraine, *La société post-industrielle* (Paris, 1969).

4. A. Giddens, *The Class Structure of the Advanced Societies* (London, 1973), p.285.

5. Giddens, *Class Structure*, p.285.

6. See Annie Kriegel, *Aux origines du communisme français 1914–1920* (Paris, 1964, 2 vols).

7. See Robert Aron, *Le socialisme français face au marxisme* (Paris, 1971), and James Joll, *The Second International* (London, 1968), introduction, for representative expressions of this point of view.

8. Figures taken from C. Hurtig, *De la SFIO au nouveau Parti Socialiste* (Paris, 1970); *Les forces politiques et les élections de mars 1973* (Paris, 1973); G. Dupeux, *French Society 1789–1970* (London, 1976), calculations based upon figures given on p.240.

9. See Willard, *Guesdistes*, pp.247, 514; Barral, *Le département de l'Isère*, p.428; Derruau-Boniol, Le socialisme dans l'Allier, p.144; Laurent, *Les vignerons de la Côte d'Or*, p.511; R. Pierre, *Les origines du socialisme et du syndicalisme dans le Drôme* (Paris, 1973), pp.124, 174.

10. See the article by Chris Johnson in Price (ed.), *Revolution and Reaction*, pp.87–115, on Economic change and artisan discontent; also J. Julliard, *Fernand Pelloutier et les origines du syndicalisme d'action directe* (Paris, 1971); E. Dolléans and G. Dehove, *Histoire du travail en France* (Paris, 1953; E. Poisson, *Socialisme et coopération* (Paris, 1922).

11. The 'invention of tradition' was the subject of a colloquium held in 1977 under the auspices of *Past & Present*.

12. On the SFIO since 1945 see R.D. Graham, *The French Socialists and Tripartism 1944–1947* (London, 1965); H. Simmons, *French Socialists in Search of a Role 1956–1967* (Ithaca, N.Y., 1970); F.L. Wilson, *The French Democratic Left 1963–1969* (Stanford, Calif., 1971); R. Quilliot, *La SFIO et l'exercice du pouvoir 1944–1958* (Paris, 1972).

13. On this see Judt, *La reconstruction*, pp.71–98.

14. See Dieter Groh, *Negative Integration und revolutionärer Attentismus* (Frankfurt am Main, 1973).

15. Cf. Giddens, *Class Structure*, p.280: 'The revolutionary potential of the working class depends upon the initial encounter with capitalism, not upon the maturity of the capitalist mode of production.'

A note on sources

The material on which this book is based has been drawn from four general categories of primary sources (as well of course as a variety of secondary writings). These are official statistics, surveys, censuses and the like; police and prefectoral reports, concerned chiefly with political conflicts and public 'order'; local newspapers; and the data collected by the various movements of the left concerning their membership, performance at elections, internal differences and the like. All of these pose particular problems for the historian in respect of their partial or incomplete nature. But it may be worth drawing the reader's attention briefly to the special difficulties for the social historian associated with official sources, printed and archival, for the period which has been studied here.

In the first place, the coming of the Third Republic marked, progressively, the dismantling of the detailed mechanisms of political control and coercion which had been so prominent a feature of French life since 1792, and which have proved such a boon to the historian who goes in search of France during the years from the First Republic to the Paris Commune. Where men and women were arrested for participation in political protests, there the historian is often faced with a superabundance of quantifiable material, as policemen and judges took infinite pains to list the occupation, background, education, political affiliation and much else of the offender. It is only necessary to refer to the works of Cobb, Soboul or Pinkney, Gossez or Rougerie, for it to be clear just how important a historical source the records of a repressive state may be for later students in search of the identity of those who were repressed.

Such material is not available to the student of the Third Republic. To be more precise, it is not available in any quantified form. Policemen in the Third Republic were no less interested in the activities of rebels of every kind (and indeed the files they kept are a good initial guide to official feeling about what was and what was not a politically innocuous activity — there are no files on the Radicals, in the Var at least, after 1880). But however much they infiltrated socialist groups and syndicalist meetings, their evidence remains confined to head-counts and impressions, however acute. What they cannot tell us is how many men from one village and not another, how many artisans, how many peasants, and in what sort of a relation, were totally committed to a particular cause. At no point during the years from 1877 to 1914 can we, using official data, produce the kind of table which Ted Margadant, in his study of the 1851 insurrection, presents to show the occupational spread of insurrection in that year. However closely we try to relate electoral results and party membership to social and economic context, we cannot *know* on any scale how each man voted, and how far his commitment went. And unlike the judge at a tribunal, we cannot ask him *why* he held the views which led him to act as he did.

Of course the sources upon which the social history of earlier protest movements is based are themselves sometimes suspect. Governments and policemen often directed their repression at certain regions and certain social categories, sometimes to provide public confirmation of their view of the causes of a given disturbance, sometimes *pour encourager les autres*, sometimes because, believing for instance that peasants do not rebel of their own accord, they went in search of the artisans, foreigners, etc., who *must* have been the leaders. Such police records, however copious, pose many difficulties of interpretation. But at least they are present, often in superabundance. One of the minor expenses in the balance-sheet of liberal democracy is that it deprives later generations of much information about people's political choices. We are forced to proceed by inference — and are thus well advised to avoid an excessive reliance on data which might tempt us into statements of a quantitative nature.

Nor is this a difficulty confined to political statistics. The centralised French state of the nineteenth century offers a wealth of material about the more static features of life — what people did, how they lived, what they produced — and this book has drawn widely upon such material. But it too is easy to misinterpret. For example, censuses and occasional reports on the state of agriculture take great care to list a man's exact occupation, and it is largely from such material that historians of France learn of the social structure of a village, or even a region. Yet it is not uncommon to find a man referred to in one source as a butcher, in another as a small-property-owning peasant. What has happened of course is that the man was indeed both of these, perhaps at different times of his life, possibly even simultaneously, though his peasant property was unlikely to be very large. Similarly a census in 1891 may describe a man as a tenant farmer, but will list him a decade later as a *petit propriétaire*. It may indeed be that in the intervening period he has bought his way into property ownership; but it is just as likely that he and his family had for many years owned property themselves, but been obliged to work the land of others on a tenancy basis in order to make ends meet. Such examples occur again and again, and should make us wary of too rigidly classifying one man, one village or a whole department as dominated by a given occupational or class category. It was not unusual at this time for men to be industrial workers and property-owning peasants simultaneously; sometimes they could be both of these *and* an agricultural labourer, depending upon the time of the year the census was taken and the state of the local economy just then. What is more, many 'peasant proprietors' were often men who had clung to a few miserable hectares in order to retain a connection with the land on which they no longer worked or lived — yet it enabled them to declare themselves to the census-taker as a *propriétaire* — thereby fooling him and misleading us.

Once we have discounted this difficulty of labels, and overcome the hurdle imposed by the French administrative distinction between rural communes (those whose population was less than 2000 people) and urban ones, a distinction which tells us nothing about true distinctions within rural communities (where a 'town' of 5000 souls could be a sleepy place full of peasants, and a rural community of 1200 people might be a bustling and noisy town), we face a further problem. Many of the facts and figures which found their way onto the pages of national statistical surveys and annual economic publications, as well as into the archives of the various ministries, were in the first place provided by a local elected official, usually the mayor of a commune, in reply to a questionnaire he had received. This accounts both for the mysteriously rounded figures we so often encounter when studying these surveys (such and such a village had 500 sheep, 1000 pigs, 200 cows and so forth), and the bizarre,

biologically unlikely variations which appear over quite brief spans of
time. A mayor could be forgiven for getting facts such as these
wrong; it cannot always have been easy to obtain them — especially
from men who had voted for a different list in the previous municipal elections! But when it comes to more sensitive material — the
effect of phylloxera in a given region, the degree of literacy in a
particular village, the state of the public buildings (especially the
school), the health of the population — the mayor often had a very
good reason of his own for over- or underestimating the figures concerned. If he was campaigning for a new school, in conflict with the
local *curé* or simply a candidate on a Radical ticket in forthcoming
elections, he would be tempted to set his educational standards high
and report to the ministry that illiteracy was rife in his commune,
the fault no doubt of the failings and ignorance of the existing
(religious) school. He might overestimate the damage caused by a
storm or by the phylloxera, the better to obtain government compensation for his commune. The mayor was probably as reliable a
source of information as anyone else — perhaps better than many in
that he knew his community very well and what he could say about
it is very important. But his bias, or at any rate his political instincts,
have to be allowed for when we conscientiously rely upon the facts
with which he has provided us, *par ministère interposée.*

One further difficulty worth noting arises in local studies such as
this. Since we cannot always attach political labels to men in these
years, both because the information is not available and also because
to do so would be too naively to adopt political categories and divisions which we are in fact seeing in the process of development, we
need to be able, wherever possible, to trace the acts and identities of
particular individuals. In doing so we can sometimes establish
patterns which might tentatively be applied to other men about
whom we have less information. As a method such an approach lacks
rigidity or numerical significance, but it can offer useful insights.
But in Provence (and this would no doubt apply elsewhere) the same
names, often the same first names, occur over and over again! As an
example of the frustrating difficulties faced by the local historian, let
me take the example of Aups, a middle-sized bourg. On the victorious
1896 municipal slate, there was one François Bagarry, baker. On the
defeated list there were three Bagarrys, initials P., M., and E. Two of

them were farmers, a *ménager* and a *fermier*, one was given as being
without occupation.

In 1900 the old municipal council was overthrown, and on the
newly successful 'rallié' list there appeared Bagarry, M., listed as a
baker. François Bagarry does not reappear until 1908 when he was
on the successful list, with his occupation given as a *marchand de
pâtisseries*. On that list of 1908 there were three other men of that
name, Bagarry, P. (*ménager*), Bagarry, P. (*cultivateur*), and Bagarry,
J. (*propriétaire*). All of this is actually quite interesting: for not
merely have we seen four kinds of peasant category listed, all but
that of *fermier* denoting some form of property-ownership (although
as I have said, none of these categories need have been exclusive);
François Bagarry has undergone a subtle change of status; most significantly, he is now on the same list as Bagarry, P., whom he
opposed in 1896. Indeed, only one politically active Bagarry,
Bagarry, M., appears on the opposite, conservative list. There is a
slight sniff of *politique du clocher*, or even of family feuding here,
and so we turn to the census lists for more information. There we
find no fewer than 32 Bagarrys listed in 1906, not including children,
and covering a wide variety of occupations. But *none* of them is
listed as being a *ménager*, and only François Bagarry is consistently
reported to earn his living from baking. In fact the only Bagarry with
the initial M. is given as being a qualified mason! All of this is complicated still further when we study the details of the membership
of the local agricultural cooperative, where *all* of the political
Bagarrys are members, including Bagarry, M., who is now neither
mason nor baker, but a simple *cultivateur*!

The point being made here is not that it is impossible to write
French social history, but that the copious sources which make the
writing of that history possible, and of which much use has been
made in this book, need to be treated with care as well as respect. No
statement which depends substantially upon material found in police
or judicial records, or in statistical surveys or even electoral results
(so far as political and occupational labels are concerned), is ever
beyond doubt. At best we may hope that the errors and inaccuracies
are in some respect consistent, so that allowance may be made for
their inbuilt weaknesses. Newspapers, another major source for
modern history, are paradoxically much more reliable, if only in that

we do not expect them to be safe and disinterested sources of information, and are thus not tempted to construct massive series and
calculations upon what we learn from them. Furthermore, their very
distortions and bias, in so far as these can be checked against other
sources, are valuable guides to the opinion and tone, both of the
period and of the audience to which a particular journal was directed.

Perhaps the most useful source of all is one which does not even
appear in the bibliography which follows. Over the years which have
been spent preparing this study, I have met many men and women
who have spoken to me of their memories of Provence in former
times, and of their direct or indirect experience of political and social
life in the region before the First World War. Little of what I have learnt
from these encounters has been in the form of verifiable historical
fact, and much of it has been little more than vague and often con-
tradictory recollections from a far-off youth. But from no other
source have I obtained anything like such a rich sense of what it was
really like to live in the last years of pre-war France, nor of the
precise sense in which, I have no doubt, politics and political activity
of a modern kind first entered into the consciousness of the rural
populations of the Var. It is because so much of the 'formal' source
material listed in the following pages confirms the impressions gained
from listening to the sons and daughters of the protagonists of this
account, that I have given it credence, and not the other way around.
Here at least the contemporary historian can steal a march, however
fleeting, on his better-documented colleague studying the earlier
years. And here too the local historian, however wide his concerns
and whatever his misgivings concerning the strengths and weaknesses
of oral history, has the advantage of the student of national entities
or long time-spans. What we shall make of the siren-like appeals of
nineteenth-century social statistics when we have only their word for
how it was is a different matter.

Sources and bibliography

1. ARCHIVAL SOURCES

(a) Archives Nationales

C3021		Enquête sur les classes ouvrières 1872–1875
BB³⁰	486–490	Aix Cour d'Appel 1871–1877 (Rapports du Procureur Général)
F⁷	12488	Congrès ouvriers 1876–1879
	12489	Congrès socialistes 1880–1882
	12494	Congrès divers (Japy 1899, Wagram 1900)
	12503	Activité socialiste dans les départements 1896–1915
	12522	Congrès divers 1876–1902
	12723	Agitation révolutionnaire par départements 1893–1914
	12886	Parti Ouvrier Français 1896–1899
	13072	SFIO Congrès 1905–1920
F¹¹	2768	Prix des grains 1889–1895
F¹²	4664	Grèves 1880–1889
	4702	Syndicats agricoles dissous
F¹⁷	14269	Instruction publique (Ecoles de hameau 1900)
	14270	Degré d'instruction des conscrits 1899
	14295	Instruction primaire. Affaires diverses 1858–1883
F¹⁹	3630 (29)	Demandes de secours après la Séparation
F²²	150	Syndicats ouvriers
	167	Grèves 1905–1906
	169	Grèves 1907

(b) Archives de la Préfecture de Police

Ba/32	Congrès régionaux jusqu'en 1882
Ba/37	Congrès de Marseille 1879
Ba/201	Le socialisme – France 1885–1892
Ba/627	Socialistes et boulangistes
Ba/1135	Dossier Lafargue
Ba/1470	Bibliothèque socialiste 1878–1884
Ba/1476	Le socialisme en province
Ba/1485	Cercles d'études socialistes (POF)

(c) Archives Départementales du Var

Série M:-

II M 1	2	Elections 1848–1850

343

II M 1	3	Plébiscite de 1851			
II M 3	15	Elections du 13 mai 1849	Résultats par commune		
	29	„ du 7 janvier 1872	„	„	„
	30	„ du 20 février 1876	„	„	„
	31	„ du 14 octobre 1877	„	„	„
	32	„ du 21 août 1881	„	„	„
	34(1)	„ du 4 octobre 1885	„	„	„
	35	„ du 22 septembre 1889	„	„	„
	37	„ du 3 septembre 1893	„	„	„
	38	„ du 8 mai 1898	„	„	„
	40	„ du 27 avril 1902	„	„	„
	41	„ du 6 mai 1906	„	„	„
	44	„ du 28 avril 1910	„	„	„
	46	„ du 26 avril 1914	„	„	„
II M 5	(120–124)	Elections du conseil général 1880			
	(128–133)	„ „ „ „ 1883			
	(138–144)	„ „ „ „ 1886			
	(207–213)	„ „ „ „ 1904			
	(218–224)	„ „ „ „ 1907			
	(227–231)	„ „ „ „ 1910			
II M 7	15 (1–2)	Elections et nominations des conseillers municipaux par commune 1871–1876			
	18 (1–5)	„ „ „ 1876–1884			
	21 (1–13)	„ „ „ 1896–1908			
IV M 40		Correspondance relative à l'esprit publique 1870–1873			
	41	„ „ „ „ 1877–1909			
	42	„ „ „ „ 1909–1913			
	43	„ „ „ „ 1914			
IV M 24 (2–3)		Condamnés politiques 1851			
IV M 52		Manifestations syndicales 1871–1914			
IV M 55 (1)		1e mai 1892–1914			
IV M 56 (1–6)		Grèves 1871–1914			
VIII M 16 (1–28)		Cercles et associations			
XI M 2 (6–260)		Dénombrement de la population 1872–1914			
XI M 3 (37)		Population agglomérée, population éparse 1893			
XIV M 7 (2)		Syndicats agricoles 1900–1909			
XIV M 7 (6)		Coopératives			
XIV M 19 (4)		Statistique agricole par commune 1871–1888			
XIV M 19 (7–8)		„ „ „ „ 1889–1898			
XIV M 19 (9–12)		„ „ „ „ 1903–1918			
XIV M 29 (1)		La production vinicole par commune 1812–1946			
XIV M 29 (8)		Le phylloxéra 1871–1881			
XIV M 29 (10)		„ „ 1886–1899			
XVI M 1 (8)		Statistique industrielle. Situation mensuelle par commune 1876–1881			
	(9)	„ „ „ „ 1882–1884			
	(10)	„ „ „ „ 1885–1886			
	(11)	„ „ „ „ 1887–1894			

XVI M 15 (1)	Salaires 1883–1912
Série T:-	
III T 1 (5)	Instruction publique. Enseignement
	Primaire — Rapports 1870–1899
(6)	„ „ „ 1900–1938
Série U:-	
VII U 29 (3)	Justice. Tribunal 1e Instance de Draguignan. Affaires politiques 1870–1895.
Série Z:-	
I Z 4 (1)	Sous-préfecture de Brignoles. Rapports sur l'esprit publique.
III Z 2 (11–12)	Sous-préfecture de Toulon. Elections Municipales.
III Z 4 (3)	Sous-préfecture de Toulon. Police politique, rapports sur l'esprit publique.
III Z 6 (15)	Sous-préfecture de Toulon. Rapports quotidiens de police.
III Z 26 (1)	Culte protestant dans le Var (sous-préfecture de Toulon).

2. PRINTED SOURCES

France. *Annuaire statistique de la France 1878–1906* (Imprimerie Nationale, Paris)

„   Ministère de l'Agriculture. *La petite propriété rurale en France 1908–1909* (Imprimerie Nationale, Paris)

„   *Recensement de la population, 1906* (Imprimerie Nationale, Paris, 1907)

„   *Statistique et atlas des forêts de France* (Imprimerie Nationale, Paris, 1912)

„   *Statistique des grèves 1890–1908* (Imprimerie Nationale, Paris)

—   *Indicateur du Var* (published annually)

J. Salvarelli *Les administrateurs du département du Var 1790–1897* (Draguignan, 1897)

3. NEWSPAPERS

Le Petit Var	Published daily. Utilised for the period 1879–1906
Le Cri du Var	Published weekly. Utilised for the period 1904–1914

4. SFIO

Rapports	1905 1e Congrès 23–25 avril (Paris)
	1905 2e Congrès 29 octobre–1 novembre (Chalon-sur-Saône)
	1906 3e Congrès 1–4 novembre (Limoges)
	1907 4e Congrès 11–14 août (Nancy)
	1908 5e Congrès 15–18 octobre (Toulouse)
	1909 6e Congrès 11–14 avril (St Etienne)

1910 7e Congrès 15—16 juillet (Paris)
1911 8e Congrès 16—19 avril (St Quentin)
1912 9e Congrès 18—21 février (Lyon)
1913 10e Congrès 23—25 mars (Brest)
1914 11e Congrès 25—28 janvier (Amiens)

5. SECONDARY SOURCES

The books and articles listed below are far from constituting an exhaustive bibliography of the subject. They represent a selection of those works which are of interest and importance, and which have been most useful in the preparation of this study. The following abbreviations of the titles of journals have been employed:

A.H.R.	*American Historical Review*
A.M.	*Annales du Midi*
Annales	*Annales E.S.C.*
A.P.S.R.	*American Political Science Review*
C.H.	*Cahiers d'Histoire*
C.I.S.	*Cahiers Internationaux de Sociologie*
Comp. Studies	*Comparative Studies in Society & History*
Ec.H.R.	*Economic History Review*
E.G.	*Economic Geography*
F.H.S.	*French Historical Studies*
H.J.	*Historical Journal*
I.H.	*Information Historique*
I.R.S.H.	*International Review of Social History*
J.Ec.H.	*Journal of Economic History*
J.I.H.	*Journal of Interdisciplinary History*
J.M.H.	*Journal of Modern History*
J.P.S.	*Journal of Peasant Studies*
J.S.H.	*Journal of Social History*
M.S.	*Le Mouvement Social*
P&P	*Past & Present*
P.H.	*Provence Historique*
P.S.N.	*Peasant Studies Newsletter*
R.Ec.	*Revue Economique*
R.F.S.	*Revue Française de Sociologie*
R.F.S.P.	*Revue Française de Science Politique*
R.H.	*Revue Historique*
R.H.E.S.	*Revue d'Histoire Economique et Sociale*

(i) *Modern French history*

M. Agulhon   *1848 ou l'apprentissage de la République* (Paris, 1973)
P. Ariès   *Histoire des populations françaises* (Paris, 1971)
A. Armengaud   *La population française au XIXe siècle* (Paris, 1971)
J.-P. Aron, P. Dumont
and E. Le Roy Ladurie *Anthropologie du conscrit français* (Paris/La Haye, 1972)

Atlas historique de la France contemporaine (Paris, 1966)
Atlas de la France rurale (Paris, 1968)

J.-P. Bardet (*et al.*)	*Sur la population française au 18ᵉ et au 19ᵉ siècles* (Paris, 1973)
P. Barral	*Les agrariens français de Méline à Pisani* (Paris, 1968)
N. Belmont	*Mythes et croyances dans l'ancienne France* (Paris, 1973)
G. Bollème	*La bibliothèque bleue. La littérature populaire en France du 16ᵉ au 19ᵉ siècle* (Paris, 1971)
J. Bouillon	Les démocrates-socialistes aux élections de 1849, *R.F.S.P.* VI, 1, jan.–mars 1956
G. Chapman	*The Third Republic of France. The First Phase 1871–1894* (London, 1962)
L. Chevalier	*Classes laborieuses et classes dangereuses à Paris pendant la première moitié du 19ᵉ siècle* (Paris, 1958)
P. Cornut	*Répartition de la fortune privée en France au cours de la première moitié du XXᵉ siècle* (Paris, 1963)
J.-J. Darmon	*Le colportage de librairie en France sous le Second Empire* (Paris, 1972)
A. Daumard	L'évolution des structures sociales en France à l'époque de l'industrialisation (1815–1914), *R.H.* CCXLVII, 502, 1972
G. Dupeux	*French Society 1789–1970* (London, 1976)
M. Duverger	*Partis politiques et classes sociales en France* (Paris, 1955)
F. Furet and W. Sachs	La croissance de l'alphabétisation en France, *Annales,* mai–juin 1974
F. Goguel	*Géographie des élections françaises sous la Troisième et la Quatrième République* (Paris, 1951)
	La politique des partis sous la Troisième République (Paris, 1946)
R. Gossez	Les antagonismes sociaux au milieu du 19ᵉ siècle, *R.Ec.* 1956
J. Gouault	*Comment la France est devenue républicaine* (Paris, 1954)
F.W. Hemmings	*Culture and Society in France 1848–1898* (London, 1971)
A. Jardin and A.-J. Tudesq	*La France des notables* (Paris, 1963, 2 vols)
A. Joanne	*Dictionnaire des communes de la France* (Paris, 1864)
J. Jolly	*Dictionnaire des parlementaires français* (Paris, 1960–)
J.T. Joughin	*The Paris Commune in French Politics 1871–1880* (Baltimore, Md., 1955)
J. Kayser (*et al.*)	*La presse de province sous la Troisième République* (Paris, 1958)
T. Kemp	*Economic Forces in French History* (London, 1971)
	The French Economy 1913–1939 (London, 1972)
C.E. Labrousse (ed.)	*Aspects de la crise et de la dépression 1846–1851* (La Roche-sur-Yonne, 1956)

C.E. Labrousse (*et al.*) *Histoire économique et sociale de la France* (vols 4, 5) (Paris, 1970)

A. Lancelot *L'abstentionnisme électoral en France* (Paris, 1968)

G. Lefebvre *La Grande Peur de 1789* (Paris, 1970)

M. Lévy-Leboyer La croissance économique en France au 19ᵉ siècle, *Annales,* juillet—août 1968
La décéleration de l'économie française dans la seconde moitié du 19ᵉ siècle, *R.H.E.S.* XLIX, 4, 1971

J. Lhomme *La grande bourgeoisie au pouvoir 1830—1880* (Paris, 1960)

T.-J. Markovitch *L'industrie française de 1789 à 1964* (Paris, 1965, 1966, 2 vols)

J.-M. Mayeur *Les débuts de la Troisième République* (Paris, 1973)

J. Merriman (ed.) *1830 in France* (New York, 1975)

F. Pisani-Ferry *Le coup d'état manqué du 16 mai 1877* (Paris, 1965)

A. Plessis *De la Fête Impériale au Mur des Fédérés 1852—1871* (Paris, 1973)

C.-H. Pouthas *La population française pendant la première moitié du 19ᵉ siècle* (Paris, 1956)

P. de Pressac *Les forces historiques de la France* (Paris, 1928)

R. Price *The French Second Republic* (London, 1972)

R. Price (ed.) *Revolution and Reaction: 1848 and the Second French Republic* (London, 1975)

A. Prost *L'enseignement en France 1800—1967* (Paris, 1968)

M. Rebérioux *La République radicale?* (Paris, 1975)

R. Rémond *La vie politique en France* (vol. 2, 1848—1879) (Paris, 1969)

J. Rougerie Faut-il départementaliser l'histoire de France?, *Annales,* jan.—fév. 1966

P. Sorlin *La société française 1840—1914* (Paris, 1969)

A.-J. Tudesq *Les grands notables en France 1840—1849* (Paris, 1964, 2 vols)

A. Young *Travels in France* (New York, 1969)

T. Zeldin *France. Ambition, Love and Politics 1848—1945* (Oxford, 1973)

(*ii*) *Socialism and the labour movement*

J.-P. Aguet *Les grèves sous la monarchie de juillet* (Geneva, 1954)

R. Aron *Le socialisme français face au marxisme* (Paris, 1971)

C. Audry *Léon Blum ou la politique du juste* (Paris, 1955)

G. Baal V. Pengam et l'évolution du syndicalisme révolutionnaire à Brest (1904—1914), *M.S.* no. 82, 1973

D.N. Baker Seven perspectives on the socialist movement of the Third Republic, *Réflexions Historiques,* vol. I, no. ii, 1974

R.P. Baker *Socialism in the Nord 1870—1924 — a regional study of French working-class organisation* (Stanford, Calif., unpub. diss. 1966)

R.P. Baker	Socialism in the Nord 1880–1914, *I.R.S.H.* XII, 3, 1967
S.H. Barnes	*Politics in an Italian Socialist Federation* (New Haven, Conn., 1967)
S. Bernstein	Jules Guesde, pioneer of Marxism in France, *Science & Society*, IV, 1, 1940
L. Blum	*Commentaires sur le programme d'action du Parti Socialiste* (dated 21 April 1919, pub. Paris, 1933)
C. Bouglé	*Socialismes français* (Paris, 1946)
H. Bourgin	*De Jaurès à Léon Blum. L'ENS et la politique* (Paris, 1938)
M. Branciard	*Société française et luttes de classe* (vol. 2) (Lyon, 1967)
J. Braunthal	*History of the International* (vols 1, 2) (London, 1967)
R. Brécy	*Le mouvement syndical en France 1871–1921. Bibliographie* (Paris, 1963)
A. Châtelain	Les migrations temporaires françaises au 19ᵉ siècle: problèmes, méthodes, documentation, *Annales de Démographie Historique*, 1967
	Les migrants temporaires et la propagation des idées révolutionnaires en France au 19ᵉ siècle, *Etudes de la Révolution de 1848*, 1951
J. Colton	*Léon Blum* (Paris, 1967)
Le Communisme en France (Paris, 1969)	
A. Compère-Morel	*Encylopédie socialiste* (vol. III) (Paris, 1921)
	Grand dictionnaire socialiste (Paris, 1924)
	La question agraire et le socialisme en France (Paris, 1912)
	Le programme socialiste des réformes agraires (Paris, 1919)
	Le socialisme et la terre (Paris, 1921)
E. Coornaert	*Les compagnonnages en France du moyen-âge à nos jours* (Paris, 1975)
J.P. Courtheoux	Naissance d'une conscience de classe dans le prolétariat textile du Nord 1830–1870, *R.Ec.* VIII, 1, 1957
L. Derfler	Reformism and Jules Guesde 1891–1904, *I.R.S.H.* XII, 1, 1967
	Socialism since Marx (London, 1973)
S. Derruau-Boniol	Le socialisme dans l'Allier de 1848 à 1914, *C.H.* II, no. 2, 1957
J. Derville	*La Fédération Socialiste SFIO du Pas de Calais* (Thèse 3ᵉ cycle, Paris, 1970)
D. Desanti	*Les socialistes de l'utopie* (Paris, 1970)
E. Dolléans	*Le mouvement ouvrier* (vols 1, 2) (Paris, 1939)
M.M. Drachkovitch	*Les socialismes français et allemand et le problème de la guerre 1870–1914* (Geneva, 1953)
	De Karl Marx à Léon Blum; la crise de la social-démocratie (Geneva, 1954)
J. Droz	*Le socialisme démocratique 1864–1960* (Paris, 1966)
J. Duclos	*Mémoires* (vol. I) (Paris, 1968)
J.-B. Dumay	*Mémoires d'un militant ouvrier du Creusot* (Paris, 1976)

M. Emérit	Le St Simonisme dans les Charentes, *M.S.* no. 88, 1974
F. Engels (and	
P. Lafargue)	*Correspondance* (vol. III, 1891—5) (Paris, 1959)
G. Fasel	Urban workers in provincial France, February—June 1848, *I.R.S.H.* XVII, 3, 1972
J.-J. Fiechter	*Le socialisme français de l'affaire Dreyfus à la Grande Guerre* (Geneva, 1965)
P. Fourchy	*Les doctrines du Parti Socialiste Français* (Thèse de Droit, Nancy, 1929)
J. Gaillard	*Les associations de production en France (1852—1870), M.S.* 52, 1965
	Communes de province, Commune de Paris (Paris, 1971)
C. Geslin	Provocations patronales et violences ouvrières: Fougères (1887—1907), *M.S.* no. 82, 1973
J. Girault	*Le guesdisme dans l'unité socialiste* (Diplôme d'Etudes Supérieures, 1964, Paris)
R. Goetz-Girey	*La pensée syndicale française. Militants et théoriciens* (Paris, 1948)
H. Goldberg	Jaurès and the formation of a socialist peasant policy, 1885—1898, *I.R.S.H.* II, 3, 1957
	Life of Jean Jaurès (Madison, Wisc., 1962)
R. Gossez	*Les ouvriers de Paris. L'organisation 1848—1851* (Paris, 1967)
J. Guesde	
(and J. Jaurès)	*Les deux méthodes* (Paris, 1945)
G. Haupt	*Le congrès manqué* (Paris, 1965)
P. Hutton	The impact of the Boulangist crisis upon the Guesdist party at Bordeaux, *F.H.S.* VIII, 2, 1971
	The rôles of the Blanquist party in left-wing politics in France, 1879—1890, *J.M.H.* XLVI, 2, 1974
J. Jaurès	*L'armée nouvelle* (Paris, 1915)
	Cahiers de la Quinzaine (troisième série 1—4) (Paris, 1901)
	Oeuvres (vols 3, 6) (ed. M. Bonnafous) (Paris, 1931—3)
	Les origines du socialisme allemand (Paris, 1959)
C. Johnson	*Utopian Communism in France: Cabet and the Icarians 1839—1951* (Cornell, N.Y. 1974)
J. Joll	*The Second International* (London, 1968)
J. Julliard	*Fernand Pelloutier et les origines du syndicalisme d'action directe* (Paris, 1971)
A. Kriegel	*Aux origines du communisme français 1914—1920* (Paris, 1964, 2 vols)
	Patrie ou Révolution: Le mouvement ouvrier français devant la guerre, *R.H.E.S.* XLIII, 3, 1965
	Le pain et les roses (Paris, 1968)
	Les internationales ouvrières (Paris, 1970)
C. Landauer	*European Socialism* (vol. 1) (Berkeley, Calif., 1959)
	The Guesdists and the small farmer, *I.R.S.H.* VI, 2, 1961

C. Landauer	The origin of socialist reformism in France, *I.R.S.H.* XII, 1, 1967
J.-M. Laux	Travail et travailleurs dans l'industrie automobile jusqu'en 1914, *M.S.* no 81, 1972
G. Lefranc	*Essais sur les problèmes socialistes et syndicaux* (Paris, 1970)
	Jaurès et le socialisme des intellectuels (Paris, 1968)
	Le mouvement socialiste sous la Troisième République, 1875–1940 (Paris, 1963)
	Le mouvement syndical sous la Troisième République (Paris, 1967)
Y. Lequin	Classe ouvrière et idéologie dans la région Lyonnaise à la fin du 19e siècle, *M.S.* no. 69, 1969
F. L'Huillier	*La lutte ouvrière à la fin du Second Empire* (Paris, 1957)
G. Lichtheim	*Marxism* (London, 1961)
	Marxism in Modern France (New York, 1966)
	A Short History of Socialism (London, 1970)
D. Ligou	*Histoire du socialisme en France 1871–1961* (Paris, 1962)
P. Louis	*Histoire du socialisme en France* (Paris, 1925)
R. Luxemburg	*Le socialisme en France 1898–1912* (Paris, 1971)
J. Maîtron (ed.)	*Dictionnaire biographique du mouvement ouvrier* (Paris, 1964–)
J. Maîtron	Un anar', qu'est-ce que c'est? *M.S.* no. 83, 1973
F.E. Manuel	*The Prophets of Paris* (Cambridge, Mass., 1962)
E. Masson	*Les Bretons et le socialisme* (Paris, 1972)
D. Mayer	*Pour une histoire de la gauche* (Paris, 1969)
T. Moodie	The reorientation of French socialism 1888–1890, *I.R.S.H.* XX, 3, 1975
B.H. Moss	*The Origins of the French Labor Movement. The Socialism of Skilled Workers 1830–1914* (Berkeley, Calif., 1976)
A. Noland	*The Founding of the French Socialist Party 1893–1905* (Cambridge, Mass., 1956)
L. Osmin	*Figures de jadis* (Paris, 1934)
Parti Socialiste	*Programme d'action 1919* (Paris, 1919)
M. Perrot	Archives policières et militants ouvriers sous la Troisième République, *R.H.E.S.* no. 2, 1959
	Etat des travaux universitaires inédits faits depuis 1945 et concernant le mouvement ouvrier en France 1815–1939, *M.S.*, 33–4, 1960–1
	Les ouvriers en grève (Paris, 1974, 2 vols)
	Les ouvriers en grève 1871–1890, *M.S.* no. 82, 1973
M. Perrot and A. Kriegel	*Le socialisme français et le pouvoir* (Paris, 1966)
J. Peyrot	Questions pédagogiques: les socialismes et le mouvement socialiste au 19e siècle, *C.H.* XVIII, no. iii, 1973
A. Philip	*Les socialistes* (Paris, 1967)
R. Pierre	*Les origines du syndicalisme et du socialisme dans le Drôme* (Paris, 1973)

E. Poisson	*Socialisme et coopération* (Paris, 1922)
M. Prélot	*L'évolution politique du socialisme français* (Paris, 1938)
F.F. Ridley	*Revolutionary Syndicalism in France* (Cambridge, 1970)
J. Rougerie	*Jalons pour une histoire de la Commune* (Paris, 1973) Remarques sur l'histoire des salaires à Paris au 19e siècle, *M.S.* 63, 1968
A. Roveri	*Dal sindicalismo rivoluzionario al fascismo: capitalismo agrario e socialismo nel Ferrarese 1870–1920* (Florence, 1972)
J. Scott	*The Glassworkers of Carmaux* (Cambridge, Mass., 1974)
W.H. Sewell	La classe ouvrière de Marseille sous la 2e République: structure sociale et comportement politique, *M.S.* 1971 Social change and the rise of working-class politics in nineteenth-century Marseille, *P&P* no. 65, 1974
E. Shorter and C. Tilly	*Strikes in France 1830–1968* (Cambridge, 1974)
P. Souyri	*Le marxisme après Marx* (Paris, 1970)
D. Stafford	*From Anarchism to Reformism* (London, 1971)
P. Stearns	National character and European labor history, *J.S.H.* IV, 2, 1970 *Revolutionary Syndicalism and French Labor* (New Brunswick, N.J., 1971)
C. Willard	*Les guesdistes* (Paris, 1965) *Socialisme et communisme français* (Paris, 1967)
A. Zévaès	*Histoire du socialisme et du communisme en France 1871–1947* (Paris, 1947)
G. Ziebura	*Léon Blum et le Parti Socialiste* (Paris, 1967)

(*iii*) *Regional studies*

J. Anglade	*La vie quotidienne dans le Massif Central au 19e siècle* (Paris, 1971)
A. Armengaud	*Les populations de l'Est-Aquitain 1845–1871* (Paris, 1961)
B. Barbier	*Villes et centres des Alpes du Sud* (Gap, 1969)
P. Barral	Aspects régionaux de l'agrarisme français avant 1930, *M.S.* no. 67, 1969 *Le département de l'Isère sous la Troisième République 1870–1940* (Paris, 1962)
J. Basso	*Les élections législatives dans le département des Alpes-Maritimes 1860–1939* (Paris, 1968)
S. Berger	*Peasants against Politics: Rural Organisation in Brittany 1911–1967* (Cambridge, Mass., 1972)
P. Bernard	*Economie et sociologie de la Seine-et-Marne 1850–1950* (Paris, 1953)
R. Bezucha	*The Lyon Uprising of 1834* (Cambridge, Mass., 1974)
R. Blanchard	*Les Alpes occidentales* (vol. IV, *Les préalpes françaises du Sud*) (Grenoble, 1945)

P. Bois   *Paysans de l'Ouest* (Paris, 1971, abridged edn)
G. Bouchard   *Le village immobile. Senneley-en-Sologne au 18ᵉ siècle*
                           (Paris, 1972)
P. Bozon   *La vie rurale en Vivarais: étude géographique* (Valence,
                           1961)
Y. Brékilien   *La vie quotidienne des paysans bretons au 19ᵉ siècle*
                           (Paris, 1966)
P. Brunet   *Structure agraire et économie rurale des plateaux*
                           tertiaires entre la Seine et l'Oise (Caen, 1960)
M. Chevalier   La 'guerre des Demoiselles' en Ariège: folklore et
                           histoire sociale, *Revue Géographique des Pyrénées et du*
                           Sud-Ouest XLV, 1, 1974
L. Clarenc   Riches et pauvres dans le conflit forestier des Pyrénées
                           centrales vers le milieu du 19ᵉ siècle, *A.M.* 79, 3, 1967
A. Corbin   *Archaïsme et modernité en Limousin au 19ᵉ siècle*
                           (1845–1880) (Paris, 1974, 2 vols)
                           Limousins migrants, Limousins sédentaires, *M.S.* no. 88,
                           1974
                           Migrations temporaires et société rurale au 19ᵉ siècle: le
                           cas du Limousin, *R.H.* CCXLVI, 500, 1971
R. Delefortrie and
J. Morice   *Les revenus départementaux en 1864 et en 1954* (Paris,
                           1959)
S. Derruau-Boniol   Le département de la Creuse. Structure sociale et
                           évolution politique, *R.F.S.P.* VII, 1, 1957
G. Desert   Les paysans du Calvados au 19ᵉ siècle, *Annales de*
                           Normandie, XXI, 2, 1971
F. Dreyfus   *La vie politique en Alsace* (Paris, 1969)
R. Dugrand   *Villes et campagnes en Bas-Languedoc* (Paris, 1963)
G. Dupeux   *Aspects de l'histoire sociale et politique du Loir-et-Cher*
                           1848–1914 (Paris, 1962)
P. Elton Mayo   *The Roots of Identity* (London, 1974)
D. Fabre and
J. Lacroix   *Communautés du Sud* (Paris, 1976, 2 vols)
                           La vie quotidienne des paysans du Languedoc au 19ᵉ
                           siècle (Paris, 1973)
A.-M. Faidutti-Rudolph *L'immigration italienne dans le Sud-est de la France*
                           (Gap, n.d.)
A. Fel   *Les hautes terres du Massif Central. Tradition paysanne*
                           et économie agricole (Paris, 1962)
G. Frêche   Etudes statistiques sur le commerce céréalier de la
                           France méridionale au 18ᵉ siècle, *R.H.E.S.* XLIX, 1 and 2,
                           1971
F. Furet and J. Ozouf   Literacy and industrialisation in the Nord, *Journal of*
                           European Economic History V, i, 1976
J. Garavel   *Les paysans de Morette. Un siècle de vie rurale dans une*
                           commune du Dauphiné (Paris, 1948)
G. Garrier   *Paysans du Beaujolais et du Lyonnais 1800–1970*
                           (Grenoble, 1973, 2 vols)

P. George	*Géographie des Alpes* (Paris, 1942)
J. Girault	*La Commune et Bordeaux* (Paris, 1971)
P. Goujon	*Le vignoble de Saône-et-Loire au 19ᵉ siècle (1815– 1870)* (Lyon, 1973)
D. Halévy	*Visites aux paysans du centre* (Paris, 1935)
J. Harvey Smith	Work routine and social structure in a French village: Cruzy in the nineteenth century, *J.I.H.* V, iii, 1975
P. Higonnet	*Pont-de-Montvert* (Cambridge, Mass., 1971)
B. Kayser	*Communes et villes de la Côte d'Azur: essai sur les conséquences du développement urbain* (Monaco, 1960)
J. Larrue	*Loisirs ouvriers chez les métallurgistes toulousains* (Paris, 1965)
R. Laurent	*Les vignerons de la Côte d'Or au 19ᵉ siècle* (Paris, 1957)
P. Léon (*et al.*)	*Structures économiques et problèmes sociaux du monde rural dans la France du Sud-Est (fin 17ᵉ siècle–1835)* (Paris, 1966)
E. Le Roy Ladurie	*Les paysans du Languedoc* (Paris, 1966, 2 vols)
L.-A. Loubère	*Radicalism in Mediterranean France 1848–1914* (New York, 1974)
C. Marcilhacy	*Le diocèse d'Orléans au milieu du 19ᵉ siècle. Les hommes et leurs mentalités* (Paris, 1964)
C. Marie	*L'évolution du comportement politique d'une ville en expansion: Grenoble 1871–1965* (Paris, 1966)

Marseille sous le Second Empire (Paris, 1961)

C. Mesliand	La fortune paysanne dans le Vaucluse 1900–1938, *Annales* jan.–fév. 1967
A. Meynier	*Géographie du Massif Central* (Paris, 1935)
M. Moissonier	*L'Internationale et la Commune à Lyon* (Paris, 1973)
A. Olivési	*La Commune de 1871 à Marseille* (Paris, 1950)
A. Olivési and M. Roncayolo	*Géographie électorale des Bouches du Rhône sous la Quatrième République* (Paris, 1961)
P. Pierrard	*La vie ouvrière à Lille sous le Second Empire* (Paris, 1965)
P. Pinchemel	*Structures sociales et dépopulation dans les campagnes picardes de 1836 à 1936* (Paris, 1957)
J. Pitié	*Exode rurale et migrations intérieures en France. L'exemple de la Vienne et du Poitou-Charentes* (Paris, 1976)
A. Siegfried	*Géographie électorale de l'Ardèche sous la Troisième République* (Paris, 1949)
	Tableau politique de la France de l'Ouest sous la Troisième République (Paris, 1913)
S. Tardieu	*La vie domestique dans le Mâconnais rural pré-industriel* (Paris, 1964)
S.G. Tarrow	*Peasant Communism in Southern Italy* (New Haven, Conn., 1967)
R. Thabault	*Education and Change in a Village Community. Mazières-en-Gâtine 1848–1914* (London, 1971)

G. Thuillier	*Aspects de l'économie nivernaise au 19ᵉ siècle* (Paris, 1966)
R. Trempé	*Les mineurs de Carmaux* (Paris, 1971, 2 vols)
D. Vasseur	*Les débuts du mouvement ouvrier dans la région de Belfort-Montbéliard 1870–1914* (Paris, 1967)
C. Vidal	Chronologie et rythmes du dépeuplement dans le département des Alpes de Haute-Provence depuis le début du 19ᵉ siècle, *P.H.* XXI, 85, 1971
P. Vigier	*La Seconde République dans la Région Alpine* (Paris 1963, 2 vols) Lyon et l'évolution politique de la province française au 19ᵉ siècle, *C.H.* XII, 1–2, 1967
L. Wylie	*Village in the Vaucluse* (Cambridge, Mass., 1957)
T. Zeldin (ed.)	*Conflicts in French Society* (London, 1970)

(iv) Provence and the Var

M. Agulhon	La diffusion d'un journal montagnard, 'le Démocrate du Var', sous la Seconde République, *P.H.* X, 39, 1960 La fin des petites villes dans le Var intérieur au 19ᵉ siècle in *Villes de l'Europe méditerranéenne et de l'Europe occidentale* (Actes du Colloque de Nice, 1969) La notion de village en Basse-Provence vers la fin de l'Ancien Régime, *Actes du 90ᵉ Congrès National des Sociétés Savantes, Nice 1965* (Paris, 1966) *La République au village* (Paris, 1970) *La sociabilité méridionale* (Aix-en-Provence, 1966, publ. de la Faculté des Lettres, 2 vols) *La vie sociale en Provence intérieure au lendemain de la Révolution* (Paris, 1970) Les chambrées de Provence: histoire et ethnologie, *R.H.* CCXLV, 498, 1971 Mise au point sur les classes sociales en Provence, *P.H.* no. 80, 1970 *Une ville ouvrière au temps du socialisme utopique. Toulon de 1815 à 1851* (Paris, 1970)
F. Allard	*Les forêts et le régime forestier en Provence* (Paris, 1901)

Atlas historique de Provence (Paris, 1969)

J.-J. Aubin	*Var, dénombrement quinquennaux de la population de 1856 à 1881* (Draguignan, 1883)
P. Audibert	*Chronique de Carcès. L'envolée du XXᵉ siècle dans un village du Var* (Draguignan, n.d.)
R. Baehrel	*Une croissance: la Basse-Provence rurale fin 16ᵉ siècle–1789* (Paris, 1961)
E. Baratier	*La démographie provençale du 13ᵉ au 16ᵉ siècle* (Paris, 1961)
E. Baratier (*et al.*)	*Histoire de la Provence* (Toulouse, 1969)

H. Baudrillart	*Les populations agricoles de la France* (vol. III) (Paris, 1893)
J. Bernès and	
S. Bernel	*Le Var agricole* (Draguignan, 1923)
F. Beslay	*Voyage aux pays rouges* (Paris, 1873)
Stendhal (H. Beyle)	*Mémoires d'un touriste* (Oxford, 1905)
M. Brandon-Albini	*Midi vivant* (Paris, 1963)
M. Brion	*Provence* (London, 1963)
G. Callon	*Le mouvement de la population dans le département du Var au cours de la période 1820–1921* (Toulon, 1932)
T. Carsignol	*L'évolution du peuplement dans le département du Var 1871–1936* (Diplôme d'Etudes Supérieures, Aix-en-Provence, 1936)
A. Celestin	*St Paul en Forêt* (Cannes, 1931)
R. Collier	Essai sur le 'socialisme' communal en Haute-Provence, in *Actes du 90ᵉ Congrès National des Sociétés Savantes, Nice 1965* (Paris, 1966)
E. Constant	Notes sur la presse dans le département du Var sous le Second Empire, *P.H.* X, nos. 39, 41, 1960
A. Dauzat	*Les argots de métiers franco-provençaux* (Paris, 1917)
P. Dominique	*Les brigands en Provence et en Languedoc* (Avignon, 1975)
C. Durandet	*Les maquis de Provence* (Paris, 1965)
J. Girard	*Nomenclature des richesses minières du département du Var* (Draguignan, 1919)
J. Girault	A la recherche du 'Var Rouge', de l'insurrection de décembre 1851 au Front Populaire, *Cahiers de la Méditerranée*, déc. 1973

Historique et vie de la Fédération Socialist du Var (Toulon, 1936)

T. Judt	The development of socialism in France: the example of the Var, *H.J.* XVIII, 1, 1975
	The origins of rural socialism in Europe: economic change and the Provençal peasantry 1870–1914, *Social History* I, 1, 1976
E. Julliard	*La Côte des Maures – son évolution économique et sociale depuis cent ans* (Grenoble, 1957)
G. Le Gall	*La population de St Nazaire 1856–1931* (Mémoire, Faculté des Lettres à Aix-en-Provence, 1970)
Y. Leroux	*Une petite ville. Brignoles – aspects humains et économiques* (Diplôme d'Etudes Supérieures, Nice, 1974)
R. Livet	*Habitat rural et structures agraires en Basse-Provence* (Aix-en-Provence, 1962)
J. Masse	Les anarchistes varois 1879–1921, *M.S.* no. 69, 1969
Y. Masurel	*La vigne dans la Basse-Provence orientale* (Thèse Complémentaire, Aix-en-Provence, 1964)
L. Nardin	*Lorgues: cité franche de Provence* (Draguignan, n.d.)
Y. Rinaudo	L'opposition à la loi de trois ans dans le Var

	(printemps–été 1913), *P.H.* XX, 80, 1970
	Quelques aspects de l'évolution démographique de deux
	communes viticoles varoises: Taradeau et le Thoronet
	1872–1911, *P.H.* XIX, 76, 1969
A.V. Roche	*Provençal Regionalism* (Evanston, Ill., 1954)
P. Rollet	*La vie quotidienne en Provence au temps de Mistral*
	(Paris, 1972)
L. Roubin	*Chambrettes des Provençaux: une maison des hommes*
	en Méditerranée septentrionale (Paris, 1970)
M. Rozycka-Glassova	Modifications de structure du système de culture dans le
	département du Var au 19e siècle et au cours de la
	première moitié du 20e siècle, in *Cahiers du Centre*
	d'Etudes des Sociétés méditerranéennes, no. 2, 1968
L. Sénéquier	*Connaissances de la Garde Freinet* (Draguignan, 1965)
L. Stouff	*Ravitaillement et alimentation en Provence aux 14e et*
	15e siècles (Paris, 1971)
R. Tresse	Les départements du Var et des Alpes-Maritimes en
	1872, *R.H.E.S.* XLVI, 1, 1968
J. Valbonne	*Villes de Provence et de Côte d'Azur* (Paris, 1966)
M. Vovelle	Essai de cartographie de la déchristianisation sous la
	Révolution française, *A.M.* 76, 1964
	Etat présent des études de structure agraire en Provence
	à la fin de l'Ancien Régime, *P.H.* XVIII, 78, 1968
	Les métamorphoses de la fête en Provence de 1750 à
	1820 (Paris, 1976)
	Piété baroque et déchristianisation en Provence au 18^e
	siècle (Paris, 1973)

(v) *Peasants and rural society*

R.T. and G. Anderson	The indirect social structure of European village com-
	munities, *American Anthropologist* LXIV, 1962
M. Augé-Laribé	*Le problème agraire du socialisme* (Paris, 1907)
M. Aymard	Rendements et productivité agricole dans l'Italie
	moderne, *Annales*, mars–avril 1973
P. Bairoch	*Révolution industrielle et sous-développement* (Paris,
	1969)
E. Banfield	*The Moral Basis of a Backward Society* (Glencoe, Ill.,
	1958)
Y.-M. Bercé	*Croquants et nu-pieds. Les soulèvements paysans en*
	France du 16e au 19e siècle (Paris, 1974)
M. Bloch	*French Rural History* (Berkeley, Calif., 1966)
A. Blok	*The Mafia of a Sicilian Village 1860–1960* (Oxford,
	1974)
J. Brögger	*Montevarese: A Study of Peasant Society and Culture in*
	Southern Italy (Bergen, 1971)
A. de Cambriaire	*L'auto-consommation agricole en France* (Paris, 1952)
P. Carrère and	
R. Dugrand	*La région méditerranéenne* (Paris, 1960)

A. Chayanov · *The Theory of Peasant Economy* (Homewood, Ill., 1966) (1st edn 1925)

L. Chevalier · *Les paysans* (Paris, 1947)

D. Chirot · The growth of the market and service labor systems in agriculture, *J.S.H.* winter, 1975

G. Cholvy · Sociétés, genres de vie et mentalités dans les campagnes françaises de 1815 à 1880, *I.H.* 36, no. 4, 1974

C. Clarke and
M. Haswell · *The Economics of Subsistence Agriculture* (London, 1964)

E.J. Collins · Migrant labour in British agriculture in the nineteenth century, *Ec.H.R.* XXIX, i, 1976

A. Dauzat · *Le village et le paysan en France* (Paris, 1941)

F. Dovring · *Land and Labor in Europe 1900–1950* (The Hague, 1956)

D. Faucher · *La vie rurale vue par un géographe* (Toulouse, 1962)

M. Faure · *Les paysans dans la société française* (Paris, 1966)

J. Fauvet and
H. Mendras (eds) · *Les paysans et la politique dans la France contemporaine* (Paris, 1958)

W. Fischer · Rural industrialisation and population change, *Comp. Studies* XV, 2, 1973

R. Forster · Obstacles to agricultural growth in eighteenth-century France, *A.H.R.* LXXV, vi, 1970

S.H. Franklin · *The European Peasantry* (London, 1969)
Rural Societies (London, 1971)

G. Friedmann (ed.) · *Villes et campagnes* (Paris, 1970)

G. Garrier · Les enquêtes agricoles du 19ᵉ siècle; une source contestée, *C.H.* XII, 1–2, 1967

M. Gervais (*et al.*) · *L'univers politique des paysans* (Paris, 1972)

P. Ginsborg · Peasants and revolutionaries in Venice and the Veneto in 1848, *H.J.* 3, XVII, 1974

L.-M. Goreux · Les migrations agricoles en France depuis un siècle et leurs relations avec certains facteurs économiques, *Etudes et Conjonctures* XI, iv, 1956

P. Gratton · *La lutte des classes dans les campagnes* (Paris, 1971)
Les paysans français contre l'agrarisme (Paris, 1972)

E. Gueit · *Exode rurale et main d'oeuvre saisonnière* (Draguignan, 1924)

E. Guillemin · *La vie d'un simple* (Paris, 1942)

H.J. Habakkuk · Family structure and economic change in nineteenth-century Europe, *J.Ec.H.* XV, 1, 1955

E.J. Hobsbawm · Peasants and politics, *J.P.S.* I, 1973

P. Hohenberg · Change in rural France in the period of industrialisation, 1830–1914, *J.Ec.H.* XXXII, 1, 1972
Les migrations dans la France rurale 1836–1901, *Annales*, mars–avril 1974

W.G. Hoskins · *Provincial England* (London, 1965)

H. Janne	Tradition et continuité dans les sociétés en évolution rapide, *C.I.S.* XLIV, 44, 1968
M. Jollivet	*Sociétés paysannes ou luttes de classes au village?* (Paris, 1974)
M. Jollivet and H. Mendras	*Les collectivités rurales françaises* (vol. I) (Paris, 1971)
E.L. Jones and S.J. Woolf (eds)	*Agrarian Change and Economic Development* (London, 1969)
E. Julliard (ed.)	*Histoire de la France rurale* (vol. III) (Paris, 1975)
T. Kaplan	The social base of nineteenth-century Andalusian anarchism in Jerez de la Frontera, *J.I.H.* VI, i, 1975
E. Kardelj	*Les problèmes de la politique socialiste dans les campagnes* (Paris, 1960)
B. Kayser	Le problème de l'autarchie dans une commune rurale (Valbonne) sous l'Ancien Régime et la Révolution, *P.H.* III, no. 2, 1953
J. Klatzmann	*Géographie agricole de la France* (Paris, 1972)
C.E. Labrousse	*Le prix du froment en France 1726–1913* (Paris, 1970) The evolution of peasant society in France from the eighteenth century to the present, in Acomb and Brown (eds) *French Society and Culture since the Old Régime* (New York, 1966)
H. Lefebvre	Perspectives de sociologie rurale, *C.I.S.* XIV, 1953
E. Le Roy Ladurie	Pour un modèle de l'économie rurale française au 18e siècle, *C.H.* XIX, 1, 1974
M. Levy	*Modernisation and the Structure of Societies* (Princeton, N.J., 1966)
J.J. Linz	Patterns of land tenure, division of labor and voting behavior in Europe, *Comparative Politics* VIII, iii, 1976
J. Lopreato	*Peasants no more: Social Class and Social Change in Southern Italy* (New York, 1967)
J.S. Macdonald	Agrarian organisations, migration and labour militancy in rural Italy, *Ec.H.R.* XVI, 1, 1963–4
A.L. Maraspini	*The Study of an Italian Village* (Paris, 1968)
T.W. Margadant	Peasant protest in the Second Republic, *J.I.H.* V, i, 1974
P. Marrès	*La vigne et le vin en France* (Paris, 1950)
H. Mendras	*Sociologie de la campagne française* (Paris, 1965) *The Vanishing Peasant – Innovation and Change in French Agriculture* (Boston, Mass., 1970) Un schéma d'analyse de paysannerie occidentale, *P.S.N.* I, 3 and 4, 1972
P. Merlin	*L'exode rurale* (Paris, 1971)
C. Mesliand	Problèmes de la recherche historique sur la paysannerie française depuis la fin du 19e siècle, *M.S.* no. 86, 1974
J.S. Migdal	*Peasants, politics and revolution* (Princeton, N.J., 1974)
G.E. Mingay	*Enclosures and the Small Farmer in the Age of the Industrial Revolution* (London, 1968)
D. Mitrany	*Marx against the Peasant* (New York, 1961)

M. Morineau   Y a-t-il eu une révolution agricole en France au 18ᵉ
                       siècle? *R.H.* CCXXXIX, 1968
R. Mousnier   *Peasant Uprisings* (London, 1971)
W.H. Newell   The agricultural revolution in nineteenth-century
                       France, *J.Ec.H.* XXXIII, 4, 1973
J. Peristiany (ed.)   *Contributions to Mediterranean Sociology* (Paris, 1968)
J. Pitt-Rivers (ed.)   *Mediterranean Countrymen* (Paris, 1963)
J. Pitt-Rivers   Social class in a French village, in C. Tilly (ed.) *An
                       Urban World* (Boston, Mass., 1974)
J.D. Powell   Peasant society and clientelist politics, *A.P.S.R.* LXIV,
                       2, 1970
R. Price   The onset of labour shortage in nineteenth century
                       French agriculture, *Ec.H.R.* 2, XXVIII, ii, 1975
P. Rambaud   *Sociologie rurale* (Paris, 1976)
P. Redfield   *The Little Community and Peasant Society and Culture*
                       (Chicago, 1960)
Revue Française de
Sociologie 1965   Numéro consacré aux *Transformations des sociétés
                       rurales françaises*
A. Rodgers   Migration and industrial development: the South Italian
                       experience, *E.G.* no. 46, 1970
D. Sabean   Markets, uprisings and leadership in peasant societies,
                       P.S.N. II, 3, 1973
G. Schachter   *The Italian South: Economic Development in
                       Mediterranean Europe* (New York, 1965)
T. Shanin (ed.)   *Peasants and Peasant Societies* (London, 1971)
T. Shanin   Peasantry: delineation of a sociological concept and a
                       field of study, *P.S.N.* II, 1, 1973
                       The peasantry as a political factor, *Sociological Review*
                       N.S. XIV, 1, 1966
J.-B. Silly   La disparution de la petite métallurgie rurale, *Revue
                       d'Histoire de Sidérurgie* II, 1961
F.M. Snowden   On the social origins of agrarian reform in Italy, *Archives
                       Européennes de Sociologie* XII, ii, 1972
A. Soboul   *Paysans, sans-culottes et jacobins* (Paris, 1967)
                       Survivances 'féodales' dans la société rurale fran çaise au
                       19ᵉ siècle, *Annales* sept.—oct. 1968
                       The French rural community in the eighteenth and
                       nineteenth centuries, *P&P*, no. 10, 1956
A.L. Stinchcombe   Agricultural enterprise and rural class relations,
                       American Journal of Sociology LXVII, 2, 1961
Structures agraires et paysages ruraux, mémoire no. 13 de la Faculté des Lettres
                       de l'Université de Nancy (Nancy, 1957)
Y. Tavernier (and
H. Mendras)   *Terre, paysans et politique* (Paris, 1969)
J. Tepicht   *Marxisme et agriculture* (Paris, 1973)
C. Tilly   Does modernisation breed revolution? *Comparative
                       Politics* V, 3, 1973

L.A. Tilly	The food riot as a form of political conflict in France, *J.I.H.* II, 1, 1971
A. Touraine and O. Ragazzi	*Ouvriers d'origine agricole* (Paris, 1961)
J.-C. Toutain	*Le produit physique de l'agriculture française de 1700 à 1958* (Paris, 1961, 2 vols)
J. Vidalenc	*La société française de 1815 à 1848: le peuple des campagnes* (Paris, 1970)
C.K. Warner	Soboul and the peasants, *P.S.N.* IV, 1, 1975 *The Wine-growers of France and the Government since 1875* (New York, 1960)
D. Warriner	*The Economics of Peasant Farming* (Oxford, 1939)
E. Weber	*Peasants into Frenchmen. The Modernisation of Rural France 1870–1914* (London, 1977)
E.R. Wolf	*Peasant Wars of the Twentieth Century* (London, 1969) *Peasants* (Englewood Cliffs, N.J., 1966) Peasants and political mobilisation, *Comp. Studies* XVII, 4, 1975

(vi) Tools and techniques

P. Barral	La sociologie électorale et l'histoire, *R.H.* CCXXXVII, juillet–sept. 1967
R.J. Bezucha (ed.)	*Modern European Social History* (Lexington, Mass., 1972)
M. Blanchard	*Géographie des chemins de fer* (Paris, 1942)
F. Boulard	*Introduction to Religious Sociology* (London, 1960)
F. Boulard and J. Rémy	*Pratique religieuse urbaine et régions culturelles* (Paris, 1968)
J. Bouvier	*Histoire économique et histoire sociale* (Paris, 1968)
H. Cavaillès	*La route française. Son histoire, sa fonction. Etude de géographie humaine* (Paris, 1946)
J. Chaurand	*Introduction à la dialectologie française* (Paris, 1972)
G. Cholvy	*Géographie religieuse de l'Hérault contemporain* (Paris, 1968)
	Conjoncture économique, structures sociales (Hommage à Ernest Labrousse) (Paris, 1974)
A. Coutrot and F. Dreyfus	*Les forces religieuses dans la société française* (Paris, 1965)
K. Deutsch	Social mobilisation and political development, *A.P.S.R.* LV, 3, 1961
J. Dubois	*Le vocabulaire politique et sociale en France de 1869 à 1872* (Paris, 1964)
R. and E. Forster	*European Diet from Pre-industrial to Modern Times* (New York, 1975)
J. Gadille	*La pensée et l'action politiques des évêques français au début de la Troisième République* (Paris, 1967, 2 vols)

P. Haggett	*Locational Analysis in Human Geography* (London, 1965)
Y.-M. Hilaire	La pratique religieuse en France de 1815 à 1878, *I.H.* 25, no. 2, 1963
	L'histoire sociale, sources et méthodes (Paris, 1967)
S.P. Huntington	*Political Order in Changing Societies* (New Haven, Conn., 1968)
F. Isambert	L'attitude religieuse des ouvriers français au milieu du 19e siècle, *Archives de Sociologie des Religions* V—VI, 1958
H. Lartilleux	*Géographie des chemins de fer français* (Paris, n.d.)
G. Le Bras	*Etudes de sociologie religieuse.* Vol. I, *Sociologie de la pratique religieuse dans les campagnes françaises* (Paris, 1955)
P. Leuilliot	Défense et illustration de l'histoire sociale (préface à G. Thuillier, *Aspects de l'économie nivernaise au 19e siècle*) (Paris, 1966)
G. Lukács	*Histoire et conscience de classe* (Paris, 1960)
J.-M. Mayeur	Géographie de la résistance aux Inventaires (février—mars 1906), *Annales*, nov.—déc. 1966
R. Mehl	*The Sociology of Protestantism* (London, 1970)
A. Meynier (*et al.*)	La carte des communes de France, *Annales* juillet—sept. 1958
R. Michels	*Political Parties* (London, 1915)
P. Pinchemel	*France: a geographical survey* (London, 1969)
M. Richter (ed.)	*Essays in Theory and History* (Cambridge, Mass., 1970)
R. Robin	Langage et idéologies, *M.S.* no. 85, 1973
G. Rudé	*The Crowd in History* (New York, 1964)
J.-Y. Tirat	Problèmes de méthode en histoire sociale, *Revue d'Histoire Moderne et Contemporaine* X, 1963
L. Trénard	L'histoire des mentalités collectives, *Revue d'Histoire Moderne et Contemporaine* XV, 1968

Index